THE THEOLOGICAL GRAMMAR OF THE ORAL TORAH

I.

VOCABULARY:
NATIVE CATEGORIES

BY

JACOB NEUSNER

Dowling Studies in the Humanities
and the Social Sciences

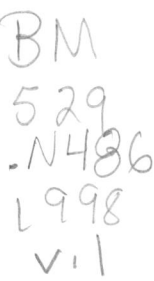

Copyright (c) 1998 by *Jacob Neusner*

All rights reserved. No portion of this publication may be duplicated in any way without the expressed written consent of the publisher, except in the form of brief excerpts or quotations for the purpose of review.

Library of Congress Cataloging-in-Publication Data

Jacob Neusner, *The Theological Grammar of the Oral Torah. I. Vocabulary: Native Categories*

1. The Torah 2. Judaic Studies 3. Religious Studies
4. Philosophy of Religion 5. Oral Tradition
6. Religious Symbolism 7. History of Religions

ISBN 1-88305871-6

Published by the Dowling College Press.

Announcement

Dowling studies in the Humanities and the Social Sciences (DSHSS) has been established to further research in the humanities and the social sciences. Manuscripts submitted undergo an external review and need not reflect the views of the Editorial Board.

On behalf of the Editorial Board, I am pleased to express appreciation for the support we have received from the Dowling College administration; we especially thank President Victor P. Meskill, Provost and College Secretary, Albert B. Donor, and Dean of Arts and Sciences, James E. Caraway.

Robert M. Berchman
Editor in Chief

Dowling Studies in the Humanities and the Social Sciences

───◆───

Sponsor
Victor P. Meskill, *ex officio*

Editor in Chief
Robert M. Berchman

Managing Editor
Parviz Morewedge

Editors

Joseph Behar	Joan Boyle
James E. Caraway	Jeffrey Cole
Andrew Karp	John D. Mullen
Byron Roth	Susan Rosenstreich
Martin Schoenhals	James O. Tate

THE THEOLOGICAL GRAMMAR OF THE ORAL TORAH

I.

VOCABULARY:
NATIVE CATEGORIES

BY

JACOB NEUSNER

Dowling College Press

Contents

Preface..1
Introduction...29
1. Atonement...63
2. Commandment..71
3. Creation...81
4. Gentiles..87
5. God...107
6. Intentionality...127
7. Israel..139
8. Justice and Mercy...171
9. Kingdom of Heaven..189
10. Land of Israel..191
11. Loving Kindness..203
12. Man...207
13. Messiah..213
14. Prayer...227
15. Prophecy, Echoes, and Other Media
    For Divine Communication..233
16. Redemption..239
17. Repentance..243
18. Resurrection..255
19. Revelation, Giving of the Torah..................................269
20. Sage, the; and the Disciple of Sages...........................273
21. Righteousness..285
22. Sanctification...289
23. Sin...293
24. Soul, the...313
25. Suffering...319
26. Temple, Holy Place..325
27. Torah, the..329
28. Torah, Oral..337
29. Torah-study...341
30. Will of God, the...359
31. Women...367
32. Zekhut..373
Cross-references..383

THE THEOLOGICAL GRAMMAR OF THE ORAL TORAH

Preface to Volumes I-III

Theology identifies the main frame, the cognitive structure, of a religion's authoritative documents or doctrines: what holds them all together and defines the message of each one. But how to identify the comprehensive theological traits and principal components? Here I turn to linguistics to supply a metaphor guiding the description and analysis of the theological structure and system of that part of Rabbinic Judaism represented by the classical documents of the Oral Torah. Rabbinic Judaism is the Judaic religious system that appeals to the myth of the dual Torah, oral and written, revealed together at Sinai and transmitted through a process of tradition from God to our rabbi, Moses, and thereafter in the same manner from master to disciple, from then to now. That Judaism finds its authoritative writings in the documents comprised by Scripture and the writings that set forth that originally-oral Torah. The documents that comprise the oral part of the Torah frame this inquiry into describing a governing theology of a corpus of kindred writings.

I

In this three-part work, as though describing the grammar of a language, I lay out data that permit a systematic account of the main lines of theology of that body of coherent writings. I ask how the theological language was correctly, that is, intelligibly, spoken, giving an account of [1] important words (head-nouns) treated as a metaphor for native categories, [2] rules of turning words into combinations (syntax), comparable to the modes of forming correct constructions of nouns and making connections between them, [3] laws permitting the formulation of a virtually-unlimited repertoire of propositions immediately intelligible to speakers of the language (semantics), counterpart to the cognitive models that govern coherent expression of thought. In a companion work, which builds upon these results, I set forth the main lines of the result: the kind of theology that this "language" -= its vocabulary, grammar, and semantics, that is, its native categories, constructions and connections, and models of coherent discourse — generates.[1] Let me now spell out these matters, to render the results that fill the shank of the work exemplary, therefore useful.

Since I compare describing a theological system to describing a language, the three questions that I deem fundamental to the theological description of the Rabbinic writings of late antiquity cover its [1] vocabulary, [2] syntax, and [3] semantics. Each entry in each volume, suitably cross-referenced, will provide in the respective volumes of the *Theological Grammar* [1] a reliable definition of a native category; [2] a theological text, its larger context; and [3] a large-scale structure, the text's still more comprehensive position within the matrix of the system as a whole. That is the theology, or, in terms of my governing metaphor, the "meaning." Each volume, accordingly, both stands on its own and serves as a reference-work for the information it is required to present, but also participates in a much larger exercise of systematic theological description.[2]

The metaphor of a grammar serves, for by grammar is meant, "an example of a discrete combinatorial system. A finite number of discrete elements (in this case, words) are sampled, combined, and permuted to create larger structures (in this case, sentences) with properties that are quite distinct from those of their elements."[3] At issue then are the rules of combination and permutation into larger structures — an ideal way of surveying the work at hand. In this three-part grammar I systematically lay out

[1] theological categories that are native to those writings;

[2] cogent statements that can be made with them; and

[3] coherent propositions that those statements set forth and (within their own terms and framework) logically demonstrate as true and self-evident, both.

To spell this out: Like a language, a theology then begins with [1] a vocabulary that permits the classification of religious knowledge and experience, the organization and categorization of that knowledge and experience into intelligible and cogent sense-units. Many things of one type will be covered by a single word, of another by a different word. So much for what is offered in a grammar that sets forth available vocabulary: the words

Theological Grammar of the Oral Torah. Vol. I   3

this language uses for these things.

The units [2] then combine and recombine in sentences. These rules of theological discourse concerning religious experience we may deem the counterpart of syntax which words combine — or do not combine — with which other words, in what inflection or signaled relationship, and why. That accounts for the second aspect of a grammar, namely, its provision of the rules of grammar governing the joining of words.

The semantics [3] then dictates how to generate meaning.[4] Semantics is what dictates intelligibility — and, as we see in Volume III of this Grammar, is best defined through cases, so primitive is our present understanding of the theology of the Oral Torah.[5]

In all three areas — vocabulary, syntax, semantics — I provide examples that exemplify the rules; to attempt more would require reproducing the bulk of the evidence of the language that is spoken and written down in the classical documents, and this I have already done and need not repeat. The grammar of vocabulary, syntax, and semantics then describe how the language works, tells us that for which it can be made to work. Finite means available for infinite use,[6] the lexical concepts and grammatical rules, finite in themselves, then can address in proper semantics an infinite number of situations, making sense of, impose meaning upon, pretty much whatever comes up. That is what I have in mind, in the interest in Volume III in models of explanation — and anticipation. And that is the point at which constructive theology commences, and systematic theology will find its language. Now to begin.

II

Here, appealing to the metaphor of a grammar that describes the working of a language, I ask a simple question. Viewed synchronically,[7] how do the assertions of the documentary components of the Oral Torah cohere? Theology responds to that question. By theology I refer specifically to the governing rationality, the rules of coherent discourse, of the foundation-documents of Rabbinic Judaism. Hence, for reasons to be specified in a moment, I explore the promise of treating theology as the counterpart for religion as is grammar for a language. For grammar in the description of a language defines the generative categories that dictate the description, analysis, and interpretation of the data of the language. So too in solving the problem of describing theology: the question before us is, How are we going to identify that governing and generative theology that systematically transforms into intellectually accessible terms and categories, subject to generalization and criticism, the attitudes and feelings and intangible but very real perceptions of the enduring religious encounter of holy Israel with God that are set forth in words by the Torah, written and oral?

That question presupposes the cogency of diverse writings, all of them assigned to "our sages of blessed memory" who in late antiquity set forth in writing the initial statement of the Oral Torah. On what basis do I undertake to address to the Oral Torah questions of cogency and coherence? The foundation of the claim that coherent thought, theology, sustains and imparts cogency to the Oral Torah and its writings comes to expression in a simple principle. I invoke a single fact of intellection: the documents examined here conduct a constant dialogue among themselves: the Talmuds with the Mishnah, the Midrash-compilations with Scripture, and sayings attributed to a given sage with other sayings assigned to the same sage. The documents seen whole further are held together by such external indicators as the appeal to common named authorities and the conviction of the community that treasures the documents that they all together form one half of the whole Torah revealed by God to Moses. In such a community of documents there can be no rationality that governs in one document of a given corpus of kindred writings that all together are identified and privileged by a determinate religious system but not in another component of the same authoritative corpus. That is why I move from the identifying the parts and their interconnections to the accounting for the whole. Here I progress from the documents to the system that the documents adumbrate.[8]

Why treat the entire body of writing as systematic, in the manner of a systemic portrait, coherent in details and cogent in the aggregate? That is because an entire religious system — a generative theory of the world-view and the way of life, as well as the theory of the social entity comprised by the faithful — comes to concrete expression in detail that repeats the message of the whole. Whether here and there, whether in this detail or that, always whole and complete, the detail recapitulates the main point of the whole. For the system repeats itself interminably and unashamedly. A few topics predominate, and a small number of propositions govern what is to be said about those topics. Then it must follow that it is not the system that recapitulates the documents, but the documents that recapitulate the system. The writings constantly refer back to, take for granted, acknowledge the presence of, the coherent, generative system, comprised by a set of interlocking paradigms. The theology I propose to describe comprises that modest corpus of coherent and encompassing truths that the system spins out in unlimited variation.

That is, a symbolic structure and a precipitating myth, a system of ideas that transcends the texts and forms the matrix of the texts demands articulation. Then what do we do when we ask the theological question of the writings? It is to undertake a search, beneath the surface of their particular messages, to uncover that statement that, all together and all at once, wherever and whenever the documents speak, the generative system sets forth in its own behalf. To ask a corpus of religious writings to reveal what holds those writings together and makes them cogent, then, we raise the question of theology. By theology I mean, the interior logic of reasoned discourse about the knowledge of God. In the case of Rabbinic Judaism knowledge of God comes to Holy Israel through God's self-manifestation in the Torah revealed by God to our rabbi, Moses, at Sinai, in two media, Oral and Written. Concretely, how are we to move from perception to proposition, from the encounter with God in the Torah to critical reflection upon the experience? This brings us back to the governing metaphor that I have selected for this initial exercise of theological description.

To undertake theological description I appeal for a metaphor to the study of a language, within the linguistic theory[9] that maintains that language imparts structure to inchoate experience, supplying categories and organizing principles to articulate the order and system of pre-verbal and even non-verbal encounter. So I describe the "logic" of God — theology — as we would the grammar of (a) language: its vocabulary, syntax, and semantics. In like manner I formulate a description of the theology of the Oral Torah, treating a language's vocabulary ("head-nouns") as counterpart to a theology's native categories; a language's syntax as comparable to a system's rules for forming constructions and making connections; and a language's semantics as comparable to a theological system's models of analysis of data, explanation of (the system's own) facts, and anticipation (among diverse types of rational statements).[10]

To state matters simply: for the purpose of this study, *theology is to religion as language is to experience and perception.*[11] Just as language turns inchoate experience into propositions subject to general intelligibility in public discourse, so theology transforms into appropriate language,[12] — into intellectually accessible forms, terms and categories, subject to generalization and systematization — the attitudes and feelings and intangible but very real perceptions of the Torah and the self-manifestation of God conducted therein. Systematic, descriptive theology in the present context therefore finds its governing elements by comparing the relationship of theology to the religious encounter of the Torah — the meeting with God in the words of the Torah — with the relationship of grammar to the reality of the living language. By some definitions of language,[13] then, theology serves as the language of religion, what makes concrete, specific, and rationally accessible the experience of religious encounter. The upshot is simple: theology ascribes meaning to otherwise random experiences and events and images that life within the Torah provokes in the way in which semantics allows otherwise random sounds to become meaningful.

In the case of Rabbinic Judaism, that premise — religious experience is to theology as grammar is to language — proves remarkably congruent with the character of the record to begin with. A common language, governed by a single grammar — vocabulary, syntax, and semantics, to use the metaphor I have chosen — governs throughout the document. That absolutely incontrovertible fact on its own validates the work of theological description[14] carried out by invoking the metaphor just now set forth, so examining the theological system sets forth rules of semantics — methods for delimiting meanings, preferring some, rejecting others.[15] Available native-categories or head-nouns, formed into theoretically-intelligible Torah's theology within the categorical structure of language: vocabulary, syntax, semantics. Exactly how do I propose to describe a theology in the model of a language?

We turn first to the matter of vocabulary, for language, or native categories, for theology. Every religion uses key-words — head-nouns, to mark the beginning of declarative sentences — just as does a language. These words constitute the religion's native categories, comparable to the head-nouns or vocabulary of a language.

Second, a religious system will select a certain cluster of words to serve in a manner particular to its needs, as a language uses a small fraction of the phonemes available. These clusters correspond to the syntax that approves the joining of words in one way and not in another, or the joining of these particular words but not those other words. To take an obvious example, "the wicked Mordecai and good Haman" form an unintelligible construction, equivalent to a phoneme lacking all sense, in the Oral Torah. That is to say, on the one side religion in general may find available an unlimited range of myths and symbols, attitudes and emotions, experiences and possible formulations of concrete encounters with God. But, on the other side, religions do make their choices. And that is just as languages make their choices among the possible phonemes. A religion thus establishes its own rules of discourse — syntax or logic, forming constructions and making connections. Violating those rules excludes a statement from the system, marking the statement of what cannot be connected or joined in a common construction as unintelligible.

And, third, every clusters or syntactically-viable constructions, may or may not bear meaning, make sense. To take a famous example, "Colorless green sleeps furiously" uses valid words (not gibberish-words) and follows the correct structure (rules of grammar). But it is unintelligible. Semantics dictates what head-nouns and combinations thereof set forth intelligible statements, and which ones are not possible. The counterpart for the theology of a religion will present itself in the models of plausible, as against unintelligible, discourse.[16]

These then are the categories that result when I invoke the analogy of language to find out how the theological structure that animates the Oral Torah's documents utilizes its counterpart to phonemes (native categories, as I explain in the Introduction of Volume I). But then do I promise a "linguistics" of the Oral Torah?[17] Not at all: the metaphor is just that. What I promise is that we ultimately will learn concerns the principles that underlie how chosen clusters of words are structured into statements. I investigate the semantics of theological thought and ask how clusters once entered into a certain structure yield meaning.

III

Why use the form of a grammar (including instructions on rules of grammar and lessons on semantics) to begin raising constructive and synchronic questions of governing logic, cogency and coherence? Since I invoke the metaphor of a language to describe a theology, I quite naturally pursue the implications of the metaphor by choosing a form for assembling data that serves well in describing a language. There is no simpler, or more rigorous medium for describing a language than the one that takes the form of a a grammar, with a syntax and lessons of semantics included. A grammar exposes the discipline of system and order, focusing upon the individual units that can serve a given language in any way that the rules of that language permit. A grammar constitutes a sustained work of factual description, systematically carried out. It turns facts into cases, and cases into the exemplifications of rules. The grammar-form imposes its own discipline: comprehensive coverage, systematic review of all pertinent evidence, and clear, cogent presentation of succinct statements of the facts.

Grammars by their nature accord a cool welcome to sustained presentations of large-scale reconstructions, hypotheses as to what "really" matters and what counts above all. Those issues, presently resting upon subjective judgment, not objective data, will come in due course and, when they do, they too are going to demand their own form. Grammars require hard facts, properly instantiated — that alone. Matters of taste and judgment here find no legitimate place. What grammars promise, and what I deliver here and in the two companion-volumes, is a reliable, factual, accurate answer to questions of fact, accessible in free-standing entries, arranged in the simplest possible way, alphabetically and thoroughly cross-referenced. These entries are comprised by the data themselves, pertinent statements portrayed in their own words. They exemplify rules and by their regularities, from one entry to the next, also show that rules do govern. At many entries I specify how I think a rule is instantiated; at others, I do not make the obvious explicit. I can think of no more efficient way of setting forth facts, within categories that have been properly defined, structures that have been identified in accord with a single criterion, repeatedly invoked, and cogent, working systems, able to deal with the movement and change of data, analyzed within one and the same descriptive model throughout.

What accounts for the order of the volumes — vocabulary, syntax, semantics? In terms of the logic of my metaphor, which treats theology as the effort to translate into coherent discourse the religious encounter preserved in religious writings, we move from [1] head-nouns among the principal parts of sentences to [2] noun-clusters among the components of paragraphs to [3] semantically-intelligible statements or theological compositions, whole statements of the type defined in Volume III. In the simplest terms, Volume I presents accounts of how the Oral Torah forms its statements, beginning with nouns that can serve as the subjects of a sentence; Volume II identifies the clusters of nouns that comprise sentences of the Oral Torah, how the several native categories cohere into cogent statements, form syllogisms, and otherwise impart (and impose) structure on otherwise inchoate facts; and Volume III spells out the way in which its entire chapters of cogent thought take shape — exercises in explanation, demonstrations of meaning. That is to say, as is already clear the present volume identifies the building blocks of thought; the logical next step, in Volume II, I ask how these building blocks are put together into intelligible and consequential statements, propositions; and in Volume III I further identify the principal presentations of large questions that are asked and models of explanation that are set forth, the main systematic compositions that the Oral Torah puts forth.

IV

Clearly, I have chosen a rather odd medium for the analysis of the systematic substrate upon which the documents of the Oral Torah are founded. Why undertake theological description within the framework of a grammar, treating the principal components of a theological system and structure as comparable to the principal parts of a language? It is because, in the Judaism of the Dual Torah, Oral and Written, religious encounter to begin with takes place in, and is handed on for generations to come, through the medium of words properly used. It is a religion of intellect, encompassing emotions within the conventions of rationality, a religion that knows God through the close analysis of what God says in so many words and in the breaths, the silences separating them. "An ignorant person cannot be pious," sages maintain. Torah-learning forms the antidote to ignorance. But more: proper learning forms an act of religious worship. God meets holy Israel in the school house more than in the synagogue, in study of the Torah more than in prayer — much more. That is the position of innumerable sayings of the sages themselves, and that points to the center of the religious experience they mean to make accessible and available. A religion that selects intellectual media for its principal encounter with God —

in this case, its record of God's meeting with Israel to be played, and, through the study of the language of the record, to be heard, again and again through eternity — that religion of language surely invites the metaphor that reigns in this study.

To understand that answer — God is made manifest in the Torah,[18] therefore Israel meets God in the Torah, that is, through study of the Torah — we have to recall a striking fact. For its account of what it knows about God, this particular religion appeals to the documentary record of God's presence in humanity. Specifically, the Torah, Oral and Written, sets forth what holy Israel knows about God in the record of God's own self-manifestation. Pointing to God's presence in nature and in history, the Torah identifies the occasions of encounter and intervention. The Torah preserves and hands on the record of God's presence in this world. There, in those words, sentences, paragraphs — the media by which theology forms its vocabulary based on its thought preferences — Israel finds the record of encounter with God. And God is to be met whenever the words that preserve the encounter are contemplated, thus:

> R. Hananiah b. Teradion says, "Two who are sitting, and words of Torah do pass between them — the Presence [of God] is with them, as it is said, 'Then they that feared the Lord spoke with one another, and the Lord hearkened and heard, and a book of remembrance was written before him, for them that feared the Lord and gave thought to His name' (Mal. 3:16). I know that this applies to two. How do I know that even if a single person sits and works on Torah, the Holy One, blessed be he, sets aside a reward for him? As it is said, 'Let him sit alone and keep silent, because he has laid it upon him' (Lam. 3:28)."
>
> Tractate Abot 3:2C-D

> Rabbi Halafta of Kefar Hananiah says, "Among ten who sit and work hard on Torah-study the Presence comes to rest, as it is said, 'God stands in the congregation of God' (Ps. 82:1) [and 'congregation' involves ten persons]. And how do we know that the same is so even of five? For it is said, 'And he has founded his vault upon the earth' (Amos 9:6). And how do we know that this is so even of three? Since it is said, 'And he judges among the judges' [a court being made up of three judges] (Ps. 82:1). And how do we know that this is so even of two? Because it is said, 'Then they that feared the Lord spoke with one another, and the Lord hearkened and heard' (Mal. 3:16). And how do we know that this is so even of one? Since it is said, 'In every place where I record my name I will come to you and I will bless you' (Ex. 20:24) [and it is in the Torah that God has recorded His name]."
>
> Tractate Abot 3:6

Not only so, but it is through Torah-study that prophecy is nurtured:

> "And it came to pass in the days of Ahaz" (Is. 7:1).

Theological Grammar of the Oral Torah. Vol. I　　　　　　　　　　　11

>　　What was the misfortune that took place at that time?
>
>　　"The Syrians on the east and the Philistines on the west [devour Israel with open mouth]" (Is. 9:12).
>
>　　The matter [the position of Israel] may be compared to a king who handed over his son to a tutor, who hated [the son]. The tutor thought, "If I kill him now, I shall turn out to be liable to the death penalty before the king. So what I'll do is take away his wet nurse, and he will die on his own."
>
>　　So thought Ahaz, "If there are no kids, there will be no he-goats. If there are no he-goats, there will be no flock. If there is no flock, there will be no shepherd. If there is no shepherd, there will be no world."
>
>　　So did Ahaz plan, "If there are no children, there will be no disciples; if there are no disciples, there will be no sages; if there are no sages, there will be no Torah; if there is no Torah, there will be no synagogues and schools; if there are no synagogues and schools, then the Holy One, blessed be he, will not allow his Presence to come to rest in the world."
>
>　　What did he do? He went and locked the synagogues and schools.
>
>　　That is in line with the following verse of Scripture: "Bind up the testimony, seal the Torah [teaching] among my disciples" (Is. 8:16).
>
>　　　　　　　　　　　　　　　　　　　　　　　Leviticus Rabbah XI:VII.3

Stated in both propositional and narrative ways, the conviction is the same: in the words of the Torah God speaks; hearing those words, Israel meets God — and finds guidance in where to look for God in nature and in history as well. Language, properly construed, therefore forms the principal medium of the revealed knowledge of God. Revealed speech also effects the direct encounter with God so far as that meeting can take place within the created world. Every meeting with God in time begins in the words of the Torah.[19] No wonder, then, that in the study and exegesis of the Torah over time Israel has met the Eternal.

　　Now to take up the thread of argument: the metaphor of comparing theology to a language thus proves especially appropriate in the study of that Judaism, because the representation of the religious life and experience of that Judaism comes to us in the sole medium of a distinctive corpus of holy texts, and those texts exhibit remarkably uniform traits of linguistic formalization and expression.[20] So to begin with we take up a religion that uses disciplined language to set down in permanent form whatever it wishes to say about knowing God. These fundamental convictions of Rabbinic Judaism explain why any account of the theology of that Judaism is going to focus upon the modes of recording in words Israel's moments of meeting God, and God's actions of self-revelation. Here we deal with the particular component of that record of the divine-human encounter, the

Oral Torah — the other half of the record, the half unique to Israel. That integral and necessary component of the one whole Torah revealed by God to Moses our rabbi at Sinai is set forth in vast documents. Their number, more than a score or more in all, scarcely conveys the enormous volume of words that all together comprise that part of the Torah. The Oral part of the Torah, like the Written part, records that encounter in its own distinctive language, which pervades the entire record. Then the theology of that part of the Torah becomes accessible when we know how to understand that language for what it is: the this-worldly record of the meeting of the Eternal in time with Israel.

V

No wonder, then, that in these pages I appeal to the construction of a language for a metaphor of the construction of a theology. Transforming what is private and, by its nature, individual into what is public and by its purpose, shared, theology for religion does what language does for experience and perception. So theology constitutes the language of religious faith, knowledge and experience. Theology sets forth the record of the encounter with God, doing so like language, in language, "with its lexicon and syntax, its capacity to generate an infinite number of propositions."[21] The lexicon encompasses the concepts as these stand on their own. What transform words into useful language are rules "by which coherent utterances — sentences, propositions — can be generated."[22] A theology properly set forth may then generate fresh propositions; people who can speak a language can say the hitherto unsaid, even the unthought, and rightly expect to find immediate comprehension — just like language. To extend the metaphor, theology forms the natural sounds of religion into intelligible speech.

Then to treat theology as the language of religion, we have to learn how to describe the vocabulary, syntax, and semantics that afford access to that language as it is spoken, that rationally embody the religion as it is lived. The task of describing the theology of a religion — in the present case, of a privileged collection of religious writings, deemed continuous with one another and held to form a cogent statement — is to discover within the documents of the Oral Torah the counterpart to the generative grammar of a language, that is, to discern what dictates the flow of thought and imposes form upon it. That generative grammar of theology renders public and subject to shared discourse the religious faith and encounter of those that value and privilege the selected writings. Through that grammar we move from the surface-use of the language in the documents of the Oral Torah to the deeper structures of the language, its formal structures and the formal operations, its rules of thought emerging from the laws of permitted expression.[23] To state matters simply, if we meet God in the Torah, what, in consequence, do we tell one another that we have learned, and how do we say it? In the case of the Judaism set forth here, what rules of intelligible discourse govern the speech that comes in consequence of the meeting?

Treating language as the governing metaphor for theology allows a link between the infinite possibilities of religious experience and encounter, on the one side, and the finite rules that govern intelligible discourse about that experience and encounter, on the other. More concretely, it is in language that religious encounter enters the cognitive part of the human mind, and, in line with Noam Chomsky's reprise of Schlegel, here too, "language, as an expression of the human mind rather than a product of nature, is boundless in scope and is constructed on the basis of a recursive principle that permits each creation to serve as the basis for a new creative act."[24] The experiment in progress here thus seeks to learn from the study of theological language something about the inherent properties of the religious system that comes to concrete expression in the diverse documents of the Oral Torah and that imparts coherence to them all.[25] To describe the theological system expressed within the writings that all together comprise the Oral Torah in its classical statement, therefore, I investigate principal traits of that language. If therefore this project comes to fruition, we shall know how ourselves to speak the language of the Oral Torah, having mastered its vocabulary, syntax, and semantics; and in accord with those rules of the language, we shall be able to speak of whatever we wish that the language can make intelligible to begin with.

Now to the details of the metaphor of language: how, exactly, does that comparison dictate the character of this project? In the model of language, this grammar is in three parts: vocabulary, syntax, semantics. What, exactly, do I mean by the tripartite description undertaken here in grammar-form?

First comes grammar itself, the metaphor of the whole. Defining matters for the purpose of the present analogy, Chomsky uses this language: "The theory of grammar is concerned with the question, What is the nature of a person's knowledge of his language, the knowledge that enables him to make use of language in the normal, creative fashion? A person who knows a language has mastered a system of rules that assigns sound and meaning in a definite way for an infinite class of possible sentences." Chomsky elsewhere says, "The grammar proposed by the linguist is an explanatory theory; it suggests an explanation for the fact that...a speaker of the language in question will perceive, interpret, form, or use an utterance in certain ways and not in other ways."[26]

By vocabulary or native categories I mean, those key-words that form the subjects of consequential sentences, sentences by which the system overall makes its statement. As I explain in the Introduction to this part of the Grammar, "vocabulary" is comprised by native categories, and how these are defined presents a range of considerations. My lexicon covers scarcely three dozen native categories. There are others; these suffice.

By syntax or indicators of construction and connection I mean a set of rules regarding permissible combinations. A dictionary-definition gives, "the means of indicating the relations of words in a sentence, the rules of employing these in accordance with established usage."[27] Syntax then should reveal the rules that constitute knowledge of a language, the principles that govern these systems.[28]

How does this pertain to our project? When we speak of the "syntax" of a theological language, as we do in Volume II, we mean, what are the rules that permit certain combinations to be made, by which a finite set of words may be formed and re-formed into a nearly-unlimited set of sense-statements. In the Introduction to the second part of this Grammar, that definition is given concrete instantiation. The matters of connection and relation form critical considerations in theological discourse: they dictate how we make connections and draw conclusions, the very heart of the matter of God with us.

Here "semantics" serves as a metaphor for those rubrics that set forth fully-comprehensible theological propositions, that exemplify the things that may be said — and the ways in which they are to be said. I introduce in this context the word "model," meaning, the generative pattern to which people refer in undertaking certain types of intelligible, persuasive discourse:

how would I say this, set forth a proposition of this kind, rather than of that kind? In the context of theological language, the rules that correspond to a language's semantics govern the combination and recombination of clauses and sentences into intelligible patterns of large-scale discourse ("paragraphs"). Intelligible patterns both organize and explain the facts we know, and also precipitate anticipation of the future that impends.

For a theological system, as I spell out in the Introduction to the third part of this Grammar, therefore, when we understand how sentences may be made into paragraphs, we know something about forming the models of propositional thought — the models of imparting intelligibility to experience, those of explanation of how things are and anticipation of what is then to happen. We move from the data of the theological language, then, to the rules of vocabulary, syntax, and semantics that permit discourse to range freely over the broad expanses of everyday religious experience and reflection: making sense of God with us, the system would say.

This theological grammar, in its three related but free-standing units, therefore sets forth, through examples of a particular order in each of the three parts, the vocabulary, syntax, and semantics or models of correct discourse. These, all together, are able to accommodate all appropriate thought, so translating faith in and encounter with God into a cogent system: the generative fact of society and culture. I have in mind to read the language of the Oral Torah as testimony to a governing grammar, its religion as evidence of an inherent theology.

Moving beyond the limits of the metaphor, then, I want to understand the logic of combinancy, of the combinational structures. If this project accomplishes its goals, as I said, we should find it possible to learn correctly to speak the theological language of the Oral Torah. We ought to know its main vocabulary. We should find it plausible to identify the rules of combining concepts into propositions: the laws of combinancy and recombinancy. We surely should grasp the uses of propositions in the formulation of correct thought concerning fresh questions and circumstances. Using the correct theological grammar to say, on an infinite number of subjects, the finite propositions of the Oral part of the Torah[29] — authentically, accurately, to speak that language — we shall know how to speak the language of the Torah, in secular terms, to talk proper Judaism. Accordingly, theology in the present framing of the problem of description investigates the interior intellectual traits and prevailing logic of coherent discourse that animate a cogent body of religious writings. With that learning in mind, the authentic constructive, even systematic, theology that is nourished by the Torah, oral and written together, will become possible for a future generation.

VI

From these matters of theory and metaphor, let us now turn to the work at hand: the Judaism of the dual Torah, oral and written, as that Judaism is set forth in its authoritative writings of the formative age, the first six centuries of the Common Era. Among all Judaic writings from Scripture through the end of late antiquity, writings standing for diverse Judaisms indeed, these particular, privileged writings speak a unique religious language, its formal traits, vocabulary, grammar, and semantics serving for its messages only. Other Judaisms used other languages to deliver other systemic statements.[30]

Why do I insist that these documents set forth a language that may be described, learned, and mastered? The language at hand is fluent and repetitive, saying in some few ways the same thing about many things. Its rules of word-choice, construction of intelligible statements, and composition of compelling and persuasive propositions ("paragraphs"), while never explicitly spelled out, prove blatant. And that is why for long centuries, to the present day, a great many sages of the Torah written and oral through these same documents inductively mastered that language and learned to speak it, saying in a fresh setting about new topics what that language permits to be said at any time about anything.

My appropriation of Chomsky's reading of natural language as the source of my governing metaphor therein finds its justification in the very character of the documents, because he helps me make sense of the single definitive fact of Rabbinic-Judaic theological discourse.

It is that the vocabulary, grammar, and semantics of the Oral Torah have made possible a vast range of discourse, on many subjects over long spans of recorded time and in diverse cultural settings, and continues in our own time to permit intelligible and coherent exchange on a nearly-unlimited repertoire of subjects.

This is a living language of religious expression, a language spoken this very morning in rabbinical circles throughout the world. The sages used and their continuators now — today — use the available words of this language to form intelligible sentences in accord with its grammar and set forth correct and compelling propositions. The documents we consider still define the program of learning; knowing what they say and how to speak in their language marks a learned person, and not knowing them stigmatizes someone as ignorant. Enter any authentic yeshiva in the world today, listen to the conversations of rabbis and their disciples, and you will hear that language, correctly spoken by literate, cultured masters of the speech. The principal Judaisms of the day, inclusive of Conservative and Reform Judaism, continue the language as well. Rabbis learned in the Torah as a matter of fact will find it possible to say anything they wish, to invent and create whatever thought they choose, within the rules of language dictated by the theology of the Oral Torah. Understanding that fact in the living religion, Judaism, comprehending the media of thought that impart coherence and intelligibility to the writings of that religion — these define what is at stake in theological description.

So vocabulary, syntax, and semantics of expression matching reflected-upon experience, rational thought, and deep reflection — these work together to provide a language that can be learned, one that is appropriate to the experience of encounter with God through the Torah. It is a language that is to be set down and conveyed in a public and commonly-comprehended manner. In line with its models of persuasive composition, its rules of evidence and argument the language embedded in the documents accommodates not only recapitulation of the known but immediately-intelligible expression of the unknown. In the world of that Judaism that is defined by the Torah, oral and written, in our own day, the language that I propose to describe is fluently spoken, producing a broad and creative range of public discourse. Many have learned it and many today speak it; the task at hand is only to identify the rationality that inductively is learned but ought articulately to be defined. When, therefore, we examine the documents, we too ought to be able to identify that theology as language: its systemic vocabulary, its rules of rational sentence-construction, its models of rationality.

VII

It remains to ask, What exactly is the Oral Torah, and why do I suppose that its components prove sufficiently cogent to yield a single comprehensive theology? The reason is, it is time to turn from differentiation to re-constitution. My reading of the writings document by document is now complete[31] and has shown the distinctive traits — formal and substantive alike — of each one.[32] For a quarter of a century I have worked to differentiate one Rabbinic document of late antiquity from another, and each from all others, insisting that a distinctive rhetoric, logic of coherent discourse, and topical and even propositional program, distinguishes one document from another, indeed, from all others. I have insisted that most documents make cogent statements. I did the work by translating each, providing it with an analytical reference system, conducting the form-analytical work, accounting for the rhetoric, logic of coherent discourse, and topical and even propositional program of each of the score of completed and free-standing documents. That work has made possible the logically consequent question: so much for the parts, what of the whole? That is, do these statements cohere and form a single cogent system and, if they do, how are we to identify the points of joining, the marks of cogency? To answer that question I want to find out what unites these individual and free-standing documents. My answer, adumbrated here, is, a common language, that of thought: theology.

The Oral Torah — the written record of the part of the revelation at Sinai to our rabbi, Moses, that is identified as revelation preserved in memory, through a process of tradition — is comprised by writings that are cogent for formal reasons. Each of the components of the Oral Torah adheres to the same protocol, e.g., citing a common canon of particularly authoritative parts of Israelite Scripture and naming (some) Scriptural and (many) Rabbinic authorities but no others. The documents all together hold together for another reason, which is that in ancient Judaism (all the more so, any other religious-cultural entity) no other corpus of writings bearing shared traits, besides those treated here, exhibited the specified indicative qualities. The documents are both like one another and different from all other writings in the same context. The named sages of Rabbinic literature occur only in that literature, and the verses of Israelite Scripture they deemed generative occur in comparable proportion and urgency no where else. The writings of other Judaisms cited a different repertoire of scriptural verses and named other authorities besides those prominent in this particular body of writings (or named no other authorities at all).

Theological Grammar of the Oral Torah. Vol. I 19

These formal traits of coherence validate asking the question at hand. But they do not by any means exhaust the reasonable grounds for asking about the shared traits of governing rationality and even coherent discourse, traits that as a matter of hypothesis ought to be internally cogent and externally distinguished from those of all other writings of the same place and time. But the specified indicative formal characteristics suffice to validate the inquiry at hand. That is because they identify the diverse writings as a coherent body of religious statements and make us wonder what else, besides the dominant indicative traits of form, holds the whole together. That is why we now inquire into how we are to describe the theological structure and system upon which the various documents of the Oral Torah are grounded and to which all of them constantly make reference. For those traits of a shared rationality do characterize the whole, as the present, systematic and complete review of all of those documents demonstrates beyond any doubt.

The grammar serves, is based upon a systematic examination of, these documents assigned to the first seven centuries C.E., the formative age of Rabbinic Judaism: the Mishnah, reaching closure at ca. 200 C.E.,Tosefta, 300, Talmud of the Land of Israel, 400, Talmud of Babylonia, 600; Mekhilta Attributed to R. Ishmael, , indeterminate; Sifra, Sifré, to Numbers, Sifré, to Deuteronomy, all ca. 300; Genesis Rabbah, Leviticus Rabbah, Pesiqta deRab Kahana, ca. 450-500; Lamentations Rabbati, Song of Songs Rabbah, Ruth Rabbah, Esther Rabbah I, all of indeterminate time but perhaps ca. 500-600; tractate Abot, ca. 250; and Abot deR. Natan, of indeterminate time but perhaps ca. 500-600. That sizable corpus encompasses the written-down record of the Oral Torah particular to the named sages who occur in those documents.[33] I know of no other documents that within the announced criteria of two indicative traits characteristic of a Rabbinic writing but no other, belong to this study.[34]

What about the writings that continuators of "our sages of blessed memory" produced in later centuries, beyond the sea-change in the world of intellect in Europe, the Middle East, and North Africa, that the rise of Islam and its renewal of Greek philosophy brought about? That is for others to say. The systematic examination of the documents that reached closure in medieval times, after the advent of Islam, may show that the same categorical structure, without material augmentation or diminution, continued to define matters. That will bear interesting implications for the study of the later history of Rabbinic Judaism, even into modern times, and even in the contemporary world. But for the formative age, the evidence considered here suffices to establish the repertoire of native categories that formed the building blocks of the structure and system of that Judaism in its time and place — *and, in systemic context, no other.*[35]

VIII

What writings are excluded at *this* stage of the work?[36] Documents not demonstrably particular to Rabbinic authorship, such as the Siddur (daily prayer book) and Mahzor (prayer book for the Days of Awe), as well as those not generally assumed to have reached pretty much their present state by the seventh century C.E., exemplified by the same items as well as a considerable corpus of medieval Midrash-compilation in the manner of Midrash-compilation of late antiquity, also are omitted. I promise a description of the language that conveys the theology of the Oral Torah, that alone. Rabbinic Judaism encompassed more than the writings treated here; but these define what characterized that Judaism and its framers alone. This is an austere enterprise. Here, therefore, I do not propose to describe the language that embodies the theology of Rabbinic Judaism in general, the theology of Judaism that may have enjoyed the approval of the sages of the Oral Torah but that they did not claim to have set forth — the Oral Torah, that alone. More will come in due course, not only liturgy but also poetry, not only halakhah and aggadah in the classical formulation but also Qabbalah, not only practical theology embodied in concrete sayings but also philosophy and theoretical theology, formulated in the more familiar idiom of Western thought. All will find its way into an account of the theology of Rabbinic Judaism. But here is where matters commence: the ground-zero of the faith, the record of God's presence in Israel in the embodiment of the Torah.

If I aimed at a theology of Rabbinic Judaism — not simply of the Oral Torah as written down in the specified documents — I therefore should have to expand the range of analysis to cover writings of which sages approved but which do not necessarily characterize their textual community in particular, or which may be shown marginal to its principal interests and characteristics. For one example, I should not for one minute suppose that writings such as the Siddur and Mahzor, which sages clearly adopted and to which they explicitly contributed prayers, do not speak, also, for "our sages of blessed memory." But though surely representative of sages' convictions as much as those of ordinary folk, those documents are not written in that language of thought that is particular to the sages, and they do not speak uniquely for them, in the way in which, e.g., Sifra or the Mishnah does. And if we wish to know how a group of writings and their writers took shape as a community of shared rational discourse, we must limit ourselves to the specified writings. It may well turn out that the categories native to the Oral Torah and only those categories also define the categorical structure of writings not demonstrably Rabbinic (within the simple sense just now stated, writings claiming the sponsorship of named sages as is implicit in constant inclusion of attributed statements of specified rabbinic authorities). If that structure recapitulates the one that characterizes the documents of the Oral Torah, then we shall have to consider the hypothesis that other writings, even though lacking the indicators of Rabbinic origination and sponsorship, also belong to the Rabbinic corpus. But for now we must honor the limits set by the simplest indicative traits of definition.

ACKNOWLEDGEMENTS

Professor David Aaron, Wellesley College, read the second, third and fourth drafts of the Preface and the Introductions to Volume I-III as well and made important corrections to my framing of the metaphor, correcting needless error in my understanding of matters. I appreciate very much his taking time to read my drafts and contribute his learning to them. He gave me a better understanding of the project than I possessed to begin with.

Professor Stephen T. Katz, Boston University, read the third draft of the Preface and gave me the benefit of a first-class philosophical-critical reading, for which I am very grateful.

Professor Brevard Childs, Yale University, read the second draft of the Preface and guided me to important works that pursue theological matters in the way that I here try to do and that I otherwise should not have known.

In earlier phases of this project I consulted Professor Maurice Wiles, Oxford University, and Dean Francis Young, University of Birmingham, both of whom answered my queries in a very helpful way. They guided me in ways they may not themselves have realized, and I found in their writings a standard to which to aspire.

Professor William Scott Green, University of Rochester, read the Preface in the final draft and made valuable comments.

The University of South Florida provides not only a Research Professorship but also a large Research Grant, which support my work. I give thanks for both. Bard College does the same. Both centers of higher learning bring me into everyday collaboration with colleagues of exceptional acumen, good will and intellect, and I learn from them day by day. Nothing could be the same without them.

Jacob Neusner
University of South Florida & Bard College

Footnotes

[1] *The Theology of the Oral Torah* (Kingston, 1999: McGill-Queens University Press).

[2] But, in the nature of the study, the entries in the later volumes will not recapitulate those in the earlier ones, and each volume will stand on its own, presenting the information pertinent to its descriptive problem. Each volume then follows its own program of entries, and, while intersecting in many directions, an entry in one cannot duplicate much that is presented in another of the volumes, though the same data will have been examined, in the explained sequence, to produce the later volumes. In general, however, I have tried not to introduce the same compositions in the several volumes, and very few passages occur in two, let alone all three, of the volumes of the *Grammar*.

[3] Steven Pinker, *The Language Instinct* (N.Y., 1995: HarperPerennial), p. 84.

[4] I find a comparable, tripartite approach to the systematic analysis and reconstruction of complex data in Edward O. Wilson, *In Search of Nature* (Washington D C & Covelo Ca, 1996: Island Press), p. 113: "Concepts, the most elementary clusters, are signaled by words or phrases...Propositions are signaled by phrases (such as 'dogs' and 'hunt'), clauses or sentences expressing objects and relationships ('dogs hunt'). Finally, schemata are signaled by sentences and larger units of text (the 'technique of hunting with dogs')." The context for the paradigm is quite different from ours, but the divisions strike me as identical. I could as well have called the volumes, Vocabulary, Syntax, Semantics, "concepts, propositions, schemata," but I find the analogy of a grammar more provocative.

[5] But our knowledge of how to speak the language of the Oral Torah is sophisticated indeed, as the intelligible statements of contemporary masters — rabbis, teachers — in yeshivot, seminaries, universities, and pulpits, prove. Linguistics is meant to describe, and the same is so of the kind of theology I attempt here: describing the vocabulary, syntax, and semantics of a living language, the language of a set of remarkably coherent documents — all of them written in the same language and in accord with the same linguistic rules.

[6] Sacks, p. 80.

[7] The now-complete, diachronic work is systematically set forth in *The Transformation of Judaism. From Philosophy to Religion*. Champaign, 1992: University of Illinois Press; *Rabbinic Judaism. The Documentary History of the Formative Age*. Bethesda, 1994: CDL Press, and *Rabbinic Judaism. Structure and System*. Minneapolis, 1996: Fortress Press.

[8] I expand on this matter later on.

[9] By no means universally affirmed!

[10] Clearly, I can have chosen models of any number of other fundamental intellectual constructions besides those governing the solution of problems of analysis, explanation, and anticipation, but these struck me as critical. Volume III also shows that the raw data are strikingly abundant. How these models form the counterpart to semantics is explained presently.

[11] I hasten to differentiate what is at issue here from the comparable conception of religion as an a priori of experience; that is not what I claim, my introduction of the metaphor serving for formal purposes only. See George A. Lindbeck, *The Nature of Doctrine. Religion and Theology in a Postliberal Age* (Philadelphia, 1984: Westminster Press), pp. 30-45. Lindbeck defines religion in a way comparable to this definition of theology, when he states, "A

religion can be viewed as a kind of cultural and/or linguistic framework of medium that shapes the entirety of life and thought. It functions somewhat like a Kantian a priori...it is similar to an idiom that makes possible the description of realities, the formulation of beliefs, and the experiencing of inner attitudes, feelings, and sentiments. Like a culture or language, it is a communal phenomenon that shapes the subjectivities of individuals rather than being primarily a manifestation of those subjectivities. It comprises a vocabulary of discursive and non-discursive symbols together with a distinctive logic or grammar in terms of which this vocabulary can be meaningfully deployed" (p. 33). Clearly, in invoking the metaphor of language when proposing to identify the principal components of the theology of the Oral Torah, I come into the orbit of Lindbeck's thought. But there are fundamental differences, which render the present exercise quite remote in character, not only in focus, from Lindbeck's. Where Lindbeck speaks of religion, I speak of theology. Not only so, but I address documents that use a single, coherent language throughout, and so the theology by its very character functions within the framework of language. He views religions "as products of those deep experiences of the divine (or the self, or the world) which most of us are accustomed to thinking of as peculiarly religious." This leads him into analysis of the nature of religion in general. But my focus is not on religion in general, but solely on the Torah — God's self-manifestation — in particular, and when I refer to language, it is for a governing analogy. I seek an appropriate medium for describing the unitary character of the documents that all together comprise the Torah. The use of the analogy drawn from language becomes obvious when the character of the Torah — the record of encounter with God set down in words of a propositional character — is taken into account. If in the Torah religious experience and knowledge are conveyed in words, sentences, and paragraphs, then language is the particular medium for religious encounter, and the rest follows. That is why I see no important points of intersection, then, between the mode of theological analysis followed in this *Grammar* and the reflections on the nature of religion that Lindbeck sets forth in his very different context. This will become still clear in my projected The Theology of the Torah that is Judaism, the second chapter of which will address the relationship between paradigm and experience — to what does the Torah make reference -- in the context of the Torah, written and oral.

[12] Whether mythic, narrative-biographical, narrative-historical, exegetical, or propositional, and, if propositional, whether articulated or implicit, in the case of the Oral Torah. In the shank of the three books, however, I have limited myself to materials of a single type; these suffice.

[13] The metaphor is amplified presently. As already indicated, I do not take a position on the controverted questions of linguistics, only use, as a metaphor, a particular position within that field, the position associated with the name of Noam Chomsky. For a prior venture into linguistics as a source of useful metaphors in the analysis of the documents of the oral Torah, see my *A History of the Mishnaic Law of Purities*. Leiden, 1977: Brill. XXI. *The Redaction and Formulation of the Order of Purities in the Mishnah and Tosefta.*

[14] Systematic, not only notional, description, as well as analysis and interpretation, the second step in the presentation of a system of thought, will follow in *The Theology of the Oral Torah*. Kingston and Montreal: McGill and Queens University Press, planned for 1999. The third step will be to show the correlations between the halakhic and aggadic statements of the common theology, that is, between norms of behavior and norms of belief. I have even now some preliminary ideas on how that critical exercise is to be undertaken.

Theological Grammar of the Oral Torah. Vol. I   25

What of constructive and systematic theology? My one effort at constructive theology is *Judaism's Theological Voice: The Melody of the Talmud.* Chicago, 1995: The University of Chicago Press. I cannot now even contemplate the requirements of a systematic theology of Rabbinic Judaism, or even the organizing categories (though the Protestant categories, dogmatics and apologetics, seem to me pertinent).

[15] I owe this formulation to Professor David Aaron, Wellesley College (personal letter, February 11, 1997).

[16] The specific types of models I have chosen — models of analysis, models of explanation, and models of anticipation — are explained in the Introduction to Volume III.

[17] My sense is that the great master of Rabbinic Judaism viewed as religion, Max Kadushin, the pioneer and pathfinder, was heading in exactly that direction.

[18] And, ultimately, only in the Torah. That is to say, all occasions of self-manifestation beyond the limits of the Torah — in nature and in history, for example — take on consequence when placed into the context of what the Torah teaches. It is the Torah that designates events of a particular order as manifestations of God's will and plan, that calls attention to nature in a particular context as the echo of God's voice. That argument is amplified, briefly, in *Judaism's Theological Voice*.

[19] I find in Sifra in particular the explicit and systematic embodiment of that theological conviction that the words of the Torah convey not only what God wishes to say but how God chooses to formulate thought, hence God's mind and not only God's message. See my *Uniting the Dual Torah: Sifra and the Problem of the Mishnah.* Cambridge and New York, 1989: Cambridge University Press.

[20] I have systematically conducted a form-analysis of each of the documents, which comes topression in my translations and the reference-system I have devised therein. My form-history is now complete in *The Documentary Form-History of Rabbinic Literature.* Atlanta, 1998: Scholars Press for South Florida Studies in the History of Judaism, in seven volumes, fourteen parts in all, covering the Mishnah and two Talmuds and the Midrash-compilations as well. The form-history is not random but built upon the free-standing testimony of the several documents, viewed discretely. I have found that forms cannot be examined in the abstract but only in documentary context. For a current review of this work see Edward Goldman, "Neusner Translating Talmud," in *Critical Review*, 1997 (Atlanta, 1998: Scholars Press).

[21] Oliver Sacks, *Seeing Voices* (N.Y., 1989:HarperCollins), p. 78.

[22] Sacks, p. 80.

[23] I paraphrase Noam Chomsky, *Language and Mind* (N.Y., 1962: Harcourt Brace Jovanovich), p. 111: "We abstract away from conditions of use of language and consider formal structures and the formal operations that relate them...This process of abstraction...expresses a point of view...the working hypothesis that we can proceed with the study of 'knowledge of language'...in abstraction from the problems of how language is used."

[24] *Language and Mind* , p. 102.

[25] I paraphrase Chomsky, p. 103, "I am primarily intrigued by the possibility of learning something, from the study of language, that will bring to light inherent properties of the human mind."

[26] Chomsky, *op. cit.*, p. 27.

[27] *Compact Edition of the Oxford English Dictionary* (Oxford, 1971: Oxford University Press), s.v. grammar.

[28] Chomsky, p. 28.

[29] That formulation is disingenuous, since the fundamental hermeneutical problem of the Oral part of the Torah is then gainsaid; it is, after all, to set forth the one whole Torah of Moses, our rabbi — written and oral as a single seamless statement. I return to this matter in *The Theology of the Oral Torah*. There I begin the entire theological project at that very point: the unity of the two parts of the Torah; there, in my view, the meeting with God in the Torah takes place, which is why, while acknowledging the power of prayer, Rabbinic Judaism promises that encounter through the act of Torah-study in particular. In this context the myth of the dual Torah proves definitive — which is hardly surprising.

[30] Indeed, I should claim that a body of writings that cannot be shown to yield a cogent system ought not to be asked to portray a Judaic religious system at all; whether or not, for example, the library at Qumran yields a system has yet to be investigated. But no one in modern times has ever doubted that the Rabbinic writings of late antiquity do cohere, as is the unchallenged premise of the works examined in my *The Theology of Rabbinic Judaism. A Prolegomenon*. Atlanta, 1997: Scholars Press for South Florida Studies on the History of Judaism.

[31] It is summarized in *Introduction to Rabbinic Literature*. N.Y., 1994: Doubleday.

[32] I have dealt with critics of this reading in my *The Documentary Foundation of Rabbinic Culture. Mopping Up after Debates with Gerald L. Bruns, S. J. D. Cohen, Arnold Maria Goldberg, Susan Handelman, Christine Hayes, James Kugel, Peter Schaefer, Eliezer Segal, E. P. Sanders, and Lawrence H. Schiffman*. Atlanta, 1995: Scholars Press for South Florida Studies in the History of Judaism. The main work of documentary description of the various components of the entire literature — the Mishnah, Tosefta, two Talmuds, and various Midrash-compilations, has taken twenty-five years and requires no recapitulation here. It suffices to state that every component of the Rabbinic corpus of antiquity has been examined in its own terms, for its formal traits, its principles of cogent discourse, and its substantive program. Having taken the whole apart, I wish now to find out how it holds together, as the faithful have always maintained it does.

[33] The history of the formation of Rabbinic Judaism yielded by a sequential, documentary reading of the writings is set forth in *The Transformation of Judaism. From Philosophy to Religion*. Champaign, 1992: University of Illinois Press. Second printing: Atlanta, 1997: Scholars Press for South Florida Studies in the History of Judaism.

[34] I close at 600, because from the advent of Islam, an entirely new set of intellectual issues enters — the articulate encounter with philosophy being the main one! — and with the new context a new set of problems have to be faced in the description, analysis, and interpretation of the writings of Rabbinic Judaism. A simple demonstration of how different the post-Islamic documents of that Judaism are will be gained by a systematic reading of the interpretation of given verses of Scripture through the classical Rabbinic writings and into those of the following period; the turning-point time and again proves to be the first post-Islamic compilation. At that point continuity is lost, and quite fresh issues and ideas emerge, precipitated by a completely unprecedented problematic of thought.

[35] I have founded the *Annual of Rabbinic Judaism, Ancient, Medieval, and Modern*, to

provide a forum for learned discussion of that Judaism as a cogent and continuous religious system, seeking the points of continuity and order that characterize the whole. The divisions, ancient, medieval, and modern, obscure the continuity, start to present, that in fact marks that Judaism.

[36]But only at this stage. Any account of Rabbinic Judaism, while encompassing and privileging the writings of the Oral Torah, will attend to documents that sages valued but did not set forth in the manner characteristic of their own, particular writings. We can read as a system the Mishnah or the Bavli, but to describe the Judaism to which these documents attest, we have also to move beyond Judaism: the evidence of the Mishnah and address Judaism: all pertinent evidence. That is a different problem from the one solved by documentary description of systems, as I explained in my *Judaism: The Evidence of the Mishnah* (Chicago, 1981: University of Chicago Press).

THE THEOLOGICAL GRAMMAR OF THE ORAL TORAH

I. Vocabulary: Native Categories

Introduction

Within the definition given at the outset that theology transforms into intellectually accessible terms and categories the substance of Israel's ancient, on-going encounter with God, how in the Oral Torah does theology carry on its work of systematization and ordering? What traits characterize theological discourse in the Oral Torah? The answer begins with an account of the organizing categories, the classification-system that permits the rational organization of the facts of religious experience that theology takes for sustained and systematic analysis. These I call native categories, because the documents take shape around them and, further, the documents themselves produce and validate them: thus, categories that are native to the ordering of religious experience that takes place in the Oral Torah.

Let me commence with a simple definition of "categories" within the framework of my governing metaphor: the category is that part of a proposition that allows the meanings of other words to be determined by virtue of its presence. In linguistics such terms are called collectively "the head noun." In descriptive theology these categories govern classification of data concerning what God has said and done, now recorded in the Torah.[37] The single word of a statement that determines the meaning and properties of the whole, out of linguistics, here corresponds to those categories that govern – dictate what fits with what, and how things hold together — everywhere.[38]

What, exactly, do I identify within the present definition as the working categories? "God" works, "idol" does not; "atonement" works, "repentance" works, 'rebellion' does not. And so for the principal entries in my vocabulary of native categories. So within the vocabulary of the documents of the Oral Torah, some words constitute organizing classifications, others do not. Then a theological structure and system has made its decisions, which emerge only in the details of on-going discourse. In due course, characterizing that structure and system will become feasible. What we know at this point is that the system identifies its useful vocabulary, and it is not a huge one. The list supplied at the Table of Contents suffices to demonstrate the presence of a highly restrictive vocabulary indeed. It is a set of words that the theological system animating the documents utilizes to dictate what may, and may not, be said. I refer, then, not to an absolute characteristic of a particular word — why should "sword" or "sponge' not stand for a native category, while "Land of Israel" or 'salvation" should? Rather, I ask how in the documents, as I read them, certain words function, how the words I list here behave.[39]

In this context Aaron states, "It may turn out that all statements with 'God' as the subject conform to certain rules of syntax such that their semantic values are highly uniform." My entry under "God" shows that within the limits of the Oral Torah that is precisely how matters turn out. The native categories form the first step toward the description of the system that all documents realize in one aspect or another: the theology of the Oral Torah, the free-standing documents now read comprehensively. So much for "category;" in due course we shall deal with the "native" part of the project.

I

Now to start from the beginning. A language is made up of these components: the smallest parts, its governing logic, and its structures that allow for the discernment of meaning (semantics). These correspond to the vocabulary (native categories), syntax, and semantics of this *Grammar*. The "smallest parts" or vocabulary correspond to the categorical structures of a theological system, and by asking the documents to dictate their own categorical structure, I follow the model of grammarians, who find the "smallest parts" within the language, not — self-evidently — beyond its own testimonies. The working tools of a language find their counterpart in the native categories of a theological system. Within some theories of language, words impose order on pre-verbal perceptions, both calling attention to and identifying data otherwise not accessible to notice (as in "the limits of my language are the limits of my world"). Along these same lines the categories of a theological system serve as the principal organizers of inchoate data, dictating how we classify data and impute meaning to them. These categories may emerge from the documents or they may take shape out of the program of questions brought to those documents; the documents may dictate their own categorical structure, or we may bring to them categories of interest to us, which we find remarkable in the document themselves.

In the model of linguistics, I classify these "smallest parts," or words, by how they behave, and that is in line with the formulation of Steven Pinker:

> "A part of speech...is not a kind of meaning; it is a kind of token that obeys certain formal rules, like a chess piece or a poker chip. A noun, for example, is simply a word that does nouny things; it is the kind of word that comes after an article, can have an 's' stuck onto it, and so on. There is a connection between concepts and parts of speech categories, but it is a subtle and abstract one. When we construe an aspect of the world as something that can be identified and counted or measured and that can play a role in events, language often allows us to express that aspect as a noun, whether or not it is a physical object [whether or not it is a person, place or thing]."[40]

The words that register here are those "that can play a role in events," and the native categories that I identify in this part of the *Grammar* identify principal and critical players in the religious events recorded by the Oral Torah. Our native categories therefore constitute items that can be identified and play a role in events or supply the topic of a sentence, in more formal terms.[41]

If not counted or measured ("person, place or thing"), the native categories I have identified nonetheless form the foci of activity and concern: Israel and the gentiles; God and man; sanctification, atonement, intentionality, Kingdom of Heaven, repentance — powerful forces all! What we can say with these categories is governed by considerations that correspond to syntax — which words can combine, and which ones cannot — and what propositions emerge to form an intelligible account of matters finds definition in the semantics to be considered in due course. Models of explanation and anticipation form the counterpart, in theological language, to the intelligible statements afforded by the semantics of a language. Thus like language theology has its building blocks (vocabulary), its syntax (conventions of discourse) and its semantics (factors that limit potential meaning).[42]

The corpus of words and other linguistic tools by which a language labels things corresponds, in a theological system, to the primary vocabulary that (formally) stands at the head of the declarative statements of that system and (categorically) defines its principal topics of cogent discourse: persons, places, principles, attitudes, ideas, affirmations. Each accomplishes the same end, in the present context, a theological one. Those media for the identification, definition, and organization of religious experience, for the naming of the actors and active powers of religious encounter with God as recorded in the Torah, oral and written, constitute the counterpart of the vocabulary of a language. What we see in the pseudo-lexicographical entries I have constructed at the shank of this volume is how a given classification holds together a number of distinct but cognate religious experiences or conceptions; the cognitive rules of a language that govern relations of words, and thus provide the metaphor for the native categories of a theological system. So far as I introduce my own comments at the several entries, it is to underscore the coherence of the components of the definition of a given category, or to address points of incoherence.

Not unlike nouns for persons, places, and things, the native categories therefore supply the name that classifies or categorizes the data of religion, whether concrete or abstract. Experiences, however discrete, of a given category are joined together, being differentiated, also, from experiences of another type. A single action may fall into more than one category, but the system will always dictate that category that pertains and exclude those that do not. These categories form that selection of the counterpart to a language's nouns, allowing us to identify as known and knowable, as subject to rational rules of relationship, the components of the otherwise-chaotic world of religious life that the theology discerns. Out of that vocabulary the religious system identifies the building blocks of thought, the topical components of its intelligible statements. That is what I mean when I propose that native categories in religious writing form the counterpart to the nouns or substantives of a language. Whether with the nouns of a language or the native categories of a religion, knowing the name that we call the data, we are able to make sense of those data, organize and categorize — and therefore understand them. Our vocabulary in both cases not only labels but creates the data. So much for systemic categories as counterparts to a language's vocabulary.

II

From categories in general, we proceed to the critical point of differentiation: "native category." A category encompasses in a single rubric diverse data. The origin of the category bears no consequence. But a native category in particular is one defined by, emerging from (in the present context) the documents themselves, not invented by us out of a later, alien system altogether. By "native category," therefore, I refer to a building block of thought and speech that in the documents of the Oral Torah is identified as imparting significance or cogency to diverse data. A native category serves in the Oral Torah to organize facts into intelligible compositions. Such a category may be, but is not necessarily a fact[43] but it always encompasses and organizes facts. A native category ought ordinarily not to be divisible or subject to classification within other categories, even though data that fit within one native-category may for other (taxonomic) reasons also fit within another.[44] Thus, for example, a critical native category, Land of Israel, also is irreducible and indivisible,[45] so too repentance or God or Israel. Diverse data may find their way to such native categories as these, but by definition and by usage "God" classifies but cannot be further classified, and so with the other items.[46]

How then do we know what belongs and what does not? A simple rule of thumb serves. If we want to test a hypothesis that a given classification serves as a native category — organizing data and imparting sense to them — we may ask about its opposite. The indicative trait of a native category is that we cannot ordinarily use its opposite in the way in which we use the native category. God is a native category, idol is not; Land of Israel is a native category, other lands (not differentiated, all unclean for instance) are not.

A constructive, positive statement meant to stand on its own and not depend upon other categories cannot be composed in the Oral Torah with "idol" at the head, or with "land of the gentiles" at the head, and so throughout. Idol will stand in a contrastive relationship to God, Land of the gentiles to Land of Israel, and so on. And then, God or Torah or Land of Israel can stand on their own and head — provide the organizing center for — a sentence, a set of sentences, a paragraph, a proposition, an entire composite. We may speak of God and and Land of Israel without invoking idol or land of the gentiles, but the contrary is rarely[47] the case.

A second criterion is not excluded by the first. What is undifferentiated is not native, e.g., gentiles except in contradistinction to Israel, and what is differentiated is native, e.g., Israel — priests, Levites, Israelites, and the like. That trait of native categories is blatant and requires no amplification.

III

To move forward, then: what makes a native category theological? Everyone knows that the documents of the Oral Torah on their own present nothing so systematic as to qualify as theology. They consist of sayings, stories, exegesis of received texts, and the like. So, as a matter of simple fact, theology in no way constitutes a native category of the writing of the Oral Torah.[48] It represents my, not sages', categorical principle. How then do we know the theological native-categories in particular? A phenomenological answer serves. A theological native category takes up a topic treated in an other-than-this-worldly or supernatural context, for example, the relationship to God of a particular type of human being, a holy person or saint or sage; or the character of an event in which God is represented as taking part, a miracle or revelation for example.[49] Three examples suffice. "Commandment" transforms an ordinary, secular action into one that sanctifies, expressing the intent of the actor to serve and obey God. Kingdom of Heaven utilizes for a transcendent purpose a political metaphor. Messiah, prayer, redemption, atonement, repentance, resurrection — all conform to the simple definition just now given; each addresses a point at which man meets God, whether in time, or in gesture, or in aspiration or intention or attitude or expectation.

How in actuality do we know a native theological category when we see one? In the documents under study and subject to theological systematization here, we recognize a native theological category if a simple condition is met. Specifically, when a sizable exercise in definition and illustration is presented by one or more documentary components, e.g., a systematic exposition of a category, an elaborate instantiation of diverse items that fall into the same category, or a topical composite held together within a single category, then we identify a category. Introduce the encounter with God, show the coherence and cogency of the data that fall into the classification, and the category self-evidently falls into the classification of theology. And since the category emerges from an analytical reading of the documents of the Oral Torah, it is native, not artificial and imposed.

To give two examples: a householder is a native category, the subject of many predicates. He would enter the classification of a theological native category at those points at which his relationship to God forms the determinative consideration in a transaction that is represented by the law, in the exposition of the theology of the laws of the first division of the Mishnah, for example, on the agricultural rules of the Torah.[50] Repentance is a native category of a theological character, since all of the usages of the category — all of the data assembled within it — involve God in the transaction. And so throughout: the data assembled for the native categories such as Israel, gentile, atonement and sin. These invariably engage God's participation.

By contrast, such candidates as the Dead Sea, or a cow that gores, or an olive tree subject to conflicting claims (among thousands of candidates) do not qualify as theological categories, though under some circumstances they may serve as native ones, indeed as representative of items beyond themselves. The theological native categories then signal that the framers of the documents of the Oral Torah identify said classifications of experience or encounter as a given and deem their irreducibility as self-evident. How do we know? As I said, we test our identification of a given category as native by examining a topical composite and asking what is primary thereto, and what is subordinate; what organizes, what is organized.

Let me broaden the matter by appealing once more to the generative metaphor. Linguistics stresses function — how words work — and that is precisely my approach to identifying native categories. I identify and classify them by reference to the way in which they work. A native category will always form the unifying taxon: repentance or sin suffice to exemplify the matter. That is a characteristic of function or behavior; it is by how native categories work that I know them.

It is also by reference to the broader context formed by the documents themselves. A word that does not affect the use or meaning of other words is not a native category; it is just a word. A word that imposes its sense and order upon other words is a native category — "something that can be identified." Prayer, righteousness, repentance — these govern. They make things happen, accomplish things, serve as the subject of a sentence, as in prayer, righteousness, repentance avert the evil decree. Persons of a given standing will serve, if not in the present volume. By contrast, nowhere in my reading of matters do places make a difference except in the instance of Land of Israel (and its type of place, that is, Jerusalem, Temple, and so on). Everywhere else is no where in particular. For the type of category I sought in the present study, my list of thirty native categories, then, is not exemplary or typical; for the type of native category I sought for the present purpose, it is exhaustive, so far as I can see.[51]

A native category will commonly serve as the subject of a predicate, as that which is modified, but uncommonly as the predicate, as that which modifies. "God will redeem" is a possible sentence in accord with the theological grammar of the Oral Torah, "the power that redeems is God" is not. Such a sentence violates the thought-rules and so produces no intelligible statement. So a native category will encompass data and impart coherence to them. But, being irreducible, it will rarely be encompassed and seldom forced to cohere with other primary data, e.g., facts or systemic givens. A native category may interact with others; indeed, that is how the structure of categories transforms itself into a system of consequential statements. But such a category will ordinarily affect the combination but be in itself unchanged therein. Native categories enjoying self-evidence include such as God, Torah, Israel, Land of Israel. God's actions and teachings, the Torah's contents and implications, Israel's adherents and experiences, the active, participative role of the enchanted Land as an active player in the supernatural drama of Israel's and God's struggle — these form examples of those irreducible classifiers of facts that in this survey of the Oral Torah's documents we come to define as native categories.[52]

IV

Now to return to the metaphor introduced in the Preface and invoked in the opening lines of this introduction. What, in particular, is it about the lexicon of a language — what we may call "the smallest parts" or phonemes — that supplies an illuminating metaphor for this effort to characterize the theological substrate of the several documents of the Oral Torah? The answer is implicit in what has already been said. It is the identification of head-words, the relations of words according to fixed rules, and the semantics that emerges from those relations, that allow rationality to be perceived. The way we form statements reflects the logic that governs our thought processes. Words and how they are arranged and used then manifest the process, the tools that change how we think into what we say. That is why I work backward from the words the theology uses to the processes of thought that govern, to try to find out something about how theology forms a vocabulary based no its thought-preferences. The governing question then is, how does a theology establish its word-choices (in this part of the study) and then how does theology govern the discourse that results (Volumes II and III)?[53]

Where does the vocabulary in particular enter in? The available theological words instantiate the power of a category to afford the possibility of generalization out of discrete data and reflection thereon. Take "redemption" for example. Israel finds itself in trouble; God intervenes, whether at the Reed Sea, whether at the crossing of the Jordan. The set of cases takes shape within a process of generalization and abstraction such as we should call analysis (what have these things in common, what rule governs them all), and explanation (how to make sense of this pattern), and, in the case of the Oral Torah, further generates the condition of anticipation (what do we learn from these facts about the future).[54] In the case of theology, native categories bring about theological discourse upon religious encounter and experience. In the present volume the categories of the Oral Torah provide an account of what takes place in meeting God in the Torah. In both realms the head-words (a.k.a., nouns) of a language, the native categories of a theological corpus Ä the generative particles of language and the structural categories of religion alike impart meaning, order, and structure to otherwise inchoate, even impalpable, data: things of the world, experiences of religious encounter, respectively.

V

How, exactly, does the process of category-formation or naming — assigning nouns to sets of persons, places, or things, designating categories to encompass varied moments of religious realization — work for language? How does its counterpart, the process of category-formation, work for theology? A noun selects and labels data, imparting to those (in some ways diverse) data the qualities of cogency and coherence and so raising them to consciousness for intellectual recognition. The process would then yield possibilities of reflection, analysis, generalization for instance.

Nouns make possible a process of *"proposition-ization,"* so to speak.

By their nature words not only label but homogenize, calling by the same word things that, in some ways, bear traits of differentiation as well, e.g., dog for the various breeds of dogs, man for diverse men, mountain for extrusions of various dimensions, match for a nearly unlimited number of sets of things that bear traits in common, or for diverse instruments for kindling a flame. At the same time categories exclude by identifying traits that differentiate all things within from all things without: species of a genus from another genus altogether. From our perspective, category-formation marks the point at which the language of a vocabulary and the category-formation of religious writings such as the documents of the Oral Torah intersect. For both language and theology, the names that label things and differentiate one from another are what permit discourse of a general character, both encompassing and transcending the cases or specific instances. Such nouns or substantives are represented, e.g., by man, mountain, match, for a person, place, or thing, respectively.

The power to organize data, to classify and to categorize what is otherwise hopelessly disparate, then illuminates the world that language informs and the eternal encounter with God that theology rationally recapitulates. With correct vocabulary in the correct structure — my "native category" — theological meaning emerges. For linguistics, the cluster of words dictate potential structures. When we know which cluster yields which structure, we have precisely what I mean by "native category." In the present work, then, my native categories join diverse data into a single cluster of congruent meanings; the native category identifies a word (or cognate words) that functions in accord with specific rules of meaning. Data that exhibit the pertinent indicative traits — even, or especially, in polythetic classification — will be rendered cogent by being given the same name, that is by being called by the same word.

Words then label in a single manner these (otherwise diverse) bipeds with proper qualities (whether physical, whether intellectual) all fall into the category of man, excluding also the bipeds that do not; they call by the right name those aspects of the landscape, mountain, and the other traits — a stick that can kindle a flame — match, respectively. It becomes possible to generalize and explain, even to compare and contrast the diverse things that bear the same name, e.g., while one is large and another small, both fit into the same genus, and the traits of the genus in general pertain to the things that fall into that genus, even though these may be speciated in some other way. In this way we may transcend cases and discuss principles. For long centuries debates have addressed the proposition that the case is all we have, so that we have only things but not thing or that the name identifies what matters in the thing and gives it consequence (nominalism vs. realism). To that debate I have no contribution to make; I invoke language as a metaphor. The analogy serves to clarify, not to complicate, the work. Then to clarify the character of the counterpart to the vocabulary of the language in theology I hardly need to review centuries of philosophical reflection on the thing-ness of "Ideas," the names of things.

VI

Now from matters of theory let us turn to the task at hand. It suffices in these few words to explain what is ahead by invoking the analogy of the vocabulary of a language. I have now to specify what I found in the documents of the Oral Torah to be comparable to the vocabulary of a language. It is my task to identify in the documents of the Oral Torah those points at which we find ourselves speaking about head-words (persons, places, or things) that make discrete data cohere — the counterpart to such words as man, mountain, and match that encompass diverse men, mountains, and matches. Just as by nouns or substantives we speak of the cases and impute to them all certain traits of cogency and coherence, so in the writings at hand, particular nouns or substantives serve. That is because they identify categories that impart form and structure and cogency to the religious experience recorded in those writings. Once a category identifies as one a range of cases, occasions, persons or events, then the traits of the cases impart definition to the category and take the measure of its dimensions.

Accordingly, within the analogy and argument at hand, religious experience within the framework of the Torah comes to expression in certain words that give shape and structure to that encounter: not the case in particular, but to the principle in general: the thing, not only the examples thereof, dog, not only yellow labrador retriever; but only dog, not dogs, cats, and other household pets. These chosen words label categories, and, by reason of the method followed here — remaining within the limits of a specified body of documents — they signify native categories, categories defined within the data. These then speak of a finite body of data and select within those data the important cases subject to recapitulation in general terms: "God forgave Israel" represents the case, "God's mercy," the categorical principle, which then is capable of encompassing a variety of kindred cases. Then on our catalogue of vocabulary we include the word, "mercy, divine."

An important qualification now enters. A variety of words will refer to a single category of phenomena, and we may supply the word, not only the translation of the documents' own word, as in the case of divine mercy or justice (*middat harahamim, middat haddin*). For instance, take the power of intentionality to dictate the outcome of a transaction. Here a word we supply — intentionality — will in fact correspond to a native category that emerges out of the documents of the Oral Torah, covered by the word "intentionality" — our word for their well-defined phenomenon. The language of the documents, e.g., *kavvanah*, will not appear invariably to signal the presence of the category. But it is, nonetheless, a cogent one.[55] One way or the other, within the corpus of words by which the language identifies out of things that happen the intelligible and consequential moments or transactions or participants we find a limited number of such substantives or nouns. These are the ones capable of holding many things together as one thing, many cases as one governing principle.

So to summarize: I regard as the vocabulary of the theological system the active categories of discourse of the Oral Torah. A "category" or "category-formation" imposes order on the chaos of inchoate data; it marks the first step toward rational description of matters. By category I mean, a classification that holds together and treats as cogent a variety of data, e.g., facts of a given order, events of a common class, persons who fit the same model, and the like. These categories function for theology as the nouns or substantives function for a language, in that they identify and name that about which the theology will conduct discourse, as nouns identify and name that about which language will speak.

VII

Now let me specify what I conceive to be at stake: what do we gain if we take this view of matters? The answer is, we gain access to the theological system and structure that the writings of the Oral Torah presuppose and instantiate. By analyzing the components of the language common

Theological Grammar of the Oral Torah. Vol. I 41

to them all, and by doing so in the manner suggested by one school of linguistics, I hope to identify what holds the whole together: the substrate of theological reflection, the system of theological inquiries, the structure of theological convictions, all together, all at once. It is not the propositions that surface hither and yon, but the language that everywhere governs consciousness, that yields an account of that system and structure: its native-categories, the ways in which it assembles and reassembles those categories, the models of thought that impart sense to, and derive meaning from, those categories.

The problem contains within itself its own solution. It is a problem comprised by a specific set of writings — not the usage of a language in general, but the particular evidences of how it is used in some few writings. Then when we know how these writings work, how their categorical structure, modes of forming constructions and drawing connections, models of coherent analysis, explanation, and anticipation, take shape — then we can say what the structure comprises and what the system does. From the usages we work our way back to the principles that govern correct usage. From what people say, we find out how they are thinking, and in that way we can reconstruct their modes of thought even on problems not explicitly addressed. The analogy to language then proves quite exact: if we know the rules of a language, with perfect confidence that we shall be understood, we can think thoughts hitherto never contemplated, we can say what has never been said before. That accounts for the appeal to the metaphor in play here: its exact correspondence to the situation before us.

My goal is to describe a theological system conveyed within a finite body of documents, and that means, as I explained in the Preface, I hope to find out what theological language serves them all, what dictionary affords access to every one, what category-formation prevails, whether on the surface or deep in the structure of thought. That accounts for the stress on vocabulary, syntax, and semantics, the components of the language throughout. Once more the chosen metaphor serves, now in a direct and unmediated manner: the limits of the language set forth in the documents of the Oral Torah set the bounds to the system and their traits of order and form adumbrate the logic and regularity thereof. They define what can be said and cannot be said. They place limits on what may be thought.[56] In theology the categories that define the range of discourse themselves form a critical component of the system; they play an active role and bear much of the systemic structure. The generative, active categories recapitulate the systemic tensions and resolve them, time and again. They make possible the statement of one thing about many things. That about which we can and are to speak to begin with defines that structure, also excluding from discourse, eliminating from consideration, a vast range of candidates for inclusion.

To make matters specific, within the language-theology of the Oral Torah, certain nouns persist in forming the center of discourse and precipitating the generative tensions, defining the recurrent questions, and others, deriving from the same repertoire supplied by the same corpus of consequential facts — the written Torah — play no consequential role. The former provoke thought, set forth propositions, define problems. The latter prove inert and neutral. Some kings matter, some do not; some places mark important events and warrant, e.g., the recitation of a blessing when one visits, others do not; some events come under close inspection and generate propositions, others prove inert. Let me briefly illustrate how the documents themselves dictate that proposition:

> A. One who sees a place where miracles were performed for Israel says, "Blessed is he who performed miracles for our fathers in this place."
> B. [One who sees] a place from which idolatry was uprooted says, "Blessed is he who uprooted idolatry from our land."
>
> M. 9:1

What we see is that the document itself dictates its theological category — that type of locale that falls within the framework of encounter with God. So too when it comes to events of nature and of everyday life, both private and public, the documents articulate how we are to classify and categorize, take note and respond, or ignore and leave uncategorized, ignore and neglect:

> A. For meteors, earth tremors, lightning, thunder, and wind, one says, "Blessed... whose power and might fill the world."
> B. For mountains, hills, seas, rivers, and deserts, he says, "Blessed... the maker of [all of] creation."
> C. R. Judah says, "He who sees the Great [Mediterranean] Sea says, 'Blessed... who made the Great Sea,'
> D. "when he sees it at intervals."
> E. For the rain and for good tidings, he says, "Blessed... who is good and does good."
> F. And for bad tidings he says, "Blessed... the true judge."

M. 9:2

These examples suffice to show how from the documents we proceed to identify working categories, those that are native and, in the nature of things, those that are theological in character. But ultimately, sufficient data having been assembled, it will become our task to formulate the system that is implicit and ubiquitous: the theology that has been constructed to take account, and make sense, of the entire repertoire of religious experiences and encounters that the Torah assembles for Israel's sustenance.

So the system identifies, and the documents replicate, the repertoire of head-words, nouns and substantives — persons, places, and things — that can stand at the head of propositions, serving as the subjects of sentences for example, or as objects of verbs. And what is at stake is obvious: when we know the native-categories, we find ourselves at the very heart of the theological system that identifies those categories and defines and organizes religious reality in accord with them.

This leads us back to our metaphor. The active vocabulary, the words that time and again dictate the head nouns — meaning, here, the topical program of a cogent set of sentences — these define the repertoire of native categories by which the Oral Torah organizes discourse and defines that which deserves rational consideration. Such a category must be deemed active in that it imposes upon the facts that fall within it a single set of rules, a governing signification. Thus *"shema"* (a prayer) and *"alenu"* (another prayer) would not constitute categories unto themselves, being taxonomically inert (within the present corpus of writing, active elsewhere), but together, and with other writings of the same order, they would fit into the category of "prayer." The native theological categories, the active, systemically-charged vocabulary of the Oral Torah, are what I list here.

VIII

That explains why the only way to describe the category-formation of the Oral Torah is to ask the documents to dictate their own categories. Any picture of the theology of the Oral Torah must begin with a reliable account of the organizing categories that the documents of the Oral Torah themselves utilize for the rationalization of the data that they set forth; these are the organizing principles of thought. These principles, which surely must strike the reader as, if unexceptionable, rather platitudinous, in fact introduce a considerable problem: whence the repertoire of categories? How do we know that a category-formation that we find indicative and active is native to the system, expressing its points of tension and recapitulation, and not imposed upon it by the on-looker out of another system? As I explain elsewhere,[57] the dogmatics of Protestant theology has conventionally assigned to and imposed upon the data of the theology of Rabbinic Judaism its own category-formation. The process has worked systematically and inexorably, producing a deeply Protestant category-formation for the consequently-formulated Judaism that is portrayed. If Protestant dogmatics set forth doctrines of justification, then justification should define a category of Rabbinic Judaism as well, so too, covenant, so too, soteriology, ethics, and on and on. That is, we know what we want to know, how we wish to organize our data, what we propose to discern therein, because the standard program of dogmatics tells us: God, ethics, salvation, and the like. The result is a profoundly Protestant Judaism, stopping short only of justification by faith alone.

Since that simple list will remind the reader how rich and dense a category-structure inheres in those enormous compilations, the question must arise: how do I know a theological category from a category-formation of some other order? That question belongs at just this point, because it brings us to a serious challenge to my insistence that I improve upon the Protestant theologians by ignoring their dogmatics — indeed, their systematics — in favor of the category-formation I insist the Oral Torah itself has framed.

First, I claim to utilize native categories. But in distinguishing holy from ordinary, theological from secular categories, I make a distinction that is certainly not native to the Oral Torah (among many representations of religion before nearly our own day)! For, clearly, the exposition of the law in the Mishnah, upon which rests the entire legal-exegetical corpus serving the Mishnah, knows sixty-two tractates, hence sixty-two topics, each of them functioning in exactly the way that I maintain categories function: organizing cogent data and offering generalizations that pertain thereto. Why then is "blessings" a theological category, but the wife accused of adultery (Sotah), or oaths (Nedarim), or animal offerings (Zebahim) or the susceptibility of utensils to cultic uncleanness (Kelim), not a theological category?

Certainly my definition of what theology does, set forth in the opening sentence of the Preface, affords no obvious answer. For as everyone knows in the world portrayed by the Oral Torah there is no distinguishing what belonged to the realm of religion from what was secular. Sages used the word sanctification for the hallowing of the Sabbath and the designation of a woman as holy to a particular man, the one religious, the other secular, in our world but not in theirs. And the same then must pertain throughout. Hence pots and pans, marital relationships, oaths, and the resolution of civil conflict, represented issues of sanctity and occasions of sanctification, as much as convictions about God, Israel, the Torah, atonement, suffering, and the soul stood for the transcendent dimensions of life. Since, moreover, the sages found in the Written Torah the rules of sanctification, all of the categories of scriptural law as much as those of scriptural lore formed integral components of the category-formation of the Oral part of the Torah that sages constructed in completion and fulfillment of the Written part. So if the categories of tractate Abot fit well, then those of tractate Nedarim or Zebahim must too.

Second, while seeking categories native to the Oral Torah, I have brought to my reading of the document a fair number of categories no more native than are justification or soteriology (or ecclesiology for that matter or Christology!). These equally alien categories are religion (as distinct from the secular), and, therefore, its intellectual byproduct, theology (as distinct from other systematizations of thought). And, within the encompassing category, theology, I include categories that sages will have found no more theological, and no less theological, than the pots and pans concerning which they legislated so reflectively. The project, then, finds its definition and destination outside the limits of the documents of the Oral Torah, bringing to those documents points of differentiation not native to them at all.

How therefore do I claim to have improved on the Protestant dogmatic theologians' reconstructive reading of the same writings? It is in insisting that, within the shared premise that we may differentiate and give emphasis to what we deem religious and not secular in writings that make no such distinction, we may still identify in those writings categories that are native. My act of extrinsic differentiation takes place within the framework only of the documents' own category-formations. I introduce none of my own, though classifying the work as a whole in my way, not in the manner of the sages. Admittedly, sages will have produced a much, much longer and more elaborate account of the governing categories of their thought than mine — sixty-two large topics of halakhah — life lived in accord with the rules of sanctification — corresponding to the number of tractates of the Mishnah, to begin with. I maintain then that I set forth native categories, but admittedly, not all of the native categories that sages will have identified for me.

But — I state with heavy emphasis — *our sages of blessed memory will have recognized and accepted all of mine.* I know that that is the fact because every category-formation listed here emerges from the data of the documents themselves, and the documents have been repeatedly read whole and complete, not merely mined for sayings pertinent to subjects important in some context other than the documents. For reasons that strike me as self-evident, sages cannot have grasped critical categories of Protestant dogmatics — justification, soteriology — that the Protestant theologians bring to bear upon these writings, any more than they will have grasped other categories of Protestant dogmatics -- ecclesiology, Christology — that they do not introduce. Or — still more important — they will have recognized those categories, but not to the proportion and position accorded to them, as in the instance of covenantal nomism. By contrast sages also will have readily acknowledged that all of the categories that enjoy prominence in these pages also enjoy prominence in their systemic discourse — God's justice, God's mercy for instance, and so throughout.

IX

What do we gain in imposing the limits — native categories, not alien ones — that define and constrict this study? I mean to make stick my critique of the use of alien category-formations that, up to the present time, have been imposed, and so have distorted, descriptions of this Judaism. Until now people have imposed the categories of Protestant dogmatic theology, so distorting their picture of the theology of the Oral Torah by laying emphasis upon matters of slight consequence therein and bypassing matters of central importance. To give a single instance, the category-formation of Protestant dogmatic theology contains no rubric for halakhah or norms of behavior (other than ethical norms) and therefore allows no exploration of how halakhah expresses in its own framework theological principles as fundamental as those contained by norms of belief or aggadah.

Theological Grammar of the Oral Torah. Vol. I   47

Marshall Sahlins cites a passage of Foucault who himself cites a zoological classification system that captures the problem:

> Better to adopt the attitude of Foucault when presented by Borges with a zoological classification from a certain Chinese encyclopaedia, in which it is written that 'animals are divided into (a) belonging to the Emperor, (b) embalmed, (c) tame, (d) suckling pigs, (e) sirens\ (f) fabulous, (g) stray dogs, (h) included in the present classification, (i) frenzied, (j) innumerable, (k) drawn with a very fine camel hair brush, (l) et cetera, (m) having just broken the water pitcher, (n) that from a long way off look like flies. In the wonderment of this taxonomy, the thing we apprehend in one great leap, the thing that, by means of the fable, is demonstrated in the exotic charms of another system of thought, is the limitation of our own, the stark impossibility of thinking *that*.58

Protestant interest in justification and soteriology in Rabbinic Judaism proves as jarring to us as do the items joined in the odd Chinese zoological classification scheme. We find ourselves in a comparable position. Faced with the classification-system that forms the foundation of the documents of the Oral Torah, our own system of thought — based as it has been on the categories of Protestant dogmatic theology — leads us to cognitive dead-ends. So we have to begin the work of theological description with a systematic and orderly account of the categories that govern in the writings of the Oral Torah themselves.

Two obvious problems left unsolved have rendered null the results of the Protestant construction of the theology of Rabbinic Judaism. First, important categories are missed, not bearing upon the Protestant program. Second, importance is assigned to categories that, in the Oral Torah, enjoy little or no importance, categories that play no systemic role, generate no tensions, resolve no points of stress. The resulting account of matters proves accurate but pointless and uncomprehending, an exercise in intellectual vacuity.

An example of the former — missing what matters — is the category, Land of Israel, which is simply missed by the Protestant reading of Rabbinic Judaism but which as I show in these pages enjoys enormous prominence in the Oral Torah and its organization of the world. The Oral Torah must be classed as a profoundly enlandized religious system, but the Protestant theological reconstruction of "Judaism" does not convey that governing fact.

An instance of the latter — distortion and disproportion in the representation of the whole — is the category, covenant, specifically, "covenantal nomism." Now that category takes an important part in the liberal Protestant apologetics in behalf of Rabbinic Judaism (or just "Judaism"). The laws are kept not as silly formalities but as expressions of the solemn covenant between Israel and God. True enough, and only a malicious person would doubt it. But that issue preoccupies no one in the entire Oral Torah; there, the commandments are supposed to purify the heart, or keeping the commandments marks us as accepting God's dominion; but to no one does the conception of the halakhah as an empty and merely formal exercise ever occur. Hence nomism/covenantal defines no native category, no systemic player. Indeed, in the documents themselves, "covenant" identifies a systemically-inert category, remarkable by its power to remain in the deep background of nearly the whole of the Rabbinic corpus. By "covenant" that corpus of writings ordinarily refers only to "circumcision." In my survey I found some important composites on the theme of circumcision, but no interesting category-formation emerged that I could define: no "word" capable of classifying but not itself subject to classification for example. True, the Written Torah's account of the covenants of God with the patriarchs and with Israel animates the whole, but so too does much else in that same component of the Torah. But in the documents in which "covenant" stands for "circumcision," in which covenantal theology plays little systemic role, to impute centrality to covenantal considerations hardly yields an account of what the documents say, only of the context that we impute to the message that they set forth.[59]

    The reason that prior scholarship has resorted to imported category formations in preference to the native ones lies in the orientation and preparation of those who have done the work. Few ever concentrated on the documents of the Oral Torah in particular; picking and choosing sayings, few actually mastered them start to finish. So while context ought to be everything, for those intent on filling up the blank spaces on a questionnaire devised for their own survey, the setting that imparted consequence to a saying meant nothing. The saying by itself sufficed for its purpose, to fill a blank space on the Protestant questionnaire. Motivated by other interests entirely, the Protestant theologians then did not trouble to master the documents in their own terms. Rather they went in search of sayings pertinent to their predetermined program. No wonder they turned up sayings that could be found in the documents but out of all context therein.

These they noticed, to them they gave heavy emphasis. Finding sayings that fit their scheme and ignoring their context produced remarkable disproportions, on the one side, and obtuse omissions, on the other.

What is to be done? When the documents speak for themselves, using their language in their context to lay down their judgment upon formations of their own devising, we may teach ourselves to hear their language, in the words and music they find proper. Clearly, defining native categories marks the starting point, because, before we can proceed to the description of the theological structure that sustained the intellectual enterprise of Rabbinic Judaism, we have to identify the building blocks. Once we do, the formations of meaning constructed out of the joining of native categories require examination. So, as the Preface makes clear, only then we may raise questions of how the blocks hold together and form larger statements of order and meaning. That is the point at which another complete pass through the entire corpus of the Oral Torah will identify the theological paradigms that are comprised by the native categories. Yet a third pass will then show us how those paradigms function, that is, how the structure formed a working system, able to function so as to accommodate the on-going intellectual adventure of Rabbinic Israel. It follows that each volume of the *Grammar* emerges from a complete reading of the Oral Torah within the framework of the task undertaken by that volume.

So to conclude: how then have I identified the nouns of the lexicon, the native categories of the Oral Torah? From start to finish, beginning with the Mishnah and ending with the Talmud of Babylonia, I simply read the documents of the Oral Torah, line by line, looking for recurrent nouns — persons, places, things, ideas, attitudes, affirmations — that repeatedly form not only the topics of discourse but the points of recurrent tension, loci of the generative problematic that precipitates thought. Repentance, atonement, resurrection, commandment, Israel, Land of Israel, righteousness, sin and suffering — these words represent one type of native category, the rock-bottom, hard-core nouns that stand at the head of many, many sentences. How they work, what they mean, why they matter — the documents give rich, dense answers.

X

From this account of what is done here, we move to the context of the work: what is not done but presupposed. I refer, specifically, to the historical premise of my entire account of Rabbinic Judaism in its formative age. It is that we understand best when we relate conviction to context, the ideas that people hold to the world in which they (imagine that they) live. But in the essentially ahistorical framework of this analysis of the components of the theological language of the Oral Torah, we pay no attention to time and place and circumstance. We do not even differentiate among the diverse documents in which sayings are located, even though I have argued that the documents form categories of consequence. What then has become of the historical given — the conviction, definitive for every line I have ever written, that circumstances of time and place enter into the description, analysis, and interpretation of documents and of the Judaism that all together they comprise? Yet here I pay no attention to context, whether documentary, whether historical.

Here the opening remarks of the Preface must be called to mind: a single language serves throughout the documents, a coherent set of rules of intelligibility governs throughout, and hence by describing that language I enter into that plane of timeless discourse in which the entire religious system of the dual Torah finds its location.[60] Not only so, but a single language has been perceived to pervade the whole, and today and for long centuries, that language has not only guided the reading of those writings, but today's discourse framed within them: it is a spoken, a living language of theology.

Why, then, seek a theology that permeates the whole, even in the face of solid evidence of intellectual change over time and in response to circumstance? The reason is that, in the end, people for long centuries have identified within the Oral Torah a single cogent system, a coherent language, a pervasive grammar of thought. While the system that everyone perceives may have taken shape over time and absorbed within itself points of contradiction and incoherence, the system in its fullness turns out in retrospect to pervade, the imperfections losing consequence when seen in the perspective of the whole. Indeed, ample evidence that a single, common theology permeates the whole comes to us out of the long centuries, including the one now closing, in which these documents were deemed to speak out of a common rationality toward a single, timeless and unchanging world. People from then to now found it reasonable to cite as facts of a common eternity sentences from hither and yon and deemed the resulting propositions amply demonstrated and obviously coherent. That is why, while I have spent many decades showing the traits of change and development in response to crisis and challenge, I have also shared the premise that the documents all together and through their several parts set forth a single cogent statement — the one whole Torah of Moses our rabbi, oral and written.

That further explains why, when we ask what holds the whole together and address the theological question, considerations of what occurs earlier or what first surfaces later on played no role in my construction of my entries; rather the logic of the category took over (so far as I could penetrate the logic that linked one component with another and imposed on all the components one order rather than another). I worked in this order for the documents: Mishnah, Tosefta, Talmud of the Land of Israel, Talmud of Babylonia; tractate Abot and Abot deR. Natan; Genesis Rabbah, Leviticus Rabbah, Pesiqta deRab Kahana; finally Song of Songs Rabbah, Lamentations Rabbati, Esther Rabbah I, and Ruth Rabbah. That is to say, I followed the exegetical tradition of the Mishnah, start to finish, and then that of privileged portions of Scripture, start to finish. But in presenting what I found, I made no effort to lay out matters in the sequence in which the documents reached closure, that is, to define my categories by appeal to a temporal sequence. So far as matters are ordered, it is within the logic that the category, or topic, itself dictates: this must be dealt with before that.

That appeal to intrinsic logic of categories is for a simple reason. Considerations of temporal sequence by definition make no difference in the account of that logical structure set forth by the theological system. [61]I maintain that the categories (the vocabulary) that I have selected and define work in all of the documents in the same manner and work equally well. Viewed from the viewpoint of the end-product, the Oral Torah seen whole, the sense and meaning encompassed by those categories cohere wherever the categories occur. I maintain that repentance bears a single meaning, whether in the Mishnah at the outset, or in the Talmud of Babylonia at the end, and so throughout. To advert to the chosen metaphor, the history of a language plays no role in how the language is used at any given point in its history; then there is no past, only a timeless present. Language contains its own history, but we do not arrange our speech —

our use of the language — in accord with the temporal sequence in which words entered a language; theology encompasses its own history — the history of its ideas. But when formed into a structure and when constituting a working system — a problem-solving entity — theology too insists upon a timeless discourse that sets forth eternal, unchanging truth. If tomorrow, truth changes, so too will theology; but the consequent structure and system will bear the same traits of timelessness as do any prior or future set.

The governing trait of the category, then, for theological purposes finds definition in a-temporality and un-contingency; it is never imputed by context but always endures not only unimpaired but intact. So when I define a category, I lay matters out in accord with that simple logic that the data impose, and what comes first is primary in sense and meaning, not in occurrence in a given document. To demonstrate that the entire enterprise rests on a dubious foundation, I should have to show that the sense and meaning of a given category in one document contradicts their counterpart in some other, and that I found myself not able to do. What one document says about repentance does not necessarily recapitulate what another has to contribute, but it also presents no contradiction.

So while we may trace the unfolding of a given idea when we follow it through the generally-assumed sequence of documents from earlier to later, in the category-formations treated here we find an inner logic that remains the same throughout: a sense for a category that accommodates everything that fits and nothing that does not fit. Readers will test that result in their examination of every line of this *Vocabulary*. If considerations of time and circumstance — the order of the documents marking the order of opinion on a given subject — enter in, then I have chosen the wrong metaphor, and a different approach to theological description will have to take over. If the static picture that I set forth places everything into a single coherent pattern, then the moment at which I take the picture — the moment at which all the documents had reached closure, from the Mishnah through the Bavli — forms that eternity within which the theological structure finds its position, the theological system, its logic and problematic.

XI

Now — in consequence of what has been said — to take up the

problem implicit in every line of this book and its successors. In *Transformation of Judaism*,[62] through the study of the shifting category-formation exhibited by the documents read in sequence, I claimed to trace the history of the formation of Rabbinic Judaism as the story of how a philosophical system was turned into a religious one. In that way I produced a documentary history of ideas, as a problem in successive category-formations and in the changes in the definition of categories and in their uses. For the case of "Israel," for example, while the Mishnah and related documents utilize that social metaphor for purposes characteristic of their treatment of all other categories (e.g., hierarchical classification) and the Talmuds and related Midrash-compilations utilize the same metaphor in a very different way, my picture of the category presented in the shank of this book yields no contradictions that I am able to discern. What one document alleges, the sense and use of the category in one venue, may not recapitulate or even form an integument of what another document maintains and how that other document defines what matters in the category. But what the documents respectively say can be read as a whole and as a logically cogent statement of matters.

In my documentary histories of ideas, I found that some fundamental ideas took on new senses over time in usages from earlier to later writings, as my *Rabbinic Judaism. The Documentary History of the Formative Age* showed.[63] Other ideas or doctrines did not. One case representative of the results of many other monographs is my *Judaism and its Social Metaphors. Israel in the History of Jewish Thought*.[64] I also found some ideas that remained essentially the same start to finish, as represented by *Vanquished Nation, Broken Spirit. The Virtues of the Heart in Formative Judaism*.[65] What I claim here is that, however the unfolding of a given category may yield variation and may show response to diverse contexts and times, the inner logic of a given category — namely, its semantic values — endures from start to finish.

New senses expanded or amplified the meanings of categories, but I cannot point to a single contradictory meaning assigned in a later document to a word important in an earlier one. The meaning of "Israel" in later writings broadened and encompassed a variety of new senses, but the meanings important in the prior documents continued, also, to serve. In the categorical definitions given in this book readers may, as I just said, challenge that allegation. The entire systematic inquiry of the documents of the Oral Torah, particularly the Talmuds, do no less, in one detail after another, and they produce a single result throughout.

So I stand in a great tradition indeed when I survey the meanings or senses imputed to a given category throughout the literature. Indeed, that tradition begins in the Talmud of Babylonia, which, in its close reading of the rules of the Mishnah and their formulation, systematically seeks points of contradiction and irons them out. An equivalent exercise for norms of belief, equivalent to that applied to norms of behavior, will identify not individual, attributed sayings in conflict on a given issue — that would produce only the banal fact that diverse authorities hold diverse opinions. It must, rather, point to large-scale and fundamental principles in conflict, e.g., why the good suffer and the evil prosper. Now, as a matter of fact, whenever we find such contradiction of principles, we discover that sages have found the same and have resolved it, e.g., the good suffer in this world but prosper in the world to come, and for the evil, it is opposite.

Not only so, but my claim, implicit everywhere and made explicit here, is that at no point does any meaning given to a native category contradict any other assigned to that same category, though the usage of a given category may stress one thing rather than another.[66] What makes it possible to read, not merely to consult, these entries from start to finish is the challenge just now set forth: each entry must appear coherent, and all entries must hold together Ä in the native categories of the theology portrayed here, as much as in the vocabulary of a language, adumbrated in the simple list of entries given in the TABLE OF CONTENTS.

XII

A glance at the table of connts leads to the next question: why so few native categories? Among the tens of thousands of words that comprise the Oral Torah, why do scarcely three dozen serve here? Surely to form its construction and to make its system work the Oral Torah demands more than a handful of category-formations for the construction of its systemic statement! By the definition of vocabulary in language and native categories in theology that stands at the head, I should provide a vocabulary-list that encompasses a much larger selection of nouns and substantives, and that selection would include important names, events, places, and other concrete data.

Let me point to categories that play no role here but that constitute common nouns in the language of the Oral Torah, its narratives and expositions and analyses. Moses serves as the head of a great many sentences indeed, but is not listed here in this Grammar. The destruction of the Temple, the Exodus from Egypt, the Fall from Eden — these define category-formations that effectively impart cogency to diverse data and commence important propositions. If repentance belongs because it defines a fundamental systemic noun (a "thing" that imparts "thingness" to many kindred things and permits discourse thereupon), why not the Crossing of the Sea of Reeds, Aaron, Nebuchadnezzar, or Daniel? Out of these things, too, vast and important compositions are formed, compositions made up of sentences that begin "Moses" or "at the Sea" or "David" or "Abraham," "Isaac," or "Jacob." If, then, my dictionary of the vocabulary of the Oral Torah covers far fewer words than the sages' counterpart would have encompassed, it is not only omission of the theological vocabulary represented by halakhic categories that must register. It is also the omission of the entire corpus of vocabulary constituted by those persons, places, things, events, ideas, and attitudes that Scripture sets forth and that my survey omits.

Nor does the list end here. The building blocks of thought in the Oral Torah take shape, also, around the names of sages themselves, and a vast variety of tales forms an important component of the repertoire of public thought and discourse. If Moses serves as a noun, so too does Aqiba, and if the event at Sinai defines the topic of many sentences and forms the subject of them all, so too do such events as the war led by Bar Kokhba, the death of a great sage, or the tale of how a master commenced his study of the Torah. But for the purposes of this volume I do not list Aqiba or Eliezer any more than I record the name of Aaron or Joshua.

I form an entry for "Israel" meaning the holy people but not for "Jacob" for two simple reasons. The first is that for the purpose of this part of the *Grammar* in my reading of the documents of the Oral Torah start to finish, I did read with my — not their — theological spectacles. Seen through them, Jacob is a person, not a theological category. He stands for no more than himself. But repentance covers a variety of transactions, always in the same way. To read Jacob in theological context we have to supply the setting, e.g., Jacob in transitive context. By contrast as the documents remind me on virtually every page, Israel is a principal, organizing theological category. It is intransitive, standing for itself, defining itself, not depending upon context for definition. That point is important in understanding the limits of the present volume.

To spell this out: while Jacob, in all his specificity, has to be recast as a paradigm and set forth as an embodiment of a concept, Israel on its own forms a given bearing self-evident meaning. The categories treated here bear in common a single trait: I could define them in their own terms, not only in relationship to other matters. To compose a theological entry on Sinai or Jacob or Nebuchadnezzar, I should have to introduce not only nouns but verbs: what so and so does, what thus and such happens, for persons and events, respectively. Atonement, commandment, creation, gentiles — these without mediation, let alone contextualization, stand for themselves, the irreducible minima of theological construction in the Oral Torah. Then an entry selecting and arranging what the documents say will permit a systematic definition. But to define Nebuchadnezzar in the Oral Torah, I should have to engage in a labor of translation from the case to what the case represents, and the category is no longer primary but, as I have explained, contextual and mediated. The same is so for all of those many specific persons, places, and things that in fact constitute the categorical data of the Oral Torah but are treated in subsequent volumes but not here. Short of providing systematic accounts of pretty much everything that is said about Moses — the figure of Moses in the Oral Torah — my theological lexicon will have had nothing of a general character to record.

XIII

This brings me to the second reason for omitting most of the nouns of the Oral Torah and focusing mainly upon those that stand on their own. It is one that directs our attention to the companion volumes of this study. These other nouns enter discourse mainly within the setting of other nouns with which they are compared and contrasted, Jacob with Esau, David with Bath Sheba, or with Torah-study, for instance. That is, figures such as Moses, events such as Creation, Exodus, Sinai, destruction of the Temple — these gain meaning when they are joined with other nouns, such as Adam, Israel, Torah, and sin, respectively. Syntax tells us how to join one word to another. Then rules of semantics — how to form an intelligible

Theological Grammar of the Oral Torah. Vol. I 57

proposition, a sentence in plain speech — intervene. Semantics defines what allows for meaning to emerge. That is to say, my native categories serve as head-nouns when joined to verbs; they gain meaning and specificity, such as render lexical study theologically consequential, when rules of syntax — the joining of words into sentences — dictate, and they form statements of meaning or remain opaque and empty symbols when rules of semantics dictate. Israel, Torah, or Land of Israel always and everywhere bear meaning intransitively, but Jacob, Moses, and Sinai, while nouns as much as Israel, Torah, or Land and in no way differentiable from them, find their definition within the semantics of correct thought: the things that can be contemplated and therefore said.

These two reasons complement one another. A noun treated here is simple and irreducible and free-standing, while those dealt with in Volume Two of this Grammar are complex and subject to deconstruction and diverse sense determined by context. Those set forth here stand on their own, those compiled in Volumes Two and Three by definition take on meaning only in combination and in a predetermined context. The one catalogued here combines data beyond itself, the other is combinant — or stands for nothing determinate. In identifying nouns in relationship, statements made of nouns (and verbs) that follow rules of construction, we deal with a different kind of problem from that presented by the simple task of identifying principal components of the theological lexicon of the Oral Torah. In my reading of the documents, start to finish, therefore, I establish my categories, my counterparts to the vocabulary of a language, by looking for those head-nouns, identifying the syntax that shows how they may function, and discovering the semantic values of everything that is juxtaposed to them, I mean to outline the logic, the cognitive structure of the cultural system that the Oral Torah exposes in detail. The word "Israel" suffices to show what is at issue.

But the careful delineation of what may be treated solely within a *Grammar* of vocabulary and not a syntax let alone an account of semantics permits the testing of a null-hypothesis. If I am right, that "Israel" or "repentance" can be defined in their own terms, and solely not transitively or contextually, then everything that I find to define those irreducible minima of thought and speech ought to fit without crowding or conflict with anything, let alone everything, else. The null-hypothesis would propose that a given theological category cannot be classed as a noun bearing a range of congruent meanings and no contradictory ones. If the same word stands for something and its opposite — Israel for a supernatural social entity and a merely-this-worldly nation like any other, for one obvious example. When I collected what I found on such a category as repentance or resurrection, priesthood or prophecy, I looked for evidence that the categories contained contradictory data and found none. Usages of these words may prove diverse, but no usage imputes to a given word a sense or meaning that contradicts that imputed elsewhere to the same word. Readers then will test this claim against the evidence that is set forth. My nearly three-dozen native categories do not remotely begin to exhaust the candidates for inclusion in this lexicon. But they do state with great force and great precision the character of the generative vocabulary of the Oral Torah. All other native categories that we may identify are going to have to exhibit the indicative traits of the items set forth here. These are the building blocks of coherent thought.

The individual entries that follow identify and define the pertinent theological native-categories. I intend the entries for reference, though readers may find illuminating the compositions and composites that I have assembled, defined, and richly instantiated. I claim that the entries are, if not complete, at least representative of the corpus as a whole; and that the elements of the entries, if not wholly coherent, do not contradict other elements of the same entries. The whole forms a labor of definition, in the manner of a vocabulary-list, with the proviso that the definitions of the words recapitulate what we find in the documents of the Oral Torah, there alone.

XIV

The upshot may be stated very briefly. By the criteria just now spelled out, I identify thirty native categories (treating the three for "Torah" as a single classification), and in fact, a closer look will turn up not much more than a score of important and encompassing classifications. If then we examine the main lines of definition of the principal categories, e.g., Torah, God, Israel, Messiah, and the like, we further find that we have indeed subdivided even these. The category, "God," for example, can and should accommodate creation, kingdom of Heaven, revelation, and the like; the category, "Torah" takes in will of God; "Israel" overspreads Land of Israel, Resurrection, and the like. The universally-acknowledged generative categories, God, Torah, and Israel, are difficult to differentiate in concrete terms, the one deeply affecting the shape and structure of the other two, and the insistence of the theologoumenon, "God, Torah, and Israel are one," finds ample instantiation in what follows. These simple facts, which the rest of this part of the *Grammar* establish beyond any reasonable doubt, underscore the proposition of the project as a whole: a simple system forms the foundation of every line of the Oral Torah, and it is a system that we can identify, the ubiquitous presence of which we can demonstrate in detail, and the fundamental cogency and unity of which validate the claim that the Oral Torah sets forth not just religious teachings about one thing and another but a whole and integral theology.

"Man" in the Oral Torah may encompass man and woman or may refer only to a male. I translate according to context. In these pages, "Man," with a capital m, ordinarily refers to both genders, so too Adam, except where Eve is also mentioned. Where the context clearly requires a male, I refer to "man," with a small m.

Footnotes

[37] The irreducible given of the Oral Torah is that the Torah supplies hard facts concerning what God has said and done in the creation and governance of the world. That is the starting point of theological inquiry. At no point do I identify, within the documents of the Oral Torah, much of an interest in apologetics within the framework of intra-Israelite discourse, only a willingness to confront and dismiss the competing facts of paganism. Before us is a theological structure utterly lacking a component of apologetics.

[38] I owe this formulation to David Aaron.

[39] And if I am to be criticized, it is because my list is too long, not too short, but that is not an issue at this point.

[40] Stephen Pinker, *The Language Instinct*, pp. 106-7.

[41] For reasons that will become clear in due course, I deal with only a single type of noun, however, since Volume II of this *Grammar* will introduce a wide array of nouns that accord with the definition before us here. So for the purposes of the present exposition of the theological language of the Oral Torah, I limit native categories of a single type alone, underscoring that other types occur in abundance and will play their role later on. I return to this matter at the end of this Introduction.

[42] Professor David Aaron, Wellesley College, frames matters in the following way (personal letter, February 11, 1997): "That domain we call 'semantics' is not so easily parsed as the other two parts of the quotient. When the parts (phonemes) are entered into relations with one another according to the governing logic (syntax rules), meaning may still not be altogether evident. That is, a statement may be perfectly 'logical' in terms of structure and the phonemes may all be discretely recognizable as legitimate words, but the statement may still make no sense. What gives it se e may not be limited to the language-act alone. Body language, intonation, common experiences, previous contexts may all contribute to a statement's potential meaning. But these aspects are also structured by those communicating, and, consequently, they also function according to certain rules...The elements that contribute to those meanings are loosely understood as belonging to what we call semantics." In our documents, the counterpart to thee other modes of communication is formed by the context, the governing problematic of discourse, the recurrent concerns that instruct a writer concerning the issues he must address.

[43] Though a type of fact, e.g., Sinai, may both function as a category and also constitute a fact within its category, a model for the rest. We return to this problem below, when I explain the criteria for inclusion here in particular.

[44] But some categories are so enormous that for the sake of clarity they have to be subdivided, e.g., "Torah."

[45] I introduce these considerations only in the context of native category; they are not borrowed from linguistics and have no place within the metaphor.

[46] Indeed, on the list of native categories belong the names of all principal players in the written Torah, e.g., Moses and Sennacherib, Israel and Egypt, the Temple and the destruction thereof — all events selected by the system as indicative within that Torah, all locations that bear symbolic meaning. These are omitted here, forming the centerpiece for the analysis of a different problem, as volume II indicates. On the other hand, I include as native categories

Theological Grammar of the Oral Torah. Vol. I 61

abstract ones that the documents do not label, e.g., intentionality, as much as the ones that the documents do identify for us, e.g., Land of Israel. The entries themselves validate this procedure and demonstrate that some abstractions do belong as native categories, even though not named by the documents themselves. The concluding section of this introduction amplifies this discussion.

[47] My claim to characterize the whole always leaves room for exceptions, in a set of documents of such enormous dimensions, reaching us in a chain of tradition via manuscripts copied over many centuries. A single example cannot prove or disprove a proposition.

[48] If it did, I should not have to write this book!

[49] I shall presently underscore that the premised distinction between religious and other-than-religious itself is not native to our documents at all!

[50] In the contemplated work, *Correspondence of Law and Lore in the Oral Torah: The Unity of Behavior and Belief*, I shall address in a more systematic way the problem of how theology comes to expression in halakhah as much as in aggadah.

[51] Obviously, I will find the judgment of others especially helpful, since, as I reviewed the entire set of documents to compose this list, my reading was guided by my own taste and judgment, and others may read the same statements and identify the head-nouns differently. But I repeat, Volumes II and III will contain an ample repertoire of native categories of a different classification from the ones prominent here.

[52] A theological description of an other-than-encyclopaedic character would also have to identify candidates for the status of native-category that do not quality. These may emerge from the documents themselves, e.g., persons, concepts, or events that in theory can have served but in actuality do not; they also may emerge from the descriptions of Rabbinic Judaism that have come from modern and contemporary scholarship, e.g,, the category of "covenantal nomism," which cannot be validated within the data though which, it seems to me, obviously is coherent with the data. But the encyclopaedic-method will not provide a proper setting for those sorts of analytical exercises.

[53] Here I assemble the data that permit answering that question. These data will serve as the foundation for *The Theology of the Oral Torah*. (Kingston and Montreal: McGill and Queens University Press, planned for 1999).

[54] I recapitulate the categories of Volume III; the logic seems to me compelling. I cannot point to models of a more basic character than those of analysis, explanation, and anticipation.

[55] Divine favor, justice, and mercy in our American language stand for words in Hebrew that are exact counterparts. But not all of my native categories correspond to available Hebrew words. To these I added such entries as creation, loving kindness, martyrdom, and intentionality — categories of experience or encounter that recur, even though some of them have no clear counterpart in the Hebrew or Aramaic of the documents. Those words name the action represented by stories about sages' surrendering their lives rather than violate the Torah, or the attitude represented by sincere affirmation or an action for its own sake, respectively. Some categories combine what for sages are clearly distinct matters, such as world to come and time of the Messiah, and I had to employ three categories to differentiate among Torah (revelation), study of the Torah, and sage. See Howard Eilberg-Schwartz, *The Human Will in Judaism* (Atlanta, 1988: Scholars Press for Brown Judaic Studies), a dissertation under my supervision that shows the variety of cases and word-choices, all of them falling within the

framework of intentionality.

[56] New thoughts, in accord with this theory of matters, will require a fresh approach to the language of theology, new vocabulary, new forms of grammar, new rules of syntax; we should then find it possible to differentiate one system from a related, even derivative one by identifying only the governing, indicative traits of language, and, of course, as everyone knows, we easily do just that, e.g., comparing a document of the Oral Torah with one produced by Qabbalah. The continuity of Rabbinic Judaism, along with the variations and amplifications and revisions thereof, should then come to systematic description in projects formulated along the lines of this one. Certainly the approach of history of ideas has run its course in any event.

[57] *The Theology of Rabbinic Judaism. A Prolegomenon.* Atlanta, 1997: Scholars Press for South Florida Studies on the History of Judaism.

[58] Marshall Sahlins, *How "Natives" Think*, p. 163, citing Michel Foucault, *The Order of Things* (N.Y., 1973: Vintage Books), p. xv.

[59] *The Theology of Rabbinic Judaism. A Prolegomenon* (Atlanta, 1997: Scholars Press for South Florida Studies on the History of Judaism) elaborates on this problem, among others, in the received work of theological description of Rabbinic Judaism.

[60] I first broached this question in *Making the Classics in Judaism: The Three Stages of Literary Formation.* Atlanta, 1990: Scholars Press for Brown Judaic Studies, speaking then of text, context, and matrix. It is that third dimension that corresponds to the work undertaken here and in the companion-projects.

[61] The profoundly indicative statement, "considerations of historical sequence play not role in the Torah" (ain muqdam umeuhar by Torah) captures the utterly a-historical character of the systemic hermeneutics. This is systematically amplified in my *The Presence of the Past, the Pastness of the Present. History Time, and Paradigm in Rabbinic Judaism.* Bethesda, 1996: CDL Press.

[62] *The Transformation of Judaism. From Philosophy to Religion.* Champaign, 1992: University of Illinois Press. Second printing: Atlanta, 1997: Scholars Press for South Florida Studies in the History of Judaism.

[63] Bethesda, 1994: CDL Press

[64] N.Y., 1988: Cambridge University Press.

[65] New York, 1987: Cambridge University Press.

[66] In appealing to the inner logic of a native category I explicitly reject any notion of a mysterious "essentialism" or "essence of Judaism."

I.

ATONEMENT

ATONEMENT: An act or event (the Day of Atonement in particular) that removes the effects of sin by bringing about God's forgiveness of sin. The forms of the Hebrew based on the root KPR do not exhaust the category, for any action that produces the result of removing the effect of a sin will fit into that category, whether or not labeled an act of Kapparah. The written Torah speaks of atoning offerings in the Temple. Atonement in this age, without the Temple and its offerings, is accomplished through charity, so b. B.B. 1:5 IV.23/9a: And said R. Eleazar, "When the Temple stood, someone would pay off his sheqel-offering and achieve atonement. Now that the Temple is not standing, if people give to charity, well and good, but if not, the gentiles will come and take it by force. And even so, that is still regarded for them as an act of righteousness: 'I will make your exactors righteousness' (Isa. 60:17)."

The principal categorical component is the atonement brought about by the advent of the Day of Atonement. So, for instance, on that day the high priest, representing all Israel, brings about atonement through the rites of the Day of Atonement, beginning with the confession, so M. Yoma 4:2: And thus did he say, "O Lord, I have committed iniquity, transgressed, and sinned before you, I and my house and the children of Aaron, your holy people. O Lord, forgive, I pray, the iniquities, transgressions, and sins which I have committed, transgressed, and sinned before you, I, my house, and the children of Aaron, your holy people, as it is written in the Torah of Moses, your servant, For on this day shall atonement be made for you to cleanse you. From all your sins shall you be clean before the Lord (Lev. 16:30)." And they responded to him, "Blessed is the name of the glory of his kingdom forever and ever." The confession was followed by an act of sacrifice, a blood-rite involving a goat that is offered up and another that is sent forth, bearing the sins of the nation, to die in the wilderness, so M. Yoma 4:3f. in line with Lev. 16. The confession recited over the goat that was to be sent forth is as follows, M. Yoma 6:2B: "O Lord, your people, the house of Israel, has committed iniquity, transgressed, and sinned before you. Forgive, 0 Lord, I pray, the iniquities, transgressions, and sins, which your people, the house of Israel, have committed, transgressed, and sinned before you, as it is written in the Torah of Moses, your servant, For on this day shall atonement be made for you to clean you. From all your sins shall you be clean before the Lord (Lev. 16:30)." And the priests and people standing in the courtyard, when they would hear the Expressed Name of the Lord come out of the mouth of the high priest, would kneel and bow down and fall on their faces and say, "Blessed be the name of the glory of his kingdom forever and ever." Various forms of self-abnegation serve also as appropriate sacrifices to atone for sin, thus M. Yoma 8:1: On the Day of Atonement it is forbidden to (1) eat, (2) drink, (3) bathe, (4) put on any sort of oil, (5) put on a sandal, (6) or engage in sexual relations.

The power of the Day of Atonement to effect atonement and forgiveness of sins is spread out through the entire month of Tishré, so Lev. R. CXXX:VII.1: "On the fifteenth day of the seventh month, when you have gathered the produce of the land, you shall keep the feast of the Lord seven days; on the first day shall be a solemn rest" (Lev. 23:40). This in fact is the fifteenth day, yet you speak of the first day! R. Mana of Sheab and R. Joshua of Sikhnin in the name of R. Levi said, "The matter may be compared to the case of a town which owed arrears to the king, so the king went to collect what was owing. When he had reached ten *mils* from the town, the great men of the town came forth and praised him. He remitted a third of their unpaid tax. When he came within five *mils* of the town, the middle-rank people came out and acclaimed him, so he remitted yet another third of what was owing to him. When he entered the town, men, women, and children, came forth and praised him. He remitted the whole of the tax. Said the king, 'What happened happened. From now on we shall begin keeping books afresh.' So on the eve of the New Year, the great men of the generation fast, and the Holy One, blessed be he, remits a third of their that is, Israel's sins. From the New Year to the Day of Atonement outstanding individuals fast, and the Holy One, blessed be he, remits a third of their that is, Israel's sins. On the Day of Atonement all of them fast, men, women, and children, so the Holy One, blessed be he, says to Israel, 'What happened. From now on we shall begin keeping books afresh.'"

The nations of the world indict Israel for committing the same sins that the nations practice, but the Day of Atonement effects atonement for Israel, so Lev. R. XXI:IV.1: Rabbis interpret the intersecting verse to speak of the New Year and Day of Atonement: "'My light' (Ps. 27):1 is on the New Year. 'And my salvation' (Ps. 27:1) is on the Day of Atonement. 'Whom shall I fear' (Ps. 27:1): 'The Lord is my strength and my song' (Ex. 15:2). 'When evildoers come near me' (Ps. 27:2) refers to the princes of heaven who represent the nations of the world. 'To eat my flesh' (Ps. 27:2): For the princes representing the nations of the world come and draw an indictment against Israel before the Holy One, blessed be he, saying before him, 'Lord of the world, these nations practice idolatry and those Jews practice idolatry. These practice fornication and those practice fornication. These shed blood and those shed blood. Why then do these nations of the world go down to Gehenna and those do not go down?' 'My adversaries and foes' (Ps. 27:2): You find that the number of days in the solar year are three hundred sixty-five, but the number of names of Satan are three hundred and sixty-four. For on all the days of the year, Satan is able to draw up an indictment, but on the Day of Atonement, Satan is not able to draw up an indictment. Said the Israelites before the Holy One, blessed be he, 'Though a host encamp against me' — the host of the nations of the world, 'My heart shall not fear' (Ps. 27:3). 'Though war arise against me' — the war of the nations of the world. 'In this I shall trust' (Ps. 27:3). In this which you have promised me: 'With this will Aaron come' Lev. 16:3 on the Day of Atonement."

Besides the Day of Atonement, atonement is also accomplished by other means, deemed comparable to sacrifices, for example, the death of the righteous or of sages, so Y. Yoma 1:1 I:2 Said R. Hiyya bar Ba, "The sons of Aaron died on the first day of Nisan. And why is their death called to mind in connection with the Day of Atonement? It is to indicate to you that just as the Day of Atonement effects expiation for Israel, so the death of the righteous effects atonement for Israel." Said R. Ba bar Binah, "Why did the Scripture place the story of the death of Miriam side by side with the story of the burning of the red cow? It is to teach you that just as the dirt of the red cow mixed with water effects atonement for Israel, so the death of the righteous effects atonement for Israel." Said R. Yudan b. Shalom, "Why did the Scripture set the story of the death of Aaron side by side with the story of the breaking of the tablets? It is to teach you that the death of the righteous is as grievous before the Holy One, blessed be he, as the breaking of the tablets." The same view is expressed at B. M.Q 3:8 III.4/28a: Said R. Eleazar, "How come the story of the death of Aaron is situated adjacent to the passage on the priestly garments Num. 20:26, 28? It is to teach you that just as the priest's garments serve to effect atonement, so the death of the righteous effects atonement."

Song too constitutes a form of atonement, so Y. Ta. 4:1 II.3: How do we know that the song in the Temple is called a form of atonement? Hinena. father of Bar Netah, in the name of R. Benaiah: "'To make atonement for the people of Israel' — this refers to the song. How do we know that the song is indispensable to the cult? R. Jacob bar Aha, R. Bulatah in the name of R. Hinena: "'To make atonement for the people of Israel' — this refers to the song.'"

The garments that the high priest wears on the Day of Atonement also signify, and effect, atonement, so Lev. R.X:VI.1:

1. A. "[The Lord said to Moses, 'Take Aaron and his sons with him,] and the garments [and the anointing oil and the bull of the sin offering, the two rams, and the basket of unleavened bread, and assemble all the congregation at the door of the tent of meeting]'" (Lev. 8:1-3).

B. R. Simon said, "Just as the sacrifices effect atonement, so [wearing of the] garments effects atonement.

C. "This is in accord with the following teaching, which we have learned in the Mishnah [M. Yoma 7:5]: 'The high priest serves in eight garments, and an ordinary priest in four: tunic, underpants, head-covering, and girdle. The high priest in addition wears the breastplate, apron, upper garment, and frontlet.'

D. "The tunic serves to effect atonement for those who wear garments made up of mixed fabrics [deriving from both vegetable matter and animal matter, such as linen and wool].

E. "That is in line with the following verse of Scripture: 'And he made from him a tunic of many colors' [Gen. 37:3].

F. "Underpants serve to effect atonement for licentiousness.

G. "That is in line with the following verse of Scripture: 'And you shall make linen underpants for them to cover the flesh of nakedness' [Ex. 28:42].

H. "The head-covering serves to effect atonement for arrogance.

I. "That is in line with the following verse of Scripture: 'And you will set the head-covering on his head' [Ex. 29:6].

J. "The girdle: There is he who maintains that it is on account of deceivers, and he who holds it is on account of thieves."

L. [Simon continues:] "The breastplate serves to effect atonement for those who corrupt justice.

M. "This is in line with the following verse of Scripture: 'And you shall put in the breastplate of judgment' [Ex. 28:30].

N. "The apron serves to effect atonement for idolatry.

O. "This is in line with the following verse of Scripture: '[For the children of Israel shall dwell many days without king or prince without sacrifice or pillar,] without apron or teraphim. [Afterward the children of Israel shall return and seek the Lord]'" (Hos. 3:4).

P. The upper garment: R. Simon in the name of R. Nathan said, "For two matters there is no possibility of atonement, yet the Torah has [still] assigned a mode of atonement to them, and these are they: gossip and unintentional manslaughter.

Q. "What is it that serves as atonement in the view of him who maintains that while there is no real possibility of atonement for gossip, yet the Torah has assigned to it a mode of atonement?

R. "It is the little bells of the priest's robe.

S. "That is in line with the following verse of Scripture: 'A golden bell and a pomegranate, a golden bell and a pomegranate, round about on the skirts of the robe. And it shall be upon Aaron when he ministers, and its voice shall be heard when he goes into the holy place before the Lord, and when he comes out, lest he die' (Ex. 28:34-5).

T. "Said the Holy One, blessed be he, 'Let the voice come and effect atonement for what the voice has done.'

W. "The frontlet:

X. "There is he who maintains that it serves to make atonement for those who are shameless, and there is he who holds that it serves to make atonement for those who blaspheme.

Y. "He who holds that it serves to make atonement for those who are shameless derives evidence from the case of the daughters of Zion.

Z. "Here it is written, 'It shall be upon Aaron's forehead' [Ex. 28:38].

AA. "There it is written, 'You [daughters of Zion] had a harlot's forehead, but you refused to be ashamed' [Jer. 3:3].

BB. "He who maintains that it serves to attain atonement for those who blaspheme draws evidence from the case of Goliath.

CC. "Here it is written, 'It will be on his forehead forever' [Ex. 28:38].

DD. "And in regard to Goliath it is written, 'and the stone sank into his forehead'" (1 Sam. 17:49).

So much for the Day of Atonement, a critical component of the category.

There are four types of atonement, so T. Yoma 1:8: R. Mattiah b. Heresh asked R. Eleazar b. Azariah, "Have you heard of the four types of atonement that R. Ishmael used to expound?" He said to him, "They are three, besides the requirement of an act of repentance." These are the three types: One Scripture says, "Return., O faithless children, says the Lord" (Jer. 3:14). And yet another verse of Scripture says, "For on this day shall atonement be made for you, to cleanse you; from all your sins you shall be clean before the Lord" (Lev. 16:30). So one verse recommends repentance, and the other grants absolution unconditionally. And one verse of Scripture says, "Then I will punish their transgression with the rod and their iniquity with scourges" (Ps. 89:32). And yet another verse of Scripture says, "Surely this iniquity will not be forgiven you till you die, says the Lord of Hosts" (Is. 22:14). Now how are these verses to be reconciled, which speak of punishment and forgiveness on the one side, and the impossibility of atonement except through death on the other? If one has violated a positive commandment but repented, he does not even leave the place before he is wholly forgiven. Concerning such a person the verse of Scripture says, "Return, O faithless children." If one has violated a negative commandment and repented forthwith, the act of repentance suspends the punishment, and the Day of Atonement effects atonement for him. In such a case the Scripture states, "For on this day shall atonement be made for you." If one has violated a commandment involving extirpation or the death penalty inflicted by a court, and has done so deliberately, repentance and the Day of Atonement effect atonement in part, and suffering effects atonement in part. Concerning such a person, the verse of Scripture states, "Then I will punish their transgression with the rod, and their iniquity with scourges." But as to him through whose action the Name of Heaven has been disgraced, repentance has not got the power to suspend punishment, nor does the Day of Atonement have the power to effect atonement, nor does suffering have the power to wipe away the guilt. But repentance and the Day of Atonement suspend the punishment, along with suffering, the man's death wipes away the sin. Concerning such a person does Scripture make the statement: "Surely this iniquity will not be forgiven you till you die"? Thus we have learned the fact that death wipes away guilt and sin.

Intentionality forms the principal criterion for effecting atonement through repentance, the rites of atonement, and the advent of the Day of Atonement itself. If one manifests the inappropriate intentionality, then the rite is null, thus M. Yoma 8:9 A. He who says, "I shall sin and repent, sin and repent" — they give him no chance to do repentance. "I will sin and the Day of Atonement will atone," — the Day of Atonement does not atone. For transgressions done between man and the Omnipresent, the Day of Atonement atones. For transgressions between man and man, the Day of Atonement atones, only if the man will regain the good will of his friend.

Atonement does not always accomplish its goals. for with genuinely evil persons repentance on its own may not suffice to accomplish atonement, so ARN XXXIX:V.1: The repentance of genuinely wicked people suspends their punishment, but the decree against them has been sealed. The prosperity of the wicked in the end will go sour. Dominion buries those that hold it. Repentance suspends punishment and the Day of Atonement achieves atonement. Repentance suspends punishment until the day of death, and the day of death atones, along with repentance.

In theory there ought to be no atonement for gossip and involuntary manslaughter, but the Torah has provided means of atonement: so Song R. XLVIII:v.5: R. Simon in the name of R. Jonathan of Bet Gubrin: "For two matters there was no atonement, but the Torah has provided atonement for them, and these are they: Gossip and involuntary manslaughter. For gossip there was no atonement, but the Torah has provided atonement for it, specifically through the bell of the robe: 'And it shall be upon Aaron to minister, and the sound thereof shall be heard' (Ex. 28:35). Let the sound that this makes come and atone for the sound of slander. For involuntary manslaughter there was no atonement, but the Torah has provided atonement for it, specifically through the death of the high priest: 'And he shall dwell therein until the death of the high priest' (Num. 35:25)."

I see no component of the category, atonement, that conflicts with any other; the datum commences with the Day of Atonement; what is then added are the considerations of intentionality and its companion, repentance, and some secondary items.

II.

COMMANDMENT

COMMANDMENT (MISVAH) refers to a religious duty that God has required of Israel as an act of sanctification and service. It is frequently accompanied by a formula of blessing that articulates the intentionality of an action to be performed and so classifies the action as a deed of service in obedience to God's will. The formula, commences, "blessed are you, Lord, our God, king of the world, who has sanctified us by his commandments and commanded us to...." Accordingly, performance of commandments represents an act of submission to the will of God, a statement of acceptance of the rule of Heaven.

The commandments mark God's love for Israel, so M. Mak. 3:16: R. Hananiah b. Aqashia says, "The Holy One, blessed be he, wanted to give merit to Israel. Therefore he gave them abundant Torah and numerous commandments, as it is said, 'It pleased the Lord for his righteousness' sake to magnify the Torah and give honor to it (Is. 42:21)." This same view is expressed at T. Ber. 6:24: Precious are Israelites, for the Holy One, blessed be he, has surrounded them with religious duties to protect them: boxes containing prayer parchments on their heads and boxes containing prayer parchments on their arms, show fringes on their garments, doorpost markers containing Torah-statements on their doors. And concerning the commandments David said, "Seven times a day I praise you for your righteous ordinances" (Ps. 119:164). When David entered the bath house and saw himself standing naked, he said, 'Woe is me, that I should stand naked, without a single religious duty. But when he remembered the circumcision that is marked in his flesh, his mind was eased. And after he went out, he said a Psalm, "To the choir master according to the Sheminit" [the eighth, here taken as a reference to circumcision on the eighth day after birth] (Ps. 12:10; and Scripture further states, "The angel of the Lord encamps around those who fear him and delivers them" (Ps. 34:8).

The commandments are what sanctify Israel to God, and even thinking about the commandments is tantamount to doing them, so Sif. Num. CXV:V.1-3: "So you shall remember and do all my commandments and be holy to your God. I am the Lord your God who brought you out of the land of Egypt to be your God. I am the Lord your God" (Num. 15:37-41): The phrasing, 'remember and do,' serves to treat remembering as tantamount to doing. "...and be holy to your God:" This refers to the sanctity of all of the religious duties [every one of which falls into the classification of remembering and doing, thus of sanctifying Israel. "I am the Lord your God who brought you out of the land of Egypt:" What relevance does the Exodus from Egypt have to the present context? It is so that someone should not say, "Lo, I shall put in dye-stuff or vegetable-matter [rather than the proper dye for the color blue, which comes from a mollusk and is difficult to get], for they produce a color similar to the required blue. And who is going to tell on me in public?" "'I am the Lord your God who brought you out of the land of Egypt,' and know what I did to the Egyptians, who acted in secret. I made public [the things that they did in secret]." Now this produces an argument *a fortiori* : now if in the case of the divine attribute of inflicting punishment, which is the lesser, he who incurs a penalty in secret finds that the Omnipresent makes the matter public, all the more so when it comes to the divine attribute of dispensing good, which is the greater of the two. God will surely grant a public reward to one who incurs divine pleasure in a private deed.

Not keeping the commandments is why Israel is punished, so Sif. Dt. CCCVI:XIII.2, XIV.1: "Give ear, O heavens, let me speak": It was because the Israelites did not carry out the religious duties that were assigned to them concerning heaven. And what were the religious duties that were assigned to them concerning heaven? The intercalation of years [by adding months to the lunar calendar to keep it even with the solar seasons]. "... the earth hear the words I utter": It was because the Israelites did not carry out the religious duties that were assigned to them concerning the earth. And what were the religious duties that were assigned to them concerning the earth? The rules of gleanings, the forgotten sheaf, the corner of the field, the priestly ration, tithes, years of release, and jubilees. It was because the Israelites did not carry out all of the religious duties that were assigned to them from heaven. "...let the earth hear the words I utter!" It was because the Israelites did not carry out all of the religious duties that were assigned to them on earth. Moses thus brought to testify against Israel two witnesses who last for ever and ever, as it is said, "I call to witness against you this day the heaven and the earth" (Dt. 30:19). And the Holy One, blessed be He, called to witness against you the song [that Moses was about to sing], as it is said, "Now therefore write this song for you" (Dt. 31:19).

Israel was sent into exile because of failure to keep the commandments: so Lam. R. XXXV:ii.2: They asked Ben Azzai, "Tell us something concerning the scroll of lamentations." He said to them, "The Israelites were sent into exile only after they had denied the Unique One of the world, the Ten Commandments, circumcision, which had been given to the twentieth generation [Abraham], and the Pentateuch. How do we know it? From the word 'how' [the letters of which stand for one, hence the Divine Unity, ten, twenty, and five.]" Said R. Levi, "The Israelites did not go into exile until they had denied the thirty-six laws in the Torah for which the penalty is extirpation. How do we know it? 'How...' [the numerical value of the letters of which add up to thirty-six]." For Israel, exile is more bitter than for nations in general, so Lam. R. XXXVII.i.1: "Judah has gone into exile:" Do not the nations of the world go into exile? Even though they go into exile, their exile is not really an exile at all. But for Israel, their exile really is an exile. The nations of the world, who eat the bread and drink the wine of others, do not really experience exile. But the Israelites, who do not eat the bread and drink the wine of others, really do experience exile. The nations of the world, who travel in litters, do not really experience exile. But the Israelites, who [in poverty] go barefoot — their exile really is an exile. That is why it is said, "Judah has gone into exile."

A symbolic figure, the sum of 248, the bones of the body, and 365, the days of the year, yields the figure of 613 commandments. But in the Oral Torah no systematic catalogue is attempted. In any event all of the commandments may be reduced to a few principles, thus B. Mak. 3:16 II.1/23b-24a: R. Simelai expounded, "Six hundred and thirteen commandments were given to Moses, three hundred and sixty-five negative ones, corresponding to the number of the days of the solar year, and two hundred forty-eight positive commandments, corresponding to the parts of man's body. David came and reduced them to eleven: 'A Psalm of David: Lord, who shall sojourn in thy tabernacle, and who shall dwell in thy holy mountain? (i) He who walks uprightly and (ii) works righteousness and (iii) speaks truth in his heart and (iv) has no slander on his tongue and (v) does no evil to his fellow and (vi) does not take up a reproach against his neighbor, (vii) in whose eyes a vile person is despised but (viii) honors those who fear the Lord. (ix) He swears to his own hurt and changes not. (x) He does not lend on interest. (xi) He does not take a bribe against the innocent' (Psalm 15)." Isaiah came and reduced them to six: '(i) He who walks righteously and (ii) speaks uprightly, (iii) he who despises the gain of oppressions, (iv) shakes his hand from holding bribes, (v) stops his ear from hearing of blood (vi) and shuts his eyes from looking upon evil, he shall dwell on high' (Isaiah 33:25-26). Micah came and reduced them to three: 'It has been told you, man, what is good, and what the Lord demands from you, (i) only to do justly and (ii) to love mercy, and (iii) to walk humbly before God' (Micah 6:8). Habakkuk further came and based them on one, as it is said, 'But the righteous shall live by his faith' (Habakkuk 2:4)."

Proper performance of the commandments demands sincerity and the proper intentionality. The purpose of the commandments is to purify the heart, so Lev. R. XIII:III.1: "Every word of God is refined; he is a shield to those who take refuge in him" (Prov. 30:5). Rab said, "The religious duties were handed over only to refine human beings through them." Why so much [engagement]? "He is a shield to those who take refuge in him" (Prov. 30:5) [and through the practice of religious duties gives people the opportunity to gain merit].

A principal result of keeping the commandments is to gain strength to overcome the impulse to do evil. The Torah and the commandments give a person power over the inclination to do evil, and abandoning them leaves a person in the power of that same inclination, so b. A.Z. 1:1 I.33 5/b: Said R. Yohanan in the name of R. Benaah, "What is the meaning of the verse of Scripture, 'Happy are you who sow beside all waters, that send forth the feet of the ox and the ass' (Isa. 32:20)? 'Happy are you, O Israel, when you are devoted to the Torah and to doing deeds of grace, then their inclination to do evil is handed over to them, and they are not handed over into the power of their inclination to do evil. For it is said, 'Happy are you who sow beside all waters.' For what does the word 'sowing' mean, if not 'doing deeds of grace,' in line with the use of the word in this verse: 'Sow for yourselves in righteousness, reap according to mercy' (Hos. 10:12), and what is the meaning of 'water' if not Torah: 'Oh you who are thirsty, come to the water' (Isa. 55:1). As to the phrase, "that send forth the feet of the ox and the ass": it has been taught by the Tannaite authority of the household of Elijah: "A person should always place upon himself the work of studying the Torah as an ox accepts the yoke, and as an ass, its burden."

The correct attitude for doing the commandments is to carry out God's will, that is, doing the commandments for their own sake and not for the sake of coercing Heaven into an exchange and so gaining a reward. Doing religious duties nonetheless brings a reward, even though one does not know what that reward will be, so Rabbi Judah the Patriarch, M. Abot 2:1: "Be meticulous in a small religious duty as in a large one, for you do not know what sort of reward is coming for any of the various religious duties. And reckon with the loss [required] in carrying out a religious duty against the reward for doing it, and the reward for committing a transgression against the loss for doing it." So too at M. Abot 4:2 Ben Azzai says, "Run after the most minor religious duty as after the most important, and flee from transgression. For doing one religious duty draws in its wake doing yet another, and doing one transgression draws in its wake doing yet another. For the reward of doing a religious duty is a religious duty, and the reward of doing a transgression is a transgression." The commandments that one carries out serve as his advocates in judgment, so M. Abot 4:11: R. Eliezer b. Jacob says, "He who does even a single religious duty gets himself a good advocate. He who does even a single transgression gets himself a prosecutor. Penitence and good deeds are like a shield against punishment."

Performance of the most inconsequential commandments of the Torah produces a reward, so Sif. Dt. CCCXXXVI:I.1: ["For this is not a trifling thing for you; it is your very life; through it you shall long endure on the land that you are to possess upon crossing the Jordan'" (Dt. 32:44-47).] "For this is not a trifling thing for you": You have in the Torah no matter so inconsequential that should you pursue it, it produces no reward in this world with enduring value for the world to come. Know that this is so, for lo, sages have said: Why is it written, 'And Lotan's sister was Timna' (Gen. 36:22), 'And Timna was concubine to Eliphaz, Esau's son' (Gen. 36:12)? It was because she said, 'I am not worthy of being wife to him. Let me be merely his concubine.' And why so? To show you the adulation that was coming to our father, Abraham. There were those that did not want [marriage into] a kingdom or a government, but ran to cleave to him. And does that not yield an argument *a fortiori*: If to Esau, who had to his credit the doing of only a single religious duty, honoring his father, royal and ruling families were running to cleave, how much the more so that they should want to cleave to Jacob, that righteous man, who carried out the entire Torah. For concerning him it is written, 'Jacob was a flawless man, dwelling in tents' (Gen. 25:27)."

These two principles — one performs commandments to accept God's rule and to serve God, and one gains a reward for doing the commandments — do not conflict, the reward of doing a commandment being the doing of another commandment. The main consideration is sincerity in doing the commandments, the right attitude governing the outcome. Not only so, but the penalty for not doing commandments is specified at some length. So the balance is a delicate one, between carrying out a religious duty for its own sake and anticipating a positive result. The matter resolves itself into the insistence that the holy actions do not compel God but may well produce a positive response from him. The consequent tension carries over into the contrast between this-worldly suffering of the righteous and prosperity of the wicked, and that contrast is suitably worked out.

Among the commandments, a scale of importance classifies some as more consequential, others less. Certainly the model of the commandments is found in the Ten Commandments. The Ten Commandments were set forth in matched pairs, indicating that each had its opposite in another, so Mekh. LIV:III.1: "How were the Ten Commandments set forth? There were five on one tablet, five on the other. On the one was written, 'I am the Lord your God.' and opposite it: 'You shall not murder.' Scripture thus indicates that whoever sheds blood is regarded as though he had diminished the divine image. The matter may be compared to the case of a mortal king who came into a town, and the people set up in his honor icons, and they made statues of him, and they minted coins in his honor. After a while they overturned his icons, broke his statues, and invalidated his coins, so diminishing the image of the king. Thus whoever sheds blood is regarded as though he had diminished the divine image, for it is said, 'Whoever sheds man's blood...for in the image of God he made man' (Gen. 9:6). One the one was written, 'You shall have no other god.' and opposite it: 'You shall not commit adultery.' Scripture thus indicates that whoever worships an idol is regarded as though he had committed adultery against the Omnipresent, for it is said, 'You wife that commits adultery, that takes strangers instead of your husband' (Ez. 16:32); 'And the Lord said to me, Go yet, love a woman beloved of her friend and an adulteress' (Hos. 3:1). One the one was written, 'You shall not take the name of the Lord your God in vain.' and opposite it: 'You shall not steal.' Scripture thus indicates that whoever steals in the end will end up taking a false oath: 'Will you steal, murder, commit adultery, and swear falsely: (Jer. 7:9); 'Swearing and lying, killing and stealing, and committing adultery' (Hos. 4:2). One the one was written, 'Remember the Sabbath day to keep it holy.' and opposite it: 'You shall not bear false witness.' Scripture thus indicates that whoever violates the Sabbath is as though he had given testimony before the One who spoke and brought the world into being, indicating that he had not created his world in six days and not rested on the seventh, and whoever keeps the Sabbath day is as though he had given testimony before the One who spoke and brought the world into being, indicating that he had created his world in six days and rested on the seventh: 'For you are my witnesses, says the Lord' (Is. 43:10). One the one was written, 'Honor your father and your mother.' and opposite it: 'You shall not covet your neighbor's wife.' Scripture thus indicates that whoever covets in the end will produce a son who curses his father and honors one who is not his father. Thus the Ten Commandments were given, five on this tablet, and five on that," the words of R. Hananiah b. Gamaliel. And sages say, "The ten were written on this tablet, and the ten on the other. For it says, 'These words...and he wrote them upon two tablets' (Dt. 5:19); 'Your two breasts are like two fawns that are twins of a gazelle' (Song 4:5); 'His hands are as rods of gold set with beryl' (Song 5:15)."

The commandments are revealed by God in the Torah. Some commandments stand to reason, and it is not necessary to rely on revelation to know them, but others are known only because of revelation, so Sifra CXCIV:II.11: "You shall keep my laws": This refers to matters that are written in the Torah. But if they had not been written in the Torah, it would have been entirely logical to write them, for example, rules governing thievery, fornication, idolatry, blasphemy, murder, examples of rules that, had they not been written in the Torah, would have been logical to include them. Then there are those concerning which the impulse to do evil raises doubt, the nations of the world, idolators, raise doubt, for instance, the prohibition against eating pork, wearing mixed species, the rite of removing the shoe in the case of the deceased childless brother's widow, the purification-rite for the person afflicted with the skin ailment, the goat that is sent forth — cases in which the impulse to do evil raises doubt, the nations of the world, idolators, raise doubt. In this regard Scripture says, "I the Lord have made these ordinances, and you have no right to raise doubts concerning them."

The commandments of God came first to Adam and his heirs, then to Noah and his, and finally to Abraham, so Song R. II.ii.14-19: R. Azariah, and some say R. Eliezer and R. Yosé, b. R. Hanina and rabbis: R. Eliezer says, "The matter may be compared to the case of a king who had a wine cellar. The first guest came to him first, and he mixed a cup for him and gave it to him. A second came and he mixed a cup for him and gave it to him. When the son of the king came, he gave him the whole cellar. So the First Man was commanded in respect to seven commandments. That is in line with this verse: 'And the Lord God commanded the man, saying, You may freely eat of every tree of the garden, [but of the tree of the knowledge of good and evil you shall not eat, for in the day that you eat of it you shall die]' (Gen. 2:16). As to Noah, a further commandment was assigned to him, not eating a limb cut from a living animal: 'O As to Abraham, a further commandment was assigned to him, circumcision. Isaac devoted the eighth day to that rite. As to Jacob, a further commandment was assigned to him, the prohibition of the sinew of the thigh-vein: 'Therefore the children of Israel do not eat the sinew of the thigh-vein' (Gen. 32:33). As to Judah, a further commandment was assigned to him, levirate marriage: 'And Judah said to Onan, Go into your brother's wife and perform the duty of a husband's brother for her' (Gen. 38:8). The Israelites, by contrast, made their own all of the religious duties, positive and negative alike."

A single action makes a big difference, whether a commandment or a sin, thus T. Qid. 1:13-17: Whoever does a single commandment — they do well for him and lengthen his days and his years and he inherits the Land [M. Qid. 1: 10A-B]. And whoever commits a single transgression — they do ill to him and cut off his days, and he does not inherit the Land. And concerning such a person it is said, One sinner destroys much good

(Qoh. 9: 18). By a single sin this one destroys many good things. A person should always see himself as if he is half meritorious and half guilty. [If] he did a single commandment, happy is he, for he has inclined the balance for himself to the side of merit. [If] he committed a single transgression, woe is he, for he has inclined the balance to the side of guilt. Concerning this one it is said, One sinner destroys much good. By a single sin this one has destroyed many good things. R. Simeon b. Eleazar says in the name of R. Meir, "Because the individual is judged by his majority [of deeds], the world is judged by its majority. And [if] one did one commandment, happy is he, for he has inclined the balance for himself and for the world to the side of merit. [If] he committed one transgression, woe is he, for he has inclined the balance for himself and for the world to the side of guilt. And concerning such a person it is said, One sinner destroys much good — By the single sin which this one committed, he destroyed for himself and for the world many good things." R. Simeon says, "[If] a man was righteous his entire life but at the end he rebelled, he loses the whole, since it is said, The righteousness of the righteous shall not deliver him when he transgresses (Ez. 33:12). [If] a man was evil his entire life but at the end he repented, the Omnipresent accepts him, as it is said, And as for the wickedness of the wicked, he shall not fall by it when he turns from his wickedness [and the righteous shall not be able to live by his righteousness when he sins] (Ez. 33:12). Whoever occupies himself with all three of them, with Scripture, Mishnah, and good conduct, concerning such a person it is said, And a threefold cord is not quickly broken (Qoh. 5:12)."

Liability to the commandments varies according to location, so T. Qid. 1:12: R. Eleazar b. R. Simeon says, "Every commandment for which the Israelites became liable before they entered the Land applies in the Land and outside of the Land, and [every commandment] for which the Israelites became liable only after they came into the Land applies only in the Land [cf. M. Qid. I:9A-C], except for the forgiveness of debts, the redemption of fields which have been sold, and the sending forth free of the Hebrew slave [in the Seventh Year]. For even though they became liable to them only after they had come into the Land, they apply in the Land and outside of the Land."

While one must carry out all commandments, both those of commission and those of omission, it is not at the cost of life. One must place the preservation of life over all considerations, except when it comes to three matters, so T. Shab. 15:17): Nothing in the whole world stands against a danger to life, except for idolatry, licentiousness, and murder. Under what circumstances? Not in a time of persecution. But in a time of persecution, for even the slightest of all the lesser commandments a man must give his life, since it says, And you shall not profane my holy name, but I will be hallowed among the people of Israel (Lev. 22:32), and it says, The Lord has made everything for its purpose (Prov. 16:4) [even the slightest of all the commandments has its purpose in a time of persecution].

III.

CREATION

CREATION, the act of bringing the world into being, is described not only in the pertinent passages of Scripture, but in a number of teachings of the Oral Torah as well. Creation is an irreducible category, never breaking down into subdivisions, always referring to that single act at the beginning of the world by which God made the world. The Oral Torah amplifies and expands the category that Scripture defined, mainly filling in gaps in the Written Torah's account.

Before creation, God contemplated a number of candidates for creation, and some were brought into being, some not, so Gen. R. I:IV.1ff.: ["In the beginning God created" (Gen. 1:1):] Six things came before the creation of the world, some created, some at least considered as candidates for creation. The Torah and the throne of glory were created [before the creation of the world]. The Torah, as it is written, "The Lord made me as the beginning of his way, prior to his works of old" (Prov. 8:22). The throne of glory, as it is written, "Your throne is established of old" (Ps. 93:2). The patriarchs were considered as candidates for creation, as it is written, "I saw your fathers as the first-ripe in the fig tree at her first season" (Hos. 9:10). Israel was considered [as a candidate for creation], as it is written, "Remember your congregation, which you got aforetime" (Ps. 74:2). The Temple was considered [as a candidate for creation], as it is written, "You, throne of glory, on high from the beginning, the place of our sanctuary" (Jer. 17:12). The name of the Messiah was kept in mind, as it is written, "His name exists before the sun" (Ps. 72:17). R. Ahbah bar Zeira said, "Also [the power of] repentance. That is in line with the following verse of Scripture: 'Before the mountains were brought forth' (Ps. 90:2). From that hour: 'You turn man to contrition and say, Repent, you children of men' (Ps. 90:3)." Nonetheless, I do not know which of these came first, that is, whether the Torah was prior to the throne of glory, or the throne of glory to the Torah. Said R. Abba bar Kahana, "The Torah came first, prior to the throne of glory. For it is said, 'The Lord made me as the beginning of his way, before his works of old' (Prov. 8:22). It came prior to that concerning which it is written, 'For your throne is established of old' (Ps. 93:2)."

Along these same lines, prior to creation of the world, God created seven things in preparation therefor, so b. Pes. 4:4 I.5/54a: Seven things were created before the world was made, and these are they: Torah, repentance, the Garden of Eden, Gehenna, the throne of glory, the house of the sanctuary, and the name of the Messiah. Torah: "The Lord possessed me in the beginning of his way, before his works of old" (Prov. 8:22). Repentance: "Before the mountains were brought forth, or even you had formed the earth and the world...you turn man to destruction and say, Repent, you sons of men" (Ps. 90:2). The Garden of Eden: "And the Lord God planted a garden in Eden from aforetime" (Gen. 2:8). Gehenna: "For Tophet is ordained of old" (Isa. 30:33). The throne of glory: "Your throne is established from of old" (Ps. 93:2). The house of the sanctuary: "A glorious high throne from the beginning is the place of our sanctuary" (Jer. 17:12). And the name of the Messiah: "His name shall endure forever and has existed before the sun" (Ps. 72:17).

God created the world with the attribute of mercy and also of justice, so that in the balance, the world might endure, s Gen. R. XII:XV.1: "The Lord God [made earth and heaven]" (Gen. 2:4): The matter [of referring to the divinity by both the names, Lord and God] may be compared to the case of a king who had empty cups. The king said, "If I fill them with hot water, they will split. If I fill them with cold water, they will contract [and snap]." What did the king do? He mixed hot water and cold water and put it into them, and the cups withstood the liquid. So said the Holy One, blessed be he, "If I create the world in accord with the attribute of mercy, sins will multiply. If I create it in accord with the attribute of justice, the world cannot endure. Lo, I shall create it with both the attribute of justice and the attribute of mercy, and may it endure!" "Thus: The Lord [standing for the attribute of mercy] God [standing for the attribute of justice] [made the earth and heavens]" (Gen. 2:4).

At twilight of the sixth day, at the very conclusion of the days of creation, ten things were made, so b. Pes. 4:4 1:7: Ten things were created on the eve of the Sabbath at twilight, and these are they: the well (Num. 21:16-18), the manna, the rainbow, writing and writing instruments, the tablets of the ten commandments, the burial cave of Moses, the cave in which Moses and Elijah stood, the opening of the ass's mouth, and the opening of the earth's mouth to swallow up the wicked. And there are those who say, "Also the staff of Aaron, its almonds and its blossoms" (Num. 17:23). And there are those who say, "Also demons." And there are those who say, "Also the garment of Adam." Three things entered God's mind for creation, and if they hadn't come into his mind, it is logical that he should have thought of them: that a corpse should stink, that a deceased person should be forgotten from the heart, and that produce should rot [so as to prevent hoarding]. And some say, also, that coins should circulate.

Creation did not produce a good result, and God nearly gave up. The failure of Creation down to Noah is not God's fault, so Gen. R. XXVIII:IV.1: "I will blot out man whom I have created" (Gen. 6:7): "I shall impose an interdict upon my creatures, but my creatures cannot impose an interdict upon me." [There are things I know that they do not. Anyone who criticizes God's destroying this generation should know that it was the best of a bad lot, as will now be shown through, first a parable and second a set of proofs of that same syllogism.] Said R. Eleazar, "The matter may be compared to the case of a king who had diverse stores [of materials and substances], and people of the city mumbled against the king, saying, 'The king is a miser, [because he will not share his stored wealth with us or even show it to us].' What did the king do? He opened up for the people the best quality [material in his storage tanks], and the entire town was filled with a stink.' People had to sweep up the material and burn it up. So these were the best among them, but only 'One man among a thousand have I found' (Qoh. 7:28). The use of one in a thousand is in line with this usage: Top grade wine [M. Men. 9:6]. [If the best quality produces a stink, the rest would have been even worse, and God did well to spare the world the stink of the other generations, which he had kept back and not revealed to the world. This point will now be made clear.] Yet this is what they have done. [Therefore:] 'I will blot out man whom I have made' (Gen. 6:7)." A thousand generations came to God's mind as candidates for creation, and how many of them were blotted out? [This in fact continues the foregoing and explains the syllogism of the whole.] R. Huna in the name of R. Eliezer b. R. Yosé, the Galilean: "There were 974 generations [that were blotted out of mind prior to the creation of man]. What is the verse of Scripture that indicates it? 'A matter that he commanded for a thousand generations' (Ps. 105:8) refers to the Torah. [That is, the Torah would be commanded after a thousand generations had lived. But in fact, we know, there were only twenty-six generations between Adam and Sinai. Hence the other 974 generations were created and destroyed in the mind of God prior to the creation of man.]" R. Levi in the name of R. Samuel bar Nahman, "There were 980. What is verse of Scripture so indicates? 'A matter that he commanded for a thousand generations' (Ps. 105:8) refers to circumcision [which applied to Abraham, six generations earlier than Sinai]."

All things that were created have and serve a purpose, however difficult it may be to discern that purpose, so Gen. R. X:VI.1ff.: Bar Sira said, "The divinity produced medicine from the earth, with which the physician heals a wound and the pharmacist mixes his medicines." Said R. Simon, "There is not a single herb which is not subject to the influence of a planet in heaven, which smites it and says to it, 'Grow!' as it is written, 'Do you know the ordinances of heaven? Can you establish the dominion thereof in the earth?' (Job 38:33). 'Can you bind the chains of Pleiades or loose the bands of Orion?' (Job 38:31)." Hinena bar Pappa and R. Simon say, "Pleides binds produce and Orion draws it out between knot and knot [Freedman], in line with the following verse of Scripture: 'Can you lead forth the constellations in their season?' (Job 38:32)." Tanhum b. R. Hiyya and R. Simon: "For it is the constellation which makes the fruit ripen." Rabbis say, "Even things that you regard as completely superfluous to the creation of the world, for instance, fleas, gnats, and flies, also fall into the classification of things that were part of the creation of the world."

One must take cognizance of how much God does to order a beneficent world, so T. Ber. 6:2: [When] Ben Zoma saw a crowd on steps of the Temple Mount, he said, "Blessed is he who is wise in knowing secrets. Blessed is he who created [all] these [people] to serve me." He would say, "How hard did Adam toil before he could taste a morsel [of food]: he seeded, plowed, reaped, made sheaves, threshed, winnowed, separated, ground, sifted, kneaded, and baked, and only then could he eat. But I arise in the morning and find all these [foods ready] before me. How hard did Adam toil before he could put on a garment: he sheared, bleached, separated, dyed, spun, and wove, and only then could he put it on. But I arise in the morning and find all these [garments ready] before me. How many skilled craftsmen are industrious and rise early [to their work] at my door. And I arise in the morning and find all these [ready] before me." And so Ben Zoma would say, "What does a good guest say? '[May my host be remembered [by God] for good!] How much trouble did he take for me! How many kinds of wine did he bring before us! How many kinds of cuts [of meat] did he bring before us! How many kinds of cakes did he bring before me! And all the trouble that he took he took for me!' But what does a bad guest say? How little trouble did this household take. [And what have I eaten of his?] I ate only a loaf of his bread. I drank only a cup of his wine. He went to all this trouble only to provide for his wife and children' [T. Ber. 6:2F-J].

IV.

Gentiles

GENTILES: A theological category, the nations, without elaborate differentiation, mean all who are not Israelites, that is, who do not belong to Israel. Israel is deemed that sector of humanity that is holy by reason of God's self-manifestation and revelation of the Torah, and the nations encompass those beyond the limits of God's revelation.

Within humanity other than Israel, differentiation is along gross lines, lacking a concrete ethnic foundation. Rather, humanity is divided between those who get a share in the world to come — Israel — and who will stand in judgment and those who will not. First, all those prior to Noah are wiped out, do not get a share in the world to come, and do not stand in Judgment. As to those after the flood, while they have no share in the world to come, they will stand in Judgment. Thus M. San. 10:3: The generation of the flood has no share in the world to come, and they shall not stand in the judgment, since it is said, My spirit shall not judge with man forever (Gen. 6:3) — neither judgment nor spirit. The generation of the dispersion has no share in the world to come, since it is said, So the Lord scattered them abroad from there — So the Lord scattered them abroad — in this world, and the Lord scattered them from there — in the world to come. The men of Sodom have no portion in the world to come, since it is said, Now the men of Sodom were wicked and sinners Wicked-in this world, And sinners-in the world to come. But they will stand in judgment. Nonetheless, particular nations that played an important role in Israel's history, such as Egypt and Canaan, Babylonia, Media, Greece, and Rome, are identified and given standing vis á vis Israel.

What separates Israel from the gentiles, and the gentiles from God, is idolatry. Idolatry is what angers God and turns him against the gentiles, co b. A.Z. 1:1 I.23/4b: "That time at which God gets angry comes when the kings put on their crowns on their heads and prostrate themselves to the sun. Forthwith the Holy One, blessed be He, grows angry." But God does not wipe out gentile idolatry, because He cannot do so in a way that would effectively demonstrate the truth of monotheism, so M. A.Z. 4:7: They asked sages in Rome, "If God is not in favor of idolatry, why does he not wipe it away?" They said to them, "If people worshipped something of which the world had no need, he certainly would wipe it away." "But lo, people worship the sun, moon, stars, and planets. "Now do you think he is going to wipe out his world because of idiots?" They said to them, "If so, let him destroy something of which the world has no need, and leave something which the world needs!" They said to them, "Then we should strengthen the hands of those who worship these which would not be destroyed, for then they would say, 'Now you know full well that they are gods, for lo, they were not wiped out!.'" It is absolutely forbidden to conduct any sort of commerce with gentiles in connection with occasions of idolatrous worship, e.g., festivals and the like, so M. A.Z. 1:1: Before the festivals of gentiles for three days it is forbidden to do business with them, (1) to lend anything to them or to borrow anything from them, (2) to lend money to them or to borrow money from them, (3) to repay them or to be repaid by them.

Gentile idolatry and consequent estrangement from God came about because the nations all rejected the Torah, each having had its opportunity to accept it. They did so because the Torah at one point or another forbad their various practices. Each gentile nation in succession gave up its opportunity, which then came to Israel; Israel accepted, so b. A.Z. 1:1 1.2/2a-b: R. Hanina bar Pappa, and some say, R. Simlai, gave the following exposition of the verse, "They that fashion a graven image are all of them vanity, and their delectable things shall not profit, and their own witnesses see not nor know" (Isa. 44:9): "In the age to come the Holy One, blessed be He, will bring a scroll of the Torah and hold it in his bosom and say, 'Let him who has kept himself busy with it come and take his reward.' Then all the gentiles will crowd together: 'All of the nations are gathered together' (Isa. 43:9). The Holy One, blessed be He, will say to them, 'Do not crowd together before me in a mob. But let each nation enter together with its scribes, 'and let the peoples be gathered together' (Isa. 43:9), and the word 'people' means 'kingdom': 'and one kingdom shall be stronger than the other' (Gen. 25:23)." The kingdom of Rome comes in first. The Holy One, blessed be He, will say to them, 'How have you defined your chief occupation?' They will say before him, 'Lord of the world, a vast number of marketplaces have we set up, a vast number of bathhouses we have made, a vast amount of silver and gold have we accumulated. And all of these things we have done only in behalf of Israel, so that they may define as their chief occupation the study of the Torah.' The Holy One, blessed be He, will say to them, 'You complete idiots! Whatever you have done has been for your own convenience. You have set up a vast number of marketplaces to be sure, but that was so as to set up whorehouses in them. The bathhouses were for your own pleasure. Silver and gold belong to me anyhow: "Mine is the silver and mine is the gold, says the Lord of hosts" (Hag. 2:8). Are there any among you who have been telling of "this," and "this" is only the Torah: "And this is the Torah that Moses set before the children of Israel' (Dt. 4:44)." So they will make their exit, humiliated. When the kingdom of Rome has made its exit, the kingdom of Persia enters afterward. The Holy One, blessed be He, will say to them, 'How have you defined your chief occupation?' They will say before him, 'Lord of the world, We have thrown up a vast number of bridges, we have conquered a vast number of towns, we have made a vast number of wars, and all of them we did only for Israel, so that they may define as their chief occupation the study of the Torah.' The Holy One, blessed be He, will say to them, 'Whatever you have done has been for your own convenience. You have thrown up a vast number of bridges, to collect tolls, you have conquered a vast number of towns, to collect the corvée, and, as to making a vast number of wars, I am the one who makes wars: "The Lord is a man of war" (Ex. 19:17). Are there any among you who have been telling of "this," and "this" is only the Torah: "And this is the Torah that Moses set before the children of Israel" (Dt. 4:44).' So they will make their exit, humiliated. And so it will go with each and every nation. They will say to him, 'Lord of the world, in point of fact, did you actually give it to us and we did not accept it?' This is what they say before him, 'Lord of the world, did you hold a mountain over us like a cask and then we refused to accept it as you did to Israel, as it is written, "And they stood beneath the mountain" (Ex. 19:17).' Then the Holy One, blessed be He, will say to them, 'Let us make known what happened first: "Let them announce to us former things" (Isa. 43:9). As to the seven religious duties that you did accept, where have you actually carried them out?' This is what the gentiles say before him, 'Lord of the world, Israel, who accepted it Ä where in the world have they actually carried it out?' The Holy One, blessed be He, will say to them, 'I shall bear witness concerning them, that they have carried out the whole of the Torah!' They will say before him, 'Lord of the world, is there a father who is permitted to give testimony concerning his son? For it is written, "Israel is my son, my firstborn" (Ex. 4:22).' The Holy One, blessed be He, will say to them, 'The Heaven and the earth will give testimony in their behalf that they have carried out the entirety of the Torah.' They will say before him, 'Lord of the world, the Heaven and earth have a selfish interest in the testimony that they give: 'If not for my covenant with day and with night, I should not have appointed the ordinances of Heaven and earth' (Jer. 33:25).' The Holy One, blessed be He, will say to them, 'Some of them may well come and give testimony concerning Israel that they have observed the entirety of the Torah. Let Nimrod come and give testimony in behalf of Abraham that he never worshipped idols. Let Laban come and give testimony in behalf of Jacob, that he never was suspect of thievery. Let the wife of Potiphar come and give testimony in behalf of Joseph, that he was never suspect of 'sin.' Let Nebuchadnessar come and give testimony in behalf of Hananiah, Mishael, and Azariah, that they never bowed down to the idol. Let Darius come and give testimony in behalf of Daniel, that he did not neglect even the optional prayers. Let Bildad the Shuhite and Zophar the Naamatite and Eliphaz the Temanite and Elihu son of Barachel the Buzite come and testify in behalf of Israel that they have observed the entirety of the Torah: "Let the nations bring their own witnesses, that they may be justified" (Isa. 43:9). They will say before him, 'Lord of the world, Give it to us to begin with, and let us carry it out.' The Holy One, blessed be He, will say to them, 'World-class idiots! He who took the trouble to prepare on the eve of the Sabbath Friday will eat on the Sabbath, but he who took no trouble on the even of the Sabbath — what in the world is he going to eat on the Sabbath! Still, I'll give you another chance. I have a rather simple religious duty, which is called "the tabernacle." Go and do that one.' Forthwith every one of them will take up the task and go and make a tabernacle on his roof. But then the Holy, One, blessed be He, will come and make the sun blaze over them as at the summer solstice, and every one of them will knock down his tabernacle and go his way: 'Let us break their bands asunder and cast away their cords from us' (Ps. 23:3). Then the Holy One, blessed be He, goes into session and laughs at them: 'He who sits in Heaven laughs' (Ps. 2:4)."

Israel's piety pleases God and saves the world, while the gentiles' impiety so outrage him as to make him consider destroying it, so Song R. CXV:ii.3: "Make haste, my beloved:" Said R. Levi, "The matter may be compared to the case of a king who made a banquet and invited guests. Some of them ate and drank and said a blessing to the king, but some of them ate and drank and cursed the king. The king realized it and considered making a public display at his banquet and disrupting it. But the matron queen came and defended them, saying to him, 'My lord, O king, instead of paying attention to those who ate and drank and cursed you, take note of those who ate and drank and blessed you and praised your name.' So is the case with Israel: when they eat and drink and say a blessing and praise and adore the Holy One, blessed be He, he listens to their voice and is pleased. But when the nations of the world eat and drink and blaspheme and curse the Holy One, blessed be He, with their fornications of which they make mention, at that moment the Holy One, blessed be He, gives thought even to destroy his world. But the Torah comes along and defends them, saying, 'Lord of the world, instead of taking note of these, who blaspheme and spite you, take note of Israel, your people, who bless and praise and adore your great name through the Torah and through song and praise.' And the Holy Spirit cries out, '"Make haste, my beloved:" flee from the nations of the world and cleave to the Israelites.'"

Then why does God tolerate gentiles, and why did he make a world that would include them? True, gentiles also are created by God, and God is the God of everyone, but God rests on Israel in greatest measure, and ultimately the gentiles will recognize that God is ruler of all, so Sif. Dt. XXXI:III.1, IV:1: "The Lord is our God": Why is this stated? Is it not said in any event, "The Lord is one"? Why then does Scripture say, "is our God"? Because the name of God rests upon us in greatest measure. "The Lord, our God": — for us. "the Lord is one: " — for everyone in the world. "the Lord, our God": — in this world. "the Lord is one": — in the world to come. And so Scripture says, "The Lord shall be king over all the earth. In that day shall the Lord be one and his name one" (Zech. 14:9).

Israel and the gentiles form a single genus, as one mankind, but are readily speciated as well. The nations of the world and Israel are both alike and different. They are called by the same name, for instance, but in the case of Israel, the name bears quite different meaning, so Lev. R.

V:VII.2: Said R. Eleazar, "The nations of the world are called a congregation, and Israel is called a congregation. The nations of the world are called a congregation: 'For the congregation of the godless shall be desolate' (Job 15:34). And Israel is called a congregation: 'And the elders of the congregation shall lay their hands' (Lev. 4:15). The nations of the world are called sturdy bulls and Israel is called sturdy bulls. The nations of the world are called sturdy bulls: 'The congregation of sturdy bulls with the calves of the peoples' (Ps. 68:31). Israel is called sturdy bulls, as it is said, 'Listen to me, you sturdy bullish of heart' (Is. 46:13). The nations of the world are called excellent, and Israel is called excellent. The nations of the world are called excellent: 'You and the daughters of excellent nations' (Ex. 32:18). Israel is called excellent: 'They are the excellent, in whom is all my delight' (Ps. 16:4). The nations of the world are called sages, and Israel is called sages. The nations of the world are called sages: 'And I shall wipe out sages from Edom' (Ob. 1:8). And Israel is called sages: 'Sages store up knowledge' (Prov. 10:14). The nations of the world are called unblemished, and Israel is called unblemished. The nations of the world are called unblemished: 'Unblemished as are those that go down to the pit' (Prov. 1:12). And Israel is called unblemished: 'The unblemished will inherit goodness' (Prov. 28:10). The nations of the world are called men, and Israel is called men. The nations of the world are called men: 'And you men who work iniquity' (Ps. 141:4). And Israel is called men: 'To you who are men I call' (Prov. 8:4). The nations of the world are called righteous, and Israel is called righteous. The nations of the world are called righteous: 'And righteous men shall judge them' (Ez. 23:45). And Israel is called righteous: 'And your people — all of them are righteous' (Is. 60:21). The nations of the world are called mighty, and Israel is called mighty. The nations of the world are called mighty: 'Why do you boast of evil, O mighty man' (Ps. 52:3). And Israel is called mighty: 'Mighty in power, those who do his word' (Ps. 103:20).

When God favors the nations, they blaspheme and do not glorify him, but when he favors Israel, they honor him, so PRK XXVIII:I.3-4: "But you have increased the nation, O Lord, you have increased the nation; you are glorified; you have enlarged all the borders of the land" (Is. 17:25): In the case of the nations of the world, if you give them a male child, he draws forward his foreskin and grows a lock that is cut off in the honor of the idol. When he grows up, he brings him to the temple of his idol and outrages you. But in the case of Israel, if you give one of them a male child, he counts eight days and circumcises him. If he was a firstborn, he redeems him after thirty days. When he grows up, he brings him to synagogues and study hours and blesses you every day: Blessed be the Lord who is to be blessed. Another interpretation of the verse But you have increased the nation, O Lord, you have increased the nation; you are glorified; you have enlarged all the borders of the land (Is. 17:25): The nations of the world, if you increase the number of festivals for them, they eat and drink and carouse and go to theaters and circuses and outrage you with their words and deeds. But in the case of Israel, if you give them festival days, they eat, drink, rejoice, go to synagogues and school houses, increase their praying and increase their prayers for additional offerings and other offerings. Therefore it was necessary for Scripture to say, On the eighth day you shall have a solemn assembly. You shall do no laborious work, but you shall offer a burnt-offering, an offering by fire, a pleasing odor to the Lord... These you shall offer to the Lord at your appointed feasts in addition to your votive-offerings and your freewill-offerings, for your burnt-offerings and for your cereal-offerings and for your drink-offerings and for your peace-offerings (Numbers 29:35-39).

The gentiles include many righteous persons, whom God will bring to Israel, so Y. Ber. 2:8 I:2: Resh Laqish expounded concerning Hiyya this verse: "My beloved has gone down to his garden, to the bed of spices, to pasture his flock in the gardens, and to gather lilies" (Song 6:2). It is not necessary for the verse to mention, 'To the bed of spices'. It is redundant if you interpret the verse literally, for most gardens have spice beds. Rather interpret the verse as follows: My beloved — this is God; has gone down to his garden — this is the world; to the beds of spices — this is Israel; to pasture his flock in the gardens — these are the nations of the world; and to gather lilies — these are the righteous whom he takes from their midst. They offer a parable relevant to this subject. To what may we compare this matter of the tragic death of his student? A king had a son who was very beloved to him. What did the king do? He planted an orchard for him. As long as the son acted according to his father's will, he would search throughout the world to seek the beautiful saplings of the world, and to plant them in his orchard. And when his son angered him he went and cut down all his saplings. Accordingly, so long as Israel acts according to God's will he searches throughout the world to seek the righteous persons of the nations of the world and bring them and join them to Israel, as he did with Jethro and Rahab. And when they the Israelites anger him he removes the righteous from their midst.

Along these same lines, if a gentile keeps the Torah, he is saved, so Sifra CXCIV:II.15: "...by the pursuit of which man shall live": R. Jeremiah says, "How do I know that even a gentile who keeps the Torah, lo, he is like the high priest? Scripture says, 'by the pursuit of which man shall live.'" And so he says, "'And this is the Torah of the priests, Levites, and Israelites,' is not what is said here, but rather, 'This is the Torah of the man, O Lord God' (2 Sam. 7:19)." And so he says, "'open the gates and let priests, Levites, and Israelites will enter it' is not what is said, but rather, 'Open the gates and let the righteous nation, who keeps faith, enter it' (Is. 26:2)." And so he says, "'This is the gate of the Lord. Priests, Levites, and Israelites...' is not what is said, but rather, 'the righteous shall enter into it' (Ps. 118:20). And so he says, "'What is said is not, 'Rejoice, priests, Levites, and Israelites,' but rather, 'Rejoice, O righteous, in the Lord' (Ps. 33:1)." And so he says, "It is not, 'Do good, O Lord, to the priests, Levites, and Israelites,' but rather, 'Do good, O Lord, to the good, to the upright in heart' (Ps. 125:4)." "Thus, even a gentile who keeps the Torah, lo, he is like the high priest." And the purpose of keeping the commandments is to live, not die, so Sifra CXCIV:II.16: "...by the pursuit of which man shall live": not that he should die by them. R. Ishmael would say, "How do you know that if people should say to someone when entirely alone, 'Worship an idol and do not be put to death,' the person should worship the idol and not be put to death? Scripture says, 'by the pursuit of which man shall live,' not that he should die by them." But even if it is in public should he obey them? Scripture says, 'You shall faithfully observe my commandments; I am the Lord. You shall not profane my holy name, that I may be sanctified in the midst of the Israelite people — I the Lord who sanctify you, I who brought you out of the land of Egypt to be your God, I the Lord' (Lev. 22:31-32). If you sanctify my name, then I shall sanctify my name through you. For that is just as Hananiah, Mishael, and Azariah did. When all of the nations of the world at that time were prostrate before the idol, while they stood up like palm trees. And concerning them it is stated explicitly in tradition: 'Your stately form is like the palm' (Song 7:8). 'I say, let me climb the palm, let me take hold of its branches; let your breasts be like clusters of grapes, your breath like the fragrance of apples, and your mouth like choicest wine' (Ps. 7:9). 'This day I shall be exalted through the in the sight of the nations of the world, who deny the Torah. 'This day I shall exact vengeance for them from those who hate them. 'This day I shall resurrect the dead among them.' "I am the Lord": "I am Judge to exact punishment and faithful to pay a reward.

God responds, also, to the acts of merit taken by gentiles, as the following narrative makes clear, so Est. R. XVIII.iii.5: Merodach-baladan was a sun-worshipper, and he ordinarily ate at the sixth hour noon and slept until the ninth hour. But on the day in the time of Hezekiah on which the sun reversed its course, he slept until the ninth hour and woke up at the fourth hour. When he woke up from his sleep, he wanted to kill all his servants. He said to them, "You let me sleep all day long and all night long!" They replied, "Not so, but the sun has reversed its course." He said to them, "Now is there a god greater than my god, who can make the sun reverse its course?" They said to him, "The God of Hezekiah is greater than your god." He immediately wrote, "Peace to Hezekiah and peace to the God of Hezekiah and peace to Jerusalem." Now when the letters and messengers had gone out, he had second thoughts and said, "This honor that I have paid to Hezekiah I have paid only on account of his God, and yet I give precedence to the greeting of peace to Hezekiah, who is a mere mortal, over the greeting of peace to his God!" He forthwith stood up from his throne and took three steps, and sent messengers and called back the letters and wrote other letters: "Peace to the great God of Hezekiah, peace to Hezekiah, and peace to Jerusalem." Said to him the Holy One, blessed be he, "You have stood up from your throne and taken three steps on account of the honor owing to my name. By your life, I shall establish on your account three kings who will be rulers from one end of the world to the other." And who are these? Nebuchadnezzar, Evil-Merodach, and Belshazzar. Therefore said to him the Holy One, blessed be he, "Your honor, and your elder's honor and that of your father — all of them came upon the throne only on account of the fact that your forebear honored this one's forebear.

Gentiles are subject to a number of commandments or religious obligations, e.g., not to curse God's name, so b. San. 7:5 I.2/56a: "Any man who curses his God shall bear his sin" (Lev. 24:15)": It would have been clear had the text simply said, "A man." Why does it specify, "Any"? It serves to encompass idolators, who are admonished not to curse the Name, just as Israelites are so admonished. And they are put to death only by decapitation, for the sole form of inflicting the death penalty in the case of the sons of Noah is by decapitation. How do we deduce from the cited verse that idolators are not to blaspheme? It derives from the following verse: "The Lord" (Gen. 2:16) signifies that cursing the divine Name is forbidden for gentiles as much as for Israelites. Said R. Isaac the Smith, "The phrase cited earlier 'any man' serves to encompass even the use of euphemisms, and it is framed in accord with the principle of R. Meir." R. Miasha said, "A son of Noah who cursed the Name by using euphemisms in the opinion of rabbis is liable to the death penalty. What is the scriptural basis for that claim? Scripture has said, 'As well the stranger as he that is born in the land when he blasphemes the name of the Lord shall be put to death' (Lev. 24:16). So in the case of the proselyte or the homeborn before we inflict the death penalty we require cursing by the use of the divine Name in particular, but in the case of the idolator, even if he uses only a euphemism he is subject to the death penalty."

In fact there are seven such religious obligations, so T. A.Z. 8:4: Concerning seven religious requirements were the children of Noah commanded: setting up courts of justice, idolatry, blasphemy, cursing the Name of God, fornication, bloodshed, thievery, and cutting a limb from a living beast (T. A.Z. 8:4). R. Hananiah b. Gamaliel says, "Also on account of blood deriving from a living beast." R. Hidqa says, "Also on account of castration." R. Simeon says, "Also on account of witchcraft." R. Yosé, says, "On account of whatever is stated in the pericope regarding the children of Noah are they subject to warning, as it is said, 'There shall not be found among you any one who burns his son or his daughter as an offering, any one who practices divination, a soothsayer or an augur or a sorcerer or a charmer or a medium or a wizard or a necromancer' (Deut. 18:10-11). Is it possible then that Scripture has imposed a punishment without imparting a prior warning.? But it provides a warning and afterward imposes the punishment. This teaches that he warned them first and then punished them." R. Eleazar says, "Also as to mixed seeds, it is permitted for a child of Noah to sow seeds which are mixed species and to wear garments of mixed species of wool and linen. But it is prohibited to breed a hybrid beast or to graft trees."

While Israelites have to accept martyrdom rather than violate the cardinal commandments against idolatry, murder, and fornication, gentiles do not have to do so, thus Y. Sheb. 4:1 V: R. Abuna asked in the presence of R. Imi, "What is the law whether or not gentiles are commanded concerning sanctification of the name of God?" {That is, do the Noahide commandments, which apply to all people, require gentiles to accept martyrdom rather than to commit idolatry? Imi said to him, "[Lev. 22:32] states, 'But I will be hallowed that is, sanctified among the people of Israel.' This means that the people of Israel are commanded concerning sanctification of the name of God, but gentiles are not commanded concerning sanctification of the name of God." If a gentile performs an act prohibited to an Israelite, and it is clear that the gentile had only his own purpose in mind, then the Israelite may benefit from the act, thus Y. Shab. 16:9 I.1: Samuel was received as a guest by a Persian. The lamp went out. The Persian went and wanted to light it. Samuel turned his face away. But when he saw the Persian working on his business papers, Samuel knew that it was not for him Samuel alone that he had lit the lamp, and Samuel turned his face back. Said R. Jacob bar Aha, "That is to say that if it was done both for the gentile's need and also for the Israelite's need, it is forbidden."

The death penalty applies to a Noahide, so b. San. 7:5 I.4-5/57a: On account of violating three religious duties are children of Noah put to death: on account of adultery, murder, and blasphemy.'" R. Huna, R. Judah, and all the disciples of Rab say, "On account of seven commandments a son of Noah is put to death. The All-Merciful revealed that fact of one of them, and the same rule applies to all of them."

Gentiles in general, however, are always suspect of the cardinal sins, bestiality, fornication, and bloodshed, as well as constant idolatry, so M. A.Z. 2:1: They do not leave cattle in gentiles' inns, because they are suspect in regard to bestiality And a woman should not be alone with them, because they are suspect in regard to fornication. And a man should not be alone with them, because they are suspect in regard to bloodshed. An Israelite girl should not serve as a midwife to a gentile woman, because she serves to bring forth a child for the service of idolatry. But a gentile woman may serve as a midwife to an Israelite girl. An Israelite girl should not give suck to the child of a gentile woman. But a gentile woman may give suck to the child of an Israelite girl, when it is by permission. The proclivity to idolatry accounts, also, for the absolute prohibition of Israelite use of wine that gentiles have at any time controlled and touched, since it is taken for granted that they will have made a libation of part of the wine, leaving the rest contaminated by the act of idolatry (M. A.Z. 2:3). The same trilogy occurs in yet another context, at Y. A.Z. 2:2 I.3: R. Jacob in the name of R. Yohanan: "With all sorts of things do they effect healing, except for an idol, fornication, or committing murder."

The nations acquire importance by reason of their dealings with Israel, and the monarchies that enjoyed prominence benefited because they ruled Israel, so Mekh. XX:II.5-7: "the mind of Pharaoh and his servants was changed toward the people:" This indicates that when the Israelites went out of Egypt, the monarchy of the Egyptians came to an end, as it is said, "Who are our servants?" and they said, 'What is this that we have done, that we have let Israel go from serving us?'" "Who are our servants?" They said, "Now all the nations of the world will be chiming in against us like a bell, saying, 'Now these, who were in their domain, they let go to leave them, how!' "Now how are we going to send to Aram Naharaim and Aram Soba officers and task-masters to bring us slave-boys and slave girls?" This indicates that Pharaoh ruled from one end of the world to the other, having governors from one end of the world to the other. This was for the sake of the honor of Israel. Of Pharaoh it is said, "The king sent and loosed him, even the ruler of peoples, and set him free' (Ps. 105:20). And so you find that every nation and language that subjugated Israel ruled from one end of the world to the other, for the sake of the honor of Israel. What does Scripture say in connection with Assyria? "And my hand has found as a nest the riches of the peoples, and as one gathers lost eggs have I gathered all the earth, and there was none that moved the wing or opened the mouth or chirped" (Is. 10:14). What does Scripture say of Babylonia? "And it shall come to pass that the nation and kingdom that will not serve this same Nebuchadnezzar, king of Babylonia" (Jer. 27:8). What does Scripture say of Media? "Then king Darius wrote to all the peoples" (Dan. 6:26). What does Scripture say of Greece? "The beast had also four heads and dominion was given to it" (Dan. 7:6). What does Scripture say of the fourth kingdom Rome? "And shall devour the whole earth and shall tread it down and break it in pieces" (Dan. 7:23). So you learn that every nation and language that subjugated Israel ruled from one end of the world to the other, for the sake of the honor of Israel.

Gentiles' deeds — idolatry, rejection of God — and not their genealogy are what define them as non-Israel. That is why Israel enters the classification of gentiles when it acts like them. Thus, if Israel conducts itself like the gentiles, Israel will be rejected and punished as were the gentiles, with special reference to Egypt and Canaan, so Sifra CXCIII:I.1-11: "The Lord spoke to Moses saying, Speak to the Israelite people and say to them, I am the Lord your God:" "I am the Lord," for I spoke and the world came into being. "I am full of mercy." "I am Judge to exact punishment and faithful to pay recompense." "I am the one who exacted punishment from the generation of the Flood and the men of Sodom and Egypt, and I shall exact punishment from you if you act like them." And how do we know that there was never any nation among all of the nations that practiced such abominations, more than did the Egyptians? Scripture says, "You shall not copy the practices of the land of Egypt where you dwelt." And how do we know that the last generation did more abhorrent things than all the rest of them? Scripture says, "You shall not copy the practices of the land of Egypt." And how do we know that the people in the last location in which the Israelites dwelt were more abhorrent than all the rest? Scripture says, "...where you dwelt, you shall not do." And how do we know that the fact that the Israelites dwelt there was the cause for all these deeds? Scripture says, "You shall not copy...where you dwelt." How do we know that there was never a nation among all the nations that did more abhorrent things than the Canaanites? Scripture says, "You shall not copy the practices...of the land of Canaan to which I am taking you; nor shall you follow their laws." And how do we know that the last generation did more abhorrent things than all the rest of them? Scripture says, "You shall not copy the practices of the land of Canaan." And how do we know that the people in the place to which the Israelites were coming for conquest were more abhorrent than all the rest? Scripture says, "...to which I am taking you." And how do we know that it is the arrival of the Israelites that caused them to do all these deeds? Scripture says, "or of the land of Canaan to which I am taking you; nor shall you follow their laws." If "You shall not copy the practices of the land of Egypt…or of the land of Canaan," might one think that they are not to build their buildings or plant vineyards as they did? Scripture says, "nor shall you follow their laws": "I have referred only to the rules that were made for them and for their fathers and their fathers' fathers." And what would they do? A man would marry a man, and a woman would marry a woman, a man would marry a woman and her daughter, a woman would be married to two men. That is why it is said, "nor shall you follow their laws." "My rules alone shall you observe and faithfully follow my laws": "my rules": this refers to laws. "…my laws": this refers to the amplifications thereof. "…shall you observe": this refers to repeating traditions. "…and faithfully follow": this refers to concrete deed. "…and faithfully follow my laws": it is not the repetition of traditions that is the important thing but doing them is the important thing. "You shall keep my laws and my rules, by the pursuit of which man shall live": This formulation of matter serves to make keeping and doing into laws, and keeping and doing into rules. "…shall live": in the world to come. And should you wish to claim that the reference is to this world, is it not the fact that in the end one dies? Lo, how am I to explain, "…shall live"? It is with reference to the world to come. "I the Lord am your God": faithful to pay a reward.

The Egyptians and Canaanites were punished for what they did to anger the Lord, and the Land of Israel is held by Israel on the stipulation that it will not follow their practice, so Sifra CCVII:II.1-13: "…that the land where I am bringing you to dwell may not vomit you out": "For I am bringing you there only so that you will inherit it, not like the Canaanites, who kept the place intact until your arrival." "And you shall not walk in the customs of the nation which I am casting out before you": this refers to the Egyptians. "…which I am casting out before you": this refers to the Canaanites. "…for they did all these things, and therefore I abhorred them": This teaches that the Canaanites were flooded with these things. "I sent them into exile only on account of these things." "…and therefore I abhorred them": "I abhorred them like someone who is repelled by his food." "But I have said to you, You shall inherit their land: "You are worthy of disinheriting them, for you were the first to open up and choose the Holy One, as it is said, "A garden locked is my own, my bride, a fountain locked, a sealed-up spring" (Song 4:12). "I am the Lord your God who has separated you from the peoples": "See how vast is the difference between you and the idolatrous nations! "One of them fixes up his wife and hands her over to someone else for sexual relations, a man fixes up himself and gives himself to someone else for sexual relations." "You shall be holy to me, for I the Lord am holy": "Just as I am holy, so you be holy. "Just as I am separate, so you be separate." "...and have separated you from the peoples, that you should be mine": "If you are separated from the nations, lo, you are for my Name, and if not, lo, you belong to Nebuchadnezzar, king of Babylonia, and his associates." R. Eleazar b. Azariah says, "How do we know that someone should not say, 'I do not want to wear mixed fibers, I don't want to eat pork, I don't want to have incestuous sexual relations.' Rather: 'I do want to wear mixed fibers, I do want to eat pork, I do want to have incestuous sexual relations. But what can I do? For my father in heaven has made a decree for me!' So Scripture says, 'and have separated you from the peoples, that you should be mine.' So one will turn out to keep far from transgression and accept upon himself the rule of Heaven."

The gentiles are incapable of acts of righteousness, so b. B.B. 1:5 IV.34/10b: Said Rabban Yohanan b. Zakkai to his disciples, "My sons, what is the meaning of Scripture: 'Righteousness exalts a nation but the kindness of the peoples is sin' (Prov. 14:34)?" R. Eliezer answered and said, "'Righteousness exalts a nation' — this refers to Israel: 'Who is like your people Israel, one nation in the earth'; (2 Sam. 7:23). '...But the kindness of the peoples is sin' — all the acts of charity and mercy that the idolatrous nations do is a sin for them, for they do it only for their own self-aggrandizement: 'They they may offer sacrifices of a sweet savor to the God of heaven and pray for the life of the king and of his sons' (Ezra 7:20)." R. Joshua answered and said, "'Righteousness exalts a nation' — this refers to Israel: 'Who is like your people Israel, one nation in the earth'; (2 Sam. 7:23). '...But the kindness of the peoples is sin' — all the acts of charity and mercy that the idolatrous nations do is a sin for them, for they do it only to prolong their dominion: 'Wherefore O king, let my counsel be acceptable to you, and break off your sins by righteousness and your iniquities by showing mercy to the poor, so there may be a lengthening of your tranquillity' (Dan. 4:27)." Rabban Gamaliel answered and said, "'Righteousness exalts a nation' — this refers to Israel: 'Who is like your people Israel, one nation in the earth'; (2 Sam. 7:23). '...But the kindness of the peoples is sin' — all the acts of charity and mercy that the idolatrous nations do is a sin for them, for they do it only to put on airs, and whoever puts on airs is thrown into Gehenna: 'The proud and haughty man, scorner is his name, he works in wrath of pride' (Prov. 21:24), and 'wrath' is Gehenna: 'A day of wrath is that day' (Zeph. 1:15)." Said Rabban Gamaliel, "We still have to hear what the Modiite has to say." R. Eliezer the Modiite answered and said, "'Righteousness exalts a nation' — this refers to Israel: 'Who is like your people Israel, one nation in the earth'; (2 Sam. 7:23). '…But the kindness of the peoples is sin' — all the acts of charity and mercy that the idolatrous nations do is a sin for them, for they do it only to reproach us: 'The Lord has brought it and done according as he spoke, because you have sinned against the Lord and have not obeyed his voice, therefore this thing is come upon you' (Jer. 40:3)." R. Nehunia b. Haqqanah answered and said, "'Righteousness exalts a nation, but the kindness' — for Israel. But 'sin' is for the peoples." Said Rabban Yohanan b. Zakkai to his disciples, "What R. Nehuniah b. Haqqanah has said makes more sense than what I have had to say and what you have had to say, since he assigns righteousness and mercy to Israel, but to gentiles, sin."

The Temple and its cult form an act of grace performed by God for Israel, which explains why Gentiles do not have the right to bring sin-offerings, and they do not atone through the cult the way Israel does, so Sifra XXXIV:I.1: Israelites bring a sin-offering, but gentiles do not bring a sin-offering. It is not necessary to say that they do not have to bring a sin-offering for inadvertently violating religious duties that were not assigned to the children of Noah, but even for violating religious duties concerning which the children of Noah were commanded, they do not have to bring a sin-offering on that account. "Say to the people of Israel:" I know that the sin-offering is owing only from Israelites. How do I know that it is owing also from proselytes and bondmen? Scripture says, "If any one sins unwittingly." Gentiles may present certain types of offerings to the altar, but no offerings that distinguish Israel as pure or elect and legitimate beneficiaries of the cult of Israel. Thus, M. Sheq. 1:5: A gentile and a Samaritan who paid the sheqel in support of the daily whole offering presented in behalf of Israel — they do not accept it from them. Nor do they accept from them bird offerings for male Zabs, bird offerings for female Zabs, bird offerings for women who have given birth, sin offerings, or guilt offerings. But offerings brought by reason of vows and freewill offerings they accept from them. This is the governing principle: Anything which is vowed or given as a freewill offering do they accept from them. Anything which is not vowed or given as a freewill offering do they not accept from them. And so is the matter explained by Ezra, since it is said, You have nothing to do with us to build a house unto our God (Ezra 4:3).

The gentiles' hatred of Israel came about because of the revelation of the Torah at Sinai, so b. Shab. 9:3-4 I.45-6/89a: Said one of the rabbis to R. Kahana, "Have you heard the meaning of the words 'Mount Sinai'?" He said to him, "The mountain on which miracles [*nissim*] were done for Israel." "But then the name should be, Mount Nisai." "Rather, the mountain on which a good omen was done for Israel." "But then the name should be, Mount Sinai." He said to him, "So why don't you hang out at the household of R. Pappa and R. Huna b. R. Joshua, for they're the ones who really look into lore." For both of them say, "What is the meaning of the name, Mount Sinai? It is the mountain from which hatred descended for the gentiles." That is in line with what R. Yosé, b. R. Hanina said, "It has five names: the wilderness of Sin, for there the Israelites were given commandments; the wilderness of Kadesh, where the Israelites were sanctified; the wilderness of Kedemot, for there the Israelites were given priority; the wilderness of Paran, for there Israel was fruitful and multiplied; and the wilderness of Sinai, for there hatred descended for the gentiles. But what really is its name? Horeb is its name." He differs from R. Abbahu, for said R. Abbahu, "It is really called Mount Sinai, but why is it called Mount Horeb? Because there desolation descended on the gentiles."

The same view is presented along these lines as well: Israel's loyalty to the Torah and commandments accounts for the nations' hostility, so PRK XIX:II.2: Rabbis interpreted the cited verse to speak of the nations of the world: "You find that when the sins of Israel made it possible for the gentiles to enter Jerusalem, they made the decree that in every place to which they would flee, they should close (the gates before them. They tried to flee to the south, but they did not let them: Thus says the Lord, for three transgressions of Gaza, yes for four, I will not reverse it because they permitted an entire captivity to be carried away captive by delivering them up to Edom (Amos 1:6). They wanted to flee to the east, but they did not let them: Thus says the Lord, for three transgressions of Damascus, yes for four, I will not reverse it (Amos 1:3). They wanted to flee to the north, but they did not let them: Thus says the Lord, for three transgressions of Tyre, yes for four, I will not reverse it (Amos 1:21). They wanted to flee to the west, but they did not let them: The burden upon Arabia (Is. 21:13). Said to them the Holy One, blessed be He, 'Lo, you outraged them.' They said before Him, 'Lord of the ages, are you not the one who did it? All my enemies, when they heard of my calamity, rejoiced at what you had done.'" They drew a parable. To what may the matter be compared? To the case of a king who married a noble lady, and gave her instructions, saying to her: "Do not talk with your neighbors, and do not lend anything to them, and do not borrow anything from them." One time she made him mad, so he drove her out and dismissed her from his palace, and she made the rounds of the households of her neighbors, but there was not a single one who would accept her. The king said to her, "Lo, you outraged them." She said to him, "My lord, king, are you not the one who did it? Did you not give me instructions, say to me, 'Do not talk with your neighbors, and do not lend anything to them, and do not borrow anything from them.' If I had borrowed something from them or had lent something to them, which one of them would have seen me pass through her household and not accept me in her home?" That illustrates the verse: All my enemies, when they heard of my calamity, rejoiced at what you had done. Said Israel before the Holy One, blessed be He, "Lord of the ages, are you not the one who did this: Did you not write for us in the Torah: You shall not make marriages with them: your daughter you shall not give to his son, nor his daughter shall you take for your son (Deut. 7:3). If we had taken children in marriage from them, or given children in marriage to them, which one of them would have seen a son or daughter standing in trouble and not receive him? That illustrates the verse: All my enemies, when they heard of my calamity, rejoiced at what you had done.

Gentiles benefit because of God's blessings of the world on account of Israel, but they repay Israel in evil ways, so Y. Sheb. 5:9 VI: R. Hanina bar Pappa and R. Samuel bar Nahman passed a certain Israelite who was plowing during the Sabbatical year. Said to him R. Samuel bar Nahman, "May you have strength so as to complete your work." R. Hanina bar Pappa said to him i.e., to Samuel bar Nahman, "Has the Rabbi that is, you not taught us (Ps. 129:8: 'And those who pass by do not say, "The blessing of the Lord be upon you"'? From here we learn that it is forbidden to say to those who plow in the Sabbatical year, 'May you have strength.'" {The Hebrew term "those who pass by" is the same as the term "sinners." Said to him Samuel bar Nahman, "You know how to read Scripture, but you do not know how to interpret it! 'And those who pass by do not say'—this refers to the nations of the world, for they pass from the world. 'And the nations do not say' to the people of Israel, 'The blessing of the Lord is upon you.' What therefore should the people of Israel say to them i.e., to the other nations? They should cite Ps. 129:8b: 'We bless you in the name of the Lord.' That verse means: Is it not enough for you that all of the blessings that come into the world are on account of our merit? And yet you other nations do not say to us, 'Come and partake of these blessings.' Rather, the other nations oppress the people of Israel and prevent them from fully enjoying the blessings they bring upon the world. And not only this, but you bring upon us town taxes, penalties, head taxes, and taxes in kind!"

Israelites are not responsible for gentiles' observance, or violation, of the commandments, so M. Shab. 16:8 A-C: A gentile who came to put out a fire — they do not say to him, "Put it out," or "Do not put it out," for they are not responsible for his Sabbath rest. On the other hand, Israelites may not employ gentiles to do what they cannot do for themselves, e.g., M. Shab. 16.8 I A. A gentile who lit a candle — an Israelite may make use of its light. But if he did so for an Israelite, it is prohibited to do so on the Sabbath. So too M. Shab. 16:8D-E: If a gentile drew water to give water to his beast, an Israelite gives water to his beast after him. But if he did so for an Israelite, it is prohibited to use it on the Sabbath.

Christians and "minim" (generally assumed to be Jews who believed in dualism) were not classified as gentiles but as apostates, that is, people who had known the faith and rejected it, so T. Shab. 13:5: The books of the Evangelists and the books of the minim they do not save from a fire. But they are allowed to burn where they are, they and the references to the Divine Name which are in them. R. Yosé, the Galilean says, "On ordinary days, one cuts out the references to the Divine Name which are in them and stores them away, and the rest burns." Said R. Tarfon, "May I bury my sons, if such things come into my hands and I do not burn them, and even the references to the Divine Name which are in them. And if someone was running after me, I should go into a temple of idolatry, but I should not go into their houses of worship. For idolators do not recognize the Divinity in denying him, but these recognize the Divinity and deny him. And about them Scripture states, 'Behind the door and the doorpost you have set up your symbol for deserting me, you have uncovered your bed' (Is. 57:8)."

A single, encompassing theory, expressed in a variety of details, governs the category, gentiles. The category itself is defined principally as not-Israel, and all of the details accommodate to that definition.

V

God

GOD: Unique, the one and only God, creator of the world, who has revealed the Torah to Israel and will at the end of time send the Messiah, raise the dead, judge mankind, and inaugurate the world to come. Recitation of the Shema, proclaiming God's unity, ("Hear O Israel") is taken to represent the affirmation that one accepts the Kingdom of God and the Yoke of the Commandments. Much creedal material is expressed in narrative form, but the narratives yield the definition just now set forth.

The fundamental creed of the Oral Torah always affirms that God is the foundation of all else, and that a violation of the Torah represents repudiation of God's rule. That basic principle is expressed in narrative form at T. Shebuot 3:5: Hanania b. Kinai says, "The Lord said to Moses, 'If any one sins and commits a breach of faith against the Lord by deceiving his neighbor in a matter of deposit or security, or through robbery, or if he has oppressed his neighbor, or has found what was lost and lied about it, swearing falsely' (Lev. 6: 1-3) — A person does not deceive his fellow before he denies the very Principle." He said to him, "What is most hateful in the world?" He said to him, "This is one who denies the One who created [the world]." He said to him, "How is it possible that God then said to Moses, 'Honor your father and your mother . . ., You shall not kill. You shall not commit adultery. You shall not steal. You shall not bear false witness against your neighbor. You shall not covet' (Ex. 20:12-17)?" He said to him, "Lo, a person does not deny a matter of detail before he already has denied the main Principle, and a person does not turn to a matter of transgression unless he already has denied the One who gave a commandment concerning it."

God is one, and Scripture itself proves that the one and unique God created the world, so Y. Ber. 9:1 I:6: The heretics — who believed there were two powers in Heaven, not just one — asked R. Simlai, "How many gods created the world?" He said to them, "Why are you asking me? Go and ask Adam himself [that is, look in the verse]. As it says, 'For ask now of the days that are past, which were before you since the day that God created man upon the earth' (Deut. 4:32). It is not written in the plural form, 'That gods created man upon the earth,' but in the singular form, 'That God created man upon the earth.'" They said to him, "Is it not written, 'In the beginning God 'lhym created' (Gen. 1:1) using what appears to be a plural noun — 'Gods'?" He said to them, "It is not written plural 'gods created,' but singular 'God created.'" Said R. Simlai, "In every instance that the heretics have raised a question out of Scripture the answer to their question is right beside it in Scripture." The heretics returned and asked him, "What is this which is written, 'Let us make man in our image, after our likeness' (Gen. 1:26)?" He said to them, "It does not say, 'The gods created — plural — man in their own images' (Gen. 1:27). But it says, 'So God created singular man in his own image.'" Simlai's students said to him, "You have deflected their question with a straw i.e. a weak argument. What will you answer us? How will you explain this verse to us?" He said to them, "At first Adam was created from dust and Eve was created from Adam's rib. From that time on man propagates, 'In our image, after our likeness.' That means a man must have a woman, a woman must have a man, and both must have the divine presence together with them in order to propagate." The heretics returned and asked him, "What is this which is written, 'The mighty one, God, the Lord! The mighty one, God, the Lord! He knows.' (Joshua 22:22)? This appears to imply that there are three powers in heaven." He said to them, "It does not say, 'They know.' But it says, 'He knows' supporting the unity, and not the trinity, of God." His students said to him, "Master you deflected their question with a straw. How will you answer us?" He said to them, "These are three titles for one individual, just the same as Basilius Caesar Augustus are three titles for the Roman Emperor."

God encompasses two attributes, the attribute of justice and the attribute of mercy, so Gen. R. LXXIII:III.3: "And God remembered Noah," (Gen. 8:1) Since the name of the divinity, God, refers to God in his attribute of justice, just as Lord refers to God in his attribute of mercy, said R. Samuel bar Nahman, "Woe to the wicked, who turn the quality of mercy into the attribute of justice. In every passage in which the divinity is called the Lord, the reference is to God in his attribute of mercy, thus: 'The Lord, the Lord is a merciful and gracious God' (Ex. 34:6). But note that it is written in connection with the destruction of the generation of the Flood, 'And the Lord saw that great was the evil.' (Gen. 6:5), 'And the Lord was sorry that he had made....,' (Gen. 6:6), 'And the Lord said, "I shall blot out man'" (Gen. 6:7). In all of these cases, while the name of the divinity indicates that it is God in his attribute of mercy, nonetheless the substance of what God does expresses his attribute of stern justice. And happy are the righteous, who turn the divinity in the attribute of justice to the attribute of mercy. In every passage in which the divinity is called 'God,' it is the divinity in the attribute of justice: 'You shall not curse God,' (Ex. 22:7), 'To God meaning, the judges will come the case of the two of them' (Ex. 22:8). But it is written, 'And God heard their cry and God remembered his covenant' (Ex. 2:24). 'And God remembered Noah' (Gen. 8:1). 'And God remembered Rachel' (Gen. 30:22)."

Man — male and female — is made in God's image, and it is a mark of divine grace that God in the Torah informed man that he is made in God's image, so M. Abot 3:14: R. Aqiba would say, "Precious is the human being, who was created in the image of God. It was an act of still greater love that it was made known to him that he was created in the image of God, as it is said, For in the image of God he made man (Gen. 9:6)." While Man is made in God's image, after God's likeness, a mark of God's power is that, nonetheless, people are all different from one another, so M. San. 4:5Nff.: "And to portray the grandeur of the Holy One, blessed be He. For a person mints many coins with a single seal, and they are all alike one another. But the King of kings of kings, the Holy One, blessed be He, minted all human beings with that seal of his with which he made the first person, yet not one of them is like anyone else. Therefore everyone is obligated to maintain, "On my account the world was created." The creation of a single Adam served to glorify God, so T. San. 8:5: Why was he created one and alone? To show the grandeur of the king of the kings of kings, blessed be he. For if a man mints many coins with one mold, all are alike. But the Holy One, blessed be he, mints every man with the mold of the first man for with a single seal, he created the entire world, and not one of them is like another from a single seal all those many diverse seals have come forth, as it is said, "It is changed as clay under the seal, and all this things stand forth as in a garment" (Job 38:14) (M. 4:5N) (T. San. 8:5A-D).

Since man is made in God's image, the advent of man confused the angels, who mistook man for God, so Gen. R. VIII:X.1: Said R. Hoshiah,

"When the Holy One, blessed be he, came to create the first man, the ministering angels mistook him for God, since man was in God's image, and wanted to say before him, 'Holy, holy, holy is the Lord of hosts.' To what may the matter be compared? To the case of a king and a governor who were set in a chariot, and the provincials wanted to greet the king, "Sovereign!' But they did not know which one of them was which. What did the king do? He turned the governor out and put him away from the chariot, so that people would know who was king. So too when the Holy One, blessed be he, created the first man, the angels mistook him for God. What did the Holy One, blessed be he, do? He put him to sleep, so everyone knew that he was a mere man. That is in line with the following verse of Scripture: 'Cease you from man, in whose nostrils is a breath, for how little is he to be accounted' (Is. 2:22)." So too Gen. R. VIII:XI.2: R. Joshua b. R. Nehemiah in the name of R. Hinena bar Isaac and rabbis in the name of R. Eleazar: "He created in him four traits applicable to beings of the upper world and four of the lower world. As to traits applicable to creatures of the upper world, he stands up straight like ministering angels, he speaks as do ministering angels, he has the power of understanding as do ministering angels, and he sees as do ministering angels. As to traits applicable to creatures of the lower world, he eats and drinks like a beast, he has sexual relations like a beast, he defecates like a beast, and he dies like a beast."

Since God is one and unique and insists upon that status, idolatry — identification of anything other than God as a god — defines the act of rebellion and estrangement that separates man from God. But Israel gave up idolatry at the Sea, so Mekh. XXXIII:I.1: "Who is like you, O Lord, among gods? Who is like you, majestic in holiness, terrible in glorious deeds, doing wonders?:" When the Israelites saw that Pharaoh and his host had perished at the Red Sea, the dominion of the Egyptians was over, and judgments were executed on their idolatry, they all opened their mouths and said, "Who is like you, O Lord, among gods? Who is like you, majestic in holiness, terrible in glorious deeds, doing wonders?" And not the Israelites alone said the song, but also the nations of the world said the song. When the nations of the world saw that Pharaoh and his host had perished at the Red Sea, the dominion of the Egyptians was over, and judgments were executed on their idolatry, they all renounced their idolatry and opened their mouths and confessed their faith in the Lord and said,

"Who is like you, O Lord, among gods? Who is like you, majestic in holiness, terrible in glorious deeds, doing wonders?" So too you find that the age to come the nations of the world will renounce their idolatry: "O Lord, my strength and my stronghold and my refuge, in the day of affliction to you the nations shall come...shall a man make himself gods" (Jer. 16:19-20); "In that day a man shall cast away his idols of silver...to go into the clefts of the rocks" (Is. 2:20-21);. "And the idols shall utterly perish" (Is. 20:18).

God is jealous and hates idolatry, but that does not prove that idols are gods, so b. A.Z. 4:6 I.3/55a: General Agrippa asked Rabban Gamaliel, "It is written in your Torah, ''For the Lord your God is a devouring fire, a jealous God' (Dt. 4:24). Is there jealousy, except on the part of a sage for another sage, on the part of a great athlete for another great athlete, on the part of a wealthy man for another wealthy man?" He said to him, "I shall give you a parable. To what is the matter to be compared? To a man who married a second wife. If she is more important than she, she will not be jealous of her. If she is less than she, she will be jealous of her."

God bears corporeal traits. God appears to Israel in various ways, not in a single image at all, so PRK XII:XXV.1f.: Another interpretation of I am the Lord your God who brought you out of the land of Egypt (Ex. 20:2): Said R. Hinena bar Papa, "The Holy One, blessed be He, had made his appearance to them with a stern face, with a neutral face, with a friendly face, with a happy face. "...with a stern face: in Scripture. When a man teaches his son Torah, he has to teach him in a spirit of awe. "...with a neutral face: in Mishnah. "...with a friendly face: in Talmud. "...with a happy face: in lore. Said to them the Holy One, blessed be He, 'Even though you may see all of these diverse faces of mine, nonetheless: I am the Lord your God who brought you out of the land of Egypt (Ex. 20:2)." Said R. Levi, "The Holy One, blessed be He, had appeared to them like an icon that has faces in all directions, so that if a thousand people look at it, it appears to look at them as well. So too when the Holy One, blessed be He, when he was speaking, each and every Israelite would say, 'With me in particular the Word speaks.' What is written here is not, I am the Lord, your plural God, but rather, I am the Lord your singular God who brought you out of the land of Egypt (Ex. 20:2)." Said R. Yosé, bar Hanina, "And it was in accord with the capacity of each one of them to listen and understand what the Word spoke with him.

It follows that Israel perceives God in many ways, and he appears to them in every sort of guise, so Mekh. XXIX:I.2: "The Lord is a man of war; the Lord is his name:" Why is this stated? Since when he appeared at the sea, it was in the form of a mighty soldier making war, as it is said, "The Lord is a man of war," and when he appeared to them at Sinai, it was as an elder, full of mercy, as it is said, "And they saw the God of Israel" (Ex. 24:10, and when they were redeemed, what does Scripture say? "And the like of the very heaven for clearness" (Ex. 24:10); "I beheld until thrones were placed and one that was ancient of days sat" (Dan. 7:9); "A fiery stream issued" (Dan. 7:10) — so God took on many forms. It was, therefore, not to provide the nations of the world with an occasion to claim that there are two dominions in heaven that Scripture says, "The Lord is a man of war, the Lord is his name." This then bears the message: The one in Egypt is the one at the sea, the one in the past is the one in the age to come, the one in this age is the one in the world to come: "See now that I, even I, am he" (Dt. 32:39); "Who has wrought and done it? He who called the generations from the beginning. I the Lord who am the first and with the last I am the same" (Is. 41:4).

Envisioning God interested sages, who invoked various metaphors to explain why God cannot be seen but nonetheless runs the world, so b. Hul 3:6-7 I.4/59b: The Caesar said to R. Joshua b. Hananiah, "I want to see your God." He said to him, "You cannot see Him." He said to him, "Really! Show him to me!" He went and pointed him towards the sun during the season of Tammuz i.e., the summer. Joshua said to him, "Look at it." He said, "I cannot." He said, "The sun is one of the attendants that attend the Holy One, blessed be He. You say you cannot look at it. All the more is it impossible to look at the Divine Presence." The Caesar said to R. Joshua b. Hananiah, "I want to make a dinner for your God." He said to him, "You cannot." He asked, "Why not?" He said, "Because he has too many in his entourage." He said, "Really! I insist!" He said, "Go set it up on the widest banks of the great sea." He worked for the six months of the summer preparing the dinner. A storm came up and washed it all into the sea. He worked for the six months of the winter. The rains came and washed it all into the sea. He said to him, "What is the meaning of this?" Joshua said to him, "These storms are like the workers who sweep and wash in preparation for his arrival." He said to him, "If that is the case, then I cannot

Theological Grammar of the Oral Torah. Vol. I 113

do it." The daughter of the Caesar said mockingly to R. Joshua b. Hananiah, "Your God must be a carpenter. For it is written, 'Who hast laid the beams of thy chambers on the waters, who makest the clouds thy chariot, who ridest on the wings of the wind' (Ps. 104:3). Tell him to make a spool for me." He said, "On my life!" He prayed and she was smitten with leprosy. They took her into the market place of Rome and they brought her a spool. For it was the custom that in Rome they brought a spool to anyone who was smitten with leprosy. And they sat her in the market place and she wound skeins of yarn so that people would see this and pray for her. One day he Joshua was passing there and she was sitting and winding skeins of yarn in the market place of Rome. He said to her, "Did my God give you a good spool?" She said to him, "Tell you God to take back what he gave me." He said to her, "Our God gives but does not take back."

At creation God formed a perfect world and took up a place within the world, but when man sinned, God was estranged and removed from the world. But then at Sinai God returned to the world. God's presence was with Adam and Eve, but gradually departed from the world of creation in response to human sin. When Abraham came, God began his return to earth, so Pes. R. V.VII.3: For so you find that from the beginning of the creation of the world, the Presence of God was among the creatures of the lower world, in line with this verse of Scripture: "And they heard the voice of the Lord God walking in the garden (Gen. 3:8). When the first man sinned, the Presence of God rose up to the first firmament. When Cain went and murdered his brother, the Presence of God went up to the second firmament. When the generation of Enosh went and sinned — then the practice of calling on the name of the Lord in vain began (Gen. 4:26) — it went up to the third firmament. When the generation of the Flood went and sinned, in line with this verse, And the Lord saw that the wickedness of man was great (Gen. 6:5), it went up to the fourth firmament. When the generation of the dispersion went and sinned — Come, let us build a city with its top in heaven (Gen. 11:4) — the Presence of God went up to the fifth firmament. When the people of Sodom went and sinned, it went up to the sixth: The men of Sodom were wicked and sinners (Gen. 13:13). When the Philistines came and sinned — and Abimelech, king of Gerar, sent and took Sarah (Gen. 20:2) — it went up to the seventh. Abraham came along and laid up a treasure of good deeds, and the Presence of God came down from the seventh firmament to the sixth. Isaac came along and stretched out his neck on the altar, and the Presence of God went down from the sixth to the fifth. Jacob came along and planted a tent for the Torah-study, in line with this verse, And Jacob was a perfect man, living in tents (Gen. 25:27), and the Presence of God came down from the fifth to the fourth firmament. Levi came along and brought it down from the fourth to the third, Kehath came along and brought it from the third to the second, Amram came along and brought it from the second to the first. Fortunate are the righteous who create on earth a dwelling place for the Presence of God. For so it is written: Truly the upright will make a dwelling place on the earth (Prov. 2:21). Moses came along and brought the Presence down, in line with this verse: The cloud covered the tent, and the glory of the Lord filled the tabernacle (Ex. 40:34)."

Another statement of the same view, that God originally took up residence with Man, but departed as successive sins drove him off; then God returned to earth through successive men of virtue, is at PRK I:I.3ff.:R. Tanhum, son-in-law of R. Eleazar b. Abina, in the name of R. Simeon b. Yosni: "What is written is not, 'I have come into the garden,' but rather, I have come back to my garden. That is, 'to my canopy.' That is to say, to the place in which the principal presence of God had been located to begin with. The principal locale of God's presence had been among the lower creatures, in line with this verse. And they heard the sound of the Lord God walking about (Gen. 3:8)." And they heard the sound of the Lord God walking about (Gen. 3:8): Said R. Abba bar Kahana, "What is written is not merely 'going,' but 'walking about,' that is, 'walking away from.'" The principal locale of God's presence had been among the lower creatures, but when the first man sinned, it went up to the first firmament. The generation of Enosh came along and sinned, and it went up from the first to the second. The generation of the flood came along and sinned, and it went up from the second to the third. The generation of the dispersion came along and sinned, and it went up from the third to the fourth. The Egyptians in the time of Abraham our father came along and sinned, and it went up from the fourth to the fifth. The Sodomites came along, and sinned, ...from the fifth to the sixth. The Egyptians in the time of Moses...from the sixth to the seventh. And, corresponding to them, seven righteous men came along and brought it back down to earth: Abraham our father came along and acquired merit, and brought it down from the seventh to the sixth. Isaac came along and acquired merit and brought it down from the sixth to the fifth. Jacob came along and acquired merit and brought it down from the fifth to the fourth. Levi came along and acquired merit and brought it down from the fourth to the third. Kahath came along and acquired merit and brought it down from the third to the second. Amram came along and acquired merit and brought it down from the second to the first. Moses came along and acquired merit and brought it down to earth. Therefore it is said, On the day that Moses completed the setting up of the Tabernacle, he anointed and consecrated it (Num. 7:1).

According to another formulation of matters, God's Presence descended to the world on ten occasions, and ascended in ten stages, so ARN XXXIV:VIII-IX.1: There were ten descents that the Presence of God made into the world. One into the Garden of Eden, as it says, And they heard the sound of God walking in the garden (Gen. 3:5). One in the generation of the tower of Babylon, as it is said, And the Lord came down to see the city and the tower (Gen. 11:5). One in Sodom: I shall now go down and see whether it is in accord with the cry that has come to me (Gen. 18:21). One in Egypt: I shall go down and save them from the hand of the Egyptians (Ex. 3:8). One at the sea: He bowed the heavens also and came down (2 Sam. 22:10). One at Sinai: And the Lord came down onto Mount Sinai (Ex. 19:20). One in the pillar of cloud: And the Lord came down in a pillar (Num. 11:25). One in the Temple: This gate will be closed and will not be open for the Lord, God of Israel, has come in through it (Ez. 44:2). And one is destined to take place in the time of Gog and Magog: And his feet shall stand that day on the mount of Olives (Zech. 14:4). In ten upward stages the Presence of God departed, from one place to the next: from the ark cover to the cherub, from the cherub to the threshold of the temple-building; from the threshold of the temple to the two cherubim; from the two cherubim to the roof of the sanctuary; from the roof of the sanctuary to the wall of the temple court; from the wall of the temple court to the altar; from the altar to the city; from the city to the Temple mount; from the temple mount to the wilderness. from the ark cover to the cherub: And he rode upon a cherub and flew (2 Sam. 22:11). from the cherub to the threshold of the temple-building: And the glory of the Lord mounted up from the cherub to the threshold of the house (Ez. 10:45). from the threshold of the temple to the two cherubim: And the glory of the Lord went forth from off the threshold of the house and stood over the cherubim (Ez. 10:18). from the two cherubim to the roof of the sanctuary: It is better to dwell in a corner of the housetop (Prov. 21:9). from the roof of the sanctuary to the wall of the temple court: And behold the Lord stood beside a wall made by a plumb line (Amos 7:7). from the wall of the temple court to the altar: I saw the Lord standing beside the altar (Amos 9:1). from the altar to the city: Hark, the Lord cries to the city (Mic. 6:9). from the city to the Temple mount: And the glory of the Lord went up from the midst of the city and stood upon the mountain (Ez. 11:23). from the temple mount to the wilderness: It is better to dwell in a desert land (Prov. 21:19). And then to on high: I will go and return to my place (Hos. 5:15).

God is present everywhere, through the Divine Presence (*Shekhinah*). The Presence of God is ubiquitous, so b. B.B. 2:9-10 I.3/25a: the Presence of God is in every place, for said R. Oshaia, "What is the meaning of the verse of Scripture, 'You are the Lord, even you alone, you made heaven, the highest heaven' (Neh. 9:6)? Your messengers are not like mortal messengers. Mortal messengers come back and report to the place from which they are sent forth, but your messengers report to the place to which they are sent: 'Can you send forth your lightnings that they may go and say to you, here we are (Job 38:35). What is said is not, 'that they may come and say,' but, 'that they may go and say,' and that shows that the Presence of God is in every place." And so, too, R. Ishmael takes the view that the Presence of God is in every place, for it has been taught by a Tannaite authority of the household of R. Ishmael: "How on the basis of Scripture do we know that the Presence of God is everywhere? 'And behold the angel that talked with me went forth and another angel went out to meet him' (Zech. 2:7). What is said is not, 'went out after him,' but, 'went out to meet him,' and that shows that the Presence of God is in every place." And so, too, R. Sheshet takes the view that the Presence of God is in every place, for said R. Sheshet to his attendant, "Set me up in any direction except east."

God certainly goes with Israel wherever Israel is located, in accord with the view of R. Simeon b. Yohai: "To every place to which the Israelites went into exile, the presence of God went with them into exile. They were sent into exile to Egypt, and the presence of God went into exile with them. What is the scriptural basis for this claim? 'And there came a man of God to Eli, and said to him, Thus the Lord has said, I revealed myself to the house of your father when they were in Egypt subject to the house of Pharaoh' (I Sam. 2:27). They were sent into exile to Babylonia, and the presence of God went into exile with them. What is the scriptural basis for this claim? 'Thus says the Lord, your Redeemer, the Holy One of Israel: For your sake I will send to Babylon and break down all the bars, and the shouting of the Chaldeans will be turned to lamentations' (Is. 43:14). They were sent into exile into Media, and the presence of God went into exile with them. What is the scriptural basis for this claim? 'And I will set my throne in Elam and destroy their king and princes, says the Lord' (Jer. 49:38). And Elam means only Media, as it is said, 'And I saw in the vision; and when I saw, I was in Susa the capital, which is in the province of Elam; and I saw in the vision, and I was at the river Ulai' (Dan. 8:2). They went into exile to Greece, and the presence of God went into exile with them. What is the scriptural basis for this claim? 'For I have bent Judah as my bow; I have made Ephraim its arrow. I will brandish your sons, O Zion, over your sons, O Greece, and wield you like a warrior's sword' (Zech. 9:13). They went into exile to Rome, and the presence of God went into exile with them. What is the scriptural basis for this claim? 'The oracle concerning Dumah. One is calling to me from Seir, "Watchman, what of the night? Watchman, what of the night?" Is. 21:11).'" (Y. Ta. 1:1 II.5).

Nonetheless, it is the Torah and those that study it that bring God's presence into the world and to the heart of Israel in particular. Specifically, the disciples of sages produce sages, sages produce elders, elders, prophets, and the prophets bring God's presence to rest within Israel, so Est. R. VIII:ii.2: "And it came to pass in the days of Ahaz" (Is. 7:1): "The Aramaeans on the east and the Philistines on the west devour Israel with open mouth" (Is. 9:12): The matter of Israel's position may be compared to the case of a king who handed over his son to a tutor, who hated the son. The tutor thought, "If I kill him now, I shall turn out to be liable to the death penalty before the king. So what I'll do is take away his wet-nurse, and he will die on his own." So thought Ahaz, "If there are no kids, there will be no he-goats. If there are no he-goats, there will be no flock. If there is no flock, there will be no Shepherd, if there is no Shepherd, there will be no world." So did Ahaz plan, "If there are no children, there will be no adults. If there are no adults, there will be no disciples. If there are no disciples, there will be no sages. If there are no sages, there will be no elders. If there are no elders, there will be no prophets. If there are no prophets, the Holy One, blessed be he, will not allow his presence to come to rest in the world." Leviticus Rabbah frames matters with Torah: If there is no Torah, there will be no synagogues and schools. If there are no synagogues and schools, then the Holy One, blessed be he, will not allow his presence to come to rest in the world. That is in line with the following verse of Scripture: "Bind up the testimony, seal the Torah among my disciples" (Is. 8:16). R. Huna in the name of R. Eleazar: "Why was he called Ahaz? Because he seized (ahaz) synagogues and schools."

Along these same lines, while God is everywhere, he may best be found in synagogues and study halls, so Y. Ber. 5:1 I:8: R. Jeremiah in the name of R. Abbahu, "'Seek the Lord while he may be found' (Isa. 55:6). Where may he be found? In the synagogues and study halls. 'Call upon him while he is near' . Where is he near? In the synagogues and study halls." Said R. Isaac b. R. Eleazar, "Moreover, it is as if God stands next to those who are in synagogues and study halls. What is the basis in Scripture for this view? 'God has taken his place in the divine congregation; in the midst of the gods he holds judgment' (Ps. 82:1)." Because God's presence is located in the schools and synagogues, those who have tried to destroy Israel therefore seek to close the schools and synagogues, so that God's presence will no longer rest within Israel, so Y. San. 10:2 II.4: R. Honiah in the name of R. Eleazar: "Why is he called 'Ahaz' seize?" Because he seized the synagogues and schools." To what is Ahaz to be compared? To a king who had a son, who handed him over to a governor. He wanted to kill him. He said, "If I kill him, I shall be declared liable to death. But lo, I'll take his wet-nurse from him, and he'll die on his own." So did Ahaz say, "If there are no lambs, there will be no sheep; if there are no sheep, there will be no flock; if there is no flock, there will be no shepherd; if there is no shepherd, there will be no world, if there is no world — as it were...." So did Ahaz reckon, saying, "If there are no children, there will be no adults; if there are no adults, there will be no sages; if there are no sages, there will be no prophets; if there are no prophets, there will be no Holy Spirit; if there is no Holy Spirit, there will be no synagogues or schoolhouses — as it were. In that case, as it were, the Holy One, blessed be he, will not let his Presence rest upon Israel."

God himself wrote and gave the Torah, and God is Israel's glory and beauty when Israel accepts the Torah, so PRK XII:XXIV.1:I [anokhi] am the Lord your God who brought you out of the land of Egypt (Ex. 20:2): What is the meaning of the word anokhi/I? Rab said, "God speaks: 'You should not treat the Torah which I have given to you. The word anokhi generates a set of words through its letters, a, n, k, and y, yielding the sense, 'I (a) myself (n) have written (k) and given (y) it.'" Another interpretation: the same letters are to be read in reverse order, that is, y, k, n, a, yielding the sense, "The Torah that is given in writing Ð pleasant are its words." Said R. Berekhiah the Priest, "The letters a n k y mean that said the Holy One, blessed be He, 'I am your light, your glory, your beauty.' When will this be so? When you accept the Ten Commandments. 'I anokhi am the Lord your God who brought you out of the land of Egypt' (Ex. 20:2)."

God makes Himself known through the Torah revealed by God to Moses at Mount Sinai in two media, writing and memory. Whatever Man knows about God, he knows through the Torah, written and oral. God is approached not only through prayer but through study of the Torah, at which point God is present and party to learning. When as few as two persons meet for Torah — study, the Presence of God is between them, so M. Abot 3:2: R. Hananiah b. Teradion says, "If two sit together and between them do not pass teachings of Torah, lo, this is a seat of the scornful, as it is said, Nor sits in the seat of the scornful (Ps. 1:2). But two who are sitting, and words of Torah do pass between them — the Presence is with them, as it is said, Then they that feared the Lord spoke with one another, and the Lord hearkened and heard, and a book of remembrance was written before him, for them that feared the Lord and gave thought to His name (Mal. 3:16)." I know that this applies to two. How do I know that even if a single person sits and works on Torah, the Holy One, blessed be he, sets aside a reward for him? As it is said, Let him sit alone and keep silent, because he hay laid it upon him (Lam. 3:28)." So too M. Abot 3:6, R. Halafta of Kefar Hananiah says, "Among ten who sit and work hard on Torah the Presence comes to rest, as it is said, God stands in the congregation of God (Ps. 82:1). And how do we know that the same is so even of five? For it is said, And he has founded his group upon the earth (Am. 9:6).

And how do we know that this is so even of three? Since it is said, And he judges among the judges (Ps. 82:1). And how do we know that this is so even of two? Because it is said, Then they that feared the Lord spoke with one another, and the Lord hearkened and heard (Mal. 3:16). And how do we know that this is so even of one? Since it is said, In every place where I record my name I will come to you and I will bless you (Ex. 20:24)." Speculation on other-than-this-worldly manifestations of God is strongly discouraged, so M. Hag. 2:2: Whoever reflects upon four things would have been better off had he not been born: what is above, what is below, what is before, and what is beyond. And whoever has no concern for the glory of his Maker would have been better off had he not been born.

But beyond the words of the Torah themselves, this world provides ample evidence concerning God and substantial knowledge of God, His will and His plan for the world that He created for Man. God is present everywhere and at all times; He, directly or through his messengers, plays an active role and intervenes in response to His wishes and plan or in response to the prayers and merits of Israel or both. God's intervention into Israelite history takes place not only in the past, but also in the present tense, and God takes up a Presence equally in all ages, so M. Pes. 10:5: "In every generation a person is duty-bound to regard himself as if he personally has gone forth from Egypt, since it is said, And you shall tell your son in that day saying, it is because of that which the Lord did for me when I came forth out of Egypt' (Ex. 13:8). Therefore we are duty-bound to thank, praise, glorify, honor, exalt, extol, and bless him who did for our forefathers and for us all these miracles. He brought us forth from slavery to freedom, anguish to joy, mourning to festival, darkness to great light, subjugation to redemption, so we should say before him, Hallelujah "

God responds to what Man says and does, to his inner feelings, attitudes, emotions, and intentionality. God feels the anguish of Man, even the most wicked of men, so M. San. 6:5: Said R. Meir, "When a person is distressed, what words does the Presence of God say? As it were: 'My head is in pain, my arm is in pain.' If thus is the Omnipresent distressed on account of the blood of the wicked when it is shed, how much the more so on account of the blood of the righteous!" In times of trouble, people must respond by beseeching God's forgiveness for their sins, e.g., M. Taanit 1:7: If these rites too have passed and they have not been answered, they cut down on commerce, building, planting, the making of betrothals and marriages, and on greeting one another, like people subject to divine displeasure. Individuals go back and fast until the end of Nisan. Once Nisan has ended, if it then rains, it is a sign of a curse, since it says, Is it not wheat harvest today? I win call unto the Lord, that he send thunder and rain, and you shall know and see that great is your wickedness which you have done in the sight of God to ask a king for yourself (I Sam. 12:17).

One should make his own will conform to God's will, so Rabban Gamaliel, son of R. Judah the Patriarch, M. Abot 2:4: Make his wishes into your own wishes, so that he will make your wishes into his wishes. Put aside your wishes on account of his wishes, so that he will put aside the wishes of other people in favor of your wishes. "God is pleased when Israelites carry out His will and perform the commandments. He is not concerned with quantity, a single commandment suffices to win God's approval, so M. Qid. 1:10: Whoever does a single commandment-they do well for him and lengthen his days. And he inherits the Land. And whoever does not do a single commandment — they do not do well for him and do not lengthen his days. And he does not inherit the Land. Carrying out the commandments expresses in action an attitude of acceptance of God's will. The proper attitude for serving God requires a person not to anticipate a reward for his service, so M. Abot 1:2: Antigonos of Sokho received the Torah from Simeon the Righteous. He would say, (1) "Do not be like servants who serve the master on condition of receiving a reward, (2) but be like servants who serve the master not on condition of receiving a reward. (3) And let the fear of Heaven be upon you."

God loves Israel, and God's judgment and wrath are matched by his mercy and forgiveness, so b. A.Z. 1:1 I;13-14: R. Abbahu praised R. Safra to the minim in context: Christian authorities of Caesarea, saying that he was a highly accomplished authority. They therefore remitted his taxes for thirteen years. One day they came upon him and said to him, "It is written, 'You only have I known among all the families of the earth; therefore I will visit upon you all your iniquities' (Amos 3:2). If one is angry, does he vent it on someone he loves?" He fell silent and said nothing at all. He said to them, "I shall tell you a parable. To what is the matter comparable? To the case of a man who lent money to two people, one a friend, the other an enemy. From the friend he collects the money little by little, from the enemy he collects all at once." Said R. Abba bar Kahana, "What is the meaning of the following verse of Scripture. 'Far be it from you to do after this manner, to slay the righteous with the wicked' (Gen. 18:25). Said Abraham before the Holy One, blessed be He, 'Lord of the world! It is a profanation to act in such a way a play on the Hebrew letters, shared by the words 'far be it' and 'profanation', 'to slay the righteous with the wicked' (Gen. 18:25)." But is it not so that God might do just that? And is it not written, "And I will cut off from you the righteous and the wicked" (Ezek. 21:8)? That speaks of one who is not completely righteous, but not of one who is completely righteous. And will he not do so to one who is completely righteous? And is it not written, "And begin the slaughter with my sanctuary" (Ezek. 9:6), in which connection R. Joseph repeated as a Tannaite version, "Read not 'with my sanctuary' but rather, 'with those who are holy to me,' namely, the ones who carried out the Torah beginning to end." There, too, since they had the power to protest against the wickedness of the others and did not do so, they were not regarded as completely righteous at all.

David's life illustrates God's power to forgive, and shows that God will forgive Israel as well, so b. A.Z. 1:1 I.26/4b: R. Yohanan said in the name of R. Simeon b. Yohai: "David was really not so unfit as to do such a deed as he did with Bath Sheva: 'My heart is slain within me' (Ps. 109:22) David's inclinations had been completely conquered by himself. And the Israelites were hardly the kind of people to commit such an act: ''O that they had such a heart as this always, to fear me and keep my commandments' (Dt. 5:26). So why did they do it? It was to show you that if an individual has sinned, they say to him, 'Go to the individual such as David, and follow his example, and if the community as a whole has sinned, they say to them, 'Go to the community such as Israel.' That is in line with what R. Samuel bar Nahmani said R. Jonathan said, "What is the meaning of the verse of Scripture, 'The saying of David, son of Jesse, and the saying of the man raised on high' (2 Sam. 23:1)? It means, 'The saying of David, son of Jesse, the man who raised up the yoke of repentance.'" The same passage is generalized to the conduct of Israel overall: Said R. Samuel bar Nahmani said R. Jonathan, "Whoever does a religious duty in this world — that deed goes before him to the world to come, as it is said, 'And your righteousness shall go before you' (Isa. 58:8). And whoever commits a transgression in this world — that act turns aside from him and goes before him on the Day of Judgment, as it is said, 'The paths of their way are turned aside, they go up into the waste and perish' (Job 6:18)." R. Eliezer says, "It attaches to him like a dog, as it is said, 'He did not listen to her to lie by her or to be with her' (Gen. 39:10). 'To lie by her' in this world. 'Or to be with her' in the world to come."

God is infinitely patient and long-suffering, though in the end he does exact justice, so M. Abot 5:2: There are ten generations from Adam to Noah, to show you how long suffering is God. For all those generations went along spiting him until he brought the water of the flood upon them. There are ten generations from Noah to Abraham, to show you how long-suffering is God. For all those generations went along spiting him, until Abraham came along and took the reward which had been meant for all of them. The reason that God tolerates the continued existence of paganism is circumstantial: he cannot destroy idols without disrupting the course of nature, so M. A.Z. 4:7: They asked sages in Rome, "If God is not in favor of idolatry why does he not wipe it away?" They said to them, "If people worshipped something of which the world had no need, he certainly would wipe it away. But lo, people worship the sun, moon, stars, and planets. Now do you think he is going to wipe out his world because of idiots?" They said to them, "If so, let him destroy something of which the world has no need, and leave something which the world needs!" They said to them, "Then we should strengthen the hands of those who worship these which would not be destroyed, for then they would say, 'Now you know full well that they are gods, for lo, they were not wiped out!'"

God's will is done, whether or not man comprehends, and it is the task of man to accept God's will without complaint, so b. Men. 3:7 II.5/ 29b: Said R. Judah said Rab, "At the time that Moses went up on high, he found the Holy One in session, affixing crowns to the letters of the words of the Torah. He said to him, 'Lord of the universe, who is stopping you from regarding the document as perfect without these additional crowns on the letters?' He said to him, 'There is a man who is going to arrive at the end of many generations, and Aqiba b. Joseph is his name, who is going to interpret on the basis of each point of the crowns heaps and heaps of laws.' He said to him, 'Lord of the Universe, show him to me.' He said to him, 'Turn around.' He went and took a seat at the end of eight rows, but he could not grasp what the people were saying. He felt faint. But when the discourse reached a certain matter, and the disciples said, 'My lord, how do you know this?' and he answered, 'It is a law given to Moses from Sinai,' he regained his composure. He went and came before the Holy One. He said before him, 'Lord of the Universe, How come you have someone like that and yet you give the Torah through me?' He said to him, 'Silence! That is how the thought came to me.' He said to him, 'Lord of the Universe, you have shown me his Torah, now show me his reward.' He said to him, 'Turn around.' He turned around and saw his flesh being weighed out at the butcher-stalls in the market. He said to him, 'Lord of the Universe, 'Such is Torah, such is the reward? He said to him, 'Silence! That is how the thought came to me.'"

Faith in God is the key to all else. By his faith in God, Joseph saved himself from the wife of Potiphar, so Gen. R. LXXXVII:X.1: "But the Lord was with Joseph and showed him steadfast love and gave him favor in the sight of the keeper of the prison. And the keeper of the prison committed to Joseph's care all the prisoners who were in the prison; and whatever was done there, he was the doer of it; the keeper of the prison paid no heed to anything that was in Joseph's care, because the Lord was with him; and whatever he did, the Lord made it prosper" (Gen. 39:21-23): R. Huna in the name of R. Hana: "His service pleased his master. When he would go out, Joseph would wash the dishes, lay out the tables, and make the beds. But in trying to entice him, Potiphar's wife said to him, 'In this matter I made your life miserable. By your life! I shall make your life miserable in other ways.' He would say to her, '"The Lord executes justice for the persecuted. He gives bread to the hungry, the Lord looses those who are bound, the Lord raises up those who are bowed down, the Lord opens the eyes of the blind" (Ps. 146:7).' We shall now see how, by his faith in God's justice and mercy as described in the verse of Psalms, Joseph found an answer to each of her threats. She said to him, 'I shall have your rations cut in half.' He said to her, '"He gives bread to the hungry."' She said to him, 'I shall have you put into chains.' He said to her, '"...the Lord looses those who are bound."' She said to him, 'I shall have you bowed down.' He said to her, '"...the Lord raises up those who are bowed down."' She said to him, 'I shall have you blinded.' He said to her, '"...the Lord opens the eyes of the blind."'" To what extent did she go? R. Huna in the name of R. Aha: "To such an extent that she put an iron fork under his neck, so that he would have to cast his eyes on her. Even so, he would not look at her. That is in line with this verse: 'His feet they hurt with fetters, his person was laid in iron' (Ps. 105:18)."

The various principles set forth in the successive paragraphs cohere and at no point contain disharmonies or inconsistencies. The basic conception of God set forth in the written Torah is reiterated, and the points at which that conception is amplified in the Oral Torah are carefully linked to data deriving from the written Torah.

VI

Intentionality

INTENTIONALITY, ATTITUDE: the attitude that motivates a given action, the intention of the person who performs the action: what he hopes to accomplish — effect or prevent. That intentionality, or expression of an attitude, governs the action's classification, e.g., as to effect or lack of effect, as to acceptability or lack of acceptability, e.g., in recitation of prayer. While a single word, *kavvanah*, corresponds, the category, intentionality, is shown by context to pertain even where that particular word does not appear.

Intentionality classifies actions, so that with one intention an action is cursed, but with the opposite, it is blessed, so T. Bik. 2:15: He who sells a Torah scroll never sees a sign of blessing. Scribes who copy Torah scrolls, tefillin-parchments, and mezuzah-parchments — they and their dealers who buy these items from scribes, and their dealers' dealers who buy them from other merchants, and all those who deal in sacred objects for the sake of making a profit will never see a sign of blessing. But if they were dealing with these objects for the sake of Heaven, lo, they shall be blessed. Dealing in holy objects for the sake of a profit is not acceptable, for the sake of Heaven is.

One's intention affects the assessment of one's deed, whether it is for good or for ill. Miriam criticized Moses and was punished, but her intention was honorable; had it been dishonorable, the punishment would have been greater, so Sif. Num. XCIX:II.2: Now it is an argument *a fortiori*: if Miriam, who intended to speak against her brother not to his detriment but to his credit, and not to lessen procreation but to increase it, and who spoke only in private, yet she was punished, if someone intends to speak ill of his fellow and not in praise, to diminish and not to increase procreation, and speaks not in private but among others — how much the more so will such a one be punished! Now it is an argument *a fortiori*: if Uzziah the king, who had no intention of arrogating greatness to himself for his own honor but for the honor of his creator, was punished as he was, one who arrogates greatness to himself for his own honor and not for the honor of his creator — how much the more so will such a one be punished!

Concrete actions take on consequence only by reference to the intention with which they are carried out. For example, what matters in the offerings is intentionality; the size of the offering makes no difference, only the intent of the person who presents it, so b. Men. 13:11 I.2/110a: It is said of the burnt offering of a beast, 'An offering by fire, a smell of sweet savor' (Lev. 1:9) and of the bird offering, 'An offering by fire, a smell of sweet savor' (Lev. 1:17) and even of the meal offering, 'An offering by fire, a smell of sweet savor' (Lev. 2:9) — to teach that all the same are the one who offers much and the one who offers little, on condition that a man will direct his intention to Heaven. Now might you say, 'Then it is because God needs the food,' Scripture states, 'If I were hungry, I would not tell you, for the world is mine and the fullness thereof' (Ps. 50:12); 'For every beast of the forest is mine and the cattle upon a thousand hills; I know all the fowl of the mountains and wild beasts of the field are mine; do I eat the meat of bulls or drink the blood of goats' (Ps. 50:10, 11, 13). I did not order you to make sacrifices so you might say, 'I will do what he wants so he will do what I want.' You do not make sacrifices for my sake but for your sake: 'you shall sacrifice at your own volition' (Lev. 19:5)."

Intentionality forms a critical theological category, since it is the actor's intention to which God responds in his evaluation of an action, its consequence, and his — God's — response. The correct attitude in serving God is on account of reverence or fear, not as an entirely votive action, out of love, e.g., M. Sot. 5:5: On that day did R. Joshua b. Hurqanos expound as follows: "Job served the Holy One, blessed be He, only out of love, since it is said, Though he slay me, yet will I wait for him (Job 13:15). But still the matter is in doubt as to whether it means, 'I will wait for him,' or 'I will not wait for him.' Scripture states, Until I die I will not put away mine integrity from me (Job. 27:5). This teaches that he did what he did out of love." Said R. Joshua, "Who will remove the dirt from your eyes, Rabban Yohanan b. Zakkai? For you used to expound for your entire life that Job served the Omnipresent only out of awe, since it is said, The man was perfect and upright and one who feared God and avoided evil (Job. 1:8). And now has not Joshua, the disciple of your disciple, taught that he did what he did out of love."

One is permitted to fear God alone, and that is the sole correct source of intentionality, as the following story indicates (Y. B.M. 2:4 I.2): Samuel bar Suseretai went to Rome. The queen had lost her jewelry. He found it. A proclamation went forth through the city: "Whoever returns her jewelry in thirty days will receive thus and so. If he returns it after thirty days, his head will be cut off." He did not return the jewelry within thirty days. After thirty days, he returned it to her. She said to him, "Weren't you in town?" He said to her, "Yes I was here." She said to him, "And didn't you hear the proclamation?" He said to her, "Yes I heard it." She said to him, "And what did it say?" He said to her. that it said, 'Whoever returns her jewelry in thirty days will receive thus-and-so. If he returns it after thirty days. his head will be cut off.'" She said to him, "And why didn't you return it within thirty days?" "So that people should not say, 'It was because I was afraid of you that I did so.' But it was because I fear the All-Merciful." She said to him. "Blessed be the God of the Jews."

The correct intentionality involves submission to God's will, and that is what governs under all conditions, so M. Rosh Hashanah 3:8: Now it happened that when Moses held up his hand, Israel prevailed, and when he let his hand fall, Amalek prevailed (Ex. 17:11). Now do Moses' hands make war or stop it? But the purpose is to say this to you: So long as the Israelites would set their eyes upward and submit their hearts to their Father in heaven, they would grow stronger. And if not, they fell. God plays a role by responding to Man's intentionality, thus: As regards a good intention — the Omnipresent, blessed be He, refines it so that it produces a corresponding deed. As for an evil intention — the Omnipresent does not refine it, so that it does not produce a corresponding deed (T. Peah 1:4).

Intentionality is critical in doing one's religious duties; one must not utilize the Torah and the commandments for an inappropriate purpose, so B. Ned. 8:3-4 II.8-9/62a: "That you may love the Lord your God and that you may obey his voice and that you may cleave to him" (Deut. 30:20): This means that someone shouldn't say, "I shall study Scripture, so as to be called a sage, I shall repeat Mishnah teachings, so as to be called 'my lord.' I shall reason critically, so that I may be an elder and take a seat at the session. Rather: Learn out of love, and honor will come on its own: "Bind them on your fingers, write them on the table of your heart" (Prov. 7:3); "Her ways are ways of pleasantness" (Prov. 3:17); "She is a tree of life to those that hold onto her, and happy is everyone who keeps her"

(Prov. 3:18). R. Eliezer b. R. Sadoq says, "Do things for the sake of the One who has made them and speak of them for their own sake, and don't turn them into a crown for self-glorification or make them into a spade with which to dig. It derives from an argument a fortiori in the case of Belshazzar, namely, if Belshazzar — who used the holy utensils that were removed from their status of sanctification, in line with the statement, 'for the robbers shall enter into it and profane it' (Ezek. 7:22), since they had broken in, the utensils were profaned — was removed from the world — 'in that night was Belshazzar slain' (Dan. 5:30) — one who makes selfish use of the crown of the Torah, which lives and endures forever, all the more so will be uprooted from this world!"

The correct intentionality is to carry out the requirements of the Torah for their own sake, not for the sake of a reward, so Sif. Dt. CCCVI:XXII.1: "May my discourse come down as the rain, my speech distill as the dew, like showers on young growths, like droplets on the grass. For the name of the Lord I proclaim": R. Benaiah would say, "If you carry out the teachings of the Torah for their own sake, the teachings of the Torah will live for you. For it is said, 'For they are life to those that find them' (Prov. 4:22). But if you do not carry out teachings of the Torah for their own sake, they will kill you. For it is said, ''My doctrine shall drop as the rain.' And the word for 'drop' yields the sense of 'killing,' in line with its usage in the following verse: 'And he shall break the heifer's neck there in the valley' (Dt. 21:4). 'For she has cast down many wounded, yes, a mighty host are all those she has slain' (Prov. 7:26)."

The right attitude furthermore involves sincerity, a total commitment to the action for its own sake, so B. Hor. 3:3 I.11/10b: Said R. Nahman bar Isaac, "A transgression committed for its own sake, in a sincere spirit, is greater in value than a religious duty carried out not for its own sake, but in a spirit of insincerity. But did not R. Judah say Rab said, "A person should always be occupied in study of the Torah and in practice of the commandments, even if this is not for its own sake but in a spirit of insincerity, for out of doing these things not for their own sake, a proper spirit of doing them for their own sake will emerge"? *Say*: it is equivalent to doing them not for their own sake.

Faith is the key. Acting in good faith, in complete sincerity, makes a person worthy of encountering the Holy Spirit, so Mekh. XXV:I.26: R.

Nehemiah says, "How do you know that whoever takes upon himself the obligation to carry out a single religious duty in faith is worth that the Holy Spirit should rest upon him? For so we find in the case of our ancestors that as a reward for the act of faith that they made, they achieved merit, so that the Holy Spirit rested on them, as it is said, 'and they believed in the Lord and in his servant Moses. Then Moses and the people of Israel sang this song to the Lord, saying, 'I will sing to the Lord, for he has triumphed gloriously; the horse and his rider he has thrown into the sea.' " So you find that Abraham our father inherited this world and the world to come only as a reward for the faith that he believed, as it is said, "And he believed in the Lord" (Gen. 15:6). So you find that the Israelites were redeemed from Egypt only as a reward for the faith that they believed, as it is said, "And the people believed" (Ex. 4:31). "The Lord preserves the faithful" (Ps. 31:25). He calls to mind the faith of the fathers.

What governs the relationship between intentionality and action? The intention to carry out one's obligation must accompany the act that effects that obligation; otherwise, the act bears no effect, so M. Ber. 2:1A-C: One who was reading the verses of the *Shema* in the Torah and the time for the recitation of the *Shema* arrived: If he directed his heart towards fulfilling the obligation to recite the *Shema*, he fulfilled his obligation to recite. And if he did not direct his heart, he did not fulfill his obligation. Whether or not the recitation of the Prayer of supplication requires intentionality is subject to discussion, e.g., M. Ber. 4:4 A. R. Eliezer says, "One who makes his prayers a fixed task — his prayers are not valid supplications of God." Intentionality may take precedence over actual activity, as at M. Ber. 4:5 A-C: If he was riding on an ass, he should dismount to recite the Prayer. But if he cannot dismount, he should turn his face toward the east. And if he cannot turn his face, he should direct his heart toward the Chamber of the Holy of Holies. When one prays, he is to direct his heart to God, e.g., M. Ber. 5:1 A-E: One may stand to pray only in a solemn frame of mind. The early pious ones used to tarry one hour before they would pray, so that they could direct their hearts to the Omnipresent. While one is praying even if the king greets him, he may not respond. And even if a serpent is entwined around his heel, he may not interrupt his prayer. Intentionality governs the effect of all rites, so M. Rosh Hashanah 3:7D-J: He who was going along behind a synagogue, or whose house was near a synagogue, and who heard the sound of the shofar or the sound of the reading of the Scroll of Esther, if he paid attention thereby intending to carry out his obligation, he has fulfilled his obligation. But if not, he has not fulfilled his obligation. That is the rule even if this one heard and that one heard, for this one paid attention, and that one did not pay attention to what he heard.

The intentional violation of the law always invalidates the consequent action. What is done in violation of the law but not by intention, by contrast, may well be accepted, since it was not an act of rebellion against the Torah, e.g., M. Ter. 2:3: One who immerses unclean utensils on the Sabbath — if he does so unintentionally, he may use them; but if he does so intentionally, he may not use them. One who tithes his produce, or who cooks on the Sabbath — if he does so unintentionally, he may eat the food he has prepared; but if he does so intentionally, he may not eat the food. One who plants a tree on the Sabbath — if he does so unintentionally, he may leave it to grow; but if he does so intentionally, he must uproot it. But in the Seventh Year of the Sabbatical cycle, whether he has planted the tree unintentionally or intentionally, he must uproot it. Along these same lines, intentionality forms the principal criterion for effecting atonement through repentance. If one manifests the inappropriate intentionality, then the rite is null, thus M. Yoma 8:9 A. He who says, "I shall sin and repent, sin and repent" — they give him no chance to do repentance. "I will sin and the Day of Atonement will atone," — the Day of Atonement does not atone. So too the law distinguishes inadvertence from deliberation in action, with appropriately diverse penalties, T. Shab. 2:17-18: He who slaughters an animal on the Sabbath — if he did so inadvertently — it may be eaten at the end of the Sabbath. If he did so deliberately, it may not be eaten. Produce which one gathered on the Sabbath — if he did so inadvertently, it may be eaten at the end of the Sabbath. If he did so deliberately, it may not be eaten.

It follows that intentionality overrides action. Thus, for example, a mere accident of speech is not binding; one must say exactly what he intended to say for the act of speech to be binding, whether in regard to oaths or offerings. Thus M. Ter. 3:8: (1) One who in designating agricultural gifts intends to say, "heave offering," but says, "tithe," "tithe," but says "heave offering," (2) or who, in designating a sacrifice, intends to say,

Theological Grammar of the Oral Torah. Vol. I 133

"burnt offering, "but says, "peace offering," "peace offering," but says, "burnt offering", (3) or who, in making a vow, intends to say, "that I will not enter this house," but says, "that house," "that I will not derive benefit from this one," but says, "from that one," has not said anything, until his mouth and heart agree. Along these same lines, to incur guilt, one must intend the action that one has carried out. If he acted in a manner different from his intended action, he is not culpable as he would have been had he accomplished his purpose, so M. San. 9:4: If he intended to kill a beast and killed a man, an untimely birth and killed an offspring that was viable, he is exempt. If he intended to hit him on his loins with a blow that was not sufficient to kill him when it struck his loins, but it went and hit his heart, and there was sufficient force in that blow to kill him when it struck his heart, and he died, he is exempt. If he intended to hit him on his heart, and there was in that blow sufficient force to kill when it struck his heart, and it went and hit him on his loins, and there was not sufficient force in that blow to kill him when it struck his loins, but he died, he is exempt.

One's intentionality further governs the effect of one's deeds when it comes to dealing with consecrated produce. For example, M. Maaser Sheni 1:5 rules, One who buys outside Jerusalem with money in the status of second tithe, which is to be eaten only in Jerusalem pieces of fruit, if he did so (1) unintentionally not realizing the coins were consecrated, let their payment be returned to its former place to the purchaser who bought them by mistake; if he did so (2) on purpose — let the pieces of fruit be brought up and eaten in the holy place Jerusalem. And if the Temple does not exist, let the pieces of fruit rot.

When the farmer has decided that he wishes to benefit from the crop, e.g., to take it to market for sale, then God's rights of ownership are activated, and the crop must be tithed. But the crop may be subjected to random nibbling and not become liable to tithing. The actions of the farmer convey his attitude and intention vis á vis the crop, e.g., once he has covered a basket, once he has filled a vessel. So M. Maaserot 1:5: At what point after the harvest must tithes be removed from produce? (1) Cucumbers and gourds-after he removes the fuzz from them. But if he does not remove the fuzz, tithes need not be removed until he stacks them up. (2) Chatemelons — after he scalds them in order to remove the fuzz. But if he does not scald them, tithes need not be removed until he makes a store of melons. (3) Green vegetables which are normally tied in bunches-after he ties them But if he does not tie them, tithes need not be removed until the vessel into which he places the picked greens is filled. But if he does not fill the vessel, tithes need not be removed until he collects all he needs. (4) The contents of a basket need not be tithed until he covers the basket. But if he does not cover it, tithes need not be removed until he fills the vessel. But if he does not fill the vessel, tithes need not be removed until he collects all he needs in that basket. Under what circumstances do these criteria apply? If he is bringing the produce to market. But if he is bringing it home, it is not liable to the removal of tithes, and) he eats some of it as a random snack until he reaches home.

The entire system of animal sacrifices in atonement of sin rests on the distinction between an intentional and an unintentional action. A sin is atoned for by a sin-offering only when the act is inadvertent. A deliberate action is not covered, so M. Shab. 11:6J-K: "This is the general principle: All those who may be liable to sin offerings in fact are not liable unless at the beginning and the end, their sin is done inadvertently. But if the beginning of their sin is inadvertent and the end is deliberate, or the beginning deliberate and the end inadvertent, they are exempt — unless at the beginning and at the end their sin is inadvertent. The matter of intentionality governs the penalty to be paid by means of an animal sacrifice or some other form of sanction, e.g., extirpation (premature death), death at the hands of Heaven, death at the hands of an earthly court, so M. Keritot 1:2: For those transgressions are people liable, for deliberately doing them, to the punishment of extirpation, and for accidentally doing them, to the bringing of a sin offering, and for not being certain of whether or not one has done them, to a suspensive guilt offering Lev. 5:17 — "except for the one who imparts uncleanness to the sanctuary and its Holy Things, because he is subject to bringing a sliding scale offering (Lev. 5:6-7, 11))" the words of R. Meir. And sages say, "Also: except for the one who blasphemes, as it is said, You shall have one law for him that does anything unwittingly (Num. 15:29)-excluding the blasphemer, who does no concrete deed."

Intentionality governs the acceptability of some classes of animal offerings but not others. Specifically, if an animal is designated for use as a Passover offering or as a sin offering, but then the officiating priest offers the animal up under some other designation, that is, in a classification other than that specified by the donor's intent, the offering is null, so M. Zeb. 1:1 = M. Men. 1:1 for meal offerings: All animal offerings which were slaughtered not for their own name are valid so that the blood is tossed, the entrails burned, etc., but they do not go to the owner's credit in fulfillment of an obligation, except for the Passover and the sin offering- the Passover at its appointed time the afternoon of the fourteenth of Nisan." So too M. Zeb. 2:3: This is the general rule: Whoever slaughters, or receives the blood, or conveys the blood, or sprinkles the blood intending to eat something which is usually eaten flesh, to burn something which is usually burned entrails, outside of its proper place the court for Most Holy Things, Jerusalem for Lesser Holy Things — it is invalid and the flesh may not be eaten. And extirpation does not apply to it. Whoever slaughters, or receives the blood, or conveys the blood, or sprinkles (the blood), intending to eat something which is usually eaten, to burn something which is usually burned outside of its proper time — it is refuse. And they are liable on its account to extirpation even if they eat the flesh within the time limit.

The intentionality of the animal offering covers six matters, and for each of these matters, the animal must be offered up under the donor's correct intentionality: M. Zeb. 4:6: For the sake of six things is the animal offering sacrificed: (1) for the sake of the animal offering, (2) for the sake of the one who sacrifices it, (3) for the sake of the Lord, (4) for the sake of the altar fires, (5) for the sake of the odor, (6) for the sake of the pleasing smell. And as to the sin offering and the guilt offering, for the sake of the sin expiated thereby. Said R. Yosé, "Even: One who was not mindful in his heart for the sake of one all of these but slaughtered without specifying these things — it is valid, for it is a condition imposed by the court, that intention follows only the mind of the one who carries out the act not the owner; and the officiant does not specify the six things at all."

The following compositions address the general problem of intentionality in matters of uncleanness, so b. Hag. 2:7 II.3-2/18b: Said R. Jonathan b. Eleazar, "If someone's head-band fell from him and he said to his fellow, 'Give it to me,' and he gave it to him, the headband is unclean" for we cannot assume that he took it upon himself to guard it from uncleanness while he handled it, since the owner did not ask whether he was clean or not, nor can we say that the owner guarded it against defilement while it was not in his possession. Said R. Jonathan b. Amram, "If one's garments for the Sabbath were mixed up with his garments for everyday and he put them on, they are made unclean." if someone protects something assuming it is one thing and finds it to be another, it is unclean.

Intentionality extends to other matters besides concrete issues of the law and its practice. Intentionality shades over into attitude, the abstract becoming concrete through feelings or emotions. The right attitude is one of accommodation of one's own will to the will of others, self-abnegation, restraint, prudence. The most prized virtue is humility, on account of which Judah merited that the monarchy be assigned to his tribe, so too Saul (T. Ber. 4:18). A person should conform to the prevailing practice of the community and not stand out, so Hillel the Elder says at T. Ber. 2:21, "Do not appear naked where others go clothed, and do not appear clothed where others go naked, and do not appear standing where others sit, and do not appear sitting where others stand, and do not appear laughing where others weep, and do not appear weeping where others laugh, because Scripture states, 'a time to weep, a time to laugh, a time to embrace, a time to refrain from embracing' (Qoh. 3:4, 5)." Along these same lines, M. Abot 3:10 advises that God is pleased by those who try to please others: "Anyone from whom people take pleasure — the Omnipresent takes pleasure. Aqiba at T. Berakhot 3:3 goes over the same ground: "One in whom mankind delights, God delights. One in whom mankind does not delight, God does not delight. One who is content with his own portion, it is a good sign for him. One who is not content with his own portion, it is a bad sign for him." And altruism is the right attitude, e.g., M. Abot 5:16: In any loving relationship which depends upon something, when that thing is gone, the love is gone. But any which does not depend upon something will never come to an end. What is a loving relationship which depends upon something? That is the love of Amnon and Tamar 11 Sam. 13:15. And one which does not depend upon something? That is the love of David and Jonathan. So too the right intention is what validates contention, M. Abot 5:17: Any dispute which is for the sake of Heaven will in the end yield results, and any which is not for the sake of Heaven will in the end not yield results. What is a dispute for the sake of Heaven? This is the sort of dispute between Hillel and Shammai. And what is one which is not for the sake of Heaven? It is the dispute of Korach and all his party. One from whom people do not take pleasure, the Omnipresent does not take pleasure."

God's response to prayer depends upon the attitude of the community. He cannot be coerced through mere recitation of the right words. Miracles respond to intentionality, so Y. Ta. 3:4 I.1: One time they had to call a fast, but it did not rain. R. Joshua carried out a fast in the South, and it rained. The Sepphoreans said, "R. Joshua b. Levi brings down rain for the people in the South, but R. Haninah holds back rain for us in Sepphoris." They found it necessary to declare a second time of fasting and sent and summoned R. Joshua b. Levi. Haninah said to him, "Let my lord go forth with us to fast." The two of them went out to fast, but it did not rain. He went in and preached to them as follows: "It was not R. Joshua b. Levi who brought down rain for the people of the south, nor was it R. Haninah who held back rain from the people of Sepphoris. But as to the Southerners, their hearts are open, and when they listen to a teaching of Torah they submit to accept it, while as to the Sepphoreans, their hearts are hard, and when they hear a teaching of Torah, they do not submit or accept it." When he went in, he looked up and saw that the cloudless air was pure. He said, "Is this how it still is? Is there no change in the weather?" Forthwith, it rained. He took a vow for himself that he would never do the same thing again. He said, "How shall I say to the creditor God not to collect what is owing to him."

It is the possibility of a minor's forming a valid intention in respect to religious obligations that determines the point at which the minor may begin to carry out those obligations, so T. Hag. 1:2: If he knows how to shake an object, he is liable to observe the commandment of the lulab. If he knows how to cloak himself, he is liable for the commandment of fringes. If he knows how to speak, his father teaches him the Shema', Torah, and the Holy Language Hebrew. And if not, it would have been better had he not come into the world. If he knows how to take care of his phylacteries, his father purchases phylacteries for him. If he knows how to take care of his person, they eat food preserved in a state of cultic cleanness depending upon the cleanness of his person. If he knows how to take care of his hands, they eat food preserved in a state of cultic cleanness depending upon the cleanness of his hands. If he has sufficient intelligence to answer a question, then a doubt involving him in private domain is resolved as unclean, and one involving him in public domain is resolved as clean. If he knows how to effect proper slaughter of an animal, then an act of slaughter on his part is valid.

The intention to do evil, even if the action is not done, is culpable and to be repented, so b. Qid. 4: 13/II.13/81b: R. Hiyya bar Ashi was accustomed, whenever he prostrated himself to his face, to say, "May the All-Merciful save us from the Evil Impulse." Once his wife heard this. She said, "Now how many years he has kept away from me, so how come he says this?" One day he was studying in his garden, and she dressed up in disguise and walked back and forth before him. He said to him, "How are you?" She said to him, "I'm Haruta the famous whore, and I've come back today." He lusted after her. She said to him, "Bring me that pomegranate from the top bough." He climbed up and got it for her. When he went back inside his house, his wife was heating the oven, so he climbed up and sat down in it. She said to him, "So what's going on?" He told her what had happened. She said to him, "So it was really me." But he wouldn't believe her until she gave him the pomegranate. He said to her, "Well, anyhow, my intention was to do what is prohibited." For the rest of the life of that righteous man he fasted in penitence until he died on that account. So too in the following: When R. Aqiba would come to this verse, he wept, saying, "If someone intended to eat ham and really had in hand veal, yet the Torah has said that he requires atonement and forgiveness, one who intends to eat ham and really had in hand ham — all the more so!" Along these same lines: "Though he knew it not, yet he is guilty and shall bear his iniquity" (Lev. 5:17) — when R. Aqiba would come to this verse of Scripture, he would weep: "If someone intended to eat permitted fat and really had in hand forbidden fat, yet the Torah has said, 'Though he knew it not, yet he is guilty and shall bear his iniquity,' one who really did intend to eat forbidden fat and had in hand forbidden fat — all the more so is he guilty!" Issi b. Judah says, "'Though he knew it not, yet he is guilty and shall bear his iniquity' (Lev. 5:17) — for such a thing as this that we are sinful even not by intent let all those who are mournful mourn."

It would be difficult to assemble a more uniform set of diverse formulations of a single principle. Intentionality forms the systemic dynamics of the entire structure of sanctification and morality that the Oral Torah constructs.

VII

ISRAEL

ISRAEL: the holy people, whom God singled out for the redemption of Mankind, variously represented in both the Written and the Oral Torah as an extended, holy family, a people or nation chosen by God for sanctification and service, God's community and venue on earth. One antonym for Israel is gentile. Gentiles worship idols, Israel worships the one, unique God. Another is Adam. Israel is Adam's counterpart, the other model for Man. Israel came into existence in the aftermath of the failure of Creation with the fall of Man, in the restoration that followed the Flood, God identified Abraham to found a supernatural social entity to realize his will in creating the world. Called, variously, a family, a community, a nation, a people, above all, Israel forms God's resting place on earth. This definition of Israel cannot be confused with any secular meanings attributed to the same word, e.g., nation or ethnic entity, counterpart to other nations or ethnic groups.

At the most profound level, Israel means, those destined to rise from the dead and enjoy the world to come. Specifically, the definition of Israel is contained in the identification of "all Israel," as those who maintain that the resurrection of the dead is a teaching of the Torah, and that the Torah comes from heaven, so M. San. 10:1A-D: All Israelites have a share in the world to come, as it is said, Your people also shall be all righteous, they shall inherit the land forever; the branch of my planting, the work of my hands, that I may be glorified (Is. 60:21). And these are the ones who have no portion in the world to come: (1) He who says, the resurrection of the dead is a teaching which does not derive from the Torah, (2) and the Torah does not come from Heaven; and (3) an Epicurean. T. San. 12:9 adds the rejection of the yoke of the commandments, the denial of the covenant, and the perversion of the Torah by maintaining that God did not reveal it. The upshot is, to be "Israel" is to rise from the dead to the world to come. Gentiles, by contrast, are not going to be resurrected when the dead are raised, but those among them who bear no guilt for their sins also will not be judged for eternal damnation, so Y. Sheb. 4:10 IX: Gentile children who did not act out of free will and Nebuchadnezzar's soldiers who had no choice but to follow the orders of the evil king will not live after the resurrection of the dead but will not be judged for their deeds.

For Israel to be holy means that Israel is to be separate, and if Israel sanctifies itself, it sanctifies God, so Sifra CXCV:I.2-3: "You shall be holy": "You shall be separate." "You shall be holy, for I the Lord your God am holy": That is to say, "if you sanctify yourselves, I shall credit it to you as though you had sanctified me, and if you do not sanctify yourselves, I shall hold that it is as if you have not sanctified me." Or perhaps the sense is this: "If you sanctify me, then lo, I shall be sanctified, and if not, I shall not be sanctified"? Scripture says, "For I...am holy," meaning, I remain in my state of sanctification, whether or not you sanctify me. Abba Saul says, "The king has a retinue, and what is the task thereof? It is to imitate the king." God is always present within Israel, wherever Israel is located, so B. Meg. 4:4 I.10: B. R. Shimon ben Yohai says: Come and see how dear the nation of Israel is before The Holy One, Blessed Be He, for wherever they were exiled, the Divine Presence was with them. When they were exiled to Egypt, the Divine Presence was with them, as is said, "was I not exiled to your father's house when they were in Egypt" (1 Sam. 2:27). When they were exiled to Babylonia, the Divine Presence was with them, as is said, "for your sake I sent to Babylonia" (Is. 43:14). And also when they will be redeemed in the future, the Divine Presence will be with them, as is said, "and the Lord your God will return your return" (Deut. 30:3). It does not say "and He will cause to return" (*ve-heshiv*) but "and He will return" (*ve-shav*). This teaches that The Holy One, Blessed Be He, will return with them from among the places of exile.

When Israel carries out God's will, Israel prospers, but when not, Israel suffers, so Mekh. XXX:I.5: "Your right hand, O Lord, glorious in power:" When the Israelites carry out the will of the Omnipresent, they turn the left into the right: "Your right hand, O Lord, glorious in power, your right hand, O Lord, shatters the enemy." But when the Israelites do not do the will of the Omnipresent, they turn the right hand into the left: "You have drawn back his right hand" (Lam. 2:3). When the Israelites do the will of the Omnipresent, there is no sleep before him: "Behold the one who watches Israel dos not slumber or sleep" (Ps. 121:4). But when the Israelites do not do the will of the Omnipresent, then, as it were, sleep comes to him: "Then the Lord awakened as one asleep" (Ps. 78:65). When the Israelites do the will of the Omnipresent, there is no anger before him: "Fury is not in me" (Is. 27:4). But when the Israelites do not do the will of the Omnipresent, then, as it were, anger is before him: "And the anger of the Lord will be kindled" (Dt. 11:17). When the Israelites do the will of the Omnipresent, he does battle for them: "The Lord will fight for you" (Ex. 14:14). But when the Israelites do not do the will of the Omnipresent, then, he fights against them: "Therefore he was turned to be their enemy, the Lord himself fought against them" (Is. 63:10). Not only so, but they make the merciful God into a sadist: "The Lord has become as an enemy" (Lam. 2:5). The same applies in reverse, so Mekh. XXVIII:II.10: R. Simeon b. Eleazar says, "When the Israelites carry out the will of the Omnipresent, then his name is made great in the world: 'And it happened that when all the kings of the Amorites ...heard' (Josh. 5:1). So too Rahab the harlot said to Joshua's messengers, 'For we have heard how the Lord dried up the water of the Red Sea before you...and as soon as we had heard it, our hearts melted' (Josh. 2:10-11). But when the Israelites do not carry out the will of the Omnipresent, then his name is profaned in the world: 'And when they came to the nations where they went, they profaned my holy name. But I had pity for my holy name which the house of Israel had profaned...therefore say to the house of Israel, Thus says the Lord God, I do not do this for your sake...and I will sanctify my great name which has been profaned among the nations' (Ez. 36:20-23)."

To take up the contrastive definition, Israel/not gentile: Israel is defined both negatively and positively. Israel means, not-gentile. Israel is fundamentally different from the nations of the world even in practical ways, so PRK V:V.2: said R. Levi, "In all their deeds the Israelites are different from the nations of the world, in their manner of ploughing, sowing, reaping, making sheaves, threshing, working at the threshing floor and at the wine press, counting and reckoning the calendar: As to ploughing: You will not plough with an ox and ass together (Deut. 22:10). ..sowing: You will now sow your vineyard with mixed seeds (Lev. 22:9). ...reaping: You will not gather the gleaning of your harvest (Lev. 19:9). ...making sheaves: And the forgotten sheaf in the field you will not recover (Deut. 24:12). ...threshing: You will not muzzle an ox in its threshing (Deut. 25:4). ...working at the threshing floor and at the wine press: You will provide liberally for the Hebrew servant out of your threshing floor and wine press (Deut. 15:14). ...counting and reckoning the calendar: The nations of the world reckon by the sun, and Israel by the moon: This month will be for you the first of the months (Ex. 12:2).

In its relationships to the nations, Israel is the victim of illegitimate violence and the nations are illegitimately empowered. All God — after all, the All-Powerful — wants is the victim, done to but never doing, so Leviticus Rabbah XXVII:V.1: "God seeks what has been driven away" (Qoh. 3:15). R. Huna in the name of R. Joseph said, "It is always the case that 'God seeks what has been driven away' favoring the victim. You find when a righteous man pursues a righteous man, 'God seeks what has been driven away.' When a wicked man pursues a wicked man, 'God seeks what has been driven away.' All the more so when a wicked man pursues a righteous man, 'God seeks what has been driven away.' The same principle applies even when you come around to a case in which a righteous man pursues a wicked man, 'God seeks what has been driven away.' R. Yosé, b. R. Yudan in the name of R. Yosé, b. R. Nehorai says, "It is always the case that the Holy One, blessed be he, demands an accounting for the blood of those who have been pursued from the hand of the pursuer. Abel was pursued by Cain, and God sought an accounting for the pursued: 'And the Lord looked favorably upon Abel and his meal offering' (Gen. 4:4). Noah was pursued by his generation, and God sought an accounting for the pursued: 'You and all your household shall come into the ark' (Gen. 7:1). And it says, 'For this is like the days of Noah to me, as I swore that the waters of Noah should no more go over the earth' (Is. 54:9). Abraham was pursued by Nimrod, 'and God seeks what has been driven away': 'You are the Lord, the God who chose Abram and brought him out of Ur' (Neh. 9:7). Isaac was pursued by Ishmael, 'and God seeks what has been driven away': 'For through Isaac will seed be called for you' (Gen. 21:12). Jacob was pursued by Esau, 'and God seeks what has been driven away': 'For the Lord has chosen Jacob, Israel for his prized possession' (Ps. 135:4). Moses was pursued by Pharaoh, 'and God seeks what has been driven away': 'Had not Moses His chosen stood in the breach before Him' (Ps. 106:23). David was pursued by Saul, 'and God seeks what has been driven away': 'And he chose David, his servant'(Ps. 78:70). Israel was pursued by the nations, 'and God seeks what has been driven away': 'And you has the

Lord chosen to be a people to him' (Deut. 14:2). And the rule applies also to the matter of offerings. A bull is pursued by a lion, a sheep is pursued by a wolf, a goat is pursued by a leopard. Therefore the Holy One, blessed be he, has said, 'Do not make offerings before me from those animals that pursue, but from those that are pursued: 'When a bull, a sheep, or a goat is born'" (Lev. 22:27). So much for relationships with gentiles.

The special character of Israel by contrast to the gentiles is displayed by the character of the prophets that God sends to Israel, by contrast to that of the ones he sends to the gentiles, so Gen. R. LII:V.1: "But God came to Abimelech in a dream by night and said to him, 'Behold, you are a dead man, because of the woman whom you have taken, for she is a man's wife'" (Gen. 20:3): What is the difference between the prophets of Israel and those of the nations? R. Hama b. R. Haninah said, "The Holy One, blessed be he, is revealed to the prophets of the nations of the world only in partial speech, in line with the following verse of Scripture: 'And God called WYQR, rather than WYQR' as at Lev. 1:1 Balaam' (Num. 23:16). On the other hand, he reveals himself to the prophets of Israel in full and complete speech, as it is said, 'And the Lord called (WYR') to Moses' (Lev. 1:1)." Said R. Issachar of Kepar Mandi, "Should that prophecy, even in partial form, be paid to them as their wage? Surely not, in fact that is no form of speech to gentile prophets, who are frauds. The connotation of the language, 'And God called to Balaam' (Num. 23:16) is solely unclean. That is in line with the usage in the following verse of Scripture: 'That is not clean, by that which happens by night' (Deut. 23:11). So the root is the same, with the result that YQR at Num. 23:16 does not bear the meaning of God's calling to Balaam. God rather declares Balaam unclean. But the prophets of Israel are addressed in language of holiness, purity, clarity, in language used by the ministering angels to praise God. That is in line with the following verse of Scripture: 'And they called one to another and said, "Holy, holy, holy is the Lord of hosts"' (Is. 6:3)." R. Yosé said, "'The Lord is far from the evil, but the prayer of the righteous does he hear' (Prov. 5:29). 'The Lord is far from the wicked' refers to the prophets of the nations of the world. 'But the prayer of the righteous does he hear' refers to the prophets of Israel. R. Yosé b. Bibah said, "The Holy One, blessed be he, appears to the prophets of the nations of the world only by night, when people take leave of one another: 'Now a word was secretly brought to me...at the time of leave-taking, from the visions of the night, when deep sleep falls on men' (Job 4:12-13)." Said R. Eleazar b. Menahem, "'The Lord is far from the evil' (Prov. 5:29) refers to the prophets of the nations of the world. 'But the prayer of the righteous does he hear' (Prov. 5:29) speaks of the prophets of Israel. You furthermore find that the Holy One, blessed be he, appears to the prophets of the nations of the world only like a man who comes from some distant place. That is in line with the following verse of Scripture: 'From a distant land they have come to me, from Babylonia' (Is. 39:3). But in the case of the prophets of Israel, he is always near at hand: 'And he appeared not having come from a great distance' (Gen. 18:1). 'And the Lord called' (Lev. 1:1). These usages bear the sense that he was right nearby."

How about a this-worldly, political definition? The secular sense of "Israel" and even "the Jews" occurs only very rarely in the Oral Torah. In the Oral Torah "Israel" bears three meanings: [1] family, that is, a social entity different from the nations because it is formed by a common genealogy; [2] nation among nations; and [3] Israel as *sui generis*, different not in contingent, indicative traits but categorically, that is to say, in its very category from all other nations. Scripture told the story of "Israel" a man, Jacob. His children therefore are "the children of Jacob." That man's name was also "Israel," and, it followed, "the children of Israel" comprised the extended family of that man. By extension upward, "Israel" formed the family of Abraham and Sarah, Isaac and Rebecca, Jacob and Leah and Rachel. "Israel" therefore invoked the metaphor of genealogy to explain the bonds that linked persons unseen into a single social entity; the shared traits were imputed, not empirical. That social metaphor of "Israel" Ä a simple one, really, and easily grasped Ä bore consequences in two ways. First, children in general are admonished to follow the good example of their parents. The deeds of the patriarchs and matriarchs therefore taught lessons on how the children were to act. Of greater interest in an account of "Israel" as a social metaphor, "Israel" lived twice, once in the patriarchs and matriarchs, a second time in the life of the heirs as the descendants relived those earlier lives. The stories of the family were carefully reread to provide a picture of the meaning of the latter-day events of the descendants of that same family. Accordingly, the lives of the patriarchs signaled the history of Israel.

Israel also found representation as beyond all metaphor. Seeing "Israel" as *sui generis* yielded a sustained interest in the natural laws governing "Israel" in particular, statements of the rules of the group's history viewed as a unique entity within time. The historical-eschatological formulation of a political teleology in that way moved from an account of illegitimate power to a formulation of the theory of the inappropriate victim, that is to say, of Israel itself. Sentences out of the factual record of the past formed into a cogent statement of the laws of "Israel"'s destiny, laws unique to the social entity at hand. Second, the teleology of those laws for an Israel that was sui generis focused upon salvation at the end of history, that is, an eschatological teleology formed for a social entity embarked on its own lonely journey through time. The conception of "Israel" as *sui generis*, third, reaches expression in an implicit statement that Israel is subject to its own laws, which are distinct from the laws governing all other social entities. These laws may be discerned in the factual, scriptural record of "Israel"'s past, and that past, by definition, belonged to "Israel" alone. It followed, therefore, that by discerning the regularities in "Israel"'s history, implicitly understood as unique to "Israel," sages recorded the view that "Israel" like God was not subject to analogy or comparison. Accordingly, while not labeled a genus unto itself, Israel is treated in that way.

The theory of Israel as *sui generis* produced a political theory in which Israel's sole legitimate ruler is God, and whoever legitimately governs does so as God's surrogate. The theory of legitimate sanctions then is recast into a religious statement of God's place in Israel's existence, but retains its political valence when we recall that the sage, the man most fully "in our image, after our likeness," governs in accord with the law of the Torah. Here is a brief statement, framed out of the materials of Leviticus Rabbah, of the successor-documents' political theory that forms also a theological creed. In it we see the definition of legitimate violence: God's alone. The theory is as follows: God loves Israel, so gave them the Torah, which defines their life and governs their welfare. Israel is alone in its category (*sui generis*), proved by the fact that what is a virtue to Israel is a vice to the nation, life-giving to Israel, poison to the gentiles. True, Israel sins, but God forgives that sin, having punished the nation on account of it. Such a process has yet to come to an end, but it will culminate in Israel's complete regeneration. Meanwhile, Israel's assurance of God's love lies in the many expressions of special concern, for even the humblest and most ordinary aspects of the national life: the food the nation eats, the sexual practices by which it procreates. These life-sustaining, life-transmitting activities draw God's special interest, as a mark of his general love for Israel. Israel then is supposed to achieve its life in conformity with the marks of God's love.

These indications moreover signify also the character of Israel's difficulty, namely, subordination to the nations in general, but to the fourth kingdom, Rome, in particular. Both food laws and skin diseases stand for the nations. There is yet another category of sin, also collective and generative of collective punishment, and that is social. The moral character of Israel's life, the treatment of people by one another, the practice of gossip and small-scale thuggery — these too draw down divine penalty. The nation's fate therefore corresponds to its moral condition. The moral condition, however, emerges not only from the current generation. Israel's richest hope lies in the merit of the ancestors, thus in the Scriptural record of the merits attained by the founders of the nation, those who originally brought it into being and gave it life.

Israel was created to carry out religious duties and perform good deeds, so Lev. R. XXIII:VI.1: "Like a rose among thorns:" Just as roses are only for occasions of rejoicing, so Israel was created only for carrying out religious duties and doing good deeds. Another interpretation of "Like a rose among thorns:" Just as a rose is only for the scent, so the righteous were created only for the redemption of Israel. Another interpretation of "Like a rose among thorns:" Just as a rose is placed on the table of kings at the beginning and end of a meal, so Israel will be in both this world and the world to come. Another interpretation of "Like a rose among thorns:" Just as a rose is made ready for the Sabbath and festivals, so Israel is made ready for the coming redemption. Another interpretation of "Like a rose among thorns:" Just as it is easy to tell a rose from the thorns, so it is easy to tell the Israelites from the nations of the world. That is in line with the following verse of Scripture: "All those who see them will recognize them" (Is. 61:9). Another interpretation of "Like a rose among thorns:" Just as a rose wilts so long as the hot spell persists, but when the hot spell passes and dew (TL for SL) falls on it, the rose thrives again, so for Israel, so long as the shadow of Esau falls across the world, as it were Israel wilts. But when the shadow of Esau passes from the world, Israel will once more thrive. That is in line with the following verse of Scripture: "I shall be like the dew for Israel. It will blossom like a rose" (Hos. 14:6).

Israel is a virtuous community, characterized by forbearance, forgiveness, and kindliness, so Y. Qid. 4:1 III.2, Then David said, "There were three good gifts that the Holy One, blessed be he, gave to Israel: forgiving people, bashful people, and kindly people." "Forgiving people," whence in Scripture? "None of the devoted things shall cleave to your hand; that the Lord may turn from the fierceness of his anger and show you mercy" (Deut. 13: 18). "Bashful people." whence in Scripture? "And Moses said to the people, 'Do not fear for God has come to prove you, and that the fear of him may be before your eyes, that you may not sin'" (Ex. 20: 20). This is a mark of a bashful person, who will not readily sin. And as to whoever is not bashful, it is a matter of absolute certainty that his forefathers did not stand before Mount Sinai. "Kindly people," whence in Scripture? "And because you hearken to these ordinances, and keep and do them, the Lord your God will keep with you the covenant and the steadfast love which he swore to your fathers to keep" (Deut. 7 :12).

To be an Israelite is defined by possessing the traits that define an Israelite. Generosity is a mark of authentic lineage within Israel, so B. Bes. 4:4 III.4 32b Said R. Nathan b. Abba said Rab, "The rich men of Babylonia will go down to Gehenna. For once Shabbetai b. Marinos came to Babylonia. He asked them for goods to trade for a commission, but they would not provide them. He asked for food. Also they would not provide him any food. He said, 'These people are descendants of the mixed multitude that left Egypt with the Israelites, Ex. 12:38, as it is written Dt. 13:17, 'And God will bestow on you the spirit of mercy and compassion as he swore to your fathers.' This means that anyone who has compassion for others is through his actions known to be of the progeny of Abraham our father. But anyone who does not show compassion to others is known not to be of the progeny of Abraham our father.'"

So too, Israel must conduct itself modestly, so Y. Suk. 5:1 I:2: Hillel the Elder: When he would see people acting arrogantly, would say to them, "If I am here, who is here? Does God need their praise? And is it not written, 'A stream of fire issued and came forth from before him; a thousand thousands served him, and ten thousand times ten thousand stood before him; the court sat in judgement, and the books were opened'" (Dan. 7:10). When he would see people acting modestly, he would say to them, "If we are not here, who is here? For even though God has before him any number of those who praise him, still, precious to him is the praise coming from Israel more than anything else. What is the scriptural basis for this statement? 'Now these are the last words of David: The oracle of David, the son of Jesse, the oracle of the man who was raised on high, the anointed of the God of Jacob, the sweet-psalmist of Israel' (2 Sam. 23:1). '...enthroned on the praises of Israel'"(Ps. 22:4).

God's love for Israel is profound and unconditional, so Sif. Num. I:X.1: "'You shall put out both male and female, putting them outside the camp, that they may not defile their camp, in the midst of which I dwell.' And the people of Israel did so and drove them outside the camp, as the Lord said to Moses, so the people of Israel did" (Num. 5:3-4). So beloved is Israel that even though they may become unclean, the Presence of God remains among them. And so Scripture states, "...who dwells with them in the midst of their uncleanness" (Lev. 16:16).. And further: "...by making my sanctuary unclean, which nonetheless is in their midst " (Lev. 15:31). And it further says: "...that they may not defile their camp, in the midst of which I dwell" (Num. 5:3-4). And it further says, "You shall not defile the land in which you live, in the midst of which I dwell, for I the Lord dwell in the midst of the people of Israel" (Num. 35:34).

God loves Israel, but Israel makes God jealous with their idolatry, so Song CVIII:ii.1: "for love is strong as death:" As strong as death is the love with which the Holy One, blessed be He, loves Israel: "I have loved you says the Lord" (Mal. 1:2). "jealousy is cruel as the grave:" That is when they make him jealous with their idolatry: "They roused him to jealousy with strange gods" (Dt. 32:16). Israel is estranged from God by its own sin, and this is a source of great anguish to sages, so B.Hag. 1:1-2 VI.4-28/5A-B: When R. Huna came to this verse, "he will see, being seen," he wept, saying, "A slave whose master yearns to see him is estranged from him: 'When you come to appear before me, who has required this of you, to trample my courts' (Is. 1:12)." When R. Huna came to this verse, he wept: "And you shall sacrifice peace offerings and shall eat there' (Dt. 27:7). A slave whose master yearns to see him is estranged from him: 'to what purpose is the abundance of your sacrifices to me, says the Lord' (Is.

1:11)." When R. Eleazar came to this verse, he wept: "'And his brothers couldn't answer him, because they were frightened in his presence' (Gen. 45:3) — if they were frightened before his rebuke, how much the more so on account of the rebuke of the Holy One, blessed be he!" When R. Eleazar came to this verse, he wept: "'And Samuel said to Saul, why have you disturbed me to bring me up' (1 Sam. 28:15) — if Samuel, a righteous man, was afraid of judgment, how much the more so should be!" When R. Ammi came to this verse, he wept: "Let him put his mouth in the dust, perhaps there may be hope" (Lam. 3:29). He said, "After all that, merely 'perhaps'?!" When R. Ammi came to this verse, he wept: "Seek righteousness, seek humility, perhaps shall you be hid in the day of the Lord's anger" (Zeph. 2:3). He said, "After all that, merely 'perhaps'?!" When R. Assi came to this verse, he wept: "Hate the evil and love the good and establish justice in the gate, perhaps the Lord, the God of hosts, will be gracious" (Amos 5:15). He said, "After all that, merely 'perhaps'?!" When R. Joseph came to this verse, he wept: "But there is he who is swept away without judgment" (Prov. 13:23). He said, "Well, is there really someone who passes away not at his proper time?" When R. Yohanan came to this verse, he wept: "'And you did incite me against him, to destroy him without a cause' (Job 2:3) — a slave whose master, when incited, yields — does he have a remedy?" When R. Yohanan came to this verse, he wept: "'Behold, he puts no trust in his holy ones' (Job 15:15) — if he doesn't have trust in his holy ones, then in whom will he trust?" When R. Yohanan came to this verse, he wept: "And I will come near to you to judgment and I will be a swift witness against the sorcerers and against the adulterers and against false swearers and against those who oppress the employee in his wages' (Mal. 3:5) — a slave whose master draws him near for judgment and also runs to testify against him — can he have any remedy?" When R. Yohanan came to this verse, he wept: "'For God shall bring every work into the judgment concerning every hidden thing whether it be good or whether it be evil' (Qoh. 12:14) — a slave whose master weighs against him equally inadvertent and deliberate sins — can he have any remedy?" When R. Yohanan came to this verse, he wept: "'And it shall come to pass, when many evils and troubles have come upon them' (Dt. 31:21) — a servant whose master brings evil and trouble upon him — can he have any remedy?" R. Ila was once walking up the stairs of Rabbah bar Shila. He heard a child's voice, reciting this verse: "For lo, he who forms the mountains and creates the wind and declares to man what his conversation was" (Amos 4:13). He said, "A slave whose master tells him what his conversation was — has he any remedy?"

Like Adam's, Israel's sin was disobedience, so Song R. CXIII:i.1: "My vineyard, my very own, is for myself:" R. Hiyya taught on Tannaite authority, "The matter may be compared to the case of a king who was angry with his son and handed him over to his servant. What did he do? He began to beat him with a club. He said to him, 'Don't obey your father.' The son said to the servant, 'You big fool! The very reason that father handed me over to you was only because I was not listening to him, and you say, "Don't listen to father"!' So too, when sin had brought it about that the house of the sanctuary should be destroyed and Israel was sent into exile to Babylonia, Nebuchadnezzar said to them, 'Do not listen to the Torah of your father in heaven, but rather, "fall down and worship the image that I have made" (Dan. 3:15).' The Israelites said to him, 'You big fool! The very reason that the Holy One, blessed be He, has handed us over to you is because we were bowing down to an idol: "She saw...the images of the Chaldaeans portrayed with vermilion" (Ezek. 23:14), and yet you say to us, "fall down and worship the image that I have made" (Dan. 3:15). Woe to you!' "It is at that moment that the Holy One, blessed be He, said, "'My vineyard, my very own, is for myself.""'"

But God's love for Israel is attested by his capacity to forgive Israel. Israel tested God ten times, and God forgave them ten times, so M. Ar. 3:5 II.3, Said R. Judah, "Ten trials did our ancestors impose upon the Holy One, blessed be he: two at the shore of the sea, two in the water, two in regard to the manna, two in regard to the quail, one in regard to the golden calf, one in the wilderness of Paran." Two at the sea:" one in going down, and one in coming up. In going down, as it is written, "Because there were no graves in Egypt you have taken us away to die in the wilderness" (Ex. 14:11). Two in the water:" at Marah and at Refidim. At Marah, as it is written, "And they came to Marah and could not drink the water" (Ex. 15:23). And it is written, "And the people complained against Moses" (Ex. 17:3). At Refidim, as it is written, "They encamped at Refidim, and there was no water to drink" (Ex. 17:1). And it is written, "And the people struggled with Moses" (Ex. 17:2). Two in regard to the manna: as it is written, 15B Do not go out, but they went out, "Do not leave any over," (Ex. 16:19) but they left some over. The first is not a direct quotation of a verse but summarizes the narrative. Two in regard to the quail: in regard to the first quail and in regard to the second quail. In regard to the first: "When we sat by the fleshpots" (Ex. 16:3). In regard to the second: "And the mixed multitude that was among them" (Num. 11:4). One in regard to the golden calf:" as the story is told. One in the wilderness of Paran:" as the story is told.

Israel is God's slave and should be regarded as such, so Sif. Num. CXV:V.4: "I am the Lord your God who brought you out of the land of Egypt to be your God": why make mention of the Exodus from Egypt in the setting of discourse on each and every one of the religious duties? The matter may be compared to the case of a king whose ally was taken captive. When the king paid the ransom and so redeemed him, he did not redeem him as a free man but as a slave, so that if the king made a decree and the other did not accept it, he might say to him, "You are my slave." When he came into a city, he said to him, "Tie my shoe-latch, carry my clothing before me and bring them to the bath house." Doing these services marks a man as the slave of the one for whom he does them. The son began to complain. The king produced the bond and said to him, "You are my slave." So when the Holy One, blessed be he, redeemed the seed of Abraham, his ally, he redeemed them not as sons but as slaves. When he makes a decree and they do not accept it, he may say to them, "You are my slaves." When the people had gone forth to the wilderness, he began to make decrees for them involving part of the lesser religious duties as well as part of the more stringent religious duties, for example, the Sabbath, the prohibition against consanguineous marriages, the fringes, and the requirement to don *tefillin*. The Israelites began to complain. He said to them, "You are my slaves. It was on that stipulation that I redeemed you, on the condition that I may make a decree and you must carry it out."

God does myriads of miracles for Israel. A single statement of that conviction suffices, at T. Sot. 8:7: Come and see how many miracles were done for Israel on that day! They crossed the water of the Jordan and came to Mount Gerizim and Mount Ebal in Samaria on the side of Shechem, near the oaks of Moreh, as it is said, And are they not on the other side of the Jordan, west of the road, toward the going down of the sun, in the land of the Canaanites who live in the Arabah, over against Gilgal, beside the oak of Moreh (Deut. 11:30) — so traversing a distance of more than sixty mils. No man stood against them, and whoever stood against them was forthwith panic-stricken, as it is said, "I will send My terror before you, and will discomfort all the people to whom you shall come" (Ex. 23:27). And it says, "Terror and dread fall upon them... until your people pass over, O Lord" (Ex. 15:16). "Until your people pass over" — this is the first passage. "Until this people which you have acquired" — this is the second passage. On this basis you must conclude: The Israelites ought to have had done for them at the Jordan what was done for them at the Sea, but they had sinned in the meantime.

External emblems of belonging to Israel serve, but only contingently. Circumcision defines who is an Israelite, but only within limits, so M. Ned. 3:11G-R: If he said, "Qonam if I derive benefit from the uncircumcised," he is permitted to derive benefit from uncircumcised Israelites but prohibited from deriving benefit from circumcised gentiles. Qonam if I derive benefit from the circumcised" - he is prohibited to derive benefit from uncircumcised Israelites and permitted to derive benefit from circumcised gentiles. For the word "uncircumcised" is used only as a name for gentiles, as it is written, "For all the nations are uncircumcised, and the whole house of Israel is uncircumcised at heart" (Jer. 9:26). And it says, "This uncircumcised Philistine" (1 Sam. 17:36). And it says, "Lest the daughters of the Philistines rejoice, lest the daughters of the uncircumcised triumph" (2 Sam. 1:20).

People nonetheless knew who was or was not an Israelite by observing the public behavior of those under examination, e.g., keeping the Sabbath, practicing circumcision, refraining from sexual relations during a woman's menstrual period, thus B. Meilah 4:3 I.2: "One time the government made a decree that people should not keep the Sabbath or circumcise their sons but must have sexual relations with their wives when they are menstruating. R. Reuben b. Istrobali went and had his hair cut in the Roman manner and went and took his place among them not being recognized as a Jew. He said to him, 'He who has an enemy — does he want him to lose money or get rich?' They said to him, 'To lose his money.' He said to them, 'In that case, let them not work on the Sabbath, so they will become impoverished.' They said to him, 'Well and good,' and he advised them to cancel the decree, and they cancelled the decree. Again he said to them, 'He who has an enemy, does he want him to get weak or grow strong?' They said to him, 'Get weak.' He said to them, 'If so, have them circumcise their sons on the eighth day, and they'll get weaken.' They said to him, 'Well and good,' and he advised them to cancel the decree, and they cancelled the decree. Again he said to them, 'He who has an enemy — does he want him to increase or decrease in numbers?' They said to him, 'Decrease.' 'If so, let them not have sexual relations with their wives when they are menstruating. They said to him, 'Well and good,' and he advised them to cancel the decree, and they cancelled the decree. Then they realized that he was a Jew, so they reinstituted the decrees.

Other indicative traits are readily discerned. For example, Israelites characteristically recited blessings throughout the day, constantly reaffirming their place in the Kingdom of Heaven. So T. Ber. 6:24-5: R. Meir used to say, "There is no person in Israel who does not perform one hundred commandments each day and recite blessings for them. One recites the Shema' and recites blessings before and after it. And one eats his bread and recites blessings before and after. And one recites the Prayer of Eighteen Blessings three times. And one performs all the other commandments and recites blessings for them." And so R. Meir used to say, "There is no person in Israel who is not surrounded by commandments. Every person wears tefillin on his head, tefillin on his arm, and has a mezuzah on his door post, the mark of circumcision in his flesh, and four fringes on his garment around him." So did David say, "Seven times a day I praise thee for thy righteous ordinances" (Ps. 119:164). And so he says, "The angel of the Lord encamps around those who fear him and delivers them" (Ps. 34:7). When he David entered the bathhouse and realized that he was naked, he said, 'Woe is me for I am stripped of the commandments.' But when he saw the mark of circumcision in his flesh he praised the Lord in his Psalm saying, "To the choirmaster according to the *sheminith*" (Ps. 12:1) The eighth, sheminith, is an allusion to circumcision on the eighth day T. 6:24-5.

Above all, Israel sacrifices this-worldly advantages to remain loyal to God, so Song R. LXXXIX:i.9: "Return that we may look upon you:" The nations of the world say to Israel, "How long are you going to die for your God and devote yourselves completely to him? For thus Scripture says, 'Therefore do they love you beyond death' (Song 1:3). And how long will you be slaughtered on his account: 'No, but for your sake we are killed all day long' (Ps. 44:23)? 'How long are you going to do good deeds on his account, for him alone, while he pays you back with bad things? Come over to us, and we shall make you governors, hyparchs, and generals, 'That we may look upon you:' and you will be the cynosure of the world: 'And you shall be the look out of all the people' (Ex. 18:21)." And the Israelites will answer, "'Why should you look upon the Shulammite, as upon a dance before two armies:' In your entire lives, have you ever heard that Abraham, Isaac, and Jacob worshipped idols, that their children should do so after them? Our fathers did not worship idols, and we shall not worship idols after them. But what can you do for us? Can it be like the dance that was made for Jacob, our father, when he went forth from the house of Laban? Or can you make a dance for us such as was made for our fathers at the sea? 'And the angel of God removed...' (Ex. 14:19). Or can you make a dance for us like the one that was made for Elisha: 'And when the servant of the man of God was risen early and gone forth, behold a host with horses and chariots was round about the city. And his servant said to him, Alas, my master, what shall we do? And he answered, Do not be afraid, for they who are with us are more than those who are with them. Forthwith Elisha prayed and said, Lord, I pray you, open his eyes that he may see And the Lord opened the eyes of the young man, and he saw, and behold, the mountain was full of horses and chariots of fire around about Elisha' (2 Kgs. 6:15). Or can you make a dance for us like the one that the Holy One, blessed be He, will make for the righteous in the age to come?"

God favors holy Israel over the gentiles, because the former accept, study, and carry out the Torah and the latter do not. Therefore at the end of days God will save Israel and destroy idolatry, so b. A.Z. I:7, 10/4a: R. Hinena bar Pappa contrasted verses of Scripture: "It is written, 'As to the almighty, we do not find him exercising plenteous power' (Job 37:23), but by contrast, 'Great is our Lord and of abundant power' (Ps. 147:5), and further, 'Your right hand, Lord, is glorious in power' (Ex. 15:6). But there is no contradiction between the first and second and third statements, for the former speaks of the time of judgment when justice is tempered with mercy, so God does not do what he could and the latter two statements refer to a time of war of God against his enemies." Raba said, "What is the meaning of the verse, 'Howbeit he will not stretch out a hand for a ruinous heap though they cry in his destruction' (Job 30:24)? Said the Holy One, blessed be He, to Israel, 'When I judge Israel, I shall not judge them as I do the gentiles, for it is written, "I will overturn, overturn, overturn it" (Ezek. 21:32), rather, I shall exact punishment from them as a hen pecks.' Another matter: 'Even if the Israelites do not carry out a religious duty before me more than a hen pecking at a rubbish heap, I shall join together all the little pecks into a great sum: "although they pick little they are saved" (Job 30:24) .' Another matter: 'As a reward for their crying out to me, I shall help them' (Job 30:24)."

Israel are God's children, and it is an act of grace that Israel is informed that they are God's children, so Aqiba, M. Abot 3:14: "Precious are Israelites, who are called children to the Omnipresent. It was an act of still greater love that they were called children to the Omnipresent, as it is said, You are the children of the Lord your God (Dt. 14:1). Precious are Israelites, to whom was given the precious thing. It was an act of still greater love that it was made known to them that to them was given that precious thing with which the world was made, as it is said, For I give you a good doctrine. Do not forsake my Torah (Prov. 4:2)." The mark of Israel's special standing before God is the Torah and the commandments, so M. Mak. 3:161: R. Hananiah b. Aqashia says, "The Holy One, blessed be he, wanted to give merit to Israel. Therefore he gave them abundant Torah and numerous commandments, as it is said, it pleased the Lord for his righteousness' sake to magnify the Torah and give honor to it (Is. 42:21)." God's love for Israel is an act of grace, not earned and not merited. Israel from the very beginning sinned against God, but God forgave them, so T. B.Q. 7:9: So too we find when the Israelites were standing at Mount Sinai, they sought to deceive the Most High, as it is said, All that the Lord has spoken we will do and we will hear (Ex. 24:7). It is as if He were the victim of stealing by them. Scripture says, Oh that they had such a mind as this always, to fear me and to keep all my commandments, that it might go well with them and with their children for ever (Deut. 5:29). Now if you should want to claim that all things are not revealed before Him, it already has been stated, But they flattered him with their mouths; they lied to him with their tongues. Their heart was not steadfast toward him; they were not true to his covenant (Ps. 78:36-37). Nonetheless: Yet he, being compassionate, forgave their iniquity, and did not destroy them (Ps. 78:38). And it says, Like the glaze covering an earthen vessel are smooth lips with an evil heart. He who hates, dissembles with his lips, and harbors deceit in his heart; when he speaks graciously, believe him not, for there are seven abominations in his heart (Prov. 26:23-25).

Israel's task is to accept its fate as destiny decreed by God, to be humble and accepting, and ultimately to triumph in God's time. Israel is similar to the dust of the earth, which is why Israel will endure forever: so Gen. R. XLI:IX.1: "I will make your descendants as the dust of the earth" (Gen. 13:16): Just as the dust of the earth is from one end of the world to the other, so your children will be from one end of the world to the other. Just as the dust of the earth is blessed only with water, so your children will be blessed only through the merit attained by study of the Torah, which is compared to water hence: through water. Just as the dust of the earth wears out metal utensils and yet endures forever, so Israel endures while the nations of the world come to an end. Just as the dust of the world is treated as something on which to trample, so your children are treated as something to be trampled upon by the government. That is in line with this verse: "And I will put it into the hand of them that afflict you" (Is. 51:23), that is to say, those who make your wounds flow. Nonetheless, it is for your good that they do so, for they cleanse you of guilt, in line with this verse: "You make her soft with showers" (Ps. 65:11). "That have said to your soul, 'Bow down, that we may go over'" (Is. 51:23): What did they do to them? They made them lie down in the streets and drew ploughs over them." R. Azariah in the name of R. Aha: "That is a good sign. Just as the street wears out those who pass over it and endures forever, so your children will wear out all the nations of the world and will live forever."

But Israel itself is differentiated in God's view, for if God particularly loves Israel, among Israel, his special love is for the righteous, so Sif. Dt. CCCXLIV:V.1: "...lover, indeed, of the people, their hallowed are all in your hand. They followed in your steps, accepting your pronouncements": This teaches that the Holy One, blessed be He, loved Israel as he did not apportion love to any other nation or kingdom. "...their hallowed are all in your hand": This refers to the souls of the righteous, who are placed in a treasury, as it is said, "And the soul of my Lord will be bound up in the bond of life with the Lord your God" (1 Sam. 25:29). "They followed in your steps": That is so, even if they step backward twelve *mils* and come forward twelve *mils*. "...accepting your pronouncements": They accept upon themselves your commandments: "Whatever the Lord has spoken we shall do and hearken" (Ex. 24:7).

God is present within Israel, so M. Meg. 4:4 I.14: Expounded Raba: "What is meant by what is written, 'Lord, you have been a dwelling place for us' (Ps. 90:1)? These are the synagogues and academies." At the same time, God is everywhere, and so those who trust in Him are always subject to his protection, so Y. Ber. 9:1 I:10: R. Zeira, son of R. Abbahu, and R. Abbahu in the name of R. Eleazar, "'Happy is he whose help is the God of Jacob, whose hope is the Lord his God.' What follows that verse? 'He made heaven and earth, the sea and all that is in them, who keeps faith forever' Ps. 146:5-6. Why are these passages juxtaposed? In accord with this parable. A person has a patron who is a human king. The king may rule over one province, but not over another. Even a king who would rule the whole world, would rule only over the dry land, but not over the seas. But the Holy One, blessed be He rules over the seas, and rules over the land. He can save one from the perils of the waters of the seas, and from the perils of the fire on dry land. He saved Moses from the sword of Pharaoh. He saved Jonah from the belly of the whale, Shadrach, Meshach and Abednego from the fiery furnace, and Daniel from the lion's den. In this regard the verse says, 'He made heaven and earth, the sea and all that is in them.'"

The most glorious moment of Israel came when the people stood at Mount Sinai and accepted the Torah, so Mekh. LI:I.1: Rabbi says, "This serves to express the praise that is coming to the Israelites. For when all of them stood before Mount Sinai to receive the Torah, they were unanimous in receiving the dominion of God with a whole heart. And not only so, but they exacted pledges for one another." And it was not only what was overt alone that the Holy One, blessed be he, revealed himself to them to make a covenant with them, but also over what is done in secret: The secret things belong to the Lord our God, and the things that are revealed" (Dt. 29:28). They said to him, "Concerning what is done openly we make a covenant with you, but we shall not make a covenant with you concerning what is done in secret, so that one of us may not commit a sin in secret and the entire community be held responsible for it."

A mark of how much God loves Israel is his intervention into the natural order of things in Israel's behalf, so Mekh. XXXVIII:I.4: Rabban Simeon b. Gamaliel says, "Come and take note of how valued are the Israelites before the One who spoke and brought the world into being. For because they are so valued to him he altered for them the course of the natural world. For them he turned the upper region into the lower and the lower into the upper. Formerly bread would come up from the earth and dew would come down from heaven: 'The earth producing grain and wine, yes, his heavens drop down dew' (Dt. 33:28). Now things were reversed. Bread began to come down from heaven, and dew to come up from the earth: 'Behold, I will rain bread;' 'and the layer of dew came up (Ex. 16:14)."

By the time that Israel left Egypt, it had become like the Egyptians, and God had to distinguish Israelite from Egyptian, and it is a mark of divine grace that, nonetheless, God did redeem Israel from Egypt, so Lev. R. XXIII:II.1: R. Eleazar interpreted the same verse to speak of those who came forth from Egypt: "'Like a rose among thorns:' Just as it is difficult to pick a rose among thorns, so it was hard to redeem the Israelites from Egypt. That is in line with the following verse of Scripture: 'Or has God tried to come to take a nation for himself from the midst of another nation'" (Deut. 4:34). R. Joshua b. R. Nehemiah in the name of R. Samuel b. Pazzi: "'A nation from the midst of a people' is not written here, nor do we find, 'a people from the midst of a nation,' but, 'a nation from the midst of a nation.' For the Egyptians were uncircumcised, and the Israelites also were uncircumcised. The Egyptians grew ceremonial locks, and so did the Israelites. The Egyptians wore garments made of mixed species, and so did the Israelites. Therefore by the measure of strict justice, the Israelites ought not have been redeemed from Egypt." Said R. Samuel b. R. Nahmani, "If the Holy One, blessed be he, had not bound himself by an oath, the Israelites would never have been redeemed from Egypt. 'Therefore say to the children of Israel, I am the Lord, and I shall take you out of the burdens of Egypt' Ex. 6:6. The language, 'therefore,' can refer only to an oath, as it is said, 'Therefore I take an oath concerning the house of Eli'" (1 Sam. 3:14).

Israel is especially beloved to God because God put special effort into acquiring Israel for his own, and the same is to be said of the Torah and of the house of the sanctuary, all of which fall into the same category, so Sif. Dt. CCCIX:V.1-VI.1: "Is not he the father who has acquired another meaning for the letters of the word created you": Said Moses to the Israelites, "You are precious to him, you are things he has acquired on his own, not merely what he has inherited." The matter may be compared to the case of someone whose father left him as an inheritance ten fields. The man went and bought a field with his own means, and that field he loved more than all of the fields that his father had left him as an inheritance. And so too, there is the case of someone whose father left him as an inheritance ten palaces. The man went and bought a palace with his own means, and that palace he loved more than all of the palaces that his father had left him as an inheritance. So did Moses say to the Israelites, "You are precious to him, you are things he has acquired on his own, not merely what he has inherited." "...who acquired you": This is one of the three items that are called acquisitions of the Omnipresent. Torah is called an acquisition of the Omnipresent, for it is said, "The Lord acquired me at the beginning of his way" (Prov. 8:22). Israel is called an acquisition of the Omnipresent, for it is said, "...who acquired you." The house of the sanctuary is called an acquisition of the Omnipresent, for it is said, "This mountain, which his right hand has acquired" (Ps. 78:54).

Only Israel was suitable to receive the Torah, so Sif. Dt. CCCXI:II.1, III:1: "...when the Most High gave nations their homes": When the Holy One, blessed be He, gave the Torah to Israel, he went and gazed and scrutinized, as it is said, "He stands and shakes the earth, he beholds and makes the nations tremble" (Hab. 3:6). But there was no nation among the nations that was suitable to receive the Torah except for Israel: "...and set the divisions of man, he fixed the boundaries of peoples in relation to Israel's numbers." "...when the Most High gave nations their homes": When the Holy One, blessed be He, gave an inheritance to the nations of the world, he gave them Gehenna as their share, as it is said, "Assyria is there and all her company" (Ez. 32:33). There are the princes of the north, all of them, and all the Sidonians" (Ez. 32:30). There is Edom, her kings" (Ez. 32:29). Now if you should say, "Who will take their wealth and the glory that is coming to these," one must say, it is Israel: "...and set the divisions of man, he fixed the boundaries of peoples in relation to Israel's numbers."

Israel's claim upon God is based upon Israel's acceptance of the Torah, which all the other nations rejected, so Song R. LXXIX:ii.1: "I am the man who has seen affliction under the rod of his wrath; he has driven and brought me into darkness without any light; surely against me he turns his hand again and again the whole day long:" Said R. Joshua of Sikhnin in the name of R. Levi, "The community of Israel says before the Holy One, blessed be He, 'Lord of the ages, I am he, and I am experienced in whatever you bring upon me' The matter may be compared to the case of a noble lady, against whom the king grew angry. He drove her out of the palace. What did she do? She went and pressed her face against the pillar. The king passed by and saw her and said to her, 'You have gall to cling to the palace after you were driven out!' She said to him, 'My lord, king, this is proper for me, this is good for me, this is right for me, for no other woman took you but for me.' The king said to her, 'No, but I am the one who rejected all other women on account of you.' She said to him, 'No, but they are the ones who did not accept you.' So the Holy One, blessed be He, said to the community of Israel, 'You have gall by praying to me after being driven into exile.' The community of Israel replied, 'Lord of the world, this is proper for me, this is good for me, this is right for me, for no other nation accepted the Torah except for us.' He said to her, 'No, but I am the one who rejected all other nations on account of you.' She said to him, 'How come you went with your Torah around to all the other nations for them to reject it?' 'And he said, The Lord came from Sinai and rose from Seir to them' (Dt. 33:2), but they rejected it. Then he offered it to the sons of Ishmael: 'He shined forth from Mount Paran' (Dt. 33:2), but they rejected it. Finally he offered it to Israel, who accepted it: 'And he came forth from the myriads holy, at his right hand was a fiery Torah for them' (Dt. 33:2), 'All that the Lord has spoken we will do and obey' (Ex. 24:7)."

God is so devoted to Israel that in his phylacteries is written a word of praise for Israel, so b. Ber. 1:1 III.23/6a: Said R. Nahman bar Isaac to R. Hiyya bar Abin, "As to the phylacteries of the Lord of the world, what is written in them?" He said to him, "'And who is like your people Israel, a singular nation on earth' (1 Chr. 17:21)." "And is the Holy One, blessed be he, praised in the praises that come to Israel? "Yes, for it is written, 'You have avouched the Lord this day... and the Lord has avouched you this day' (Deut. 26:17, 18). Said the Holy One, blessed be he, to Israel, 'You have made me a singular entity in the world, and I shall make you a singular entity in the world. 'You have made me a singular entity in the world,' as it is said, 'Hear O Israel, the Lord, our God, the Lord is one' (Deut. 6:4). 'And I shall make you a singular entity in the world,' as it is said, 'And who is like your people, Israel, a singular nation in the earth' (1 Chr. 17:21)."

God and Israel sing to one another, so Sif. Dt. CCCLV:XVII.1-2: "O Jeshurun, there is none like God": The Israelites say, "There is none like God," and the Holy Spirit says, "O Jeshurun." The Israelites say, "Who is like you, O Lord among the mighty" (Ex. 15:11). And the Holy Spirit says, "Happy are you, Israel, who is like you" (Is. 33:29). The Israelites say, "Hear O Israel, the Lord our God, the Lord is one" (Dt. 56:4). And the Holy Spirit says, "And who is like your people, Israel, a unique nation in the earth" (1 Chr. 17:21). The Israelites say, "As an apple tree among the trees of the wood..." (Song 2:3). And the Holy Spirit says, "As a lily among thorns" (Song 2:2). The Israelites say, "This is my God and I will glorify him" (Ex. 15:2). And the Holy Spirit says, "The people which I formed for myself" (Is. 43:21). The Israelites say, "For you are the glory of their strength" (Ps. 89:18). And the Holy Spirit says, "Israel, in whom I will be glorified" (Is. 49:3)

How then to account for Israel's present condition? The reason the gentiles rule is that Israel sinned. When Israel repents, they will regain dominion. so Est. R. XI.i.11: Said R. Aibu, "It is written, 'For the kingdom is the Lord's and he is the ruler over the nations' (Ps. 22:29). And yet you say here, 'when King Ahasuerus sat on his royal throne'? In the past dominion reigned in Israel, but when they sinned, its dominion was taken away from them and given to the nations of the world. That is in line with the following verse of Scripture: 'I will give the land over into the hand of evil men' (Ez. 30:12). In the future, when the Israelites repent, the Holy One, blessed be he, will take dominion from the nations of the world and restore it to Israel. When will this come about? 'When saviors will come up on Mount Zion' (Obadiah 1:21)."

Israel is punished for its failures and sins, and all of nature conspires to inflict the punishment and testify against them. Thus, when the Israelites enjoy merit, they testify against themselves, and when not, the prophets testify against them, so Sif. Dt. CCCVI:I.1: "Give ear, O heavens, let me speak": R. Meir says, "When the Israelites enjoyed merit, they would give testimony against themselves. So it is said, 'And Joshua said to the people, "You are witnesses against yourselves"' (Josh. 24:22). When they went wrong, as it is said, 'Ephraim surrounds me with lies, and the house of Israel with deceit' (Hos. 12:1), the tribes of Judah and Benjamin gave testimony against them. So it is said, 'and now, inhabitants of Jerusalem and men of Judah, judge, I ask, between me and my vineyard. What could have been done more to my vineyard?' (Is. 5:3-4). When the tribes of Judah and Benjamin went wrong, as it is said, 'Judah has dealt treacherously' (Mal. 2:11), the prophets gave testimony against them. So it is said, 'Yet the Lord forewarned Israel and Judah by the hand of every prophet' (2 Kgs. 17:13). When they did wrong to the prophets, as it is said, 'But they mocked the messengers of God' (2 Chr. 36:16), the heavens gave testimony against them. So it is said, 'I call heaven and earth to witness against you this day' (Dt. 4:26). When they did wrong to heaven, as it is said, 'Do you not see what they do...the children gather wood, the fathers kindle fire, the women knead the dough, to make cakes to the queen of heaven' (Jer. 7:17-18), the earth gave testimony against them. So it is said, 'Hear, O earth, see I will bring evil' (Jer. 6:16). When they did wrong to the earth, as it is said, 'Yes, their altars shall be as heaps in the furrows of the field' (Hos. 12:12), the roads gave testimony against them. So it is said, 'Thus says the Lord, Stand in the ways and see' (Jer. 6:16). When they did wrong to the roads, as it is said, 'You have built your high place at every head of the way' (Ez. 16:26), the gentiles gave testimony against them. So it is said, 'Therefore hear, you nations, and know, O Congregation, what is against them,' (Jer. 6:18). When they did wrong to the gentiles, as it is said, 'But our fathers mixed with the nations and learned their works' (Ps. 106:35), he called the mountains to give testimony against them. So it is said, 'Hear, O you mountains, the Lord's controversy' (Mic. 6:2). When they did wrong to the mountains, as it is said, 'They sacrifice upon the tops of the mountains' (Hos. 4:13), he called the oxen to give testimony against them. So it is said, 'The ox knows his owner...' (Is. 1:3). When they did wrong to the oxen, as it is said, 'Thus they exchanged their glory for the likeness of an ox that eats grass' (Ps. 106:20), he called the fowl to give testimony against them. So it is said, 'Yes, the stork in heaven knows her appointed times...' (Jer. 8:7). When they did wrong to the domesticated beasts, wild beasts, and fowl, as it is said, 'So I went in and saw and behold, every detestable form of creeping things and beasts' (Ez. 8:10), he called the fish to give testimony against them. So it is said, 'Or speak to the earth and it shall tea_., you, and the fishes of the sea shall declare you' (Job 12:8). When they did wrong to the fish, as it is said, 'And make man as the fish of the sea' (Hab. 1:14), he called the ant to give testimony against them: 'Go to the ant, you sluggard...which provides her bread in the summer' (Prov. 6:6-8)." R. Simeon b. Eleazar says, "Sad indeed is the man who has to learn from an ant Had he learned and done what he learned, he would have been sad, but he had to learn from the ant's ways and did not even learn!"

But then is Israel not just another Adam — rebellious and punished on that account? There is a distinction, which makes all the difference, and that comes in the entry of repentance into Israel's condition. Israel is the Last Adam, the opposite of Adam. Israel is the counterpart to the first man, and what happened to Adam happened to Israel, so Gen. R. XIX:IX.2ff.: R. Abbahu in the name of R. Yosé, bar Haninah: "It is written, 'But they are like a man Adam, they have transgressed the covenant' (Hos. 6:7). 'They are like a man,' specifically, like the first man. [We shall now compare the story of the first man in Eden with the story of Israel in its land.] 'In the case of the first man, I brought him into the garden of Eden, I commanded him, he violated my commandment, I judged him to be sent away and driven out, but I mourned for him, saying "How..."' which begins the book of Lamentations, hence stands for a lament, but which, as we just saw, also is written with the consonants that also yield, 'Where are you'. 'I brought him into the garden of Eden,' as it is written, 'And the Lord God took the man and put him into the garden of Eden' (Gen. 2:15). 'I commanded him,' as it is written, 'And the Lord God commanded...' (Gen. 2:16). 'And he violated my commandment,' as it is written, 'Did you eat from the tree concerning which I commanded you' (Gen. 3:11). 'I judged him to be sent away,' as it is written, ''And the Lord God sent him from the garden of Eden' (Gen. 3:23). 'And I judged him to be driven out.' 'And he drove out the man' (Gen. 3:24). 'But I mourned for him, saying, "How..."'. 'And he said to him, "Where are you"' (Gen. 3:9), and the word for 'where are you' is written, 'How....' 'So too in the case of his descendants, God continues to speak, I brought them into the Land of Israel, I commanded them, they violated my commandment, I judged them to be sent out and driven away but I mourned for them, saying, "How...."' 'I brought them into the Land of Israel.' 'And I brought you into the land of Carmel' (Jer. 2:7). 'I commanded them.' 'And you, command the children of Israel' (Ex. 27:20). 'Command the children of Israel' (Lev. 24:2). 'They violated my commandment.' 'And all Israel have violated your Torah' (Dan. 9:11). 'I judged them to be sent out.' 'Send them away, out of my sight and let them go forth' (Jer 15:1). '....and driven away.' 'From my house I shall drive them' (Hos. 9:15). 'But I mourned for them, saying, "How...."' 'How has the city sat solitary, that was full of people' (Lam. 1:1)."

When Israel is sent into exile, it is not the end of the matter, but exile involves one exile after another, so Sif. Dt. XLIII:XV.1: "...and you will soon perish from the good land that the Lord is assigning to you" (Dt. 11:13-17): It will involve exile after exile. And so you find in the case of the ten tribes that they suffered exile after exile. And so you find in the case of Judah and Benjamin that they suffered exile after exile. They went into exile in the seventh year of Nebuchadnezzar, and in the eighteenth, and in the twenty-third. But Israel retains its distinctive character through keeping the commandments, and that is why they do not perish, so Sif. Dt. XLIII:XVI.1: "...and you will soon perish from the good land that the Lord is assigning to you" (Dt. 11:13-17): God says, "Even though I shall exile you from the land to overseas, keep yourself distinguished from other nations through performing the religious duties, so that when you return, performing the religious duties will not prove new to you." The matter may be compared to the case of a mortal king who grew angry with his wife and drove her back to the house of her father. He said to her, "Keep yourself adorned with your jewelry, so that when you come back, they will not prove new to you." So said the Holy One, blessed be He, to Israel, "My children, keep yourself distinguished from other nations through performing the religious duties, so that when you return, performing the religious duties will not prove new to you."

Israel in exile is called back to the service of the Lord through prophets, so Sifra CCLXIX:II.3: "...and brought them into the land of their enemies": This is a good deal for Israel. For the Israelites are not to say, "Since we have gone into exile among the gentiles, let us act like them." God speaks: "I shall not let them, but I shall call forth prophets against them, who will bring them back to the right way under my wings." And how do we know? "What is in your mind shall never happen, the thought, 'Let us be like the nations, like the tribes of the countries, and worship wood and stone.' 'As I live,' says the Lord God, 'surely with a might hand and an outstretched arm and with wrath poured out, I will be king over you. I will bring you out from the peoples and gather you out of the countries where you are scattered, with a mighty hand and an outstretched arm and with wrath poured out'" (Ez. 20:33-3). "Whether you like it or not, with or without your consent, I shall establish my dominion over you."

Though God punishes Israel through the gentiles, nonetheless, God will avenge the wrongs done to Israel, because God avenges the blood of those who are pursued and persecuted, so PRK IX:IV.3-4: God seeks what has been driven away (Qoh. 3:15): R. Huna in the name of R. Joseph said, "The Holy One, blessed be He, is destined to avenge the blood of the pursued through punishing the pursuer. You find that when a righteous man pursues a righteous man, God seeks what has been driven away. When a wicked man pursues a wicked man, God seeks what has been driven away. All the more so when a wicked man pursues a righteous man, God seeks what has been driven away. The same principle applies even when you come around to a case in which a righteous man pursues a wicked man, God seeks what has been driven away.'" R. Yosé, b. R. Yudan in the name of R. Yosé, b. R. Nehorai says, "It is always the case that the Holy One, blessed be He, demands an accounting for the blood of those who have been pursued from the hand of the pursuer. You may know that this is the case, for lo, Abel was pursued by Cain, God seeks what has been driven away and God sought an accounting for the pursued: And the Lord looked favorably upon Abel and his meal offering (Gen. 4:4). Noah was pursued by his generation, God seeks what has been driven away: Noah found favor in the eyes of God (Gen. 6:8). Leviticus Rabbah adds: You and all your household shall come into the ark' (Gen. 7:1). And it says, For this is like the days of Noah to me, as I swore that the waters of Noah should no more go over the earth (Is. 54:9). Abraham was pursued by Nimrod, God seeks what has been driven away: You are the Lord, the God who chose Abram and brought him out of Ur (Neh. 9:7). Isaac was pursued by the Philistines Leviticus Rabbah: Ishmael, God seeks what has been driven away. And they said, We have certainly seen that the Lord is with you (Gen. 26:28) Leviticus Rabbah: For through Isaac will seed be called for you (Gen. 21:12). Jacob was pursued by Esau, God seeks what has been driven away. For the Lord has chosen Jacob, Israel for his prized possession (Ps. 135:4). Joseph was pursued by his brothers, God seeks what has been driven away. The Lord was with Joseph, and he was a successful man (Gen. 39:2). Moses was pursued by Pharaoh, but Moses, the man God had chosen, threw himself into the breach to turn back his wrath lest it destroy them (Ps. 106:23). David was pursued by Saul, God seeks what has been driven away. And he chose David, his servant (Ps. 78:70). Israel is pursued by the nations, God seeks what has been driven away. And you has the Lord chosen to be a people to Him (Deut. 14:2). R. Judah bar Simon in the name of R. Yosé, bar Nehorai, "And the rule applies also to the matter of offerings. A bull is pursued by a lion, a sheep is pursued by a wolf, a goat is pursued by a leopard. Therefore the Holy One, blessed be He, has said, 'Do not make offerings before me from those animals that pursue, but from those that are pursued: When a bull, a sheep, or a goat is born (Lev. 22:27).

It follows that what happens to Israel comes about by reason of Israel's own character, not because of what the nations do; they serve only to carry out God's will. Accounting for Israel's recent calamities, T. Men. 13:23 links specific failures to concrete events: Said R. Yohanan b. Torta, "On what account was Shiloh destroyed? Because of the disgraceful disposition of the Holy Things which were there. As to Jerusalem's first building, on what account was it destroyed? Because of idolatry and licentiousness and bloodshed which was in it. But as to the latter building we know that they devoted themselves to Torah and were meticulous about tithes. On what account did they go into exile? Because they love money and hate one another. This teaches you that hatred of one for another is evil before the Omnipresent, and Scripture deems it equivalent to idolatry, licentiousness and bloodshed. But as to the final building which is destined to be built -- may it be in our lifetime and in our days! — what is stated? And it shall come to pass in the latter days that the mountain of the house of the Lord shall be established as the highest of the mountains, and shall be raised above the hills, and all the nations shall flow to it, and many people shall come and say, 'Come, let us go up to the mountain of the Lord, to the house of the Cod of Jacob' (Is. 2:2-3). For there shall be a day when watchmen will call in the hill country of Ephraim: 'Arise, and let us go up to Zion our God' Jer. 31:6.

Israel's history, chapter by chapter, is written in terms of its virtue, and the relationship between Israel's vice and Israel's decline is constant, so T. Sot. 14:3-10: When hedonists became many fierce wrath came upon the world, and glory of Torah ceased. When those who went about whispering in judgment multiplied, conduct deteriorated. When those who displayed partiality in judgment multiplied, the commandment, You shall not respect persons in judgment (Deut. 1:17) was annulled, and You shall not be afraid of anyone (Deut. 1:17) ceased. And they removed the yoke of Heaven from themselves, and accepted the authority of the yoke of mortal man. When those who went about whispering in judgment multiplied, fierce wrath multiplied for Israel, and the Presence of God went away. For it is said, "He judges among the judges" (Ps. 82:1). When people multiplied whose "heart goes after their gain" (Ez. 33:31), those who call "bad good and good bad" (Is. 5:20) multiplied. When those who call bad good and good bad multiplied, there multiplied also those who cry, "Woe, woe, for the world." When those who draw out their spit became many, the arrogant became many, and disciples became few, and the Torah reverted only to those who study it. When the arrogant became many, Israelite girls began to accept marriage with the arrogant, for our generation sees only the surface. When they who compel people to be their business-agents became many, bribing became commonplace, and justice was perverted, And they went backward and not forward (Jer. 7:24). And about them is said what is said about the sons of Samuel, "Yet his sons did not walk in his ways, but turned aside after gain; they took bribes and perverted justice" (I Sam. 8:3). When there multiplied judges who say, "I accept your favor," and "I appreciate your favor," there was a multiplication of: Every man did that which was right in his own eyes (Judges 17:6). And the whole kingdom went rotten, declining more and more. And when there multiplied: Every man did that which was right in his own eyes, common sorts became exalted, and people of stature became humbled. And the whole kingdom went rotten, declining more and more. When envious men and plunderers multiplied (— they are those who shed blood —) those who hardened their heart multiplied, everybody closed his hand, and transgressed that which is written in the Torah, Take heed lest there be a base thought in your heart... and your eyes be hostile to your poor brother and you give him nothing (Deut. 15:9). When there multiplied those "who stretched forth necks and wanton eyes" (Is. 3:16), the ordeal of the bitter water became common. When the haughty of heart became many, contentiousness increased in Israel (— they are those who shed blood). When those who accept gifts became many, the days became few, and the years were shortened. When the proud of heart became many, disputes multiplied in Israel. When disciples of Shammai and Hillel who had not served the masters sufficiently well became many, disputes became many in Israel, and the Torah was made into two Torahs. When those who accept charity from gentiles became many — as it were — did the gentiles begin to become smaller and the Israelites to become exalted? Quite the opposite: it is not easy for Israel in the world.

Gentiles are not encouraged to become part of Israel, because of the rigors of such a commitment and the disadvantages incurred thereby; if he still persists, he is welcomed, so b. Yeb. 4:12 I.37/47a-b: A person who comes to convert at this time — they say to him, "How come you have come to convert? Don't you know that at this time the Israelites are forsaken and harassed, despised, baited, and afflictions come upon them?" If he said, "I know full well, and I am not worthy of sharing their suffering," they accept him forthwith. And they inform him about some of the lesser religious duties and some of the weightier religious duties. He is informed about the sin of neglecting the religious duties involving gleanings, forgotten sheaf, corner of the field, and poorman's tithe. They further inform him about the penalty for not keeping the commandments. They say to him, "You should know that before you came to this lot, if you ate forbidden fat, you would not be penalized by extirpation. If you violated the Sabbath, you would not be put to death through stoning. But now if you eat forbidden fat, you are punished with extirpation. If you violate the Sabbath, you are punished by stoning." And just as they inform him about the penalties for violating religious duties, so they inform him about the rewards for doing them. They say to him, "You should know that the world to come is prepared only for the righteous, and Israel at this time is unable to bear either too much prosperity or too much penalty." They do not press him too hard, and they do not impose too many details on him. If he accepted all this, they circumcise him immediately. If any shreds that render the circumcision invalid remain, they do it a second time. Once he has healed, they immerse him right away. And two disciples of sages supervise the process and inform him about some more of the lesser religious duties and some of the weightier religious duties. He immerses and comes up, and lo, he is an Israelite for all purposes. In the case of a woman, women sit her in the water up to hear neck, and two disciples of sages stand therefor her outside, and inform her about some more of the lesser religious duties and some of the weightier religious duties. All the same are a proselyte and a freed slave. And in a place in which a woman immerses a proselyte and a freed slave immerse. And whatever would be deemed an invalidating interposition in the case of an immersion is deemed an invalidating interposition in the case of a proselyte and a freed slave.

Many nations claim to be Israel, but in the end Israel will have the final say, so Song XCI:i.12-14 : R. Hunia commented, "Just as the householder does not take heed of baskets of dung or baskets of straw or chaff or stubble — why not? because they are not regarded as worth a thing, so the Holy One, blessed be He, does not take heed of the nations of the world — why not? because they are not regarded as worth a thing: 'All the nations are as nothing before him' (Isa. 40:17). And to whom does he pay heed? To Israel: 'When you take the sum of the children of Israel' (Ex. 30:12); 'Take the sum of all the congregation of the children of Israel' (Num. 1:2)." R. Nehemiah in the name of R. Abun says, "The nations of the world have no planting, nor sowing, nor root. The three matters derive from a single verse of Scripture: 'They are scarcely planted, scarcely sown, scarcely has their stock taken root in the earth' (Is. 40:24). But the Israelites have a planting: 'And I will plant them in this land' (Jer. 32:41); they have a sowing: 'And I will sow her to me in the land' (Hos. 2:25); they have a root: 'In days to come Jacob shall take root' (Isa. 27:6)." To what may the matter be compared? The straw, chaff, and stubble argued with one another. This one says, "On my account the field is sown," and that one says, "On my account the field is sown." The wheat said to them, "Wait for me until the threshing floor arrives, and we shall see for whom the field is sown." The threshing floor arrived, and when they were brought into the threshing floor, the household came out to winnow it. The chaff was gone with the wind. He took the straw and tossed it on the ground. He took the stubble and burned it up. He took the wheat and made it into a pile. Those who passed by, whoever saw it, kissed it: "Kiss the wheat" (Ps. 2:12). So it is with the nations of the world: These say, "We are Israel, and on our account the world has been made," and those say, "We are Israel, and on our account the world has been made," so Israel says to them, "Wait until the day of the Holy One, blessed be He, comes, and we shall then know on whose account the world has been made: 'For behold the day comes, it burns as a furnace' (Mal. 4:1); 'You shall fan them and the wind shall carry them away' (Isa. 41:16). "But of Israel Scripture says, 'And you shall rejoice in the Lord, you shall glory in the Holy One of Israel' (Isa. 41:16)."

This vast repertoire of propositions holds together to make just a few, entirely coherent points, showing how the system as a whole elaborates in diverse ways a small number of governing propositions. Not a single proposition just now set forth stands in unresolved contradiction with any other.

VIII.

Justice and Mercy

JUSTICE AND MERCY, DIVINE: While the principles of justice and mercy appear contradictory, in fact God balances justice with mercy. Otherwise, the world could not endure.

But justice comes first, only then to be tempered by mercy. It is through justice that God is known and exalted, and that is when God becomes great in this world, so Lev. R. XXIV:I.1: "You shall be holy for I the Lord your God am Holy" (Lev. 19:2). "But the Lord of hosts is exalted in justice, and the holy God shows himself holy in righteousness" (Is. 5:16). Said R. Simeon b. Yohai, "When is the name of the Holy One, blessed be he, magnified in his world? When he applies the attribute of justice to the wicked. And there are many verses of Scripture that prove that point: 'Thus I shall magnify myself and sanctify myself and make myself known in the eyes of many nations' (Ez. 38:23). 'The Lord has made himself known, he has executed judgment' (Ps. 9:7). 'I will make myself known among them when I judge you' (Ez. 35:11). 'And it shall be known that the hand of the Lord is with his servants, and his indignation is against his enemies' (Is. 66:14). 'This time I shall make them know my hand and my might' (Jer. 16:21). 'That you may know the hand of the Lord' (Hos. 4:24). And this verse: 'But the Lord of hosts is exalted in justice'" (Is. 5:16).

Being bound by fairness, by the rules of justice and mercy that man comprehends, God acts in a manner that is rational and subject to human comprehension. For example, God's favoring Abraham is not capricious but an act that responds to Abraham's own virtue, so Gen. R. LV:I.1: "And it came to pass after these things God tested Abraham" (Gen. 22:1): "You have given a banner to those that fear you, that it may be displayed because of the truth, *selah* " (Ps. 60:6). Since the word for "banner" shares the consonants of the word for "test," we interpret: test after test, one attainment of greatness after another, so as to test them in the world and so as to endow them with greatness in the world, like the ensign of a ship. And all this why? "...because of the truth, *selah*" (Ps. 60:6).

Since the word for "truth" and the word for "validate" share the same consonants, we interpret: it is so that the attribute of justice may be validated in the world. For if someone should say, "He gives riches to whomever he wishes, and he impoverishes whomever he wishes, and whomever he wishes he makes king all this without justice, and so too as to Abraham, when he wanted, he made him rich, and when he wanted, he made him king and all this without justice, you may reply to him, saying, "Can you do what Abraham did?" "Abraham was a hundred years old when Isaac, his son, was born to him" (Gen. 21:5). And after all that anguish, it was stated to him, "Take your son" (Gen. 22:2). And he did not demur. Accordingly: "You have given a banner to those that fear you, that it may be displayed because of the truth, *selah*" (Ps. 60:6). "And it came to pass after these things God tested i.e., displayed Abraham" (Gen. 22:1).

First comes justice: even at the moment of creation, God foresaw the future deeds of righteousness and sin that would be committed, and the day of judgment was prepared at the very outset, so Gen. R. III:VIII.1: Said R. Yannai, "At the beginning of the creation of the world the Holy One, blessed be he, foresaw the deeds of the righteous and the deeds of the wicked. 'And the earth was unformed and void' refers to the deeds of the wicked. 'And God said, "Let there be light"' refers to the deeds of the righteous. 'And God saw the light, that it was good,' refers to the deeds of the righteous. 'And God divided between the light and the darkness' means, he divided between the deeds of the righteous and the deeds of the wicked. 'And God called the light day' refers to the deeds of the righteous. 'And the darkness he called night' refers to the deeds of the wicked. 'And there was evening' refers to the deeds of the wicked. 'And there was morning' refers to the deeds of the righteous. 'One day,' for the Holy One, blessed be he, gave them one day, and what day is that? It is the day of judgment."

Divine Providence works inexorably to bring justice, however long delayed, so Hillel at M. Abot 2:6: He saw a skull floating on the water and said to it, "Because you drowned others, they drowned you, and in the end those who drowned you will be drowned." Once God has made a decree, it is going to be carried out, but it might be mitigated in some way, so Y. R.H. 1:3 III.2: Taught R. Simeon bar Yohai, "Behold, if Israel was worthy on the New Year, so that plentiful rain was decreed for them, and then they sinned, then, to diminish the rain is not possible, for the decree has already been issued. So what does the Holy One, blessed be he, do? He scatters the rain to the sea, desert, and river, so that the land will not benefit from it. What is the proof? 'To cause it to rain on a land where no man is, on the wilderness in which there is no man' (Job 38:26). Behold, if Israel was not worthy on the New Year, so that diminished rain was decreed for them, but in the end they repented, well, to add to the rain is not possible, for the decree was already issued. So what does the Holy One, blessed be he, do for them? He brings them as much as is needed for the land and calls down dew and wind so that the land will benefit from the rain. What is the proof? "Watering her ridges abundantly, settling down the furrows thereof, you make her soft with showers, you bless the growth thereof' (Ps. 65:11)." "Drought and heat consume the snow waters, so does the nether world those who have sinned" (Job 25:19) — because of transgressions done by Israel in the summer, they are deprived of the snow waters.

    The First Man brought down upon his head his own fate, and time and again, the one who is punished has no complaint, but others register a complaint; God's justice is acknowledged throughout, so PRK XIV:V.1: It is written, Thus said the Lord, What wrong did your fathers find in me that they went far from me and went after worthlessness and became worthless? (Jer. 2:5) Said R. Isaac, "This refers to one who leaves the scroll of the Torah and departs. Concerning him, Scripture says, 'What wrong did your fathers find in me that they went far from me.' Said the Holy One, blessed be He, to the Israelites, 'My children, your fathers found no wrong with me, but you have found wrong with me. 'The first Man found no wrong with me, but you have found wrong with me.' To what may the first Man be compared? To a sick man, to whom the physician came. The physician said to him, 'Eat this, don't eat that.' When the man violated the instructions of the physician, he brought about his own death. As he lay dying, his relatives came to him and said to him, 'Is it possible that the physician is imposing on you the divine attribute of justice?' He said to them, 'God forbid. I am the one who brought about my own death. This is what he instructed me, saying to me, 'Eat this, don't eat that,' but when I violated his instructions, I brought about my own death. So too all the generations came to the first Man, saying to him, 'Is it possible that the Holy One, blessed be He, is imposing the attribute of justice on you?' He said to them, 'God forbid. I am the one who has brought about my own death. Thus did he command me, saying to me, Of all the trees of the garden you may eat, but of the tree of the knowledge of good and evil you may not eat (Gen. 2:17). When I violated his instructions, I brought about my own death, for it is written, On the day on which you eat it, you will surely die (Gen. 2:17).' God's speech now continues: 'Pharaoh found no wrong with me, but you have found wrong with me.' To what may Pharaoh be likened? To the case of a king who went overseas and went and deposited all his possessions with a member of his household. After some time the king returned from overseas and said to the man, 'Return what I deposited with you.' He said to him, 'I did not such thing with you, and you left me nothing.' What did he do to him? He took him and put him in prison. He said to him, 'I am your slave. Whatever you left with me I shall make up to you.' So, at the outset, said the Holy One, blessed be He, to Moses, "Now go and I shall send you to Pharaoh" (Ex. 3:10). That wicked man said to him, "Who is the Lord that I should listen to his voice? I do not know the Lord" (Ex. 2:5). But when he brought the ten plagues on him, The Lord is righteous and I and my people are wicked (Ex. 9:27). God's speech now continues: 'Moses found no wrong with me, but you have found wrong with me.' One time the teacher belittled the boy and called him a moron. Said the king to him, 'With all my authority I instructed you, saying to you, Do not call my son a fool,' and yet you have called my son a fool. It is not the calling of a smart fellow to go along with fools. You're fired!' Thus it is written, And the Lord spoke to Moses and to Aaron and commanded them concerning the children of Israel (Ex. 6:13). What did he command them? He said to them, 'Do not call my sons morons.' But when they rebelled them at the waters of rebellion, Moses said to them, Listen, I ask, you morons (Num. 20:10). Said the Holy One, blessed be He, to them, 'With all my authority I instructed you, saying to you, Do not call my sons fools,' and yet you have called my sons fools. It is not the calling of a smart fellow to go along with fools. You're fired!' Therefore, what is written is not You (singular) therefore shall not bring, but you (plural) therefore shall not bring (Num. 20:12). For God said, 'Neither you nor your brother nor your sister will enter the Land of Israel.' God's speech now continues: Said the Holy One, blessed be He, to Israel, 'Your fathers in the wilderness found no wrong with me, but you have found wrong with me. I said to them, One who makes an offering to other gods will be utterly destroyed (Ex. 22:19), but they did not do so, but rather, They prostrated themselves to it and worshipped it (Ex. 32:8). After all the wicked things that they did, what is written, And the Lord regretted the evil that he had considered doing to his people (Ex. 32:14)."

God gives tranquillity, so no one condemns the sinner, but then God exacts the penalty, and no one can justly complain, so Lev. R. V:I.1ff.: "When he is quiet, who can condemn? When he hides his face, who can set him right?" (Job 34:29) When he gave tranquility to the generation of the flood, who could come and condemn them? What sort of tranquility did he give them? "Their children are established in their presence, and their offspring before their eyes. Their houses are safe from fear, and no rod of God is upon them" (Job 21:8). "And no rod of God is upon them" — for their houses are free from suffering. And this further illustrates that which is said: "When he is quiet, who can condemn, when he hides his face, who can put him right" (Job 34:30). When God hides his face from them, who can come and say to him, "You have not done right." And how, indeed, did he hide his face from them? When he brought the flood on them. That is in line with the following verse of Scripture: "And he blotted out every living substance which was upon the face of the earth" (Gen. 7:23).

When divine justice takes over, what a person wants is not given to him, and what he does not want is given to him, in an acute working out of exact judgment, so Gen. R. XX:V.5ff.: R. Isi and R. Hoshaia in the name of R. Hiyya the Elder said, "There are four things on the basis of Gen. 3:14, which the Holy One said to the snake: "Said the Holy One, blessed be he, to him, 'I made you to be king over all domesticated and wild beasts, but you did not want it: "Cursed are you above all cattle and above all wild animals" (Gen. 3:14). 'I made you to walk upright like a man, but you did not want it: "Upon your belly you shall go" (Gen. 3:14). 'I made you to eat the sort of food humans eat, but you did not want it: "And you shall eat dirt" (Gen. 3:14). 'You wanted to kill man and marry his wife: "I will put enmity between you and the woman, and between your seed and her seed" Gen. 3:15).' So what turns out is that what he wanted was not given to him, and what he had was taken away from him. And so we find in the case of Cain, Korach, Balaam, Doeg, Gihazi, Ahitophel, Absalom, Adonijah, Uzziah, and Haman: what they wanted was not given to them, and what they had was taken away from them."

The righteous suffer in this world and get their just reward in the world to come, but the wicked enjoy this world and suffer in the world to come, so B. Hor. 3:3 I./11a: Expounded R. Nahman bar Hisda, "What is the meaning of the verse of Scripture, 'There is a vanity that occurs on the earth, for there are the righteous who receive what is appropriate to the deeds of the wicked, and there are the wicked who receive what is appropriate to the deeds of the righteous' (Qoh. 8:14). Happy are the righteous, for in this world they undergo what in the world to come is assigned as recompense for the deeds of the wicked, and woe is the wicked, for in this world they enjoy the fruits of what is assigned in the world to come to the deeds of the righteous." Said Raba, "So if the righteous enjoy both worlds, would that be so bad for them?" Rather, said Raba, "Happy are the righteous, for in this world they get what is set aside for the deeds of the wicked in this world, and woe to the wicked, for in this world they get what is assigned for the deeds of the righteous in this world."

Even small gestures enjoy the appropriate reward, divine justice extending to every deed, so b. B.Q. 4:3 II.6-7/38b: Said R. Hiyya bar Abba said R. Yohanan, "The Holy One, blessed be He, does not hold back from any creature the reward that is coming to it, even the reward for a few appropriate words, for in the case of the elder daughter of Lot, who named her son Moab (= from father) (Gen.19:30-38), said the Holy One, blessed be He, to Moses, 'Do not distress the Moabites, neither contend with them in battle' (Deut. 2:9). The sense then is, it is war in particular that one is not to make against them, but one may well exact taxes from them. But in the case of the younger daughter of Lot, who named her son Ben Ammi son of my people, the Holy One, blessed be He, said to Moses, 'And when you come near against the children of Ammon, do not distress them or meddle with them at all' (Deut. 2:19) — not even exacting taxes from them." Said R. Hiyya bar Abba said R. Joshua b. Qorha, "One should always give precedence to a matter involving a religious duty, since, on account of the one night by which the elder daughter of Lot came prior to the younger, she came prior to her by four generations: Obed, Jesse, David, and Solomon via Ruth. As to the younger, she had none until Rehoboam: 'And the name of his mother was Naamah the Ammonitess' (1 Kgs. 14:31)."

God's punishments and rewards work themselves out in acute detail, pertaining to one man and his field, but not to another and his, all the time responding to the specific moral condition of a particular man, thus Y. B.M. 9:5 I.1: R. Huna said, "It is deemed a general calamity when the fields were blighted in that entire direction." Simeon bar Vava in the name of R. Yohanan, "And the stated rule applies in a case in which one had actually sown the field prior to the blight or locusts. For the landlord has the right to say to the tenant-farmer, 'If you had planted the field, it might have produced a large crop, part of which would have survived the blight.'" Now take note: There were other fields which were planted and were blighted and so produced no crop. So how can he make such a claim? But he has the right to say to him, "The Holy One, blessed be he, is long-suffering with the evil, and God may have shown mercy and protected his field, so that while one field was blighted, another was spared." If there were other fields, and they were smitten, it would indicate that the stated claim is null. He has the right to say to him, "To this extent I was liable and so my fields were smitten. But beyond this point, I was not liable and consequently, my moral condition would have led to the sparing of my fields from the blight, since I should have been amply punished for my sins by what happened to the fields of mine which were blighted."

God's justice is exact and metes out measure for measure. Man, moreover, has the capacity to correlate sin and penalty, e.g., M. Shab. 2:6 On account of three transgressions do women die in childbirth: because they are not meticulous in the laws of (1) menstrual separation, (2) in those covering the dough offering, and (3) in those covering the kindling of a lamp for the Sabbath. Divine judgment governs all things, and works systematically through all chapters of the ordinary world. Thus M. Rosh Hashanah 1:2: At four seasons of the year the world is judged: at Passover for grain; at Pentecost for fruit of the tree; at the New Year all who enter the world pass before Him like troops, since it is said, He who fashions the hearts of them all who considers all their works (Ps. 33:15); and on the Festival of Tabernacles they are judged in regard to water. The trait of divine justice is expressed in these terms at M. Sot. 1:9: By that same measure by which a man metes out to others, they mete out to him: She primped herself for sin, the Omnipresent made her repulsive. She exposed herself for sin, the Omnipresent exposed her. With the thigh she began to sin, and afterward with the belly, therefore the thigh suffers the curse first, and afterward the belly. (But the rest of the body does not escape punishment.) Samson followed his eyes where they led him, therefore, the Philistines put out his eyes, since it is said, And the Philistines laid hold on him and put out his eyes (Judges 16:21). Absalom was proud of his hair, therefore, he was hung by his hair. And since he had sexual relations with ten concubines of his father, therefore, they thrust ten spears into his body, since it is said, And ten young men that carried Joab's armor surrounded and smote Absalom and killed him (11 Sam. 18:15). And since he stole three hearts — his father's, the court's, and the Israelites' — since it is said, And Absalom stole the heart of the men of Israel, therefore, three darts were thrust into him, since it is said, And he took three darts in his hand and thrust them through the heart of Absalom (II Sam. 18:14). And so is it on the good side: Miriam waited a while for Moses, since it is said, And his sister stood afar off (Ex. 2:4), therefore, Israel waited on her seven days in the wilderness, since it is said, And the people did not travel on until Miriam was brought in again. Joseph had the merit of burying his father, and none of his brothers was greater than he, since it is said, And Joseph went up to bury his father...and there went up with him both chariots and horsemen (Gen. 50:7,9). We have none so great as Joseph, for only Moses took care of his bones. Moses had the merit of burying the bones of Joseph, and none in Israel was greater than he, since it is said, And Moses took the bones of Joseph with him (Ex. 13:19). We have none so great as Moses, for only the Holy One blessed be He took care of his bones, since it is said, And he buried him in the valley (Dt. 34:6). And not of Moses alone have they stated this rule, but of all righteous people, since it is said, And your righteousness shall go before you. The glory of the Lord shall gather you in death (Is. 58:8).

    A similar picture of the match of sin and punishment is at ARN XXXVIII:II.1: R. Josiah says, "On account of the sin of neglecting the dough offering, a blessing does not come upon the produce, so that people labor but do not suffice. On account of the sin of neglecting the separation of a portion of the crop for the priestly ration and the separation of tithes, the heavens will be closed up so as not to yield dew and rain, and people will be handed over to the government to be sold into slavery for nonpayment of their taxes in kind." The same view is at ARN XXXVIII:VI.1: Exile comes into the world because of those who worship idols, because of fornication, and because of bloodshed, and because of the neglect of the release of the Land in the year of release. On account of idolatry, as it is said: And I will destroy your high places...and I will scatter you among the nations (Lev. 26:30,33). Said the Holy One, blessed be he, to Israel, "Since you lust after idolatry, so I shall send you into exile to a place in which there is idolatry. Therefore it is said, And I will destroy your high places...and I will scatter you among the nations . Because of fornication: Said R. Ishmael b. R. Yosé, "So long as the Israelites are lawless in fornication, the Presence of God takes its leave of them," as it is said, That he not see an unseemly thing in you and turn away from you (Deut. 23:15). Because of bloodshed: So you shall not pollute the land in which you are located, for blood pollutes the land (Num. 35:33). Because of neglect of the release of the Land in the year of release: how do we know that that is the case? Then shall the land be paid her Sabbaths (Lev. 26:34). Said the Holy One, blessed be he, to Israel, "Since you do not propose to give the land its rest, it will give you a rest. For the number of months that you did not give the land rest, it will take a rest on its own. That is why it is said, Even then shall the land rest and repay her Sabbaths, As long as it lies desolate it shall have rest, even the rest that it did not have on your Sabbaths, when you lived on it (Lev. 26:35).

The same capacity to link the sin to the penalty reveals itself in connection with Saul, so Lev. R. XXVI:VII.5: It was for five sins that Saul died: "And Saul died on account of the sacrilege, which he did against the Lord" (1 Chron. 10:13). Because he slew Nob, the city of the priests, because he had pity for Agag, king of Amalek. "On account of the word of the Lord, which he did not keep" (1 Chron. 10:13). Because he did not listen to Samuel, who said to him, "Seven days you shall wait, until I come to you" (1 Sam. 10:8), but he did not do so. "And also because he consulted a medium, seeking guidance" (1 Chron. 10:13), "and he did not seek guidance from the Lord. Therefore the Lord slew him and turned the kingdom over to David, the son of Jesse" (1 Chron. 10:14).

Divine justice focuses upon the character of the sin, which defines the punishment. Thus, T. Sot. 3:10-12, that with which one sins is the source of the penalty: The men of the Tower acted arrogantly before the Omnipresent only on account of the good which he lavished on them, since it is said, Now the whole earth had one language and few words. And as men migrated from the east, they found a plain in the land of Shinar and settled there (Gen. 2). And settling refers only to eating and drinking, since it is said, And the people settled down to eat and drink and rose up to play (Ex. 32:6). That is what caused them to say, Come, let us build ourselves a city, and a tower with its top in the heavens (Gen. 11:4). And what does Scripture say thereafter? From there the Lord scattered them abroad over the face of the earth (Gen. 11:8). The men of Sodom acted arrogantly before the Omnipresent only on account of the good which he lavished on them, since it is said, As for the land, out of it comes bread . . . Its stones are the place of sapphires, and it has dust of gold . . . That path, no bird of prey knows . . . The proud beasts have not trodden it (Job 28:5—8). Said the men of Sodom, "Since bread comes forth from our land, and silver and gold come forth from our land, and precious stones and pearls come forth from our land, we do not need people to come to us. They come to us only to take things away from us. Let us go and forget how things are usually done among us." The Omnipresent said to them, "Because of the goodness which I have lavished upon you, you deliberately forget how things are usually done among you. I shall make you be forgotten from the world." What does it say? They open shafts in a valley away from where men live. They are forgotten by travelers. They hang afar from men, they swing to and fro (Job 28:4). In the thought of one who is at ease there is contempt for misfortune, it is ready for those whose feet slip. The tents of robbers are at peace, and those who provoke God are secure, who bring their god in their hand (Job 12:5—6). And so it says, As I live, says the Lord God, your sister Sodom and her daughters have not done as you and your daughters have done. Behold, this was the guilt of your sister Sodom: she and her daughters had pride, surfeit of food, and prosperous ease, but did not aid the poor and needy. They were haughty and did abominable things before me. Therefore I removed them when I saw it (Ez. 16:48—50).

Divine justice is so exact that when one sins, he does not gain what he wants but loses what he has. This is shown in the case of the wife convicted of unfaithfulness, T. Sot. 4:6-18: Just as she is prohibited to her husband, so she is prohibited to her lover (M. Sot. 5:1). You turn out to rule in the case of an accused wife who set her eyes on someone who was not available to her: What she wanted is not given to her, and what she had in hand is taken away from her. And so you find in the case of the snake of olden times, who was smarter than all the cattle and wild beasts of the field, as it is said, Now the serpent was smarter than any other wild creature that the Lord Cod had made (Gen. 3:1). He wanted to slay Adam and to marry Eve. The Omnipresent said to him, "I said that you should be king over all beasts and wild animals. Now that you did not want things that way, You are more cursed than all the beasts and wild animals of the field" (Gen. 3:14). "I said that you should walk straight-up like man. Now that you did not want things that way, Upon your belly you shall go (Gen. 3:14). I said that you should eat human food and drink human drink. Now: And dust you shall eat all the days of your life (Gen. 3:14). You wanted to kill Adam and marry Eve? And l will put enmity between you and the woman (Gen. 3:15)." You turn out to rule, What he wanted was not given to him, and what he had in hand was taken away from him. And so you find in the case of Cain, Korah, Balaam, Doeg, Ahitophel, Gahazi, Absalom, Adonijah, Uzziah, and Haman, all of whom set their eyes on what they did not have coming to them. What they wanted was not given to them, and what they had in hand was taken away from them.

A further accounting of how penalties fit crimes or sins is spelled out at M. Abot 5:8: There are seven forms of punishment which come upon the world for seven kinds of transgression. (1) If some people give tithes and some people do not give tithes, there is a famine from drought. So some people are hungry and some have enough. (2) If everyone decided not to tithe, there is a famine of unrest and drought. (3) If all decided not to remove dough offering, there is a famine of totality. (4) Pestilence comes to the world on account of the death penalties which are listed in the Torah but which are not in the hands of the court to inflict; and because of the produce of the Seventh Year which people buy and sell, (5) A sword comes into the world because of the delaying of justice and perversion of justice, and because of those who teach the Torah not in accord with the law. (6) A plague of wild animals comes into the world because of vain oaths and desecration of the Divine Name. (7) Exile comes into the world because of those who worship idols, because of fornication, and because of bloodshed, and because of the neglect of the release of the Land in the year of release.

Another effort to show the relationship of cause and effect in inflicting divine justice concerns the withholding of rain, so Y. Qid. 4:1 III.2:

David said, "It is on account of four sins that the rain is withheld: for the sins of idolatry, fornication, bloodshed, and publicly pledging charity but not paying it." How do we know that the sin of idolatry is involved? "Take heed lest your heart be deceived and you turn aside and serve other gods and worship them" (Deut. 11:16). What is written thereafter? "And the anger of the Lord be kindled against you, and he shut up the heavens, so that there be no rain" (Deut. 11:17). How do we know that the sin of fornication is involved? "You have polluted the land with your vile harlotry" (Jer. 3: 2). What is the punishment for that matter? "Therefore the showers have been withheld, and the spring rain has not come" (Jer. 3: 3). On account of murder? "You shall not thus pollute the land in which you live; for blood pollutes the land" (Num. 35: 33). As to the sin of publicly pledging to give to charity and not giving? "Like clouds and wind without rain is a man who boasts of a gift he does not give" (Prov. 25 :14).

Along these same lines, judgment takes place at appropriate points in the year, and through offerings Israel puts itself in the best possible light, as the season requires, so T. R.H. 1:12/T. Suk. 3:18: Said R. Judah said R. Aqiba, "Why does the Torah state that the Israelites must offer the omer at the time of Passover? Because Passover is the season of the harvest of grain. "The holy one, blessed be he, said, 'Offer before me an omer at the time of Passover so that the grain in the fields might be blessed for you.' "And why does the Torah state that the Israelites must offer two loaves at Pentecost? Because Pentecost is the season for fruit of the tree. The connection between the loaves and fruit lies in the fact that firstfruits were not brought to the Temple before Pentecost. "The holy one, blessed be he, said, 'Offer before me two loaves at Pentecost so that the fruit of the trees might be blessed for you.' "And why does the Torah state that the Israelites must pour out a water libation at the Festival of Tabernacles? "Said the holy one, blessed be he, 'Pour out a water libation before me at the Festival of Tabernacles so that the rains of the year will be blessed for you.' "God further said, 'Also, say before me on New Year the Scriptural passages concerning kingship, remembrance, and the blowing of the ram's horn: "'Kingship—so that you will proclaim me king over you. "'Remembrance—so that memory of you may rise favorably before me. "'And through what will that memory be made to rise? Through the ram's horn.'"

God responded to the sin of Israel by destroying the Temple, which was the point at which God and Israel met, so b. Yoma 1:1:1 IV.5/9b: Why was the first sanctuary destroyed? Because in it were practiced three vices: idolatry, fornication, and murder. Idolatry: "'For the bed is shorter than that a man can stretch himself on it, and the covering narrower than that he can wrap himself in it" (Is. 28:20). Fornication: "Moreover the Lord said, Because the daughters of Zion are haughty and walk with stretched-forth necks and wanton eyes, walking and mincing as they go, and make a tinkling with their feet' (Is. 3:16). Murder: "Moreover Manasseh shed innocent blood in great volume until he had filled Jerusalem from one end to another" (2 Kgs. 21:16). Therefore the Holy One, blessed be he, brought down upon them three evil decrees as against the three vices that were theirs: "Therefore shall Zion for your sake be plowed as a field and Jerusalem shall become heaps and the mountain of the house as the high places of a forest" (Mic. 3:12). But as to the second sanctuary, in which the people were engaged in Torah and practice of the commandments and acts of loving kindness, on what account was it destroyed? It was because of gratuitous hatred. That fact serves to teach you: gratuitous hatred weighs in the balance against the three cardinal sins of idolatry, fornication, and murder.

It is better for a person to die innocent than guilty, which is why justice may require preemptive punishment, e.g., M. San. 8:5: A rebellious and incorrigible son is tried on account of what he may end up to be. Let him die while yet innocent, and let him not die when he is guilty. Consequently, some people may be put to death to save them from doing evil, so M. San. 8:7: And these are those who are to be saved from doing evil even at the cost of their lives: he who pursues after (1) his fellow in order to kill them — after (2) a male, or after (3) a betrothed girl; but he (1) who pursues a beast, he (2) who profanes the Sabbath, he (3) who does an act of service to an idol — they do not save them even at the cost of their lives. The ones put to death preemptively all wish to commit rape in violation of the Torah's laws.

Man is constantly subject to divine judgment; he has free choice, hence may sin; God judges the world in a generous way; but judgment does take place, so Aqiba, M. Abot 3:15: "Everything is foreseen, and free choice is given. In goodness the world is judged. And all is in accord with the abundance of deeds." He would say, "(1) All is handed over as a pledge,

(2) And a net is cast over all the living. (3) The store is open, (4) the storekeeper gives credit, (5) the account book is open, and (6) the hand is writing. (1) Whoever wants to borrow may come and borrow. (2) The charity collectors go around every day and collect from man whether he knows it or not. (3) And they have grounds for what they do. (4) And the judgment is a true judgment. (5) And everything is ready for the meal."

Punishment in the world comes about by reason of wicked people, but once bad times take over, the righteous are affected as well, so b. 6:4 I.2-5/60a-b: Said R. Simeon bar Nahmani said R. Jonathan, "Punishment comes into the world only when there are wicked people in the world, but it begins only with the righteous first of all, as it is said, 'If fire breaks out and catches in thorns...' (Ex. 22:6). When does fire break out? Only when there are thorns. But it begins only with the righteous: 'so that the sheaves of wheat or the standing grain or the field be consumed...' What is said is not 'it consumes the sheaves of wheat,' but, sheaves of wheat are consumed' — meaning, it has already been consumed before the thorns are touched." R. Joseph repeated as a Tannaite statement: "What is the meaning of the verse of Scripture: 'And none of you shall go out at the door of his house until the morning' (Ex. 12:22)? Once permission is given to the destructive angel to do his work, he does not distinguish between righteous and wicked. And not only so, but so far as he is concerned, he begins with the righteous first: 'And I will cut off from you the righteous and the wicked' (Ezek. 21:8)." If there is an epidemic in town, stay indoors: "And none of you shall go out at the door of his house until the morning" (Ex. 12:22). And further: "Come my people, enter you into your chambers and shut your doors about you" (Isa. 26:20). And further: "The sword without, the terror within shall destroy" (Deut. 32:25).

Now as to the matter of divine mercy: God's mercy vastly exceeds His justice, so when God metes out reward, he does so very lavishly. So T. Sot. 4:1: I know only with regard to the measure of retribution that by that same measure by which a man metes out, they mete out to him (M . Sot. I :7A). How do I know that the same is so with the measure of goodness (M. Sot. I :9A)? Thus do you say: The measure of goodness is five hundred times greater than the measure of retribution. With regard to the measure of retribution it is written, "Visiting the sin of the fathers on the sons and on the grandsons to the third and fourth generation" (Ex. 20:5). And with regard to the measure of goodness it is written, "And doing mercy for thousands" (Ex. 20:6). You must therefore conclude that the measure of goodness is five hundred times greater than the measure of retribution. And so you find in the case of Abraham that by that same measure by which a man metes out, they mete out to him. He ran before the ministering angels three times, as it is said, "When he saw them, he ran to meet them' (Gen. 18:2), 'And Abraham hastened to the tent" (Gen. 18:6), "And Abraham ran to the herd' (Gen. 18:7). So did the Omnipresent, blessed be He, run before his children three times, as it is said, "The Lord came from Sinai, and dawned from Seir upon us; he shone forth from Mount Paran" (Deut. 33:2). Of Abraham it is said, "He bowed himself to the earth" (Gen. 18:2). So will the Omnipresent, blessed be He, respond graciously to his children in time to come, 'Kings will be your foster-fathers, and their queens your nursing mothers. With their faces to the ground they shall bow down to you and lick the dust of your feet" (Is. 49:23). Of Abraham it is said, "Let a little water be brought" (Gen. 18:4). So did the Omnipresent, blessed be He, respond graciously and give to his children a well in the wilderness, which gushed through the whole camp of Israel, as it is said, 'The well which the princes dug, which the nobles of the people delved" (Num. 21:18) teaching that it went over the whole south and watered the entire desert, which looks down upon the desert (Num. 21:20). Of Abraham it is said, "And rest yourselves under the tree" (Gen. 18:4). So the Omnipresent gave his children seven glorious clouds in the wilderness, one on their right, one on their left, one before them, one behind them, one above their heads, and one as the Presence among them. And the pillar of cloud the seventh which went before them would kill snakes and scorpions and burn off thorns, brambles, and prickly bushes and level down high places and raise up low places for them, so making

God's power to forgive sin, however formidable, and to reward virtue, however slight, is expressed in his acts of mercy. The mercy of God comes to expression in his deeds, so Gen. R. XXXIII:III.1: "The Lord is good to all, and his tender mercies are over all his works" (Ps. 145:9): Said R. Joshua b. Levi, "'The Lord is good to all, and his tender mercies are over all, for they are his works.'" Said R. Samuel bar Nahman, "'The Lord is good to all, and his tender mercies are over all, for lo, by his very nature, he extends mercy.'" R. Joshua in the name of R. Levi: "'The Lord is good to all, and out of his store of tender mercy he gives mercy to his creatures.'" R. Abba said, "Tomorrow a year of scarcity will come, and people will show mercy to one another, on account of which the Holy One, blessed be he, is filled with mercy for them."

God will ultimately forgive Israel when Israel throws itself on God's mercy, so b. Shab. 9:3-4 II.2: Raba expounded, "What is the meaning of this verse of Scripture: 'Go now and let us reason together, shall the Lord say' (Isa. 1:18)? Instead of 'go' what is required is 'come.' In the time to come the Holy One, blessed be He, will say to Israel, 'Go to your fathers and they will rebuke you.' And they shall say to him, 'Lord of the world, to whom shall we go? Should it be to Abraham, to whom you said, "Know for sure that your seed shall be a stranger...and they shall afflict them..." (Gen. 15:23) Ä and he didn't seek mercy for us? To Isaac, who blessed Esau, "And it shall come to pass that when you shall have dominion" (Gen. 27:40), and yet he did not seek mercy for us? To Jacob, to whom you said, "I will go down with you to Egypt" (Gen. 46:4), and he didn't ask for mercy for us? So to whom shall we go now? Rather let the Lord say!' The Holy One, blessed be He, will say to them, 'Since you have thrown yourselves on me, "though your sins be as scarlet, they shall be as white as snow" (Isa. 1:18).'" Said R. Samuel bar Nahmani said R. Jonathan, "What is the meaning of the verse of Scripture: 'For you are our father, though Abraham doesn't know us, and Israel doesn't acknowledge us, you Lord are our father, our redeemer, from everlasting is your name' (Isa. 63:16)? In the time to come the Holy One, blessed be He, will say to Abraham, 'Your children have sinned against me.' He will answer him, 'Lord of the world, let them be wiped out for the sake of the sanctification of your name.' And he will say, 'So I'll go and say this to Jacob, who went through the pain in raising children, maybe he'll ask for mercy for them.' So he will say to Jacob, 'Your children have sinned against me.' He will answer him, 'Lord of the world, let them be wiped out for the sake of the sanctification of your name.' He will say, 'There's no good sense in old men and no good counsel in young ones.' I'll go tell Isaac, 'Your children have sinned against me.' He will answer him, 'Lord of the world, are they my children and not your children? At the moment when they said to you first "'we will do" and then "we will hearken," you called them "Israel, my son my firstborn" (Ex. 4:22). Now you're calling them my sons, not your sons! And furthermore, how much have they sinned, how many years does a man live? Seventy. Take off twenty for which you don't impose punishment (Num. 14:29: Those who rejected the gift of the land were punished from twenty years of age and upward, leaving fifty. Take off twenty-five that cover the nights, when people don't sin. Take off twelve and a half for praying, eating, and shitting — and all you've got is twelve and a half. So if you can take it, well and good, and if not, then let half be on me and half on you And if you should say, they all have to be on me, well, now, I offered myself up to you as a sacrifice.' They therefore open prayers saying, 'For you are our father.' Then will Isaac say to them, 'Instead of praising me, praise the Holy One, blessed be He,' and Isaac will show them the Holy One, blessed be He, with their own eyes. "On the spot they will raise up their eyes to the heavens and say, 'You Lord are our father our redeemer, from everlasting is your name' (Isa. 63:16)."

The balance of justice and mercy, this world and the next world, proves exact, and the whole holds together in a cogent, indeed predetermined, way.

IX

KINGDOM OF HEAVEN

KINGDOM OF HEAVEN: God's rule, extending to this world. The kingdom of Heaven does not take place only at the end of time or in Heaven. God rules now, and those who acknowledge and accept his rule, performing his commandments and living by his will, live under God's rule, as in the language of the blessing, "Blessed are you, Lord our God, king of the world, who has sanctified us by his commandments and commanded us to...."

Israel is subject to the dominion of God and if properly motivated now lives in the Kingdom of Heaven. This is accomplished in various ways. First of all, it takes place through the declaration of the unity of God in the Shema-prayer, so A person should first accept upon himself the yoke of the kingdom of heaven i.e. recite the Shema' and then accept upon himself the yoke of the commandments e.g. the obligation to wear tefillin (M. Ber. 2:2 I) The holy people has accepted God's kingship at Sinai and has not got the right to serve any other, so T. B.Q. 7:5: On what account is the ear among all the limbs designated to be pierced? Because it heard from Mount Sinai, For unto me are the children of Israel slaves, they are my slaves (Lev. 25:55). Yet the ear broke off itself the yoke of Heaven and took upon itself the rule of the yoke of mortal man. Therefore Scripture says, "Let the ear come and be pierced, for it has not observed the commandment which it heard." Another matter: He did not wish to be enslaved to his true master. Therefore let him come and be enslaved even to his daughters. God's dominion, the arena of God's rule; when one accepts the commandments as representing God's revealed will, he enters the kingdom of Heaven, thus M. Ber. 2:2H-J: Said R. Joshua b . Qorha, "Why does the passage of Shema precede that of 'And it shall come to pass if you keep my commandments'? So that one may first accept upon himself the yoke of the kingdom of heaven and afterwards may accept the yoke of the commandments."

The recitation of a blessing also entails recognition of God's kingship, with the phrase, "...king of the world, who has commanded us...," and that clause is deemed essential to any blessing, so Y. Ber. 9:1 I:3: R. Zeira and R. Judah in the name of Rab, "Any blessing which does not include a reference to God's kingdom, is not a valid blessing."

The kingdom of God is no abstraction. Certain concrete sins or crimes (the system knows no distinction between them) are referred to Heaven for judgment. These include, for example, the following, at T. B.Q. 6:16: He who frightens his fellow to death is exempt from punishment by the laws of man, and his case is handed to Heaven. If he shouted into his ear and deafened him, he is exempt. If he seized him and shouted into his ear and deafened him, he is liable. He who frightens the ox of his fellow to death is exempt from punishment by the laws of man, and his case is handed over to Heaven. If one force-fed the ox of his fellow with assafoetida, creeper-berries, a poisonous ointment, or chicken shit, he is exempt from punishment under the laws of man, and his case is handed over to Heaven. He who performs an extraneous act of labor while preparing purification-water or a cow for purification belonging to his fellow thus spoiling what has been done is exempt from punishment by the laws of man, and his case is handed over to Heaven. A court-official who administered a blow by the decision of a court and did injury is exempt from punishment by the laws of man, and his case is handed over to Heaven. He who chops up the foetus in the belly of a woman by the decision of a court and did damage is exempt from punishment by the laws of man, and his case is handed over to Heaven. A seasoned physician who administered a remedy by a decision of a court and did damage is exempt from punishment by the laws of man, and his case is handed over to Heaven.

The Kingdom of Heaven is a phenomenon of this age as well as the world to come, and it involves everyday life, not only abstract existence. The doctrines in detail hold together in the conviction that God rules here and now, for those who, with a correct act of will and with proper conduct, accept his rule.

X.

LAND OF ISRAEL, JERUSALEM

LAND OF ISRAEL, JERUSALEM: The only territories differentiated in world geography are the Land of Israel and, therein, the metropolis of Jerusalem. These are heavily differentiated, e.g., as to levels of sanctification, while no other territory or city is differentiated in any way at all. But these are holy, and no other territory or city is holy. The Land of Israel is that territory that God promised to Abraham and gave to the children of Israel on condition that they keep the covenant, so Scripture made clear. Still more indicative of its enchanted standing, the Land of Israel is the counterpart of Eden, as Israel is the counterpart of Adam. Israel can make of the Land of Israel its own Eden. But losing the Land is the counterpart to the Fall from Eden.

Israel's claim to the Land of Israel derives from Abraham, so Simeon b. Yohai at T. Sot. 6:9: "Now if Abraham, who had received only a few commandments, inherits the land, we, who have been commanded concerning all of the commandments, surely should inherit the land." The Land of Israel is so distinguished because the dead who are buried there will be the first to come to life in the messianic era, being the land that gives breath to the people upon it, so Y. Kil. 9:3 VI. Dying in the Land of Israel is preferable to dying anywhere else, so Y. Kil. 9:3 VI.

The point of the story of Creation is to explain why Israel possesses the Land of Israel, so Gen. R. I:II.1: R. Joshua of Sikhnin in the name of R. Levi commenced discourse by citing the following verse: "'He has declared to his people the power of his works, in giving them the heritage of the nations' (Ps. 111:6). What is the reason that the Holy One, blessed be he, revealed to Israel what was created on the first day and what on the second? It was on account of the nations of the world. It was so that they should not ridicule the Israelites, saying to them, 'Are you not a nation of robbers having stolen the land from the Canaanites?' It allows the Israelites to answer them, 'And as to you, is there no spoil in your hands? For surely: "The Caphtorim, who came forth out of Caphtor, destroyed them and dwelled in their place" (Deut. 2:23)! 'The world and everything in it belongs to the Holy One, blessed be he. When he wanted, he gave it to you, and when he wanted, he took it from you and gave it to us.' That is in line with what is written, '....in giving them the heritage of the nations, he has declared to his people the power of his works' (Ps. 111:6).. So as to give them the land, he established his right to do so by informing them that he had created it. He told them about the beginning: 'In the beginning God created...'" (Gen. 1:1).

The Land is choice and elect, just as is Israel. God examined all lands, nations, mountains, cities, and the like, and chose the Land of Israel, Israel, Jerusalem, and the like because these measured at the top, so Lev. R. XIII:II.1: R. Simeon b. Yohai opened discourse by citing the following verse: "'He stood and measured the earth; he looked and shook (YTR = released) the nations; then the eternal mountains were scattered as the everlasting hills sank low. His ways were as of old' (Hab. 3:6). The Holy One, blessed be he, took the measure of all the nations and found no nation but Israel that was truly worthy to receive the Torah. The Holy One, blessed be he, further took the measure of all generations and found no generation but the generation of the wilderness that was truly worthy to receive the Torah. The Holy One, blessed be he, further took the measure of all mountains and found no mountain but Mount Moriah that was truly worthy for the Presence of God to come to rest upon it. The Holy One, blessed be he, further took the measure of all cities and found no city but Jerusalem that was truly worthy in which to have the house of the sanctuary built. The Holy One, blessed be he, further took the measure of all mountains and found no mountain but Sinai that was truly worthy for the Torah to be given upon it. The Holy One, blessed be he, further took the measure of all lands and found no land but the Land of Israel that was truly worthy for Israel. That is in line with the following verse of Scripture: 'He stood and took the measure of the earth.'"

God took an oath to give the Land to Israel, and that is not only a gift out of times past, but a gift day by day, so Mekh. XVIII:I.3-4: "as he swore to you:" Where had he taken the oath to you? "And I shall bring you into the land concerning which I raised up my hand in an oath" (Ex. 6:8). "and your fathers:" Where had he taken an oath to your fathers? Abraham: "In that day the Lord made a covenant with Abram" (Gen. 15:18). Isaac: "Sojourn in this land" (Gen. 26:3). Jacob: "The land on which you lie" (Gen. 28:13). "and shall give it to you:" It should not seem to you like an inheritance from ancestors but it should seem to you as though that very day it was given to you.

Merely living in the Land is a form of atonement for sin, so Sif. Dt. CCCXXXIII:VI.1: R. Meir would say, "For whoever lives in the land of Israel the land of Israel atones. For it is said, 'The people who live there will be forgiven their iniquity' (Is. 33:24). Still, the matter is not entirely settled, for we do not know whether they bear their sins upon it or whether their sins are forgiven upon it. When Scripture says, 'and cleanse the land of his people,' one must conclude that they bear their sins upon it, and their sins are not forgiven upon it." And so did R. Meir say, "Whoever lives in the land of Israel, recites the Shema morning and evening, and speaks the Holy Language, lo, such a one is destined for the world to come."

Israel's story in the Land of Israel is the counterpart to Adam's in Eden, so the Land of Israel is the counterpart, after the Flood, to Eden before, as we see when we compare Israel in its Land with Adam in Eden, so Lamentations R. IV.i.1: R. Abbahu in the name of R. Yosé, bar Haninah commenced discourse by citing this verse: "'But they are like a man, they have transgressed the covenant. There they dealt treacherously against me "(Hos. 6:7). They are like a man, specifically, this refers to the first man Adam. [We shall now compare the story of the first man in Eden with the story of Israel in its land.] Said the Holy One, blessed be He, 'In the case of the first man, I brought him into the garden of Eden, I commanded him, he violated my commandment, I judged him to be sent away and driven out, but I mourned for him, saying "How..."'which begins the book of Lamentations, hence stands for a lament, but which also is written with the consonants that also yield, Where are you . 'I brought him into the garden of Eden,' as it is written, And the Lord God took the man and put him into the garden of Eden (Gen. 2:15). 'I commanded him,' as it is written, And the Lord God commanded... (Gen. 2:16). 'And he violated my commandment,' as it is written, Did you eat from the tree concerning which I commanded you (Gen. 3:11). 'I judged him to be sent away,' as it is written, And the Lord God sent him from the garden of Eden (Gen. 3:23). 'And I judged him to be driven out.' And he drove out the man (Gen. 3:24). 'But I mourned for him, saying, How....' And He said to him, Where are you (Gen. 3:9), and the word for 'where are you' is written, How... 'So too in the case of his descendants, God continues to speak, I brought them into the Land of Israel, I commanded them, they violated my commandment, I judged them to be sent out and driven away but I mourned for them, saying, How...' 'I brought them into the Land of Israel:' 'And I brought you into the land of Carmel' (Jer. 2:7). 'I commanded them: ' 'And you, command the children of Israel' (Ex. 27:20). 'command the children of Israel' (Lev. 24:2). 'They violated my commandment:' 'And all Israel have violated your Torah' (Dan. 9:11). 'I judged them to be sent out:' 'Send them away, out of my sight and let them go forth' (Jer. 15:1). '....and driven away:' 'From my house I shall drive them' (Hos. 9:15). 'But I mourned for them, saying, How...:' How lonely sits the city that was full of people! How like a widow has she become, she that was great among the nations! She that was a princess among the cities has become a vassal. She weeps bitterly in the night, tears on her cheeks, among all her lovers she has none to comfort her; all her friends have dealt treacherously with her, they have become her enemies (Lamentations 1:1-2)."

God abandoned the Temple, then the Land, in stages, when the Temple was destroyed, so Lam. R. XXV.i.3: In ten upward stages the Presence of God departed: from the cherub to the cherub, from the cherub to the threshold of the temple-building; from the threshold of the temple to the two cherubim; from the two cherubim to the eastern gate of the sanctuary; from the eastern gate of the sanctuary to the wall of the temple court; from the wall of the temple court to the altar; from the altar to the roof; from the roof to the city wall, from the city wall to the city, from the city to the Mount of Olives. ...from the ark cover to the cherub: "And he rode upon a cherub and flew"(2 Sam. 22:11). ...from the cherub to the cherub: "And the glory of the Lord mounted up from the cherub to the threshold of the house" (Ezek. 10:45). ...from the cherub to the threshold of the house: "And the glory of the God of Israel was gone up from the cherub, whereupon it was to the threshold of the house" (Ezek. 9:3). ...from the threshold of the temple to the two cherubim: "And the glory of the Lord went forth from off the threshold of the house and stood over the cherubim" (Ezek. 10:18). Lo, it was necessary to say only, And the glory of the Lord came.... And you say, "went forth"? What is the meaning of "went forth"? ...from the two cherubim to the eastern gate of the sanctuary: "The cherubs raised their wings and flew above the earth before my eyes" (Ezek.

10:9). ...from the eastern gate of the sanctuary to the wall of the temple court: "And the courtyard was filled with the splendor of the glory of the Lord" (Ezek. 10:4). ...from the wall of the temple court to the altar: "I saw the Lord standing beside the altar" (Amos 9:1). ...from the altar to the roof: "It is better to dwell on the corner of the roof" (Prov. 21:9). ...from the roof to the altar: "I saw the Lord standing beside the altar" (Amos 9:1). ...from the altar to the wall: "and behold, the Lord was standing on the wall made by a plumb line " (Amos 7:7).

God mourned over Jerusalem like a mortal king, performing the same rites in nature that the king does in his palace, so PRK XV:III.1: Bar Qappara opened discourse by citing the following verse: In that day the Lord God of hosts called to weeping and mourning, to baldness and girding with sackcloth; and behold, joy and gladness, slaying oxen and killing sheep, eating meat and drinking wine. 'Let us eat and drink for tomorrow we die.' The Lord of hosts has revealed himself in my ears: 'Surely this iniquity will not be forgiven you until you die,' says the Lord of hosts (Is. 15:12-14): Said the Holy One, blessed be He, to the ministering angels, 'When a mortal king mourns, what does he do?' They said to him, 'He puts sack over his door.' He said to them, 'I too shall do that. I will clothe the heavens with blackness and make sackcloth for their covering (Is. 50:3).' He further asked them, 'When a mortal king mourns, what does he do?' They said to him, 'He extinguishes the torches.' He said to them, 'I too shall do that. 'The sun and moon will become black and the stars stop shining' (Joel 4:15) He further asked them, 'When a mortal king mourns, what does he do?' They said to him, 'He goes barefooted.' He said to them, 'I too shall do that. The Lord in the whirlwind and in the storm will be his way and the clouds the dust of his feet (Nahum 1:3). He further asked them, 'When a mortal king mourns, what does he do?' They said to him, 'He sits in silence.' He said to them, 'I too shall do that. He will sit alone and keep silence because he has laid it upon himself (Lam. 3:28).' He further asked them, 'When a mortal king mourns, what does he do?' They said to him, 'He overturns the beds.' He said to them, 'I too shall do that. I beheld to the seats of thrones having been overturned, now were placed right side up (Dan. 7:9).' He further asked them, 'When a mortal king mourns, what does he do?' They said to him, 'He tears his royal purple garment.' He said to them, 'I too shall do that. The Lord has done that which he devised, he tore his word (Lam. 2:17).'" He further asked them, 'When a mortal king mourns, what does he do?' They said to him, 'He sits and laments.' He said to them, 'I too shall do that. How lonely sits the city that was full of people! How like a widow has she become, she that was great among the nations! She that was a princess among the cities has become a vassal. She weeps bitterly in the night, tears on her cheeks, among all her lovers she has none to comfort her; all her friends have dealt treacherously with her, they have become her enemies (Lamentations 1:1-2).'"

Israel truly worships the Lord only when situated in the Land of Israel, so. T. A.Z. 4:5: And it says, "I am the Lord your God, who brought you forth out of the land of Egypt to give you the land of Canaan, and to be your God" (Lev. 25: 38). So long as you are in the Land of Canaan, lo, I am your God. If you are not in the Land of Canaan, it is as if I am not God for you. And so it says, "About forty thousand ready armed for war passed over before the Lord for battle to the plains of Jericho (Joshua 4:13). And would it ever enter your mind that the Israelites would conquer the Land before the Omnipresent? But the meaning is this: so long as they are located upon it, it is as if it is conquered. Lo, if they are not located upon it, it is as if it is not conquered. And so Scripture says, "For they have driven me out this day, that I should have no share in the heritage of the Lord, saying, 'Go, serve other gods' (I Sam. 26:19). Now would it ever enter your mind that David would go and worship idols? But David made the following exegesis: Whoever leaves the Land in a time of peace and goes abroad is as if he worships idolatry, as it is said, "I will plant them in this land in faithfulness, with all my heart and all my soul" (Jer. 33:31). So long as they are located upon it, it is as if they are planted before me in faithfulness with all my heart and all my soul. Lo, if they are not located upon it, they are not placed before me in faithfulness with all my heart and all my soul. Israelites living outside of the Land worship idols and do not even know it, so ARN XXVI:VI.1: R. Simeon b. Eliezer says, "Israelites who live outside of the Land worship idols in all innocence. How so? A gentile who makes a banquet for his son sends and invites all the Jews in his town. Even though they bring and eat their own food and drink their own wine and take along their own servant who stands over them and pours for them, Scripture regards them as though they had eaten from sacrifices of corpses, as it is said, 'And they will invite you and you will eat of their sacrifice' (Ex. 34:15)."

Dwelling in the Land of Israel secures Torah-learning of the highest quality, so ARN XXVIII:I.1-II.1: R. Nathan says, "You have no love like the love for the Torah, wisdom like the wisdom of the Land of Israel, beauty like the beauty of Jerusalem, wealth like the wealth of Rome, power like the power of Persia, lewdness like the lewdness of the Arabs, arrogance like the arrogance of Elam, hypocrisy like the hypocrisy of Babylonia or witchcraft like the witch-craft of Egypt." R. Simeon b. Eleazar says, "A sage who has dwelled in the Land of Israel and then left for overseas becomes flawed. One who remains in the Land is more praiseworthy than he. And even though the former is flawed, he is nonetheless more praiseworthy than all those who live in other lands never having lived in the Land. The matter yields a parable. To what may it be likened? To Indian iron that comes from overseas. Even though it is less than it was, it is still better than the best iron made in all other lands."

It is best to be buried in the Land of Israel, so ARN XXVI:III.1: He would say, "Whoever is buried in other lands is as though he were buried in Babylonia. Whoever is buried in Babylonia is as if he were buried in the Land of Israel. Whoever is buried in the Land of Israel is as if he were buried under the altar. For the whole of the Land of Israel is suitable as a location for the altar. And whoever is buried under the altar is as if he were buried under the throne of glory. As it is said, 'You throne of glory, on high from the beginning, you place of our sanctuary' (Jer. 17:12)." Living in the Land of Israel guarantees entry into the world to come, thus Y. Shab. 1:3 V.3: It has been taught in the name of R. Meir, "Whoever lives permanently in the Land of Israel, eats his unconsecrated produce in a state of cultic cleanness, speaks in the Holy Language of Hebrew, and recites the *Shema* morning and night may be certain that he belongs among those who will live in the world to come."

For the Oral Torah the union of Israelites and the promised Land marks the Land and its produce as holy, with God claiming a share as partner of the Israelite householder (farmer). The disposition of the crops is governed by the wishes of both partners, that is, God and the farmer. In the Written Torah God specified a variety of ways in which His share of the Land was to be distributed. Firstfruits, for example, are to be designated and set aside and brought to Jerusalem, to the Temple, but only by an Israelite who actually owns the land on which the produce is grown, thus M. Bik. 1:2, "You shall bring the first of the firstfruits of your land" (Dt. 26:2). You may not bring firstfruits unless all of their growth takes place on your land. (1) Sharecroppers, (2) tenant farmers, (3) a holder of confiscated property, and (4) a robber do not bring firstfruits, for the same reason: because it is written, "the first of the firstfruits of your land." Not only so, but only the seven species by which the Land is distinguished are subject to the requirement, wheat, barley, grapes, figs, pomegranates, olives used for oil, and dates for honey. A declaration of faith is made when the firstfruits are presented, in line with Dt. 26:3: "A wandering Aramean was my father, and he went down into Egypt and sojourned there, few in number, and there he became a nation, great, mighty, and populous. And the Egyptians treated us harshly and afflicted us...Then we cried to the Lord...and the Lord heard our voice...and he brought us into this place and gave us this land...and behold now I bring the first of the fruit of the ground, which you, O Lord has given me" (Dt. 26:5-10). At that point, M. Bik. 3:7: "And then he places the basket beside the altar, and he bows down and departs." So too, dough-offering is to be separated from Loaves of bread made from five types of grain grown in the Land of Israel: 1) wheat, (2) barley, (3) spelt, (4) oats, and (5) rye (M. Hal. 1:1 A).

The manner in which the Land of Israelite is to be farmed by Israelites is specified in Scripture and carefully elaborated in the Oral Torah. Diverse genera are not to be mixed together in the same field, but diverse species of the same genus may (M. Kil. 1:1 etc.). The laws of the Seventh Year, requiring that the Land be left fallow, are augmented, so that farm work carried out before the advent of the Seventh Year that benefits the crop in the Seventh Year may not be performed (M. Sheb. 1:1). The rule amplified by sages is this (M. Shebiit 7:1): They stated an important general rule concerning the laws of the Sabbatical year: All produce which is (1) fit for human consumption, animal consumption, or is a species of plant used for dyeing, (2) and which does not continue to grow in the ground for longer than one season, i.e. , plants which are not perennials is subject to the laws of the Sabbatical year, and the money receive when the produce is sold is subject to the laws of the Sabbatical year. This produce also is subject to removal the produce must be removed from one's possession when similar produce is no longer available in the fields, and the money received when the produce is sold is subject to removal. The rule of leaving a corner of the field for the gleaning of the poor is to be observed, so M. Peah 1:2: And even though they said, "Peah has no specified measure," the quantity designated should always accord with: (1) the size of the field, (2) the number of poor people, (3) and the extent of the yield. The prohibition against using the produce of a fruit tree for the first three years of its growth is enforced, so M. Orlah.

The Land of Israel enjoys supernatural grace, as shown by its remarkable productivity, so b. Ket. 13:13:11 III.33-50/111b-113a: Hiyya bar Adda was an elementary teacher for the children of R. Simeon b. Laqish. He took a three-day absence and did not come. When he came, he said to him, "Why were you absent?" He said to him, "Because my father left me one espalier, and on the first day I was absent, I cut three hundred grape clusters from it, each yielding a keg; on the second, three hundred, each two of which yielded a keg. On the third day, three hundred, three each of which yielded a keg. And I renounced my ownership of more than half of the yield." He said to him, "Well, if you hadn't been absent, it would have yielded even more." R. Ammi bar Ezekiel visited Bené, Beraq. He saw goats grazing under fig trees, with honey flowing from the figs, and milk running from the goats, and the honey and milk mingled. He said, "That is in line with 'a land flowing with milk and honey' (Ex. 3:8, Num. 13:27)." Said R. Jacob b. Dosetai, "From Lud to Ono is three Roman miles. Once I got up early at down and I walked up to my ankles in fig honey." Said R. Simeon b. Laqish, "I personally saw the flood of milk and honey of Sepphoris, and it extended over sixteen square miles." Said Rabbah bar bar Hannah, "I personally saw the flood of milk and honey of the entirety of the Land of Israel, and it extended from Be Mikse to the Fort of Tulbanqi, twenty-two parasangs long, six parasangs wide." R. Helbo, R. Avira, and R. Yosé, bar Hanina came to a certain place. They brought before them a peach as large as a pot of Kefar Hino — and how big is that? Five seahs. A third of the peach they ate, a third they declared ownerless, and a third they placed before their animals. The next year R. Eleazar came there. They brought one to him. He took it into his one hand and said, "'A fruitful land into a salt waste, for the wickedness of them that dwell therein (Ps. 107:34).'" R. Joshua b. Levi came to Gabela. He saw vines heavy with grape clusters, standing up like calves. He said, "Calves among the vines?" They said to him, "All they are are clusters of ripe grapes." He exclaimed, "Land, land, hold back your produce? To whom do you yield it? To those Arabs who stood against us on account of our sins?" A year later R. Hiyya came there. He saw them standing like goats. He said, "Goats among the vines?" They said to him, "All they are are clusters of ripe grapes. Get out of here, don't do to us what your friend did." What is the extent of the blessings that are bestowed on the Land of Israel? A bet seah produces fifty thousand kor. Said R. Yosé, "A seah's land in Judah would yield five seahs: a seah of flour, a seah of fine flour, a seah of bran, a seah of coarse bran, and a seah of cibarium ." A certain Sadducee said to R. Hanina, "It is quite right that you should sing the praises of your land. My father left me one bet seah in it, and from that ground I get oil, wine, grain, pulse, and my cattle feed on it." Said an Amorite to someone who lives in the Land of Israel, "How much do you collect from that date tree on the bank of the Jordan?" He said to him, "Sixty kor." He said to him, "You haven't improved it, you've ruined it, because we used to collect from it a hundred and twenty kor." "Well, I was talking to you about the yield of only one side." Said R. Hisda, "What is the meaning of the verse of Scripture: 'I give you a pleasant land, the heritage of the deer' (Jer. 3.19)? How come the Land of Israel is compared to a deer? To tell you, just as a deer's hide cannot, when flayed, contain its flesh, so the Land of Israel cannot contain its produce there being insufficient facilities to store that much. "Another explanation: Just as the deer is swiftest of all wild beasts, so the Land of Israel is the swiftest among all the lands in ripening its fruit. "Might you say, just as the deer is swift but its meat is not fat, so the Land of Israel ripens swiftly, but its produce is not fat, Scripture says, 'flowing with milk and honey,' which are richer than milk, sweeter than honey." When R. Eleazar went up to the Land of Israel, he said, "I have escaped one thing." When he was ordained, he said, "Now I have escaped two." When they seated him on the council for intercalating the year, he said, "Now I have escaped three: 'And my hand shall be against the prophets that see vanity...they shall not be in the council of my people' (Ezek. 13:9) — this refers to the council for intercalating the year. '...neither shall they be written in the register of the house of Israel' (Ezek. 13:9) — this refers to ordination. '...neither shall they enter into the Land of Israel'

(Ezek. 13:9) — this means what it says." When R. Zira went up to the Land of Israel, he did not find a ferry to cross the river, so he took hold of a rope bridge and crossed. A Sadducee said to him, "Hasty people, you put your mouths before your ears 'we shall do and we shall listen', you still as always hold on to your rashness." He said to him, "A place that Moses and Aaron did not have the heavenly favor of seeing — as for me, who is going to tell me that I am going to have the grace of entering it which accounts for my haste!" R. Abba would kiss the cliffs of Akko. Hanina would go out and repair the roads. Ammi and R. Assi would get up and move from sun to shade and from shade to sun. Hiyya bar Gameda would roll himself in the dust of the land: "For your servants take pleasure in her stones and love her very dust." Said R. Zira said R. Jeremiah bar Abba, "'The generation to which the son of David will come will be marked by persecution of disciples of sages.' Now, when I said this before Samuel, he said, 'Test after test: "And if there be yet a tenth of it, it shall again be eaten up" (Isa. 6:11).'" R. Joseph repeated as a Tannaite statement, "Plunderers and plunderers of the plunderers." Said R. Hiyya bar Ashi said Rab, "All of the barren trees that are located in the Land of Israel are destined to bear fruit: 'For the tree bears its fruit, the fig tree and vine yield their strength' (Joel 2:22)."

In the end of days Jerusalem will receive all the nations, so ARN XXXV:IV.3: Rabban Simeon b. Gamaliel says, "Jerusalem is destined to have all the nations and kingdoms gathered together in its midst. For it is said, 'And all the nations shall be gathered into it, to the name of the Lord, to Jerusalem' (Jer. 3:17). And further: 'Let the waters under the heaven be gathered together to one place' (Gen. 1:9). Just as the gathering stated in that passage refers to a gathering of all the waters of creation to one place, so the gathering referred to here means the gathering of all the nations and kingdoms into it, as it is said, And all the nations shall be gathered into it." Many miracles were done there, so ARN XXXV:I.1: Ten wonders were done for our fathers in the Jerusalem: A woman never miscarried on account of the stench of the meat of Holy Things. No one was ever attacked in Jerusalem. No one ever stumbled in Jerusalem. A conflagration never broke out in Jerusalem. No building ever collapsed in Jerusalem. No one ever said to his fellow, "I have not found in Jerusalem an oven in which to roast Passover-offerings." No one ever said to his fellow, "I have not found in Jerusalem a bed in which to sleep." And no one ever said to his fellow, 'The place is too crowded for me (Is. 49:20) to sleep over in Jerusalem.

I see no points of conflict among the propositions expressed in this compilation. In detail they express the same main point, as stated at the outset.

XI.

LOVING KINDNESS

LOVING KINDNESS: An attitude of forbearance and commitment to the other, modeled after God's conduct.. An act of loving kindness is one that cannot be coerced but is all the ore appreciated by God; it is an act of generosity of spirit and shows an attitude of love for the other. Loving kindness is still more valued than charity, which is more valued than all the sacrifices: M. Suk. 4:9-10 V.7-10/49A: Said R. Eleazar, "Greater is the one who carries out an act of charity more than one who offers all the sacrifices. For it is said, 'To do charity and justice is more desired by the Lord than sacrifice' (Prov. 21:3)." And R. Eleazar said, "An act of loving kindness is greater than an act of charity. For it is said, 'Sow to yourselves according to your charity, but reap according to your loving kindness' (Hos. 10:12). If a man sows seed, it is a matter of doubt whether he will eat a crop or not. But if a man harvests the crop, he most certainly will eat it." And R. Eleazar said, "An act of charity is rewarded only in accord with the loving kindness that is connected with it. For it is said, 'Sow to yourselves according to your charity, but reap according to your loving kindness' (Hos. 10:12)." Our rabbis have taught on Tannaite authority: In three aspects are acts of loving kindness greater than an act of charity. An act of charity is done only with money, but an act of loving kindness someone carries out either with his own person or with his money. An act of charity is done only for the poor, while an act of loving kindness may be done either for the poor or for the rich. An act of charity is done only for the living. An act of loving kindness may be done either for the living or for the dead. And R. Eleazar has said, "Whoever does an act of charity and justice is as if he has filled the entire world with mercy."

Acts of loving kindness are illustrated in Scripture, so Lev. R. XXIV:VIII.2: R. Simon in the name of R. Eleazar stated four R. Simon in the name of R. Eleazar said, "Who is he who did a deed of kindness for someone who did not need kindness? It was Abraham with the ministering angels. For it is written, 'And he was standing over them under the tree, and they ate' (Gen. 18:8). Now did the angels really eat? Now see how the

Holy One, blessed be he, paid back his sons: the manna, the well, the quail, and the clouds of glory that surrounded them. Now it is a matter of an argument *a fortiori*: if in the instance of someone who did a deed of kindness for someone who did not require it, we see how lavishly the Holy One, blessed be he, repaid his sons, he who carries out a deed of kindness for someone who really needs it — how much the more so will God pay back his descendants!" R. Simon in the name of R. Eleazar gave yet another example. R. Simon in the name of R. Eleazar said, "Who are they who did not do a deed of kindness with those who did not need kindness? It was Ammon and Moab with Israel. For it is written, 'It is because of the fact that they did not greet you with bread and water' (Deut. 23:5). Now did the Israelites actually need these things? And is it not so that during the entire period of forty years that the Israelites were in the wilderness the manna came down for them, and the well spurted up, and the quail was everywhere available, and the clouds of glory surrounded them. So did the Israelites really need these things? Now how did the Holy One, blessed be he, pay them back? 'An Ammonite and a Moabite shall not enter the congregation of the Lord' (Deut. 23:4). Now this fact produces an argument *a fortiori*: If in the case of one who did not do an act of kindness to someone who did not need such an act of kindness, we see how the Holy One, blessed be he, paid them back for what was coming to them, he who does not do an act of kindness for someone who really does need an act of kindness — how much the more so will God punish him!" R. Simon in the name of R. Eleazar gave yet a third example. Who did an act of kindness with someone to whom he owed it? It was Jethro with Moses. For it is written, 'He said to his daughters, "Where is he? Call him and let him eat bread"'" (Ex. 2:20). Now did Jethro show kindness to all the children of Israel? Was it not only with to Moses alone that he showed kindness. But this serves to teach you that whoever does an act of kindness for one of the great authorities of Israel is credited as if he had done it for all Israelites. It is then a matter of an argument *a fortiori*: Now if in the case of someone who did an act of kindness for someone to whom he owed it, we see how the Holy One, blessed be he, repaid him with an ample reward, how much the more so will one be rewarded who does an act of kindness for someone to whom he is not indebted at all!" R. Simon in the name of R. Eleazar gave yet a further example: "Who is he who did an act of kindness for someone who needed that act of kindness? It was Boaz with Ruth. For it is said, 'And Boaz said to her at mealtime, "Come here"' (Ruth 2:14), that is to say, draw nigh.

Love of one's brother or neighbor involves not holding a grudge; but one must rebuke one's neighbor, so Sifra CC:III.1-2, 4-7: "You shall not hate your brother in your heart, but reasoning, you shall reason with your neighbor, lest you bear sin because of him. You shall not take vengeance or bear any grudge against the sons of your own people, but you shall love your neighbor as yourself: I am the Lord" (Lev. 19:17-18). Might one suppose that one should not curse him, set him straight, or contradict him? Scripture says, "in your heart." I spoke only concerning hatred that is in the heart. And how do we know that if one has rebuked him four or five times, he should still go and rebuke him again? Scripture says, "reasoning, you shall reason with your neighbor." Might one suppose that that is the case even if one rebukes him and his countenance blanches? Scripture says, "lest you bear sin." "You shall not take vengeance or bear any grudge": To what extent is the force of vengeance? If one says to him, "Lend me your sickle," and the other did not do so. On the next day, the other says to him, "Lend me your spade." The one then replies, "I am not going to lend it to, because you didn't lend me your sickle." In that context, it is said, "You shall not take vengeance." "...or bear any grudge": To what extent is the force of a grudge? If one says to him, 'Lend me your spade," but he did not do so. The next day the other one says to him, "Lend me your sickle," and the other replies, "I am not like you, for you didn't lend me your spade but here, take the sickle!" In that context, it is said, "or bear any grudge." "You shall not take vengeance or bear any grudge against the sons of your own people": "You may take vengeance and bear a grudge against others." "...but you shall love your neighbor as yourself: I am the Lord": R. Aqiba says, "This is the encompassing principle of the Torah." Ben Azzai says, "'This is the book of the generations of Adam' (Gen. 5:1) is a still more encompassing principle."

XII.

MAN

MAN=ADAM AND EVE: Adam — "man" —may represent both genders, but when Eve is mentioned in context, Adam refers only to the male of the species.

God created Man at his own volition, against the counsel of the angels, so b. San. 4:5 V.4/38b: Said R. Judah said Rab, "When the Holy One, blessed be he, proposed to create man, he created a group of ministering angels. He said to them, 'Shall we make man in our image?' They said to him, 'Lord of the ages, what sort of things will he do?' He said to them, 'These are the sorts of the things he will do.'" They said before him, 'Lord of the ages, 'What is man that you are mindful of him, and the son of man that you think of him' (Ps. 8:5)? He poked his little finger among them and burned them up, and so too did he do with the second group of ministering angels. The third group said to him, 'Lord of the ages, As to the first two groups that spoke to you, what good did they do? The whole world is yours. Whatever you want to do in your world, go and do it.' When he reached the time of the men of the generation of the flood and the men of the generation of the division of languages, whose deeds were corrupt, they said to him, 'Lord of the worlds, did not the first groups of ministering angles speak well to you?' He said to them, 'Even to old age, I am the same, and even to hoary hairs will I carry' (Is. 46:4)."

The creation of man involved much deep thought on God's part, so Gen. R. VIII:IV.1: Said R. Berekhiah, "When God came to create the first man, he saw that both righteous and wicked descendants would come forth from him. He said, 'If I create him, wicked descendants will come forth from him. If I do not create him, how will the righteous descendants come forth from him?' What did the Holy One, blessed be he, do? He disregarded the way of the wicked and joined to himself his quality of mercy and so created him. That is in line with this verse of Scripture: 'For the Lord knows the way of the righteous, but the way of the wicked shall perish' (Ps. 1:6). What is the sense of 'shall perish'? He destroyed it from before his presence and joined to himself the quality of mercy, and so created man."

Not only so, but the angels were divided on the project, so Gen. R. VIII:V.1: Said R. Simon, "When the Holy One, blessed be he, came to create the first man, the ministering angels formed parties and sects. Some of them said, 'Let him be created,' and some of them said, 'Let him not be created.' That is in line with the following verse of Scripture: 'Mercy and truth fought together, righteousness and peace warred with each other' (Ps. 85:11). Mercy said, 'Let him be created, for he will perform acts of mercy.' Truth said, 'Let him not be created, for he is a complete fake.' Righteousness said, 'Let him be created, for he will perform acts of righteousness.' Peace said, 'Let him not be created, for he is one mass of contention.' What then did the Holy One, blessed be he, do? He took truth and threw it to the ground. The ministering angels then said before the Holy One, blessed be he, 'Master of the ages, how can you disgrace your seal which is truth? Let truth be raised up from the ground!' That is in line with the following verse of Scripture: 'Let truth spring up from the earth' (Ps. 85:2)." All the rabbis say the following in the name of R. Haninah, R. Phineas, R. Hilqiah in the name of R. Simon: "'Very' [at Gen. 1:31], 'And God saw everything that he had made, and behold it was very good,' refers to man. The sense is, 'And behold, man is good.'" R. Huna the elder of Sepphoris said, "While the ministering angels were engaged in contentious arguments with one another, keeping one another preoccupied, the Holy One, blessed be he, created him. He then said to them, 'What good are you doing [with your contentions]? Man has already been made!'"

God erred in making man, so Gen. R. XXVII:VI.1: "And the Lord was sorry that he had made [man on the earth, and it grieved him to his heart]" (Gen. 6:6): R. Judah said, "[God said,] 'It was a blunder before me that I created him below [out of earthly elements], for if I had made him of the elements of heaven, he would never have rebelled against me.'" R. Nehemiah said, "[God said,] 'I take comfort in the fact that I created him below, for if I had created him above, just as he brought rebellion against me from the creatures below, so he would have led a rebellion against me among the creatures above.'" R. Aibu said, "'It as a blunder that I created in him the impulse to do evil, for if I had not created the impulse to do evil in him, he would never have rebelled against me.'" Said R. Levi, "'I am comforted that I made him from the earth [mortal, so he will go back to the dust].'"

Man is created out of nothing in which to take pride, so Lev. R. XVIII:I.1: Aqabiah b. Mehalalel says, "Contemplate three things, and you will not come to commit a transgression. Know whence you have come, from a fetid drop; and where you are going, to worms and corruption; and before whom you are going to have to give a full accounting of yourself, before the King of kings of kings, the Holy One, blessed be he" [M. Abot 3:1). R. Abba b. R. Kahana in the name of R. Pappi and R. Joshua of Sikhnin in the name of R. Levi: "All three matters did Aqabiah derive by exegesis from a single word [that is, BWRK, 'your Creator']: Remember your well (beerka), your pit (BRK), and your Creator (BWRK). 'Remember your well' — this refers to the fetid drop. Remember your pit' — this refers to worms and corruption. 'Remember your Creator' — this refers to the King of kings of kings, the Holy One, before whom one is destined to render a full accounting."

Man was created because he had greater wisdom than the angels, so PRK IV:III.5: He was wiser than all man (1 Kgs. 5:11): [Since the verse uses for man the word Adam, we conclude that] this refers to the first Man. And what constituted the wisdom of the first Man? You find that when the Holy One, blessed be He, planned to create the first Man, he took counsel with the ministering angels, saying to them, "Shall we make man" (Gen. 1:26). They said to him, "Lord of the ages, what is man that you remember him, and the son of man that you think of him (Ps. 8:5)." He said to them, "This man whom I am planning to create in my world has wisdom greater than yours." What did he do? He collected all the domesticated beasts and the wild beasts and fowl and brought them before them and said to them, "What are the names of these?" But they did not know. When he created the first Man, he collected all the domesticated beasts and the wild beasts and fowl and brought them and said to him, "What are the names of these?" He said, "This one it is proper to call, 'horse,' and that one it is proper to call, 'lion,' and that one it is proper to call, 'camel,' and that one it is proper to call, 'ox,' and that one it is proper to call, 'eagle,' and that one it is proper to call, 'ass.'" That is in line with this verse: And Man assigned names to all domesticated beasts and wild beasts and fowl (Gen. 2:20). He said to him, "And as to you, what is your name?" He said to him, "Man." He said to him, "Why?" He said to him, "Because I have been created from the earth [adam, adamah, respectively]." He said to him, "And what is my name? He said to him, "The Lord," He said to him, "Why?" He said to him, "For you are the Lord over all those things that you have created."

Man is created as the counterpart to the natural world, so that whatever characterizes the creation of nature also marks the creation of man, so ARN XXXI:III.1: R. Yosé, the Galilean says, "Whatever the Holy One, blessed be he, created on earth, he created also in man. To what may the matter be compared? To someone who took a piece of wood and wanted to make many forms on it but had no room to make them, so he was distressed. But someone who draws forms on the earth can go on drawing and can spread them out as far as he likes. But the Holy One, blessed be he, may his great name be blessed for ever and ever, in his wisdom and understanding created the whole of the world, created the heaven and the earth, above and below, and created in man whatever he created in his world. In the world he created forests, and in man he created forests: the hairs on his head. In the world he created wild beasts and in man he created wild beasts: lice. In the world he created channels and in man he created channels: his ears. In the world he created wind and in man he created wind: his breath. In the world he created the sun and in man he created the sun: his forehead. Stagnant waters in the world, stagnant waters in man: his nose, [namely, rheum]. Salt water in the world, salt water in man: his urine. Streams in the world, streams in man: man's tears. Walls in the world, walls in man: his lips. Doors in the world, doors in man, his teeth. Firmaments in the world, firmaments in man, his tongue. Fresh water in the world, fresh water in man: his spit. Stars in the world, stars in the man: his cheeks. Towers in the world, towers in man: his neck. masts in the world, masts in man: his arms. Pins in the world, pins in man: his fingers. A King in the world, a king in man: his heart. Grape clusters in the world, grape clusters in man: his breasts. Counsellors in the world, counsellors in man: his kidneys. Millstones in the world, millstones in man: his intestines [which grind up food]. mashing mills in the world, and mashing mills in man: the spleen. Pits in the world, a pit in man: the belly button. Flowing streams in the world and a flowing stream in man: his blood. Trees in the world and trees in man: his bones. Hills in the world and hills in man: his buttocks. pestle and mortar in the world and pestle and mortar in man: the joints. Horses in the world and horses in man: the legs. The angel of death in the world and the angel of death in man: his heels. Mountains and valleys in the world and mountains and valleys in man: when he is standing, he is like a mountain, when he is lying down, he is like a valley. Thus you have learned that whatever the Holy One, blessed be he, created on earth, he created also in man."

The creation of Adam and Eve and their fall took place rapidly, within a short period of time, so ARN I:XII.1: What was the order of the creation of the first Man? [The entire sequence of events of the creation and fall of Man and Woman took place on a single day, illustrating a series of verses of Psalms that are liturgically utilized on the several days of the week.] In the first hour [of the sixth day, on which Man was made] the dirt for making him was gathered, in the second, his form was shaped, in the third, he was turned into a mass of dough, in the fourth, his limbs were made, in the fifth, his various apertures were opened up, in the sixth, breath was put into him, in the seventh, he stood on his feet, in the eighth, Eve was made as his match, in the ninth, he was put into the Garden of Eden, in the tenth, he was given the commandment, in the eleventh, he turned rotten, in the twelfth, he was driven out and went his way. This carries out the verse: But Man does not lodge overnight in honor (Ps. 49:13). And why [was man created last]? So that [immediately upon creation on the sixth day] he might forthwith take up his Sabbath meal So too ARN I:XIV.1: On the very same day Man was formed, on the very same day man was made, on the very same day his form was shaped, on the very same day he was turned into a mass of dough, on the very same day his limbs were made and his various apertures were opened up, on the very same day breath was put into him, on the very same day he stood on his feet, on the very same day Eve was matched for him, on the very same day he was put into the Garden of Eden, on the very same day he was given the commandment, on the very same day he went bad, on the very same day he was driven out and went his way, thereby illustrating the verse, "Man does not lodge overnight in honor" (Ps. 49:24).

These several propositions hold together and yield a few simple and coherent principles of theological anthropology.

XIII.

THE MESSIAH

MESSIAH, THE: an anointed man who will rebuild the Temple and inaugurate the end of days. There is more than one anointed, and more than a single Messianic task. The Messiah moreover is not the final player in the drama of the end of time.

The name of the Messiah was selected before the creation itself. For prior to creation of the world, God created seven things in preparation therefor, so b. Pes. 4:4 I.5/54a: Seven things were created before the world was made, and these are they: Torah, repentance, the Garden of Eden, Gehenna, the throne of glory, the house of the sanctuary, and the name of the Messiah. Torah: "The Lord possessed me in the beginning of his way, before his works of old" (Prov. 8:22). Repentance: "Before the mountains were brought forth, or even you had formed the earth and the world...you turn man to destruction and say, Repent, you sons of men" (Ps. 90:2). The Garden of Eden: "And the Lord God planted a garden in Eden from aforetime" (Gen. 2:8). Gehenna: "For Tophet is ordained of old" (Isa. 30:33). The throne of glory: "Your throne is established from of old" (Ps. 93:2). The house of the sanctuary: "A glorious high throne from the beginning is the place of our sanctuary" (Jer. 17:12). And the name of the Messiah: "His name shall endure forever and has existed before the sun" (Ps. 72:17).

The time of the Messiah will last for three generations, so Sif. Dt. CCCX:V.1: "...consider the years of ages past": This refers to the generation in which the messiah will be, which encompasses, in time, three generations, as it is said, "They shall fear you while the sun endures and so long as the moon, throughout all generations" (Ps. 72:5). This conviction has to be set into the context of the periods of the history of creation: those marked by chaos, Torah, and Messiah. Specifically, the history of the world is divided into three units of two thousand years each, the age of chaos, Torah, and Messiah: with the Torah succeeding the age of chaos, and the Messiah the age of the Torah: so b. A.Z. 1:1 II.5/9a: The Tannaite authority of the household of Elijah stated, "The world will last for six thousand years: two thousand years of chaos, two thousand years of Torah, two thousand years of the time of the Messiah. But because of the abundance of our sins, what has passed of the foreordained time has passed." As to the two thousand years of Torah, from what point do they commence? If one should say that it is from the actual giving of the Torah at Mount Sinai, then up to this time there has not been so long a span of time. For if you look into the matter, you find that, from the creation to the giving of the Torah, the years comprise two thousand and part of the third thousand specifically, 2,448; from Adam to Noah, 1,056; from Noah to Abraham, 891; from Abraham to the Exodus, 500, from the Creation to Exodus and the giving of the law at Sinai, 2,448 years. Therefore the period is to be calculated from the time that Abraham and Sarah 'had gotten souls in Haran,' for we have learned by tradition that Abraham at that time was fifty-two years old. Now to what measure does the Tannaite calculation deduct? Since the Tannaite teaching is 448 years, you find that from the time that Abraham and Sarah 'had gotten souls in Haran,' to the giving of the Torah were 448 years."

We can calculate the time of the coming of the Messiah, so b. A.Z. 1:1 II.9/9a: Said R. Hanina, "When four hundred years have passed from the destruction of the Temple, if someone says to you, 'Buy this field that is worth a thousand denars for a single denar, don't buy it." In a Tannaite formulation it was repeated: From the year 4231 after the creation of the world, if someone says to you, 'Buy this field that is worth a thousand denars for a single denar, don't buy it." What is the difference between these two formulations? The difference is three years, the latter being three years longer.

Other speculation on the length of the rule of the Messiah presents matters differently, so Pes. R. I:VII.1: How long are the days of the Messiah? R. Aqiba says, "Forty years, in line with this verse: 'And he afflicted you and allowed you to hunger' (Deut. 8:3), and it is written, 'Make us glad according to the days in which you afflicted us' (Ps. 90:15). Just as the affliction lasted forty years in the wilderness, so the affliction here is forty years with the result that the glad time is the same forty years." R. Eliezer says, "Four hundred years, as it is written, 'And they shall enslave them and torment them for four hundred years' (Gen. 15:13), and further it is written, 'Make us glad according to the days in which you afflicted us'

(Ps. 90:15)." R. Berekhiah in the name of R. Dosa the Elder says, "Six hundred years, as it is written, 'As the days of a tree shall be the days of my people' (Is. 65:22). How long are the days of a tree? A sycamore lasts for six hundred years." R. Eliezer b. R. Yosé, the Galilean says, "A thousand years, as it is written, 'For a thousand years in your sight as are but as yesterday when it has passed' (Ps. 90:40), and it is written, 'The day of vengeance as in my heart but now my year of redemption is come' (Is. 63:4). The day of the Holy One, blessed be he, is the same as a thousand years for a mortal." R. Joshua says, "Two thousand years, 'according to the days in which you afflicted us' (Ps. 90:15). For there are no fewer days as in the cited verse than two, and the day of the Holy One, blessed be he, is the same as a thousand years for a mortal." R. Abbahu says, "Seven thousand years, as it is said, 'As a bride groom rejoices over his bride will your God rejoice over you' (Is. 62:5), and how long does a groom rejoice over his bride? It is seven days, and the day of the Holy One, blessed be he, is the same as a thousand years for a mortal." Rabbi says, "You cannot count it: 'For the day of vengeance that was in my heart and my year of redemption have come' (Is. 63:4). How long are the days of the Messiah? Three hundred and sixty-five thousand years will be the length of the days of the Messiah."

There will be more than a single Messiah, There will be a Messiah, son of David, following the Messiah, son of Joseph, who will be called: so M. Suk. 5:1-4 II.5/b. 52a: To the Messiah, son of David, who is destined to be revealed — speedily, in our days! — the Holy One, blessed be he, will say, "Ask something from me, and I shall give it to you." So it is said, "I will tell of the decree... this day have I begotten you, ask of me and I will give the nations for your inheritance" (Ps. 2:7-8). When the Messiah, son of David sees the Messiah, son of Joseph, killed, he will say before God, "Lord of the Age, I ask of you only life." He will say to him, "Life? Before you spoke of it, David your father had already prophesied about you, as it is said, 'He asked life of you, you gave it to him, even length of days forever and ever' (Ps. 21:5)."

The task of the king-messiah is to gather the exiles, so Gen. R. XCVIII:IX.2: Said R. Hanin, "Israel does not require the learning of the king-messiah in the age to come, as it is said, 'Unto him shall *the nations* seek' (Is. 11:1) — but not Israel. If so, why will the king-messiah come?

And what will he come to do? It is to gather together the exiles of Israel and to give them thirty religious duties: 'And I said to them, If you think good, give me my hire, and if not, forbear. So they weighed for my hire thirty - pieces of silver' (Zech. 11:12)." Rab said, "These refer to thirty heroes." R. Yohanan said, "These refer to thirty religious duties." They said to R. Yohanan, "Have you not accepted the view of Rab that the passage speaks only of the nations of the world?"

The Messiah was born on the day that the Temple was destroyed, as proven by the verse, "Lebanon with its majestic trees will fall" (Isa. 10:34). And what follows this? "There shall come forth a shoot from the stump of Jesse" (Isa. 11:1). Right after an allusion to the destruction of the Temple the prophet speaks of the Messiah. The same view is contained within the following story at Y. Ber. 2:6 II.4: Once a Jew was plowing and his ox snorted once before him. An Arab who was passing and heard the sound said to him, "Jew, Jew. Loosen your ox, and loosen your plow and stop plowing. For today your Temple was destroyed." The ox snorted again. He the Arab said to him, "Jew, Jew. Bind your ox, and bind your plow. For today the Messiah-king was born." He said to him, "What is his name?" The Arab replied, "Menahem." He said to him, "And what is his father's name?" He the Arab said to him, "Hezekiah." He said to him, "Where is he from?" He said to him, "From the royal capital of Bethlehem in Judea." He the Jew went and sold his ox and sold his plow. And he became a peddler of infants' clothes diapers. And he went from place to place until he came to that very city. All of the women bought from him. But Menahem's mother did not buy from him. He heard the women saying, "Menahem's mother, Menahem's mother, come buy for your child." She said, "I want to choke this enemy of Israel. For on the day he was born the Temple was destroyed." This Jew said to her, "We are sure that on this day it was destroyed, and on this day of the year it will be rebuilt. Do not abandon the child. Provide for him." She said to him the peddler, "I have no money." He said to her, "It is of no matter to me. Come and buy for him and if you have no money, pay me when I return." After a while he returned. He went up to that place. He said to her, "What happened to the infant?" She said to him, "Since the time you saw him a spirit came and carried him up and took him away from me."

The same view is set forth in a comparable narrative, at Lam. R.

L.:i:14: There was a man who was ploughing, and one of his oxen lowed. An Arab came by and said to him, "What are you?" He said to him, "I am a Jew." He said to him, "Untie your ox and your plough." He said to him, "Why?" He said to him, "Because the house of the sanctuary of the Jews has been destroyed." He said to him, "How do you know?" He said to him, "I know from the lowing of your ox." While he was engaged with him, the ox lowed again. He said to him, "Harness your ox and tie on your plough, for the redeemer of the Jews has been born." He said to him, "What is his name?" He said to him, "His name is Menahem Redeemer." "And as to his father, what is his name?" He said to him, "Hezekiah." He said to him, "And where do they live? He said to him, "In Birat Arba in Bethlehem in Judah." That man went and sold his oxen and sold his plough and bought felt clothing for children. He went into one city and left another, went into one country and left another, until he got there. All the villagers came to buy from him. But the woman who was the mother of that infant did not buy from him. He said to her, "Why didn't you buy children's felt clothing from me?" She said to him, "Because a hard fate is in store for my child." He said to her, "Why?" She said to him, "Because at his coming the house of the sanctuary was destroyed." He said to her, "We trust in the Master of the world that just as at his coming it was destroyed, so at his coming it will be rebuilt." He said to her, "Now you take for yourself some of these children's felt garments." She said to him, "I haven't got any money." He said to her, "What difference does it make to you! Take them now, and after a few days I'll come and collect." She took the clothes and went away. After a few days that man said, "I'm going to go and see how that infant is doing." He came to her and said to her, "As to that child, how is he doing?" She said to him, "Didn't I tell you that a hard fate is in store for him? Misfortune has dogged him. "From the moment you left, strong winds have come and a whirlwind and swept him off and have gone on." He said to her, "Did I not say to you that just as at his coming it was destroyed, so at his coming it will be rebuilt?"

The nations will bring gifts to the Messiah, and it will be a great honor to them that they are permitted to do so, so b. Pes. 10:7 II.22/118b: "Egypt is destined to bring a gift to the Messiah. He will think that he should not accept it from them. The Holy One, blessed be He, will say to the Messiah, 'Accept it from them, they provided shelter for my children in Egypt.' Forthwith: 'Nobles shall come out of Egypt, bringing gifts' (Ps. 68:32). The Ethiopians will propose an argument a fortiori concerning themselves, namely: 'If these, who subjugated them, do this, we, who never subjugated them, all the more so!' The Holy One, blessed be He, will say to the Messiah, 'Accept it from them.' Forthwith: 'Ethiopia shall hasten to stretch out her hands to God' (Ps. 68:32). Wicked Rome will then propose the same argument a fortiori in her own regard: 'If these, who are not their brethren, are such, then we, who are their brethren, all the more so!' The Holy One, blessed be He, will say to Gabriel, 'Rebuke the wild beast of the reeds, the multitude of the bulls' (Ps. 68:32) — 'rebuke the wild beast and take possession of the congregation.' Another interpretation: 'Rebuke the wild beast of the reeds' — who dwells among the reeds, 'the boar out of the wood ravages it, that which moves in the field feeds on it' (Ps. 80:14)."

The Messiah will come whenever Israel wants, specifically, if Israel repents on day, that will conclude the matter, so Y. Ta. 1:1 II.5: The Israelites said to Isaiah, "O our Rabbi, Isaiah, What will come for us out of this night?" He said to them, "Wait for me, until I can present the question." Once he had asked the question, he came back to them. They said to him, "Watchman, what of the night? What did the Guardian of the ages say a play on 'of the night' and 'say'?" He said to them, "The watchman says: 'Morning comes; and also the night. If you will inquire, inquire; come back again'" (Is. 21:12). They said to him, "Also the night?" He said to them, "It is not what you are thinking. But there will be morning for the righteous, and night for the wicked, morning for Israel, and night for idolaters." They said to him, "When?" He said to them, "Whenever you want, He too wants it to be — if you want it, he wants it." They said to him, "What is standing in the way?" He said to them, "Repentance: 'come back again'" (Is. 21:12). R. Aha in the name of R. Tanhum b. R. Hiyya, "If Israel repents for one day, forthwith the son of David will come. What is the scriptural basis? 'O that today you would hearken to his voice!'" (Ps. 95:7). Said R Levi, "If Israel would keep a single Sabbath in the proper way, forthwith the son of David will come. What is the scriptural basis for this view? 'Moses said, Eat it today, for today is a Sabbath to the Lord; today you will not find it in the field' (Ex. 16:25). And it says, 'For thus said the Lord God, the Holy One of Israel, 'In returning and rest you shall be saved; in quietness and in trust shall be your strength.' And you would not'" (Is. 30:15). By means of returning and Sabbath rest you will be redeemed.

The Messiah will come at the right time, which is when Israel is in greatest need of his advent, so b. San. 11:1 I.81-2, 87, 90-92, 97/96b-97a: Said R. Nahman to R. Isaac, "Have you heard when the son of 'the fallen one' will come?" He said to him, "Who is the son of 'the fallen one'?" He said to him, "It is the Messiah." "Do you call the Messiah 'the son of the fallen one'?" He said to him, "Yes, for it is written, 'On that day I will raise up the tabernacle of David, the fallen one' (Amos 9:11)." He said to him, "This is what R. Yohanan said, 'The generation to which the son of David will come will be one in which disciples of sages grow fewer, 'and, as to the others, their eyes will wear out through suffering and sighing, and troubles will be many, and laws harsh, forever renewing themselves so that the new one will hasten onward before the old one has come to an end.'" The seven year cycle in which the son of David will come: As to the first one, the following verse of Scripture will be fulfilled: "And I will cause it to rain upon one city and not upon another" (Amos 4:7). As to the second year, the arrows of famine will be sent forth. As to the third, there will be a great famine, in which men, women, and children will die, pious men and wonder-workers alike, and the Torah will be forgotten by those that study it. As to the fourth year, there will be plenty which is no plenty. As to the fifth year, there will be great prosperity, and people will eat, drink, and rejoice, and the Torah will be restored to those that study it. As to the sixth year, there will be rumors. As to the seventh year, there will be wars. As to the end of the seventh year (the eighth year), the son of David will come. "For the Lord shall judge his people and repent himself of his servants, when he sees that their power has gone, and there is none shut up or left" (Deut. 32:36). The son of David will come only when traitors are many. Another matter: Only when disciples are few. Another matter: Only when a penny will not be found in anyone's pocket. Another matter: Only when people will have given up hope of redemption, as it is said, "There is none shut up or left" (Deut. 32:36), as it were, when there is none God being absent who supports and helps Israel. Said Elijah to R. Sala the Pious, "The world will last for no fewer than eighty-five Jubilees of fifty years each, and the son of David will come in the last one." He said to him, "Will it be in the first or the last year of the last Jubilee?" He said to him,

"I do not know." "Will it come at the end or not come at the end of the fiftieth year?" He said to him, "I do not know." R. Hanan, son of Tahalipa, sent to R. Joseph, "I came across a man who had in hand a scroll, written in Assyrian block letters in the holy language. I said to him, 'Where did you get this?' He said to me, 'I was employed in the Roman armies, and I found it in the Roman archives.' In the scroll it is written that after four thousand two hundred ninety-two years from the creation of the world, the world will be an orphan. As to the years to follow in some there will be wars of the great dragons, and in some, wars of Gog and Magog, and the rest will be the days of the Messiah. And the Holy One, blessed be he, will renew his world only after seven thousand years." R. Nathan says, "This verse of Scripture pierces to the depth: 'For the vision is yet for an appointed time, but at the end it shall speak and not lie; though he tarry, wait for him; because it will surely come, it will not tarry' (Hab. 2:3)." This is not in accord with our rabbis, who interpreted, "Until a time and times and the dividing of time" (Dan. 7:25). Nor does it accord with R. Simlai, who would interpret, "You feed them with the bread of tears and given them tears to drink a third time" (Ps. 80:6). Nor does it accord with R. Aqiba, who would interpret the verse, "Yet once, it is a little while, and I will shake the heavens and the earth" (Hag. 2:6). Rather, the first kingdom will last for seventy years, the second kingdom for fifty-two years, and the kingdom of Ben Koziba will be for two and a half years. Said R. Hanina, "The son of David will come only when a fish will be sought for a sick person and not be found, as it is said, 'Then I will make their waters deep and cause their rivers to run like oil' (Ez. 32:14), and it is written, 'In that day I will cause the horn of the house of Israel to sprout forth' (Ez. 29:21)." Said R. Hama bar Hanina, "The son of David will come only when the rule over Israel by the least of the kingdoms will come to an end, as it is said, 'He shall both cut off the springs with pruning hooks and take away and cut down the branches' (Is. 18:5), and further: 'In that time shall the present be brought to the Lord of hosts of a people that is scattered and peeled' (Is. 18:7)." Said Zeiri said R. Hanina, "The son of David will come only when arrogant people will no longer be found in Israel, as it is said, 'For then I will take away out of the midst of you those who rejoice in your pride' (Zeph. 8:11), followed by: 'I will also leave in the midst of you an afflicted and poor people, and they shall take refuge in the name of the Lord'

(Zeph. 3:12)." Said R. Simlai in the name of R. Eliezer b. R. Simeon, "The son of David will come only when all judges and rulers come to an end in Israel, as it is said, 'And I will turn my hand upon you and purely purge away your dross and take away all your tin, and I will restore your judges as at the first' (Is. 1:25-26)." Said Ulla, "Jerusalem will be redeemed only through righteousness, as it is written, 'Zion shall be redeemed with judgment and her converts with righteousness' (Is. 1:27)." Said R. Yohanan, "If you see a generation growing less and less, hope for him, as it is said, 'And the afflicted people will you save' (2 Sam. 22:28)." Said R. Yohanan, "If you see a generation over which many troubles flow like a river, hope for him, as it is written, 'When the enemy shall come in like a flood, the spirit of the Lord shall lift up a standard against him' (Is. 59:19), followed by: 'And the redeemer shall come to Zion' (Is. 59:20)." And said R. Yohanan, "The son of David will come to a generation that is either entirely righteous or entirely wicked. A generation that is entirely righteous, as it is written, 'Your people also shall be all righteous, they shall inherit the land for ever' (Is. 60:21), or a generation that is entirely wicked, as it is written, 'And he saw that there was no man and wondered that there was no intercessor' (Is. 59:16), and it is written, 'For my own sake, even for my own sake I will do it' (Is. 60:22)."

Further speculation on when the Messiah will come includes the following, at b. San. 11:1 I.103-104, 110/98a-99a: His disciples asked R. Yosé, b. Qisma, "When is the son of David coming?" He said to them, "I am afraid to answer, lest you ask an omen from me that my answer is right." They said to him, "We shall not ask for an omen from you." He said to them, "When this gate falls and is rebuilt, falls and is rebuilt, and falls a third time. They will not suffice to rebuild it before the son of David will come." They said to him, "Our master, give us an omen." He said to them, "But did you not say to me that you would not ask for an omen from me?" They said to him, "Even so." He said to them, "Then let the waters of the grotto of Banias turn to blood," and they turned to blood. When he died, he said to them, "Dig my bier deep into the ground, for there is not a palm tree in Babylonia on which a Persian horse has not been tied, nor is there a bier in the land of Israel from which a Median horse will not eat straw." Said Rab, "The son of David will come only when the monarchy of Rome will spread over Israel for nine months, as it is said, 'Therefore will he give them up, until the time that she who travails has brought forth; then the remnant of his brethren shall return to the children of Israel' (Mic. 5:2)." R. Simlai interpreted the following verse: "What is the meaning of that which is written, 'Woe to you who desire the day of the Lord! to what end is it for you? the day of the Lord is darkness and not light' (Amos 5:18)? The matter may be compared to the case of the cock and the bat who were waiting for light. The cock said to the bat, 'I am waiting for the light, for the light belongs to me, but what do you need light for?'" That is in line with what a min said to R. Abbahu, "When is the Messiah coming?" He said to him, "When darkness covers those men." He said to him, "You are cursing me." He said to him, "I am merely citing a verse of Scripture: 'For behold, the darkness shall cover the earth, and great darkness the people, but the Lord shall shine upon you, and his glory shall be seen upon you' (Is. 60:2)."

When the Messiah comes, he will gather the exiles back to the land, so Song R. LII:ii.1ff.: "Depart from the peak of Amana, from the peak of Senir and Hermon, from the dens of lions, from the mountains of leopards:" Said R. Hunia in the name of R. Justus, "When the exiles returning to Zion when the Messiah brings them back reach Taurus Munus, they are going to say a Song. And the nations of the world are going to bring them like princes to the Messiah." What verse of Scripture indicates it? 'Depart from the peak of Amana.' The sense of the word for 'depart' is only 'offering,' as in the following verse: 'There is not a present to bring to the man of God' (1 Sam. 9:7)." God speaks, 'Have I not done as much in the time of Hazael: "So Hazael went to meet him and took a present with him, even of every good thing of Damascus, forty camels' burden" (2 Kgs. 8:9).' But the nations of the world are going to bring them as gifts to the royal messiah: 'And they shall bring all your brethren out of all the nations for an offering to the Lord, upon horses and in chariots and in litters and on mules and upon swift beasts' (Isa. 66:2). That view, that the nations will present Israel as a gift to the Messiah, is in line with this verse of Scripture: 'Give to the Lord families, you peoples' (Ps. 96:7)." Said R. Aha, "What is written is not, 'Peoples, give to the Lord the families,' but 'give...families, you peoples, give to the Lord glory and strength.' The meaning is, 'When you bring them, do not bring them in a casual way, but with 'glory and strength.'"

It follows that one's location when the Messiah comes makes a difference. Where one is located when the Messianic age or the age to come dawns is an open question. b. Ket. 13:11 III.16-17/111a-b: Said Abbayye, "We hold a tradition that Babylonia will not see the birth pangs of the Messiah." He explained this to speak to Husal in Benjamin, which he called, "the corner of refuge." Said R. Eleazar, "The dead that are abroad will not come back to life: 'And I will set glory in the land of the living' (Ezek. 26:20) — the dead buried in the land where I have my desire will live, but the dead of the land in which I have no desire won't live." Objected R. Abba bar Mammal, "'Your dead shall live, my dead bodies shall arise' (Isa. 26:19) — doesn't 'your dead shall live' mean, they will live among the dead that are in the Land of Israel, and doesn't 'my dead bodies shall arise' mean, to the dead outside of the Land; and doesn't 'and I will give glory in the Land of Israel' refer to Nebuchadnezzar, concerning whom the All-Merciful has said, 'I will bring against them a king who is as swift as a stag'?" He said to him, "My lord, I expound another verse of Scripture: 'He who gives breath to the people upon it, and spirit to them that walk therein' (Isa. 42:5)." But isn't it written, My dead bodies shall arise? That refers to abortions. And R. Abba bar Mammal— how does he interpret the verse, He who gives breath to the people upon it, and spirit to them that walk therein? He requires it in line with what R. Abbahu said, for said R. Abbahu, "Even a Canaanite slave girl located in the Land of Israel is certain that she will belong to the world to come. Here it is written, 'He who gives breath to the people upon it,' and elsewhere, 'Abide you here with the ass' (Gen. 22:5) — 'a people that are like an ass.'" "And spirit to them that walk therein": Said R. Jeremiah bar Abbah said R. Yohanan, "Whoever walks four cubits in the Land of Israel is certain that he will belong to the world to come." "You shall carry me out of Egypt and bury me in their burial ground" (Gen. 47:30): Said Qarna, "There is something hidden here. Jacob our father knew full well that he was completely righteous, and, if the dead who are outside of the Land will live, why in the world did he make so much trouble for his children? It is since he might not have sufficient grace accorded to him to roll through the paths."

The Messiah's age will be brief and will come to an end, so b. San. 11:1 I.111/99a: R. Eliezer says, "The days of the Messiah will last forty years, as it is said, 'Forty years long shall I take hold of the generation' (Ps.

95:10)." R. Eliezer b. Azariah says, "Seventy years, as it is said, 'And it shall come to pass in that day that Tyre shall be forgotten seventy years, according to the days of one king' (Is. 23:15). Now what would be a one and singular king? We must say that it is the Messiah." Rabbi says, "Three generations, as it is said, 'They shall fear you with the sun and before the moon, a generation and generations' (Ps. 72:5)." R. Eliezer says, "The days of the Messiah will last for forty years. Here it is written, 'And he afflicted you and made you hunger and fed you with manna' (Deut. 8:3), and elsewhere: 'Make us glad according to the days forty years in the wilderness in which you have afflicted us' (Ps. 90:15)." R. Dosa says, "Four hundred years. Here it is written, 'And they shall serve them and they shall afflict them four hundred years' (Gen. 15:13), and elsewhere: 'Make us glad according to the days wherein you have afflicted us' (Ps. 90:15)." Rabbi says, "Three hundred and sixty-five years, according to the number of days in the solar year, as it is said, 'For the day of vengeance is in my heart and the year of my redemption has come' (Is. 63:4)." Abimi, son of R. Abbahu, stated on Tannaite authority, "The days of the Messiah for Israel will be seven thousand years, as it is said, 'And as the bridegroom rejoices over the bride a week, so shall your God rejoice over you' (Is. 62:5)." Said R. Judah said Samuel, "The days of the Messiah are the same as the days that have passed from the day of the creation of the world even to now, as it is said, 'As the days of heaven upon earth' (Deut. 11:21)." R. Nahman bar Isaac said, "As the days from Noah to now, as it is said, 'For this is as the waters of Noah, which are mine, so I have sworn it' (Is. 54:9)."

So much for the authentic Messiah, what about the false one? It was arrogance that marked Ben Kosiba as a false messiah, so Song R. LVIII.ii.8: When they went out to battle, he would say, "Lord of all ages, don't help us and don't hinder us!" That is in line with this verse: "Have you not, O God, cast us off? And do not go forth, O God, with our hosts" (Ps. 60:12). The same view occurs at so Song R. LVIII.ii.19: There were two brothers in Kefar Haruba, and no Roman could pass by there, for they killed him. They decided, "The whole point of the thing is that we must take the crown and put it on our head and make ourselves kings." They heard that the Romans were coming to fight them. They went out to do battle, and an old man met them and said, "May the Creator be your help against them." They said, "Let him not help us nor hinder us!"

What we see, in summary, is that difference of opinion marked discussions on when the Messiah would come and how long the Messiah's time would last. But the basic outline of the Messiah-doctrine — conviction that an anointed savior would come, at some indeterminate moment at the end of time, and that he would rule for a period of time, during which he would restore Israel to its land and fortunes — encompasses all parties to disputed points. The emphasis on the requirement that Israel show appropriate humility, remorse, and repentance, for the coming of the Messiah, is equally widely shared. The Messiah-doctrine therefore accommodates diverse opinion within the main lines of a coherent position characteristic of all authorities in all pertinent documents.

XIV.

Prayer

PRAYER: The act of directing one's words (whether spoken or silent) to God in supplication, thanksgiving, or praise. Prayer forms a composite category along with repentance and righteousness/charity, all three bearing the power to annul a divine decree. Repentance pertains to an attitude, righteousness/charity to an action, and prayer to a mode of speech: direct discourse with God. The primary media for overcoming an unwanted fate are prayer, charity, and repentance. To these God may respond with an act of forgiveness, so Y. Ta. 2:1 III.5: Said R. Eleazar, "Three acts nullify the harsh decree, and these are they: prayer, charity, and repentance." And all three of them are to be derived from a single verse of Scripture: 'If my people who are called by my name humble themselves, pray and seek my face, and turn from their wicked ways, then I will hear from heaven and will forgive their sin and heal their land' (2 Chron. 7:14). Pray — this refers to prayer. 'And seek my face'— this refers to charity, as you say, 'As for me, I shall behold thy face in righteousness; when I awake, I shall be satisfied with beholding thy form' (Ps. 17:15). 'And turn from their wicked ways'— this refers to repentance."

Prayer is to constitute an act of supplication, but it also must conform to the regulations of the Torah, so M. Abot 2:13, R. Simeon says, "(1) Be meticulous in the recitation of the *shema* and the Prayer. And (2) when you pray, don't treat your praying as a matter of routine. But let it be a plea for mercy and supplication before the Omnipresent, blessed be he, as it is said, For he is gracious and full of compassion, slow to anger and full of mercy, and repents of the evil (Joel 2:13)." Prayer presupposes that God can and does intervene in the course of natural and human life and change that course in response to human supplication. One may say a prayer concerning what will take place in the future, but may not say a prayer concerning what is already decided, e.g., M. Ber. 9:3E-F: If one's wife was pregnant and he said, "May it be thy will that she give birth to a male" — lo, this is a vain prayer. If he was coming along the road and heard a noise of crying in the city and said, "May it be thy will that those who are crying are not members of my household" — lo, this is a vain prayer.

Prayer is the principal road to God and takes priority even over good deeds, so b. Ber. 5:1 I.38/32b: Said R. Eleazar, "Prayer is more important than good deeds. For you have no one who excelled in good deeds more than Moses, our master. Even so, he was answered only when he prayed. For it is said, 'Speak no more to me' (Deut. 3:26), and forthwith, 'Get you up to the top of Pisgah' (Ex. Deut. 3:27)." And R. Eleazar said, "Fasting is more important than philanthropy. What is the reason? This is done with one's body, while that, only with his money." And R. Eleazar said, "Prayer is more important than offerings, for it is said, 'To what purpose is the multitude of your sacrifices to me' (Is. 1:11). And forthwith: 'And when you spread forth your hands' (Is. 1:15)."

That God hears and answers prayers is explained at T. M. S. 5:24: The mouths of all those who fulfill the commandments are open in prayer to the Omnipresent and their prayers are answered, and it says in Scripture, "You shall pray to him and he will hear you, you shall pay your vows, when you decide on a matter, it will be established for you" (Job 22:27f.); and it says in Scripture, "And Hezekiah turned his face toward the wall land prayed to the Lord, saying, 'Please, God, remember that I conducted myself before you in truth and with proper intention and did what you favor.' Then the word of the Lord came to Isaiah, 'Go say to Hezekiah, thus says the Lord, the God of David your father: I have heard your prayers. . .'" (Isa. 38:2Ä5). And it says in Scripture, "Look down from your holy dwelling place" (Deut. 26:15). This is the place of looking down referred to in the passage: "Truth will spring up from the ground and righteousness will look down from the heavens. God will surely grant the good, our land will give her full yield" (Ps. 85: 12). "From the heavens" — from the storehouse of good in the heavens, as it says in Scripture, "May the Lord open for you his storehouse of good, the heavens, to give the land rain in its season and to bless all your labors" (Deut. 28:12).

Several metaphors explain or account for the obligatory prayers, first, that the patriarchs instituted them, so b. Ber. 4:4 I.5 26b: R. Yosé, b. R. Hanina said, "As to the recitation of Prayer, the patriarchs ordained them." R. Joshua b. Levi said, "As to the recitation of the Prayers, they were ordained as the counterpart of the daily whole-offering." Abraham ordained the recitation of the Prayer in the morning, as it is said, "And

Abraham got up early in the morning to the place where he had stood" (Gen. 19:27), and "standing" refers only to reciting the Prayer, as it is said, "Then Phineas stood up and prayed" (Ps. 106:30). Isaac ordained the recitation of the Prayer in the afternoon, as it is said, "And Isaac went out to meditate in the field at eventide" (Gen. 24:63), and "meditation" refers to prayer, as it is said, "A prayer of the afflicted when he faints and pours out his meditation before the Lord" (Ps. 203:1). Jacob ordained the recitation of the Prayer in the evening, as it is said, "And he lighted upon the place" (Gen. 28:11), and "lighting" refers only to prayer, as it is said, "Therefore do not pray for this people nor lift up pray nor cry for them nor light upon me in their regard" (Jer. 7:16) And it has been taught on Tannaite authority in accord with the view of R. Joshua b. Levi: Why did they say, The morning Prayer may be recited until midday (M. Ber. 4:1A)? For so the daily morning sacrifice was offered until midday. R. Judah says, "It may be offered until the fourth hour (M. Ber. 4:1B) for so the daily morning sacrifice was offered until the fourth hour." Why did they say, The afternoon Prayer may be recited until the evening (M. Ber. 4:1C)? For so the daily afternoon sacrifice was offered until the evening. R. Judah says, "Until the mid-afternoon (M. Ber. 4:1D) for so the daily afternoon sacrifice was offered until the mid-afternoon." And why did they say, "The evening Prayer had no fixed time" (M. Ber. 4:1E)? For so the limbs and fat pieces not burned up in the evening were offered all night. And why did they say, "The additional Prayer may be recited all day" (M. Ber. 4:1F)? For so the additional sacrifice was offered all day. R. Judah says, "Until the seventh hour (M. Ber. 4:1G), for so the additional sacrifice was offered until the seventh hour." And what is considered the greater part of the afternoon? From six and one-half hours onward i.e., from 12:30 p.m., since daylight is reckoned at 6 a.m. When is the mid-afternoon? At the eleventh hour less a quarter -hour (i.e., 4:45p.m.).

It is obligatory to recite the Prayer three times a day. These acts of prayer correspond to changes in the natural world; to the actions of the patriarchs; and to the course of offerings in the Temple, so Y. Ber. 1:4 I:4: Whence did they derive the obligation to recite daily three prayers? R. Samuel bar Nahmani said, "They parallel the three changes people undergo each day. In the morning a person must say, 'I give thanks, Lord, my God and God of my fathers, for you have brought me forth from darkness into light!' In the afternoon a person must say, 'I give thanks to you,

Lord, my God and God of my fathers, for just as I have merited seeing the sun rise in the east, now may I merit seeing it set in the west.' In the evening he must say, 'May it be thy will, Lord, my God and God of my fathers, that just as I have been in darkness before and you have brought me forth to light, so shall you once again bring me forth from darkness to light.'" R. Joshua ben Levi said, "They learned the obligation to recite the three daily prayers from the actions of the patriarchs. They derived the obligation to recite the Morning Prayer from the action of our forefather Abraham: 'And Abraham went early in the morning to the place where he had stood before the Lord' (Gen. 19:27). And 'Standing' must refer to the recitation of the) Prayer. As it says, 'Then Phineas stood up and prayed' (Ps. 106:30). They derived the obligation to recite the Afternoon Prayer, from the action of our forefather Isaac: 'And Isaac went out to meditate in the field in the evening' (Gen. 24:63). And 'meditation' must refer to the recitation of the Prayer. As it says, 'A prayer of one afflicted, when he is faint and pours out his meditation before the Lord' (Ps. 101:1). They derived the obligation to recite the Evening Prayer, from the action of our forefather Jacob: 'And he came to (wypg') a certain place, and stayed there that night because the sun had set' (Gen. 28:11). And the Hebrew term for 'Coming to' (pgy'h) must refer to the recitation of the Prayer. As it says, 'Let them intercede (ypg'w) with the Lord of hosts' (Jer. 28:18). And it says, 'As for you, do not pray for this people, or lift up cry or Prayer for them, and do not intercede (tpg') with me, for I do not hear you' (Jer. 7:16)." And our rabbis said. "The obligation to recite three daily Prayers is derived from the comparison to the order of the daily sacrifices. The obligation to recite the Morning Prayer, is derived from the daily morning sacrifice. The obligation to recite the Afternoon Prayer, is derived from the daily evening sacrifice. For the Evening Prayer, they found no support. So they just taught that one is obliged to recite it without elaborating on the sources of the obligation. "

The prayers of the saints and virtuous persons are what save Israel, so b. Sot. 9:12 V.2-: Said R. Ilai son of Yebarekhia, "Were it not for David's prayer's effectiveness, all Israelites would be garbage-dealers, for it is said, 'Grant fear of them, O Lord' (Ps. 9:21)." Said R. Ilai, son of Yebarekhia, "If it were not for the prayer of Habakkuk, two disciples of sages would have to cloak themselves in a single garment when studying Torah. For it is said, 'O Lord, I have heard the report of you and I am afraid, O Lord, revive your work in the midst of the years' (Hab. 3:2). Do not read 'in the midst of the years' but 'in the drawing together of two.'"

XV.

Prophecy

PROPHECY, echoes, and other media effect divine communication with Man, as matters are represented in the documents of the Oral Torah. Among them, prophecy represented only one medium of direct communication between God and man, both for Israel and for the gentiles, yielding statements by the recipient, the prophet, in the language he directly attributes to God. God in times past communicated with Israel through prophets, so indicated by their speaking direct quotations from God. The prophets not only interpreted events of the past and present but also predicted what would take place in the future. But in the Oral Torah media for direct communication with Heaven did not include prophecy. That point is made in so many words on the Babylonian Talmud's commentary at Mishnah-tractate Sotah 9:12A. The Mishnah's rule states, "When the former prophets died out, the Urim and Tummim were cancelled." In that context, the Talmud cites a Tannaite formulation that alleges that with the end of the latter prophets, Haggai, Zechariah, and Malachi, the Holy Spirit came to an end in Israel. What that means is that in the Oral Torah there were no further holy writings, beyond those of the Hebrew Scriptural canon (as then understood), in which it would be alleged, "God spoke to me, saying...." The system could find ample space for teachings of the Torah not in writing, that is, documents alleged to originate in the oral tradition that formed part of the revelation of Sinai — but no more written ones.

But sages claim that their group possessed media for direct communication with Heaven. These were two, one of which is not readily discerned from prophecy or the workings of the Holy Spirit, the other of which represents a distinctive and very particular means for communication with Heaven, one that defines the very character and essence of this Judaism. That is the view stated at T. St. 13:3-4/B. Sotah 48B: When the latter prophets died, that is, Haggai, Zechariah, and Malachi, then the Holy Spirit came to an end in Israel. But even so, they made use of an echo. Sages gathered together in the upper room of the house of Guria in Jericho, and a heavenly echo came forth and said to them, "There is a man among you who is worthy to receive the Holy Spirit, but his generation is unworthy of such an honor." They all set their eyes upon Hillel, the elder. And when he died, they said about him, "Woe for the humble man, woe for the pious man, the disciple of Ezra" (T. Sot. 13:3). Then another time they were in session in Yabneh and heard an echo saying, "There is among you a man who is worthy to receive the Holy Spirit, but the generation is unworthy of such an honor." They all set their eyes upon Samuel the younger. At the time of his death what did they say? "Woe for the humble man, woe for the pious man, the disciple of Hillel the Elder!" Also: he said at the time of his death, "Simeon and Ishmael are destined to be put to death, and the rest of the associates will die by the sword, and the remainder of the people will be up for spoil. After this, the great disasters will fall." Also concerning R. Judah b. Baba they ordained that they should say about him, "Woe for the humble man, woe for the pious man, disciple of Samuel the Small." But the times did not allow it (T. Sot. 13:4). How sages differentiated "the Holy Spirit" from the "echo" is not clear in the passage before us. The two serve the same purpose and with the same effect; and both are relied upon.

Since sages maintained that the Holy Spirit and prophecy no longer serve to convey to Israel Heaven's wishes on any given occasion, we have to ask ourselves what media did sages identify for the same purpose, that is, what served Israel in its diminished capacity — unworthy of having the Holy Spirit represented in its midst — for the delivery of Heaven's views. The answer to that question is made explicit at B. Makkot 23A-B, in a comment on the Mishnah-passage of M. Makkot 3:15A-D, which is as follows: "All those who are liable to extirpation who have been flogged are exempt from their liability to extirpation, as it is said, 'And your brother seem vile to you' (Dt. 25:3) — once he has been flogged, lo, he is tantamount to your brother," the words of R. Hananiah b. Gamaliel. Said R. Hananiah b. Gamaliel, "Now if one who does a single transgression — Heaven takes his soul on that account, he who performs a single religious duty — how much the more so that his soul will be saved for handed over to him on that account!" Now the statement attributed to Hananiah maintains that Heaven weighs in the balance a single transgression and a single religious duty. The latter saves the soul. Others, by contrast, require repentance. The discussion is as follows: Said R. Hananiah b. Gamaliel, "Now if one who does a single transgression — Heaven takes his soul on that account, he who performs a single religious duty — how much the more so that his soul will be saved for him on that account!": Said R. Yohanan, "R. Hananiah b. Gamaliel's colleagues Aqiba and Ishmael, who insist upon repentance, not punishment, as the condition of avoiding extirpation differed from him." Said R. Adda bar Ahbah, "They say in the household of the master, 'We have learned in the Mishnah: There is no difference between the Sabbath and the Day of Atonement except that deliberately violating this one is punishable at the hands of an earthly court, while deliberately violating that one is punishable through extirpation (M. Meg. 1:5C). Now if Hananiah b. Gamaliel were right, then both the one and the other should be punishable in the hands of an earthly court." R. Nahman bar Isaac says, "Lo, who is the authority behind this Mishnah-passage? It is R. Isaac, who has said, 'There is no flogging of those who are subject to the penalty of extirpation. For it has been taught on Tannaite authority: R. Isaac says, 'All those violations of the law that are punishable by extirpation were subject to a single encompassing statement 'For whoever shall do any of these abominations — the persons that do them shall be cut off from among their people' (Lev. 18:29)), and why was the penalty of extirpation made explicit in particular in the case of his sister? It was to impose in that case the penalty of extirpation and not mere flogging.'" R. Ashi said, "You may even say the opinion accords with the view of rabbis. In the case of the Sabbath, the principal penalty is inflicted by the earthly court, in the case of the Day of Atonement, the principal penalty is inflicted by the heavenly court." So far, the presentation represents a standard Rabbinic dispute on a point of law. The interesting initiative now takes place: Said R. Adda bar Ahbah said Rab, "The decided law is in accord with R. Hananiah b. Gamaliel." Said R. Joseph, "Well, who has gone up to heaven and 'said' that is, returned and made this definitive statement?!" Said to him Abbayye, "But then, in line with what R. Joshua b. Levi said, 'Three rulings were made by the earthly court, and the court on high concurred with what they had done,' ask the same question — who has gone up to heaven and returned and 'said' made this definitive statement?! Rather, we expound verses of Scripture to reach dependable conclusions, and in this case, too, we expound verses of Scripture."

For our purpose the interesting point comes at Joseph's (sarcastic) statement that he thinks it unlikely that sages possess direct knowledge of Heaven's will in a given point of law. Abbayye's reply in the name of Joshua b. Levi provides us with the key to the way in which, in this Judaism, people know Heaven's will: sages do not have to go to Heaven on consultations, because they have direct access to God's will as expressed in Scripture. The Holy Spirit, or prophecy, give way to another medium for communication between Heaven and earth, although, as we shall see presently, prophecy retains a critical position for itself. The issue then becomes subtle: at what point does Heaven communicate for which purpose? And the first part of the answer is, when it comes to the determination of law, it is by the correct exposition of Scripture, that sages have an accurate and reliable picture of Heaven's will. The upshot, in so many words, and in the exact context at hand, is then simply stated: study of the Torah for sages has now replaced prophecy. For the age at which prophecy is no longer available, Torah-learning substitutes quite nicely. But that is only for the stated purpose and takes place only in the single context: the nature of norms and how they are determined. Here, masters of Torah enter into communion with Heaven through their knowledge of the Torah, its traditions but also its logic.

The passage proceeds to expand on that claim by giving three examples of occasions on which the earthly court, that is, sages, made a ruling that was then confirmed by the corresponding court in Heaven. This view is expressed in the continuation of the foregoing passage: R. Joshua b. Levi said, 'Three rulings were made by the earthly court, and the court on high concurred with what they had done,' ask the same question:" And what were these? Reciting the scroll of Esther, greeting people with the divine name, and the presentation of the Levite's tithe to the Temple chamber. Reciting the scroll of Esther, as it is written, "They confirmed, and the Jews took upon them and their descendants" (Est. 9:27) — "they confirmed" above what they had "taken upon themselves" below. greeting people with the divine name: as it is written, "As it is said, "And behold Boaz came from Bethlehem; and he said to the reapers, 'The Lord be with you' And they answered, 'The Lord bless you'" Ruth 2:4). And Scripture says, "The Lord is with you mighty man of valor" (Judges 6:12). What is striking in the same composite is a matching composition, inserted immediately after the allegation that sages below made decrees that Heaven accepted and confirmed. We are given three examples in which, in ancient times, the Holy Spirit did operate.

Sages of the Oral Torah affirms prophecy and recognizes the presence in the midst of its Israel of the Holy Spirit. They explicitly reject the intervention or prophecy or the Holy Spirit in matters of the determination of law, because their position maintains that these matters are resolved through the interplay of practical reason and applied logic, on the one side, and accurate tradition, on the other. The Torah is the medium for communication from Heaven to earth, not only way back in the time of Moses, but also in the here and now of sages' own day. It is important to note, moreover, that the interplay of Heaven and earth takes place not only in matters of law, but also theology and the interpretation of events and prediction of the future, certainly critical matters in the conception of prophecy that sages set forth for themselves. When, moreover, the prophets — for so Solomon and Samuel and David are explicitly classified — made their rulings, the same media of heavenly confirmation that serves sages came into play. Since sages represent Solomon and David as sages, the point is clear: Heaven has a heavy stake in sages' deliberations, follows them, responds to them. In this context we recall the story of how Heaven calls up Rabbah bar Nahmani, requiring his knowledge of a matter of purity law! In the view of Rabbinic Judaism, nothing ended with the cessation of prophecy — not direct communication from Heaven to earth, not prediction of the future, not divine guidance for especially-favored persons concerning the affairs of the day. Canonical prophecy ended, but the works of prophecy continued in other forms, both on Heaven's side with the Holy Spirit and later on with the echo, and on earth's side with sages joining in conversation with Heaven through the echo, on the one side, and through Torah-learning, on the other. That the whole doctrine coheres and contains no loose ends is obvious.

XVI.

REDEMPTION

REDEMPTION: saving Israel from its enemies. Redemption will take place when Israel has fully repented from its sins and atoned, and God responds by intervening and restoring Israel's fate. This will be done through the agency of the Messiah. Israel's redemption depends on repentance, so Y. Ta. 1:1 II.1: R. Eliezer says, "If the Israelites do not repent, they will not be redeemed forever, since it is said, 'For thus said the Lord God, the Holy One of Israel, 'in returning and rest you shall be saved; in quietness and in trust shall be your strength.' And you would not'" (Is. 30:15). Said to him R. Joshua, "And is it so that if Israel should stand and not repent, they will not be redeemed forever?" Said to him R. Eliezer, "The Holy One, blessed be He, will appoint over them a king as harsh as Haman, and forthwith they will repent and so will be redeemed." So too Y. Ta. 1:1 II.2: On account of five matters were the Israelites redeemed from Egypt: Because the end had come, because of oppression, because of their outcry, because of the merit of the fathers, and because of repentance.

The redemption of Israel involves an innovation in the very conduct of history, so PRK V:XI.1, 4: "This month is for you the first of months, you shall make it the first month of the year" (Ex. 12:2): Reading the letters for month to sound like the word, innovation: R. Berekhiah in the name of R. Yudan b. R. Simeon: "Said the Holy One, blessed be He, to Israel, 'There will be an innovation as to redemption for you in the age to come. 'In the past I never redeemed one nation from the midst of another nation, but now I am going to redeem one nation from the midst of another nation.' That is in line with this verse of Scripture: Has God tried to go and take for himself a nation from the midst of another nation (Deut. 4:34)." "This month is for you the first of months, you shall make it the first month of the year" (Ex. 12:2): Said R. Joshua b. Levi, "The matter may be compared to the case of a king whose son was taken captive, and he put on the garb of vengeance and went and redeemed his son, and he said, 'Count the years of my reign as beginning from the time of the redemption of my son.' So said the Holy One, blessed be He, 'Count the years of my reign as beginning from the time of the Exodus from Egypt.'"

The redemption of Israel must take place at the right time, not too soon, not too late, so Song R. CXV:ii.6: To four matters the redemption (reading *ge'ulatan* rather than *ge'utan*) of Israel is comparable: harvest, vintaging, spices, and a woman in labor. To a harvest, for if a field is harvested not at its right season, it does not produce even decent straw, but if it is harvested in its right season, then the entire crop is first class: "Put in the sickle, for the harvest is ripe" (Joel 3:13). It is comparable to vintaging, for if the grapes of a vineyard are not harvested at the right time, they do not produce even good vinegar, but if it harvested at the right time, then even the vinegar is first rate: "Sing you of her, a vineyard of foaming wine" (Isa. 27:2), when it produces foaming wine, then pick the grapes. It is comparable to spices, for when spices are picked when they are soft and moist, their fragrance does not give a scent, but when they are picked dry, then their fragrance gives a scent. It is comparable to a woman in labor, for when a woman gives birth before term, the foetus cannot live, but when she gives birth at term, the foetus can live: "Therefore he will give them up until the time that she who is in labor has brought forth" (Mic. 5:2) R. Aha in the name of R. Joshua b. Levi said, "'I the Lord will hasten it in its time' (Isa. 60:22): if you have not attained merit, then 'in its time.' But if you have attained merit, then 'I will hasten it.'"

Redemption depends upon righteousness, just as the present age comes about by reason of arrogance, so b. Shab. 20:1 III.10-12/139a: R. Yosé, b. Elisha says, "If you see a generation on which great troubles break, go and examine the judges of Israel, for any punishment that comes into the world comes only on account of the judges of Israel, as it is said, 'Hear this, please you heads of the house of Jacob and rulers of the house of Israel, who abhor judgment and pervert all equity. They build up Zion with blood and Jerusalem with iniquity. The heads thereof judge for reward, and the priests thereof teach for hire, and the prophets thereof divine for money, yet will they lean upon the Lord?' (Mic. 3:9-11). They are wicked, yet they put their trust in him who by speaking brought the world into being. Therefore the Holy One, blessed be He, will bring upon them three punishments for three transgressions for which they bear responsibility, as it is said, 'Therefore shall Zion for your sake be ploughed as a field, and Jerusalem shall become heaps, and the mountain of the house as the high places of a forest' (Mic. 3:12). And the Holy One, blessed be He, will bring his Presence to rest on Israel only when the wicked judges and rulers will come to an end in Israel, as it is said, 'And I will turn my hand upon you and thoroughly purge away your dross and will take away all your tin, and I will restore your judges as at the first and your counsellors as at the beginning' (Isa. 1:25-26)." Said Ulla, "Jerusalem will be redeemed only through righteousness, as it is written, 'Zion shall be redeemed with judgment and her converts with righteousness' (Isa. 1:27)." Said R. Pappa, "If the arrogant end in Israel, the Magi will end in Iran, if the judges end in Israel, the rulers of thousands will come to an end in Iran. If the arrogant end in Israel, the magi will end in Iran, as it is written, 'And I will purely purge away your haughty ones and take away all your tin' (Isa. 1:25). If judges end in Israel, the rulers of thousands will come to an end in Iran, as it is written, 'The Lord has taken away your judgments, he has cast out your enemy' (Zeph. 3:15)." Said R. Milai in the name of R. Eleazar b. R. Simeon, "What is the meaning of the verse, 'The Lord has broken the staff of the wicked, the scepter of the rulers' (Isa. 14:5)? 'The Lord has broken the staff of the wicked': This refers to judges who become a staff for their court officers; 'The scepter of the rulers' refers to disciples of sages who belong to families of the judges." Mar Zutra said, "This refers to disciples of sages who teach public law to ignorant judges." Said R. Milai in the name of R. Eleazar b. R. Simeon, "What is the meaning of the verse, 'For your hands are defiled with blood, and your fingers with iniquity; your lips have spoken lies, your tongue speaks wickedness' (Isa. 59:3)? 'For your hands are defiled with blood' speaks of judges; 'and your fingers with iniquity' speaks of the scribes of the judges; 'your lips have spoken lies' refers to the court clerks of the judges; 'your tongue speaks wickedness' means litigants."

How redemption will take place is spelled out at Y. Ber. 1:1 I:10. It will begin slowly but then grow greater. And once R. Hiyya the Elder and R. Simeon ben Halafta were walking in the valley Arbel at daybreak. And they saw the first rays of dawn 'hind of dawn' as the daylight broke forth into the sky. Said R. Hiyya the Elder to R. Simeon ben Halafta b. Rabbi, "Like the break of day so is the redemption of Israel. It begins little by little and, as it proceeds, it grows greater and greater." What is his basis for this comparison of daybreak and redemption? Scripture says, "When I sit in darkness the Lord will be a light to me" (Micah 7:8, i.e. he will redeem me). By way of illustration of this last teaching: So it was at the outset the redemption of Israel in the time of Esther, for example, proceeded slowly as it says, "And Mordecai was sitting at the king's gate" (Esther 2:21). And thereafter it grew greater as the passage indicates, "So Haman took the robes and the horse and he arrayed Mordecai" (Esther 6:11). And thereafter, "Then Mordecai went out from the presence of the king in royal robes" (Esther 8:15). And thereafter, "The Jews had the light of redemption and gladness and joy and honor" (Esther 8:16). Thus the redemption proceeds slowly at first and then quickly shines forth like light, a term used in the last verse. The age to come will mark a moment comparable to the exodus from Egypt, and in the age to come Israel will no longer make mention of the exodus, which will have been overshadowed by the final redemption, this time from "the kingdom of the North" or from Gog and Magog," (Jer. 23:7-8), thus Y. Ber. 1:6 I:7: Ben Zoma says, "Israel is destined not to mention the exodus from Egypt in the future age." What is the basis for this statement? "And thus the days are coming says the Lord, you shall no longer say, 'God lives, who took us out of the Land of Egypt;' but 'God lives, who took out and who brought the seed of the House of Israel from the Land in the North'" (Jeremiah 23:7-8). And so its says, "Do not mention the first redemption" — this refers to the redemption from Egypt. "And pay no heed to the early redemption" — this refers to the redemption from the Kingdom of the North. "Lo, I am making a new redemption" — this refers to the redemption to come in the time of Gog. Afterwards he met up with a lion and was saved from it. He forgot the story of his salvation from the wolf and began to tell the story of his salvation from the lion. Afterwards he met up with a serpent and was saved from it. He forgot both the previous incidents and began to tell the story of his salvation from the serpent. Just so was the case for Israel. Their salvation from the later troubles caused them to forget to mention the story of their salvation from the earlier troubles.

While readily differentiated philologically, salvation and redemption in function bear the same meanings in the Oral Torah. The entire set of allegations hold together, further blending with those concerning the coming of the Messiah and the end of history and the resurrection of the dead.

XVII.

REPENTANCE

REPENTANCE, in Hebrew, *teshubah*, in the Oral Torah effects an act of transformation. It is closely related to the categories, atonement and Day of Atonement and integral to them. Through the act of repentance, a person who has sinned leaves the status of sinner, atones, and gains forgiveness, so that such a person is no longer deemed a sinner. The act involves a statement of regret or remorse, resolve never to repeat the act, and, finally, the test (where feasible) of entering a situation in which the original sin is possible but is not repeated.

The definition of repentance in the context of atonement is systematically worked out in Fathers According to R. Nathan XXIX:VIII.1: In Rome R. Matia b. Harash asked R. Eleazar b. Azariah, ""Have you heard about the four types of atonement that R. Ishmael expounded?" He said to him, "I heard indeed, but they are three, but with each of them repentance is required. One verse of Scripture says, 'Return, you backsliding children, says the Lord, I will heal your backsliding' (Jer. 3:22). A second says,' For on this day shall atonement be made for you to cleanse you' (Lev. 16:30). And a third says, 'Then I will visit their transgression with the rod and their iniquity with strokes' (Ps. 89:33), and a fourth: 'Surely this iniquity shall not be expiated by you until you die' (Is. 22:14). How so? If someone has violated a religious duty involving an act of commission but has repented, he does not move from that spot before he is forgiven forthwith. In this regard it is said, 'Return, you backsliding children, says the Lord, I will heal your backsliding' (Jer. 3:22). If someone has transgressed a negative commandment but has repented, repentance suspends the punishment and the Day of Atonement atones. In this regard it is said, 'For on this day shall atonement be made for you to cleanse you' (Lev. 16:30). If someone has transgressed a rule, the penalty of which is extirpation or judicially inflicted capital punishment, but has repented, the repentance and the Day of Atonement suspend the matter, and suffering on the other days of the year effect atonement, and in this regard it is said, 'Then I will visit their transgression with the rod and their iniquity with strokes' (Ps. 89:33). But one who has profaned the name of heaven — repentance has not got the power to effect suspension of the punishment, nor suffering to wipe it out, nor the Day of Atonement to atone, but repentance and suffering suspend the punishment, and death will wipe out the sin with them, and in this regard it is said, 'Surely this iniquity shall not be expiated by you until you die' (Is. 22:14)"

Repentance is required if one is to be resurrected at the end of time and gain a portion in the world to come, so Y. Sheb. 4:10 VI: Said R. Jonah in the name of R. Hama bar Hanina, "One who dies during the seven year battle of Gog so as not to suffer fully the troubles of the nation does not have a portion in the coming world. R. Yosé, heard this and said, "Now, is this really true? For there is always repentance as a method of earning a place in the world to come." This applies even if the individual has not suffered along with the Israelite nation.

The power of repentance overcomes all else, so PRK XXIV:XII.1: R. Judah the Patriarch in the name of R. Judah bar Simon: "Under ordinary circumstances if someone shoots an arrow, it may go a distance of a kor or two. But so great is the power of repentance that it reaches the throne of glory." Said R. Yosé, "It is written, 'Open to me' (Song 5:2). Said the Holy One, blessed be He, Open to me an opening as small as a hole of a needle and I shall open for you a space through which military camps and siege engines can enter." R. Tanhuma in the name of R. Haninah, R. Aibu in the name of R. Simeon b. Laqish: "'Repent for a brief moment and know that I am the Lord' (Ps. 46:11)." Said R. Levi, "If the Israelites repented for a single day, they would be redeemed." Said R. Judah bar Simon, "'Return, Israel, to the Lord your God' (Hosea 14:2), even if you have denied the very principle of the faith." Said R. Eleazar, "Under ordinary circumstances, if someone humiliates his fellow in public and after a while wants to conciliate him, the other says, 'Are you going to humiliate me in public and then conciliate me in private? Go and bring those people before whom you humiliated me and in their presence I shall be conciliated with you.' But the Holy One, blessed be He, is not that way. Rather, a person may go and blaspheme and curse in the market place, but the Holy One, blessed be He, says to him to repent 'even between you and me and I shall accept you.'"

It is God who instituted repentance as the medium of atonement, so PRK XXIV:VII.1-3: Good and upright is the Lord, because he teaches sinners in the way (Ps. 25:78): They asked wisdom, "As to the sinner, what is his punishment?" She said to them, "Evil pursues sinners (Prov. 13:21)." They asked prophecy, "As to the sinner, what is his punishment?" She said to them, "The soul that sins shall die (Ez. 18:4)." They asked the Torah, "As to the sinner, what is his punishment?" She said to them, "Let him bring a guilt-offering and it will attain atonement for him." They asked the Holy One, blessed be He, "As to the sinner, what is his punishment?" He said to them, "Let him repent, and it will attain atonement for him," That is in line with the verse of Scripture: Good and upright is the Lord, because he teaches sinners in the way (Ps. 25:78). Good and upright is the Lord, because he teaches sinners in the way (Ps. 25:78): Said R. Phineas, "Why is he good? Because he is upright. Why is he upright? Because he is good."..because he teaches sinners in the way (Ps. 25:78): For he teaches sinners the way in which to repent. Therefore Hosea admonishes Israel saying to them, "Return O Israel to the Lord your God, for you have stumbled because of your iniquity. Take with you words and return to the Lord and say to him, Take away all iniquity; accept that which is good, and we will render the fruit of our lips. Assyria shall not save us, we will not ride upon horses; and we will say no more, Our God to the work of our hands. In you the orphan finds mercy" (Hosea 14:1-3).

Repentance overrides even the violation of negative commandments, brings redemption, changes the character of sins that have been committed, so b. Yoma 8:9 III.8-13: /86b: Said R. Yohanan, "Great is repentance, for it overrides a negative commandment that is in the Torah: 'If a man put away his wife and she go from him and become another man's wife, may he return to her again? Will not that land be greatly polluted? But you have played the harlot with many lovers, and would you then return to me, says the Lord' (Jer. 3:1)." Said R. Jonathan, "Great is repentance, for it brings redemption near: 'And a redeemer shall come to Zion and to those who return from transgression in Jacob' (Is. 59:20) — how come 'a redeemer shall come to Zion'? Because of 'those who return from transgression in Jacob.'" Said R. Simeon b. Laqish, "Great is repentance, for by it sins that were done deliberately are transformed into those that were done inadvertently: 'And when the wicked turns from his wickedness and does that which is lawful and right, he shall live thereby' (Ez. 33:19)

— now 'wickedness' is done deliberately, and yet the prophet calls it stumbling!" Is this so? But said R. Simeon b. Laqish, "Great is repentance, for by it sins that were done deliberately are transformed into those that were merits 'And when the wicked turns from his wickedness and does that which is lawful and right, he shall live thereby' (Ez. 33:19)"! There is no contradiction between these versions, the one refers to repentance out of love, the other, out of fear. Said R. Samuel bar Nahmani said R. Jonathan, "Great is repentance, for it lengthens the years of a person: 'And when the wicked turns from his wickedness...he shall live thereby' (Ez. 33:19)." Said R. Isaac, or} they say in the West in the name of Rabbah bar Mari, "Come and take note of how the characteristic of the Holy One, blessed be he, is not like the characteristic of mortals. If a mortal insults his fellow by something that he has said, the other may or may not be reconciled with him. And if you say that he is reconciled with him, he may or may not be reconciled by mere words. But with the Holy One, blessed be he, if someone commits a transgression in private, he will be reconciled with him in mere words, as it is said, 'Take with you words and return to the Lord' (Hos. 14:3). And not only so, but God credits it to him as goodness: 'and accept that which is good' (Hos. 14:5); and not only so, but Scripture credits it to him as if he had offered up bullocks: 'So will we render for bullocks the offerings of our lips' (Hos. 14:5). R. Meir would say, "Great is repentance, for on account of a single individual who repents, the whole world is forgiven in its entirety: 'I will heal their backsliding, I will love them freely, for my anger has turned away from him' (Hos. 14:5). What is said is not 'from them' but 'from him.'"

Repentance overcomes harsh decrees and even oaths, so Song R. CVIII.i.8: R. Aha b. R. Abin b. R. Benjamin in the name of R. Aha b. R. Pappi said, "Great is the power of repentance, for it can annul a harsh decree and annul even the power of an oath. How do we know that it can annul a harsh decree? 'Write this man childless, a man who shall not prosper in his days' (Jer. 22:30), and further, 'In that day says the Lord of hosts will I take you, O Zerubbabel, my servant, son of Shealtiel, says the Lord, and I will make you as a signet' (Hag. 2:23). How do we know that it can annul even the power of an oath? 'As I live, says the Lord, though Coniah son of Jehoiakim king of Judah were the signet upon my right hand, yet I would pluck you hence' (Jer. 22:24), and yet, 'The sons of

Jeconiah, the same is Assir Shealtiel, his son' (1 Chr. 3:17)."

The power of repentance is unlimited so b. A. Z. 1:7 II.10/17a: They say concerning R. Eleazar b. Dordia that he did not neglect a single whore in the world with whom he did not have sexual relations. One time he heard that there was a certain whore in one of the overseas towns, and she charged as her fee a whole bag of denars. He took a bag of denars and went and for her sake crossed seven rivers. At the time that he was with her, she farted, saying, "Just as this fart will never return to its place, so Eleazar b. Dordia will never be accepted in repentance." He went and sat himself down between two high mountains and said, "Mountains and hills, seek mercy in my behalf." They said to him, "Before we seek mercy for you, we have to seek mercy for ourselves: 'For the mountains shall depart and the hills be removed' (Isa. 54:10)." He said, "Heaven and earth, seek mercy for me." They said to him, "Before we seek mercy for you, we have to seek mercy for ourselves: 'the Heavens shall vanish away like smoke, and the earth shall wax old like a garment' (Isa. 51:6)." He said, "Sun and moon, seek mercy for me." They said to him, "Before we seek mercy for you, we have to seek mercy for ourselves: 'Then the moon shall be confounded and the sun ashamed' (Isa. 24:23)." He said, "Stars and constellations, seek mercy for me." They said to him, "Before we seek mercy for you, we have to seek mercy for ourselves: 'All the hosts of Heaven shall moulder away' (Isa. 34:4)." He said, "The matter depends only on me." He put his head between his knees and he wept a mighty weeping until his soul expired. An echo came forth and said, "R. Eleazar b. Dordia is destined for the life of the world to come." Now here was a case of a sin other than *Minut* [heresy] and yet he did die. There, too, since he was so much given over to that sin, it was as bad as *Minut*. Upon hearing this story Rabbi wept and said, "There is he who acquires his world in a single moment, and there is he who acquires his world in so many years." And said Rabbi, "It is not sufficient for penitents to be received, they even are called 'rabbi.'"

The act of repentance involves only the attitude, specifically substituting feelings of regret and remorse for the arrogant intention that lead to the commission of the sin. If the person declares regret and undertakes not to repeat the action, the process of repentance gets underway. When the occasion to repeat the sinful act arises and the penitent refrains from doing it again, the process comes to a conclusion. So it is through the will and attitude of the sinner that the act of repentance is realized; the entire process is carried on beyond the framework of religious actions, rites or rituals. The power of repentance overcomes sins of the most heinous and otherwise-unforgivable character. The following (B. Gittin 57B) is explicit that no sin overwhelms the transformative power of repentance: Grandsons of Haman studied Torah in Bene Beraq. Grandsons of Sisera taught children in Jerusalem. Grandsons of Sennacherib taught Torah in public. And who were they? Shemaiah and Abtalion teachers of Hillel and Shammai. This remarkable statement from the Talmud shows that sin is not indelible either upon one's family or upon oneself.

The classic statement of repentance occurs at M. Yoma 8:8-9: A sin offering and an unconditional guilt offering atone. Death and the Day of Atonement atone when joined with repentance. Repentance atones for minor transgressions of positive and negative commandments. And as to serious transgressions, repentance suspends the punishment until the Day of Atonement comes along and atones. He who says, "I shall sin and repent, sin and repent" — they give him no chance to do repentance. If he said, "I will sin and the Day of Atonement will atone," — the Day of Atonement does not atone. For transgressions done between man and the Omnipresent, the Day of Atonement atones. For transgressions between man and man, the Day of Atonement atones, only if the man will regain the good will of his friend.

There is no such thing as preemptive repentance, that is, planning in advance to atone for a sin, so ARN XL:V.1: He who says, "I shall sin and repent" will never suffice to carry out repentance. "I will sin and the Day of Atonement will accomplish atonement" — the Day of Atonement will not accomplish atonement. "I shall sin and the day of death will wipe away the sin" — the day of death will not wipe away the sin. R. Eliezer b. R. Yosé, says, "He who sins and repents and then proceeds in an unblemished life does not move from his place before he is forgiven. He who says, 'I shall sin and repent' is forgiven three times but no more."

The Hebrew word is *teshubah*, from the root for return, and the concept is generally understood to mean, returning to God from a situation of estrangement. The turning is not only from sin, for sin serves as an indicator of a deeper pathology, which is, utter estrangement from God.

Teshubah then involves not humiliation but reaffirmation of the self in God's image, after God's likeness. It follows that repentance forms a theological category encompassing moral issues of action and attitude, wrong action, arrogant attitude, in particular. Repentance forms a step in the path to God that starts with the estrangement represented by sin: doing what I want, instead of what God wants, thus rebellion and arrogance. Sin precipitates punishment, whether personal for individuals or historical for nations, punishment brings about repentance for sin, which, in turn, leads to atonement for sin and, it follows, reconciliation with God. That sequence of stages in the moral regeneration of sinful humanity, individual or collective, defines the context in which repentance finds its natural home.

True, repentance is a far cry from loving and forgiving one's unrepentant enemy. God forgives sinners who atone and repent and asks of humanity that same act of grace — but no greater. For forgiveness without a prior act of repentance violates the rule of justice but also humiliates the law of mercy, cheapening and trivializing the superhuman act of forgiveness by treating as compulsive what is an act of human, and divine, grace. Sin is to be punished, but repentance is to be responded to with forgiveness, as the written Torah states explicitly: "You shall not bear a grudge nor pursue a dispute beyond reason, nor hate your brother in your heart, but you shall love your neighbor as yourself" (Lev. 19:18). The role of the sinful other is to repent, the task of the sinned-against is to respond to and accept repentance, at which point, loving one's neighbor as oneself becomes the just person's duty, so repentance forms the critical center of the moral transaction in a contentious and willful world.

A sizable abstract allows the Talmud of Babylonia, the final and authoritative statement of the Torah of Sinai, to portray the conception in its usual, systematic way. For, organizing topical presentations on such theological themes, the Talmud makes its statement on the subject in the following terms, a sequence of sayings expressing the main components of the concept: (B. Yoma 86A-B): Said R. Yohanan, "Great is repentance, for it overrides a negative commandment that is in the Torah: 'If a man put away his wife and she go from him and become another man's wife, may he return to her again? Will not that land be greatly polluted? But you have played the harlot with many lovers, and would you then return to me, says the Lord' (Jer. 3:1)." Said R. Jonathan, "Great is repentance, for it brings redemption near: 'And a redeemer shall come to Zion and to those who return from transgression in Jacob' (Is. 59:20) — how come 'a redeemer shall come to Zion'? Because of 'those who return from transgression in Jacob.'" Said R. Simeon b. Laqish, "Great is repentance, for by it sins that were done deliberately are transformed into those that were done inadvertently: 'And when the wicked turns from his wickedness and does that which is lawful and right, he shall live thereby' (Ez. 33:19) — now 'wickedness' is done deliberately, and yet the prophet calls it stumbling!" Said R. Isaac, or} they say in the West in the name of Rabbah bar Mari, "Come and take note of how the characteristic of the Holy One, blessed be he, is not like the characteristic of mortals. If a mortal insults his fellow by something that he has said, the other may or may not be reconciled with him. And if you say that he is reconciled with him, he may or may not be reconciled by mere words. But with the Holy One, blessed be he, if someone commits a transgression in private, he will be reconciled with him in mere words, as it is said, 'Take with you words and return to the Lord' (Hos. 14:3). And not only so, but God credits it to him as goodness: 'and accept that which is good' (Hos. 14:5); and not only so, but Scripture credits it to him as if he had offered up bullocks: 'So will we render for bullocks the offerings of our lips' (Hos. 14:5). Not you might say that reference is made to obligatory bullocks, but Scripture says, 'I will heal their backsliding, I love them freely' (Hos. 14:5)." How is a person who has repented to be recognized? Said R. Judah, "For example, if a transgression of the same sort comes to hand once, and second time, and the one does not repeat what he had done." Judah defined matters more closely: "With the same woman, at the same season, in the same place."

The act of repentance commences with the sinner, but then compels divine response; the attitude of the penitent governs, the motive — love, fear — making the difference. The power of repentance to win God over, even after recurring sin, forms the leading theme — the leitmotif — of the composite. Israel's own redemption depends upon Israel's repentance. The concluding statement proves most concrete. Repentance takes place when the one who has sinned and declares his regret ("in words") faces the opportunity of repeating the sinful action but this time refrains, so No. 14. That we deal with the critical nexus in the relationship between God and humanity emerges in one composition after another, e.g., repentance overrides negative commandments of the Torah (the more important kind); brings redemption; changes the character of the already-committed sins; lengthens the life of the penitent. Not only so, but the power of repentance before the loving God of grace is such that mere words suffice. The upshot is, we deal with a matter of attitude that comes to the surface in concrete statements; but as to deeds, the penitent cannot repeat the sin, so no deed can be required; the penitent has a more difficult task: not to do again what he has done before. The whole complex then draws us deep into an enchanted and transcendent universe.

The primary media for overcoming an unwanted fate are prayer, charity, and repentance. To these God may respond with an act of forgiveness, so Y. Ta. 2:1 III.5: Said R. Eleazar, "Three acts nullify the harsh decree, and these are they: prayer, charity, and repentance." And all three of them are to be derived from a single verse of Scripture: 'If my people who are called by my name humble themselves, pray and seek my face, and turn from their wicked ways, then I will hear from heaven and will forgive their sin and heal their land' (2 Chron. 7:14). Pray — this refers to prayer. 'And seek my face'— this refers to charity, as you say, 'As for me, I shall behold thy face in righteousness; when I awake, I shall be satisfied with beholding thy form' (Ps. 17:15). 'And turn from their wicked ways'— this refers to repentance."

Whether or not repentance accomplishes the whole of atonement is subject to some uncertainty, so Lev. R. X:V.1: Judah b. Rabbi said, "Repentance achieves only part, while prayer achieves the complete atonement." R. Joshua b. Levi said, "Repentance achieves the whole of atonement, while prayer achieves only part of atonement." In the view of R. Judah b. Rabbi, who has said that repentance achieves only part of the needed atonement, from whom do you derive proof? It is from Cain, against whom a harsh decree was issued, as it is written, "A fugitive and a wanderer will you be on the earth" (Gen. 4:12). But when Cain repented, part of the harsh decree was removed from him. That is in line with the following verse of Scripture: "Then Cain went away from the presence of the Lord and dwelt in the land of the wanderer Nod, east of Eden" (Gen. 4:16). "In the land of a fugitive *and* a wanderer" is not written here, but rather, only "in the land of the wanderer." The matter of being a fugitive is thus annulled. "Then Cain went away" (Gen. 4:16). When he had left God, the first man met him, saying to him, What happened at your trial? He said to him, "I repented and copped a plea." When the first man heard this, he began to slap his own face, saying, "So that's how strong repentance is, and I never knew!" At that moment, the first man pronounced this Psalm, "A Psalm, the song for the Sabbath day" (Ps. 92:1) which says, "It is a good thing to make a confession to the Lord" (Ps. 92:2). In the view of Judah b. Rabbi, who said that prayer accomplishes the whole of the necessary atonement? From whence do you derive proof? It is from Hezekiah. The allotted time for Hezekiah's rule was only fourteen years. That is in line with the following verse of Scripture: "And it happened in the fourteenth year of King Hezekiah Sennacherib, king of Assyria came up against all the fortified cities of Judah and took them" (Is. 36:1). But when Hezekiah prayed, fifteen more years were added to his rule. That is in line with the following verse of Scripture: "Behold, I will add fifteen years to your life" (Is. 38:5). In the view of R. Joshua b. Levi, who has said that repentance effects the whole of the required atonement, from whom do you derive evidence? From the inhabitants of Anathoth: Therefore thus says the Lord concerning the men of Anathoth, who seek your life and say, Do not prophecy . . . , Behold, I will punish them; the young men shall die by the sword; their sons and their daughters shall die by famine; and none of them shall be left. For I will bring evil upon the men of Anathoth, the year of their punishment" (Jer. 11:21-23). But because they repented, they enjoyed the merit of being listed in the honorable genealogies: "The men of Anathoth were one hundred twenty-eight" (Ezra 2:23; Neh. 7:27).

The relationship between repentance and the final judgment made of a person is worked out at b. R.H. 1:2 I.25/17b: Said R. Yohanan, "Great is the power of repentance, which obliterates a person's final judgment. This is as it says (Is. 6:10): 'Make the heart of this people fat and their ears heavy and shut their eyes, lest they see with their eyes and hear with their ears and understand with their hearts and turn and be healed.'" Said Rab Pappa to Abbayye, "But perhaps (Is. 6:10's notion that, if people 'turn' they will be 'healed,' applies only before the final decree is made?" In this view, contrary to Yohanan, once final judgment has been passed, repentance does not have the power to obliterate that judgment. Abbayye said to him, "At Is. 6:10 'and be healed' is written. Which thing leads the individual to require healing? Let us say it is the final decree!" Hence the power of repentance is as Yohanan said. They objected: "We know a teaching which states that if a wrongdoer repented between New Year and the Day of Atonement, his transgressions are forgiven. If he did not repent, even if he brought as sacrifices all of the rams of Nebayot, he will not be forgiven." Accordingly, the efficacy of repentance is restricted to a specific period. Repentance does not have the power Yohanan ascribes to it. There is no contradiction. This latter statement, refers to an individual. This former statement refers to a community. They objected on the basis of a prior teaching, "Referring to the land of Israel, Dt. 11:12 states: 'The eyes of the Lord your God are always upon it'—which means sometimes for good and sometimes for evil. 'Sometimes for good'—how so? Lo, if at New Year the people of Israel were in the category of people who are thoroughly evil, so that insubstantial rains were decreed for them, but, in the end, they turned and changed their ways — for God to supply additional rain is impossible, since the judgment already has been decreed. Rather, the holy one, blessed be he, brings down the rain at the proper time, upon the land that requires it, entirely according to the needs of the particular plot of land. But the amount of rain, previously decreed, does not change. 'Sometimes for evil'—how so? Lo, if at New Year the people of Israel were in the category of people who are thoroughly righteous, so that substantial rains were decreed for them, but, in the end, they turned and changed their ways— for God to supply less rain is impossible, since the judgment already has been decreed. Rather, the Holy One, blessed be he, brings down the rain at the wrong time, upon land that does not require it. The previously decreed quantity of rain does not change. But the rain is made to fall in areas in which it is wasted. If, as Yohanan claims, in response to repentance, the decree will be rescinded, for the case of individuals who changed their ways to the good, at least, let the judgment be rescinded so as to increase for them the quantity of rain!" The fact that the quantity of rain is not increased proves that repentance does not have the power Yohanan ascribes to it. There in the case of a decree regarding the quantity of rain it is different, since it is possible to solve the problem by doing that . In this case actually altering the decree is not necessary and therefore is not done. This reflects the special nature of the circumstance, not a limitation of the power of repentance. Come and learn a further challenge to Yohanan's position: Ps. 107:23-31 states: "Some went down to the sea in ships, doing business on the great waters. They saw the deeds of the Lord, his wondrous works in the deep. For he commanded and raised the stormy wind, which lifted up the waves of the sea. They mounted up to heaven, they went down to the depths. Their courage melted away in their evil plight. They reeled and staggered like drunken men and were at their wits' end. Then they cried to the Lord in their trouble, and he delivered them from their distress. He made the storm be still, and the waves of the sea were hushed. Then they were glad because they had quiet, and he brought them to their desired haven. Let them thank the Lord for his steadfast love, for his wonderful works to the sons of men!" The psalmist made them signs corresponding to the "but's" and "only's" in the Torah, so as to teach you that if they cried in supplication to the Lord prior to the passing of their final judgment, they were answered. Reference is to an inverted Hebrew letter ("nun") that appears in the Masoretic text before a number of the verses of this psalm. But if they cried to the Lord after their final judgment was passed, they were not answered. Accordingly, we see that repentance does not have the unmitigated power Yohanan ascribes to it. The challenge to Yohanan's understanding of the power of repentance is rejected. Here too the people are treated as individuals! We already know that for individuals, repentance is not invariably efficacious. Yohanan's view applies only to the case of a community. That accordingly does not disprove Yohanan's theory.

    The same motifs recur, intentionality, atonement, remorse, now in the context of the governing category of them all. That the various categories are formed of coherent materials is now joined with the further fact that the categories we identify themselves form large and coherent groups. A single statement of the whole clearly comes into view.

XVIII.

RESURRECTION OF THE DEAD
ETERNAL LIFE, WORLD TO COME

RESURRECTION OF THE DEAD, ETERNAL LIFE, WORLD TO COME: Beyond the grave, at a determinate moment, man rises from death in resurrection and enjoys the world to come. The exact sequence of events, involving the Messiah, the restoration of all Israel to the Land of Israel, the days of the Messiah, the age or world to come, and the final judgment, proves somewhat unclear. But the main point registers: death does not mark the end of the individual human life. Not only so, but man is judged individually, and there is a last judgment as well.

The nature of the world to come is not fully clarified; it is to last forever, and in it one's fate is determined by his conduct in this world. Thus T. Hullin 10:16 amplifies the matter in the context of the prohibition against taking the dam with the young: R. Jacob says, "You find no other commandment in the Torah, the specification of the reward for which is (not) located by its side, and the promise of the resurrection of the dead is written alongside it as well, as it is said, 'You will surely send forth the dam …so that it will be good for you And so that your days may be prolonged — If this one went up to the top of a tree and fell and died, or to the top of a building and fell and died, where has the good of this one gone, and where is the prolonging of his life? One must therefore conclude: So that it will be good for you — in this world. And so that your days may be prolonged — in the world of endless time."

It certainly is assumed that the age to come commences with the resurrection of the dead. A sequence of virtues, properly carried out, will lead to the resurrection of the dead, so M. Sot. 9:15MM: R. Pinhas b. Yair says, "Heedfulness leads to cleanliness, cleanliness leads to cleanness, cleanness leads to abstinence, abstinence leads to holiness, holiness leads to modesty, modesty leads to the fear of sin, the fear of sin leads to piety, piety leads to the Holy Spirit, the Holy Spirit leads to the resurrection of the dead, and the resurrection of the dead comes through Elijah, blessed be his memory, Amen." Belief both in the resurrection of the dead and that it is the Torah that reveals that the dead will rise are fundamental to the Oral Torah, so M. San. 10:1A-D: All Israelites have a share in the world to come, as it is said, Your people also shall be all righteous, they shall inherit the land forever; the branch of my planting, the work of my hands, that I may be glorified (Is. 60:21). And these are the ones who have no portion in the world to come: (1) He who says, the resurrection of the dead is a teaching which does not derive from the Torah, (2) and the Torah does not come from Heaven; and (3) an Epicurean. One who rejects the yoke of the commandments, denies the covenant, or perverts the Torah also loses a share in the world to come (T. San. 12:9). Such a one holds that the Torah was not revealed by God.

People enjoy a continuous existence in both this world and the world to come, so that what they do in this world affects their situation in the world to come, thus M. Peah 1:1: These are things the benefit of which a person enjoys in this world, while the principal remains for him in the world to come: (1) deeds in honor of father and mother, (2) performance of righteous deeds, (3) and acts which bring peace between a man and his fellow. But the study of Torah is as important as all of them together. That explains why in the world to come disciples of sages will continue their Torah-study, so Y Sheb. 4:10 VII: R. Jonah in the name of R. Hiyya bar Ashi, "In the world to come the rabbinical colleagues still will toil at their studies in the synagogues and study houses. Great sages were believed to know about the fate of named individuals in regard to the world to come, so T. Yeb. 3:1, Eliezer's disciples are represented as asking him, "What is the fate of Mr. So-and-so as to the world to come? What is the fate of Mr. Such-and-such as to the world to come?"

Man's destiny is to die and to be resurrected, so Eliezer Haqqappar, M. Abot 4:21: Those who are born are destined to die, and those who die are destined for resurrection.. And the living are destined to be judged so as to know, to make known, and to confirm that (1) he is God, (2) he is the one who forms, (3) he is the one who creates, R "(4) he is the one who understands, (5) he is the one who judges, (6) he is the one who gives evidence, (7) he is the one who brings suit, (8) and he is the one who is going to make the ultimate judgment. Blessed be he, for before him are not (1) guile, (2) forgetfulness, respect for persons, (4) bribe taking, for everything is his. And know that everything is subject to reckoning. And do not let your evil impulse persuade you that Sheol is a place of refuge for you. For (1) despite your wishes were you formed, (2) despite your wishes were you born, (3) despite your wishes do you live, (4) despite your wishes do you die King of kings of kings, the Holy One, blessed be he." Not only so, but death at specified ages expresses divine judgment, e.g., death at fifty represents extirpation (death before one's time); at sixty is normal; at seventy is death as an act of love; at eighty is death at true old age, and from that age onward, life is one of pain (Y. Bik. 2:1 II).

Everything that God is going to do in the world to come, he already has done in this world through the righteous, so Gen. R. LXXVII:I.1: "And Jacob was left alone" (Gen. 32:24): "There is none like unto God, O Jeshurun" (Deut. 33:26): R. Berekhiah in the name of R. Judah bar Simon, "The sense of the verse is this: 'There is none like God. But who is like God? It is Jeshurun, specifically, the proudest and the noblest among you." You find that everything that the Holy One, blessed be he, is destined to do in the age to come he has already gone ahead and done through the righteous in this world. The Holy One, blessed be he, will raise the dead, and Elijah raised the dead. The Holy One, blessed be he, will hold back rain, and Elijah held back rain. The Holy One, blessed be he, made what was little into a blessing and so increased it in volume, and Elijah made what was little into a blessing. The Holy One, blessed be he, visits barren women and makes them fruitful, and Elisha visits barren women and makes them fruitful. The Holy One, blessed be he, made what was little into a blessing and so increased it in volume, and Elisha made what was little into a blessing. The Holy One, blessed be he, made the bitter sweet, and Elisha made the bitter sweet. The Holy One, blessed be, he made the bitter sweet through something that was bitter, and Elisha made the bitter sweet through something that was bitter."

It is the Israelite dead who are going to be raised. Thus: all Israel have a portion in the world to come, hence will be resurrected. But in the final cataclysm before the resurrection, suffering will be acute, and the general suffering of Israel at that time is what, in the opinion of some, guarantees resurrection, by way of recompense. But others hold that repentance is the key, and that takes effect at any time in life, so Y. Sheb. 4:10 VI: Said R. Jonah in the name of R. Hama bar Hanina, "One who dies during the seven year battle of Gog so as not to suffer fully the troubles of the nation does not have a portion in the coming world. R. Yosé, heard this and said, "Now, is this really true? For there is always repentance as a method of earning a place in the world to come." This applies even if the individual has not suffered along with the Israelite nation.

The resurrection of the dead will take place at the hand of the righteous, and Israel alone will be resurrected, so b. Pes. 6:1-2 II.3-5/68b: Said R. Samuel bar Nahmani said R. Jonathan, "The righteous are destined to resurrect the dead, as it is said, 'There shall yet old men and old women sit in the broad places of Jerusalem, every man with his staff in his hand for very age' (Zech. 8:4), and, 'and lay my staff upon the face of the child' (1 Kgs. 4:29)." Ulla contrasted these verses: "'He will swallow up death for ever' (Isa. 25:8) and by contrast, 'for the youngest shall die a hundred years old' (Isa. 65:20). No problem: the one speaks of Israel, the other, gentiles. And what are gentiles doing in that context at all? 'And strangers shall stand and feed your flocks, and aliens shall be your plowmen and your vine dressers' (Isa. 56:5)." The resurrection will mark the advent of the Messiah and the world to come: R. Hisda contrasted these verses: "'Then the moon shall be confounded and the sun ashamed' (Isa. 24:23), and by contrast, 'Moreover the light of the moon shall be as the light of the sun, and the light of the sun seven-fold as the light of the seven days' (Isa. 30:26). No problem: the one speaks of the world to come, the other, the days of the Messiah." And from the view of Samuel, who has said, "The only difference between this age and the days of the Messiah is Israel's subjugation to the kingdoms alone," what is to be said? Both speak of the world to come, but there is no problem, the one speaks of the camp of the Presence of God, the other, the camp of the righteous.

Those who die in the Land of Israel, and the righteous overseas, will enjoy the resurrection of the dead at the end of days, but gentiles are explicitly excluded, so Pes. R. I:VI.4: Thus you have learned that (1) those who die in the Land of Israel live in the days of the Messiah, and (2) the righteous who die overseas come to it and live in it. If that is the case, then will the gentiles who are buried in the Land also live? No, Isaiah has said, The neighbor shall not say, I too have suffered pain. The people who dwell therein shall be forgiven their sin (Is. 33:24). The sense is, "My evil neighbors are not going to say, "We have been mixed up with Israel and will share their fate, so we too shall live with them." But that one that was the people dwelling therein is the one that will live, and what is that people? It is the people that has been forgiven its sin, namely, those concerning whom it is said, Who is God like you, who forgives sin and passes over transgression for the remnant of his inheritance (Mic. 7:18) which can only be Israel.

Being born into Israel the holy people guarantees participation in the resurrection of the dead, but the issue is raised, at what point is an infant deemed an Israelite, so Y Sheb. 4:10 IX Israelite children who die will live again after the resurrection of the dead if they had attained what age? R. Hiyya the elder and R. Simeon b. Rabbi disputed this question. One said, "As soon as they are born they are guaranteed resurrection." But the other said, "Only once they speak are they guaranteed resurrection." It is taught on Tannaitic authority in the name of R. Meir, "An Israelite child is guaranteed resurrection if he dies anytime after he knows how to answer 'Amen' to the prayers recited in the synagogue." There in Babylonia they state: "An Israelite child is guaranteed resurrection if he dies anytime after he is circumcised." But the rabbis from here in the land of Israel say, "An Israelite child is guaranteed resurrection if he dies anytime after he is born." R. Eleazar said, "Even miscarried fetuses are guaranteed resurrection." So too Israelites living in the Land of Israel are sure to enter the world to come, thus Y. Shab. 1:3 V.3: It has been taught in the name of R. Meir, "Whoever lives permanently in the Land of Israel, eats his unconsecrated produce in a state of cultic cleanness, speaks in the Holy Language of Hebrew, and recites the *Shema* morning and night may be certain that he belongs among those who will live in the world to come."

The coming resurrection of the dead is called to mind whenever one is located in a cemetery, so Y. Ber. 9:1 III:8: One who passes between graves in a cemetery, what does he recite? "Blessed art Thou, O Lord, our God, King of the Universe, who resurrects the dead." R. Hiyya in the name of R. Yohanan says he recites, "Blessed art Thou, O Lord, our God, King of the Universe who is true to his word to resurrect the dead." R. Hiyya in the name of R. Yohanan says he recites, "He who knows your numbers, He shall awaken you, He shall remove the dust from your eyes. Blessed art Thou, O Lord, our God, King of the Universe, who resurrects the dead." R. Eliezer in the name of R. Hanina says he recites, "He who created you with justice, and sustained you with justice, and removed you from the world with justice, and will resurrect you with justice; He who knows your numbers, He shall remove the dust from your eyes. Blessed art Thou, O Lord, our God, King of the Universe, who resurrects the dead." This is the case that one recites this blessing only if he passes among the graves of the Israelite dead. But concerning one who passes among the graves of the gentile dead, he says, "Your mother shall be utterly shamed, and she who bore you shall be disgraced. Lo, she shall be the last of the nations, a wilderness dry and desert" (Jer. 50:12).

Israel in particular heads toward the world to come, by reason of its loyalty to God in this world: T. Sot. 7:10: "You have declared this day concerning the Lord that he is your God, and that you will walk in his ways and keep his statutes and his commandments and his ordinances and will obey his voice; and the Lord has declared this day concerning you that you are a people for his own possession (Deut. 26:17—18). Said the Holy One blessed be He to them, 'Just as you have made me the only object of your love in the world, so I shall make you the only object of my love in the world to come."

In the age to come, God will lead the rejoicing, as head of the dance, so Y. Meg. 2:4 I:3: R. Berekhiah, R. Helbo, Ulla Biriayyah, R. Eleazar in the name of R. Haninah: "In time to come the Holy One, blessed be he, will be made into the head of the dance of the righteous in time to come." What is the scriptural basis for this view? "Consider well her ramparts" (HYLH) — "Her dance" is what is written. And the righteous will point to him in a gesture of respect with their finger and say, "That this is God, our God for ever and ever. He will be our guide for ever" (Ps. 48:14). He is our guide (almuth)" — with youthfulness, with liveliness. Aqila translated the word *almut* as *athanasia*, that is, immortality: a world in which there is no death. And the righteous will point to him in a gesture of respect with their finger and say, "'That this is our God, our God for ever and ever. He will be our guide for ever' (Ps. 48:14). He will be our guide in this world, he will be our guide in the world to come."

In the world to come people will go out at night by the light of God, so PRK XXI:V.2: R. Samuel bar Nahman: "While in this age people go by day in the light of the sun and by night in the light of the moon, in the coming age, they will undertake to go only by the light of the sun by day, and not by the light of the moon by night. What verse of Scripture indicates it? The sun shall no longer be your light by day, nor the moon shine on

Theological Grammar of the Oral Torah. Vol. I   261

you when evening falls; the Lord shall be your everlasting light, your God shall be your glory. Never again shall your sun set, nor your moon withdraw her light; but the Lord shall be your everlasting light and the days of your mourning shall be ended (Is. 60:19-20). By what light will they walk? By the light of the Holy One, blessed be He, in line with the passage: the Lord shall be your everlasting light."

One can lose his share in the world to come through improper actions and attitudes, so Y. Hag. 2:2 III.11: R. Yosé, ben Hanina said, "He who exalts himself at the cost of his fellow's humiliation has no share in the World to Come. How much more he who exalts himself against the Life of the Worlds! What is written after it? 'How abundant is your goodness, which you have laid up for those who fear you' (Ps. 31:20). Let him have no share in your abundant goodness."

In order to inherit the world to come, one must practice restraint in this world; one may lose his portion in the world to come by self-indulgence in this world, as the following story, B. Bes. 2:1 I.4/15b, illustrates: There once was an incident involving R. Eliezer, who was sitting and expounding the whole festival day concerning the laws of the festival day. When the first group of individuals walked out in the middle of his lecture he said, "These are owners of large vats of wine." Eliezer indicated that these were rich gluttons, who preferred going home to a large festival meal than sitting and listening to rabbinic discourse. When the second group of people walked out, he said, "These are owners of smaller vats." When the third group of individuals walked out, he said, "These are owners of pitchers." When the fourth group of people walked out, he said, "These own flasks." When the fifth group of people walked out, Eliezer said, "These own glasses." When the sixth group began to walk out, he said in anger, "These people are cursed." He cast his eyes upon his disciples, the only ones left in the hall, and their faces began to change. They paled, thinking that perhaps Eliezer's remark was directed at them, since, by remaining for so long, they forced him to continue lecturing. He said to them, "My sons, not of you did I say it. Rather of those who left. For they relinquish an everlasting life in order to occupy themselves with immediate gratification." When, at the conclusion of the lecture, the students were leaving, he said to them (citing Neh. 8:10), "'Go your way, eat the fat and drink the sweet wine and send portions to him for whom nothing is prepared; for this day is holy to our Lord and do not be grieved, for the joy of the Lord is your strength.'" In this context, study of the Torah constitutes eternal life.

One is lucky to suffer in this world so as to enjoy the world to come, so B. Ar. 3:5 II.21/16b: To what trivial degree do penitential troubles extend? That is, there are chastisements for sin which one suffers in this world, so that, in the world to come, there is no unpenalized sin, and one will enjoy the world to come. The question then is what are the most trivial sorts of inconvenience that constitute adequate chastisement in this world for some sort of sin, so that, on their account, one may be confident of enjoying the world to come? There follows a catalogue of the most trivial sorts of inconvenience. Said R. Eleazar, "Such would be any case in which people wove a garment for the man, which turns out not to fit." Raba Zeira objected — and some say, R. Samuel bar Nahmani: "They gave a still more extreme case than this. Even if people planned to mix wine for him to drink hot, and they mixed it cold, or to mix it to drink cold, and they mixed it hot, it would count as a penitential trouble, and you say this!" Mar, son of Rabina, said, "Even if his shirt was turned inside out." Raba, and some say, R. Hisda, and some say, R. Isaac, and there are those who report that it was repeated in a Tannaite teaching: "Even if one put his hand into his pocket to take out three coins and only two came up in his hand it would count as a penitential chastisement." That would apply if it was three that he planned to take and only two came up in his hand, but if he planned to take two and three came up, that would not constitute appropriate chastisement, for there is no element of inconvenience to toss one coin back. But why transmit all of this information? It is in accord with that which a Tannaite authority of the house of R. Ishmael taught, "Anyone who has passed forty days without any sort of penitential chastisement may know that he has received his entire reward in this world and will suffer in the world to come."

The wicked enjoy this world but suffer in the world to come, the righteous suffer in this world but enjoy the next world, so b. Yoma 8:9 III.22/86b: "It is not good to respect the person of the wicked" (Ps. 18:5) — It is not good for the wicked to be shown respect in this world. It was not good for Ahab that he was shown favor in this world: "Because he humbled himself before me, I will not bring evil in his days" (1 Kgs. 21:29). It is good for the righteous not to be shown favor in this world. It was good for Moses not to be shown favor in this world: "Because you did not believe in me, to sanctify me" (Dt. 20:13). Lo, had you believed in me, the time for you to take leave of this world would not yet have come. Happy are the righteous, for it is not sufficient for them only to acquire uncoerced grace in their own behalf but they bestow unmerited grace to their children and their grandchildren to the end of all generations. For how many sins did Aaron have who were worthy of being burned up like Nadab and Abihu, as it is said, "That were left..." (Lev. 10:12), but the uncoerced grace attained by their father stood up for them. Woe are the wicked, for it is not sufficient for them only to suffer condemnation on their own account, but they bring about the condemnation of their children and their grandchildren to the end of all generations. Canaan had many sons who were worthy of being ordained like Tabi, Rabban Gamaliel's slave, but the guilt of their ancestor caused them to lose out.

Gehenna may or may not figure in the fate of souls after death. Its precise character is unclear, so Gen. R. XXVI:VI.2: R. Yannai and R. Simeon b. Laqish say, "Gehenna in point of fact is nothing other than a day which will burn up the wicked. What is the scriptural evidence? 'For lo, a day comes, it burns as a furnace' (Mal. 3:19)." Rabbis say, "In point of fact there is really such a thing, as it is said, 'Whose fire is in Zion, and his furnace in Jerusalem' so Gehenna is in Jerusalem (Is. 31:9)." R. Judah b. R. Ilai: "Gehenna is neither a day nor a real place. But it is a fire that goes forth from the body of a wicked person and consumes him. What is the scriptural evidence for that proposition? 'You conceive chaff, you shall bring forth stubble, your breath is a fire that shall devour you' (Is. 33:11).
"

In the world to come or the time of the Messiah, there will be celebrations for the righteous. For example, God will make a banquet for the righteous; he will lead the dancing; he will prepare a tabernacle for the righteous, so b. B.B. 5:1 IV.28-29/75a: Rabbah said R. Yohanan said, "The Holy One, blessed be He, is destined to make a banquet for the righteous out of the meat of Leviathan: 'Companions will make a banquet of it' (Job 40:30). The meaning of 'banquet' derives from the usage of the same word in the verse, 'And he prepared for them a great banquet and they ate and drank' (2 Kgs. 6:23)." "'Companions' can refer only to disciples of sages, in line with this usage: 'You that dwells in the gardens, the companions hearken for your voice, cause me to hear it' (Song 8:13). The rest of the creature will be cut up and sold in the markets of Jerusalem: 'They will part him among the Canaanites' (Job 40:30), and 'Canaanites' must be merchants, in line with this usage: 'As for the Canaanite, the balances of deceit are in his hand, he loves to oppress' (Hos. 12:8). If you prefer: 'Whose merchants are princes, whose traffickers are the honorable of the earth' (Isa. 23:8)." Rabbah said R. Yohanan said, "The Holy One, blessed be He, is destined to make a tabernacle for the righteous out of the hide of Leviathan: 'Can you fill tabernacles with his skin' (Job 40:31). If someone has sufficient merit, a tabernacle is made for him; if he does not have sufficient merit, a mere shade is made for him: 'And his head with a fish covering' (Job 40:31). If someone has sufficient merit, a shade is made for him, if not, then a mere necklace is made for him: 'And necklaces about your neck' (Prov. 1:9). If someone has sufficient merit, a necklace is made for him; if not, then an amulet: 'And you will bind him for your maidens' (Job 40:29). And the rest of the beast will the Holy One, blessed be He, spread over the walls of Jerusalem, and the glow will illuminate the world from one end to the other: 'And nations shall walk at your light, and kings at the brightness of your rising' (Isa. 60:3)."

Along these same lines, God will make canopies for the righteous, so b. B.B. 5:1 IV.33/5a: And said Rabbah said R. Yohanan, "The Holy One, blessed be He, is destined to make seven canopies for every righteous person: 'And the Lord will create over the whole habitation of Mount Zion and over her assemblies a cloud of smoke by day and the shining of a flaming fire by night, for over all the glory shall be a canopy' (Isa. 4:5). This teaches that for every one will the Holy One create a canopy in accord with the honor that is due him." This restores the condition of Man as it was in Eden, so ibid. IV.35: Said R. Hama bar Hanina, "Ten canopies did the Holy One, blessed be He, make for the First Man in the garden of Eden: 'You were in Eden, the garden of God; every precious stone was your covering, the cornelian, the topaz, the emerald, the beryl, the onyx, the jasper, the sapphire, the carbuncle, and the emerald and gold' (Ezek. 28:13)."

Resurrection of the dead is a doctrine set forth by the written Torah and demonstrable within the framework of the Torah. That proposition is demonstrated over and over again. That the dead are going to rise up to life is indicated in various passages of Scripture, so Sif. Dt. CCCXXIX:II.1: Another interpretation of the phrase, "I deal death and give life; I wound and I will heal, none can deliver from my hand": This is one of the four promises in which to the Israelites is given an indication of the resurrection of the dead. The others are these: "Let me die the death of the righteous, and let my end be like his" (Num. 23:10) "Let Reuben live and not die" (Dt. 33:6) "After two days he will revive us" (Hos. 6:2). Might I suppose that the death applies to one person, the life to another? Scripture says, "I wound and I will heal." Just as the wounding and healing pertain to a single individual, so the death and life pertain to a single individual thus showing that Scripture contains evidence for the belief in the resurrection of the dead.

Further proofs of the same proposition are abundant, with the following instances representative of the larger corpus, b. San. 11:1/I.2-14/ 90b-91b, pass.: How, on the basis of the Torah, do we know about the resurrection of the dead? As it is said, "And you shall give thereof the Lord's heave-offering to Aaron the priest" (Num. 18:28). And will Aaron live forever? And is it not the case that he did not even get to enter the Land of Israel, from the produce of which heave-offering is given? So there is no point in Aaron's life at which he would receive the priestly rations. Rather, this teaches that he is destined once more to live, and the Israelites will give him heave-offering. On the basis of this verse, therefore, we see that the resurrection of the dead is a teaching of the Torah. It has been taught on Tannaite authority: Simai says, "How on the basis of the Torah do we know about the resurrection of the dead? As it is said, 'And I also have established my covenant with the patriarchs to give them the land of Canaan' (Ex. 6:4). 'With you' is not stated, but rather, 'with them,' indicating on the basis of the Torah that there is the resurrection of the dead." Romans asked R. Joshua b. Hananiah, "How do we know that the Holy One will bring the dead to life and also that he knows what is going to happen in the future?" He said to them, "Both propositions derive from the following verse of Scripture: As it is said, 'And the Lord said to Moses, Behold you shall sleep with you fathers and rise up again, and this people shall go awhoring ...' (Deut. 31:16). But perhaps the sense is, 'the people will rise up and go awhoring' He said to them, "Then you have gained half of the matter, that God knows what is going to happen in the future." It has also been stated on Amoraic authority: Said R. Yohanan in the name of R. Simeon b. Yohai, "How do we know that the Holy One, blessed be he, will bring the dead to life and knows what is going to happen in the future? As it is said, 'Behold, you shall sleep with you fathers, and ... rise again ... (Deut. 31:16)." It has been taught on Tannaite authority: Said R. Eliezer b. R. Yosé, "In this matter I proved false the books of the minim. For they would say, 'The principle of the resurrection of the dead does not derive from the Torah.' I said to them , 'You have forged your Torah and have gained nothing on that account. 'For you say, "The principle of the resurrection of the dead does not derive from the Torah." 'Lo, Scripture says, "Because he has despised the Lord of the Lord ... that soul shall be cut off completely, his iniquity shall be upon him" (Num. 15:31). "'... shall be utterly cut off ...," in this world, in which case, at what point will "... his iniquity be upon him ..."? 'Will it not be in the world to come?'" Caesar said to Rabban Gamaliel, "You maintain that the dead will live. But they are dust, and can the dust live?" His daughter said to him, "Allow me to answer him: There are two potters in our town, one who works with water, the other who works with clay. Which is the more impressive?" He said to her, "The one who works with water." She said to him, "If he works with water, will he not create even more out of clay?" A Tannaite authority of the house of R. Ishmael taught, "Resurrection is a matter of an argument a fortiori based on the case of a glass utensil. Now if glassware, which is the work of the breath of a mortal man, when broken, can be repaired, A mortal man, who is made by the breath of the Holy One, blessed be he, how much the more so that he can be repaired, in the resurrection of the dead."

Further proofs from the written Torah that the dead will be resurrected include the following, b. San. 11:1 I.27ff./91bff.: R. Meir says, "How on the basis of the Torah do we know about the resurrection of the dead As it is said, 'Then shall Moses and the children of Israel sing this song to the Lord' (Ex. 15:1). What is said is not 'sang' but 'will sing,' on the basis of which there is proof from the Torah of the resurrection of the dead." Said R. Joshua b. Levi, "How on the basis of Scripture may we prove the resurrection of the dead? As it is said, 'Blessed are those who dwell in your house, they shall ever praise you, selah' (Ps. 84:5). What is said is not 'praised you' but 'shall praise you,' on the basis of which there is proof from the Torah of the resurrection of the dead." And R. Joshua b. Levi said, "Whoever recites the song of praise in this world will have the merit of saying it in the world to come, as it is said, 'Happy are those who dwell in you house, they shall ever praise you, selah' (Ps. 84:5)." Said R. Hiyya b. Abba said R. Yohanan, "On what basis do we know about the resurrection of the dead from Scripture." As it says, 'Your watchman shall lift up the voice, with the voice together they shall sing (Is. 52:8).'" What is said is not 'sang' but 'will sing' on the basis of which there is proof from the Torah of the resurrection of the dead. Said Raba, "How on the basis of the Torah do we find evidence for the resurrection of the dead? As it is said, 'Let Reuben live and not die' (Deut. 33:6). 'Let Reuben live' in this world, and 'not die', in the world to come."

The resurrection of the dead means that death itself will die, so b. San. 11:1 I.22-23/91b: R. Simeon b. Laqish contrasted these two verses: "It is written, 'I will gather them ... with the blind and the lame, the woman with child and her that trail travails with child together' (Jer. 31:8), and it is written, 'Then shall the lame man leap as a hart and the tongue of the dumb sing, for in the wilderness shall waters break out and streams in the desert' (Is. 35:6). How so will the dead both retain their defects and also be healed? They will rise from the grave bearing their defects and then be healed." Ulla contrasted these two verses: "It is written, 'He will destroy death forever and the Lord God will wipe away tears from all faces' (Is. 25:9), and it is written, 'For the child shall die a hundred years old ... there shall no more thence an infant of days' (Is. 65:20). There is no contradiction. The one speaks of Israel, the other of idolators."

Once more, a fairly complex body of opinion coalesces within a few fundamental affirmations, themselves wholly coherent.

XIX.

Revelation
Giving of the Torah at Sinai

Revelation, giving of the Torah at Sinai: The act of giving of the Torah marked the meeting of Israel and God at Sinai, where, via Moses, God revealed the Torah, written and oral, to Israel. The importance of the giving of the Torah derives from Israel's acceptance thereof.

At the revelation at Sinai, Israel accepted God's rule and so completed the natural course of creation, so b. Shab. 9:3-4 I.25-6/88a: "And they stood under the mount" (Ex. 19:17): Actually underneath the mountain. Said R. Abdimi bar Hama bar Hasa, "This teaches that the Holy One, blessed be He, held the mountain over Israel like a cask and said to them, 'If you accept the Torah, well and good, and if not, then there is where your grave will be.'" Said Hezekiah, "What is the meaning of the verse, 'You caused sentence to be heard from Heaven, the earth feared and was tranquil' (Ps. 76:9)? If it feared, why was it tranquil, and if it was tranquil, why did it fear? But to begin with there was fear, but at the end, tranquillity." Why the fear? It is in line with what R. Simeon b. Laqish said, for said R. Simeon b. Laqish, "What is the meaning of the verse of Scripture, 'And there was evening, and there was morning, the sixth day' (Gen. 1:31)? This teaches that the Holy One, blessed be He, made a stipulation with all of the works of creation, saying to them, 'If Israel accepts my Torah, well and good, but if not, I shall return you to chaos and void.'" Sinai marked the moment of God's and Israel's union, so b. Shab. 9:3-4 I.27-9: Expounded R. Simai, "At the moment that the Israelites first said, 'we shall do,' and then, 'we shall listen,' six hundred thousand ministering angels came to each Israelite and tied on to each of them two crowns, one for the 'we shall do' and the other for the 'we shall listen.' When the Israelites sinned, however, a million two hundred thousand angels of destruction came down and took them away: 'and the children of Israel stripped themselves of their ornaments from Mount Horeb' (Ex. 33:6)." Said R. Hama bar Hanina, "At Horeb they put them on, at Horeb they took them off. Said R. Eliezer, "At the moment that the Israelites first said, 'we shall do,' and then, 'we shall listen,' an echo came forth and proclaimed to them, 'Who has told my children this secret, which the ministering angels take advantage of: 'bless the Lord, you angels of his, you mighty in strength who fulfil his word, who hearken to the voice of his word' (Ps. 103:2) — first they do, then they hear." Said R. Hama b. R. Hanina, "What is the meaning of the verse of Scripture, 'As the apple tree among trees of the wood, so is my beloved among the sons' (Song 2:3)? Why are the Israelites compared to an apple? To tell you, just as an apple Ä its fruit appears before the leaves, so the Israelites gave precedence to 'we shall do' over 'we shall hearken.'"

Revelation took place in all languages, so that every nation had the same opportunity to hear it, so b. Shab. 9:3-4 I.34-5/88a: Said R. Yohanan, "What is the meaning of this verse of Scripture: 'The Lord gives the word, they who publish the good news are a great host' (Ps. 68:12)? Every act of speech that came forth from the mouth of the Almighty was divided into seventy languages." A Tannaite statement of the household of R. Ishmael: "'And like a hammer that breaks the rock into pieces' (Jer. 23:29) — just as a hammer yields ever so many sparks, so every work that came forth from the mouth of the Holy One, blessed be He, was divided into seventy languages."

The giving of the Torah involved death and rebirth for Israel: b. Shab. 9:3-4 I.39-41/88a: And said R. Joshua b. Levi, "At every word that came forth from the mouth of the Holy One, blessed be He, the souls of the Israelites went forth, as it is said, 'My soul went forth when he spoke' (Song 5:6). But since their souls departed at the first word, how could they receive the next? He brought down dew, with which he will resurrect the dead, and brought them back to life: 'Your God sent a plentiful rain, you confirmed your inheritance when it was weary' (Ps. 68:10)." And said R. Joshua b. Levi, "At every word that came forth from the mouth of the Holy One, blessed be He, the Israelites retreated for twelve miles, but the ministering angels led them back: 'The hosts of angels march, they march' (Ps. 68:13) — read the word as though its consonants yielded 'they lead.'" Moses on high confronted the angels, who were jealous that the Torah was to be given to Israel, so I.41: And said R. Joshua b. Levi, "When Moses came up on high, the ministering angels said before the Holy One, blessed be He, 'Lord of the world, what is one born of woman doing among us?' He said to them, 'He has come to receive the Torah.' They said before him, 'This secret treasure, hidden by you for nine hundred and seventy-four generations before the world was created, are you now planning to give to a mortal? "What is man, that you are mindful of him, and the son of man, that you think of him, O Lord our God, how excellent is your name in all the earth! who has set your glory upon the heavens" (Ps. 8:5, 2)!' Said the Holy One, blessed be He, to Moses, 'Answer them.' He said before him, 'Lord of the world, I'm afraid lest they burn me with the breath of their mouths.' He said to him, 'Hold on to my throne of glory and answer them.' So Scripture says, 'He makes him to hold on to the face of his throne and spreads his cloud over him' (Job 26:9)." And in this connection R. Tanhum said, "This teaches that the All-Mighty spread over him some of the splendor of his Presence and his cloud." He said to him, 'Lord of the world, the Torah that you are giving me — what is written in it?' 'I am the Lord your God who brought you out of the land of Egypt' (Ex. 20:2). He said to the angels, 'To Egypt have you gone down. To Pharaoh have you been enslaved? Why should the Torah go to you?' He again said to him, 'Lord of the world, the Torah that you are giving me — what is written in it?' 'You will have no other gods' (Ex. 20:3). 'So do you live among the nations who worship idols?' He again said to him, 'Lord of the world, the Torah that you are giving me — what is written in it?' 'Remember the Sabbath day to keep it holy' (Ex. 20:8). 'So do you do work that you need rest?' He again said to him, 'Lord of the world, the Torah that you are giving me — what is written in it?' 'You shall not take the name of the Lord your god in vain' (Ex. 20:7). 'So is there any give or take among you?' He again said to him, 'Lord of the world, the Torah that you are giving me — what is written in it?' 'Honor your father and your mother' (Ex. 20:12). 'So do you have fathers and mothers?' He again said to him, 'Lord of the world, the Torah that you are giving me — what is written in it?' 'You shall not murder, you shall not commit adultery, you shall not steal' (Ex. 20:13-15). 'So is there envy among you, is there lust among you?' Forthwith they gave praise to the Holy One, blessed be He: 'O Lord our God, how excellent is your name' (Ps. 8:10), but they didn't add, 'who has set your glory upon the heavens.' On the spot everyone of them became a friend of his and gave him something: 'You have ascended on high, you have taken the spoils, you have received gifts on account of man' (Ps. 68:19). In reparation for their calling you a man, you received gifts. So, too, the angel of death handed over something to him: 'and he put on the incense and made atonement for the people' (Num. 16:47), 'and he stood between the dead and the living' (Num. 16:48). If the other hadn't told him where, would he have known what to do?"

The doctrine of the giving of the Torah forms a chapter in the much larger category, Torah, which, owing to its massive character, is treated in a number of entries. What is critical here is the engagement of heaven and earth, the angels and Israel, the gentiles and Israel, God's self-manifestation, and the other paramount themes at hand.

XX

SAGE, DISCIPLE OF SAGES

SAGE, THE, AND THE DISCIPLE OF SAGES: a man sanctified through study of the Torah in discipleship, a link in the chain of Oral Torah from Sinai. Because they embody the law of the Torah, the actions of the sage define norms and supply exemplary models; the sage then constitutes a native category, holding together a vast corpus of exemplary statements, e.g., of what this or that named master did or refrained from doing. Because of his mastery of the Torah, a disciple of a sage is equivalent to an actual Torah-scroll, the physical object, and is treated with the same respect that is paid to the Torah, so T. Ta. 3:7 I.10, He who sees a disciple of a sage who has died is as if he sees a scroll of the Torah that has been burned. Said R. Abbahu, "May a bad thing happen to me, if I tasted any food all that day on which I saw a deceased disciple of a sage." The sage is treated like a scroll of the Torah, so b. Ket. 23:1-2 I.19/17a: With special reference to the death of a sage, R. Sheshet, and some say, R. Yohanan, said, "Removing the Torah contained in the sage must be like the giving of the Torah: just as the giving of the Torah involved six hundred thousand, so taking away the Torah involves six hundred thousand. But this is with regard to one who has recited Scripture and repeated Mishnah traditions. But in the case of one who repeated Tannaite statements to others, there is no upper limit at all."

To deny the teachings of the sages is to deny God. This proposition is worked out in the following way at Sifra CCLXIV:I.1: "But if you will not hearken to me and will not do all these commandments": What is the point of Scripture in saying, "will not do"? You have someone who does not learn but who carries out the teachings of the Torah. In that connection, Scripture says, "But if you will not hearken to me and will not do ." Lo, whoever does not learn the Torah also does not carry it out. And you have someone who does not learn the Torah and also does not carry it out, but he does not despise others who do so. In that connection, Scripture says, "if you spurn my statutes." Lo, whoever does not learn the Torah and does not carry it out in the end will despise others who do so. And you furthermore have someone who does not learn the Torah, and also does not carry it out, and he does despise others who do so, but he does not hate the sages. In that connection, Scripture says, "and if your soul abhors my ordinances" - Lo, whoever does not learn the Torah, also does not carry it out, and does despise others who do so, in the end will hate the sages. And you furthermore have someone who does not learn the Torah, does not carry it out, despises others who do so, and hates the sages, but who lets others carry out the Torah. Scripture says, "so that you will not do all my commandments but break my covenant" - lo, whoever does not learn the Torah, does not carry it out, despises others who do so, and hates the sages, in the end will not let others carry out the Torah. Or you may have someone who does not learn the Torah, does not carry it out, despises others who do so, hates the sages, does not let others carry out the Torah, but he confesses that the religious duties were spoken from Sinai. Scripture says, "all my commandments" - lo, whoever does not learn the Torah, does not carry it out, despises others who do so, hates the sages, does not let others carry out the Torah, in the end will deny that the religious duties were spoken from Sinai. Or you may have someone who exhibits all these traits but does not deny the very Principle of God's existence and rule. Scripture says, "but break my covenant" - lo, whoever exhibits all these traits in the end will deny the very Principle of God's existence and rule.

Study of the Torah changed the one who studied because through it he entered into the mind of God, learning how God's mind worked when God formed the Torah, written and oral alike and (in the explicit view of Genesis Rabbah 1:1) consulted the Torah in created the world. And there, in the intellect of God, in their judgment humanity gained access to the only means of uniting intellect with existential condition as to salvation. The Mishnah had set forth the rules that governed the natural world in relationship to Heaven. But knowledge of the Torah now joined the one world, known through nature, with the other world, the world of supernature, where, in the end, intellect merely served in the quest for salvation. Through Torah-study sages claimed for themselves a place in that very process of thought that had given birth to nature; but it was a supernatural process, and knowledge of that process on its own terms would transform and, in the nature of things, save. That explains the integrative power of imputing supernatural power to learning.

The capacity of the sage himself to participate in the process of revelation is illustrated in two types of materials. First of all, tales told about rabbis' behavior on specific occasions immediately are translated into rules for the entire community to keep. Accordingly, he was a source not merely of good example but of prescriptive law. Reports of what rabbis had done enjoyed the same authority, as statements of the law on eating what Samaritans cooked, as did citations of traditions in the names of the great authorities of old or of the day. What someone did served as a norm, if the person was a sage of sufficient standing. Even the ordinary actions of sages serve to exemplify the correct conduct of the law, so M. Suk. 3:9D: Said R. Aqiba, "I was watching Rabban Gamaliel and R. Joshua, for all the people waved their palm branches, but they waved their palm branches only at, Save now, we beseech thee, 0 Lord (Ps. 118:25)."

God confirms decisions of sages, even when these are in error. For example, sages' declaration of the timing of holy days must be accepted by the disciples, even though they have evidence that the declaration errs. So Aqiba instructs Joshua, M. Rosh Hashanah 2:9C: "I can provide grounds for showing that everything that Rabban Gamaliel has done is validly done, since it says, 'These are the set feasts of the Lord, even holy convocations, which you shall proclaim' (Lev. 23:4). Whether they are in their proper time or not in their proper time, I have no set feasts but these which you shall proclaim." That is because the sages' court at any one moment represents the authority of Sinai, once more M. Rosh Hashanah 2:9E-G: "Now if we're going to take issue with the court of Rabban Gamaliel, we have to take issue with every single court which has come into being from the time of Moses to the present day, since it says, 'Then went up Moses and Aaron, Nadab and Abihu, and seventy of the elders of Israel' (Ex. 24:9). Now why have the names of the elders not been given? To teach that every group of three elders who came into being as a court of Israel — lo, they are equivalent to the court of Moses himself." Naming a particular sage, however, also serves to validate a teaching, and if one can cite a tradition in the name of an approved figure, that will settle an argument, so Y. Shab. 19:1 I.4: R. Zeira in the name of R. Eleazar: "Any teaching of Torah which is not attached to the authority of a named source is not a valid teaching of Torah." To settle an argument: When Hillel saw what they had done, he remembered the law. He said to them, "This is what I heard from the instruction of Shemayah and Abtalion." At that point the controversy was resolved.

The sages of the Torah are to be respected as God himself is respected, so B. Ar. 1:2 II.3/6b: Simeon the Imsonite would derive a lesson from the use of every accusative particle that is in the Torah. When he reached the verse that places the accusative particle before the word "Lord," namely, "the Lord your God you shall fear" (Dt. 10:20), he refrained from doing so since he did not wish to suggest there was more than one God. He disciples said to him, "My lord, what then will be the fate of all the other accusative particles from which you have drawn lessons if you pick and choose among them?" He said to them, "Just as I have received a reward for the lessons that I have derived, so I shall receive a word for refraining from deriving a lesson." And that was the situation that prevailed until R. Aqiba came along and taught concerning the verse that places the accusative particle before the word "Lord," namely, "the Lord your God you shall fear" (Dt. 10:20), "The accusative particle serves to encompass within the commandment the disciples of sages themselves."

The sage is the highest earthly authority of the Torah, thus T. Hor. 2:8: A sage takes precedence over a king. For if a sage dies, we have none who is like him. If a king dies, any Israelite is suitable to mount the throne. What the sage did had the status of law; the sage was the model of the law, thus having been changed, transformed, regenerated, saved, turned by studying the Torah into the human embodiment of the Torah. That view of Torah-study as transformative and salvific — now without explicit appeal to deeds in conformity to the law, though surely that is taken for granted — accounts for the position that the sage was a holy man. For what made the sage distinctive was his combination of this-worldly authority and power and otherworldly influence. The clerk in the court and the holy man on the rooftop praying for rain or calling Heaven to defend the city against marauders, in the Yerushalmi's view were one and the same. The tight union between salvation and law, the magical power of the sage and his law giving authority, was effected through the integrative act of studying the Torah. And that power of integration accounts for the successor-system's insistence that if the sage exercised supernatural power as a kind of living Torah, his very deeds served to reveal law, as much as his word expressed revelation.

Theological Grammar of the Oral Torah. Vol. I 277

The disciple of a sage indicates his knowledge by his deeds, for example, by the way in which he carries out his religious obligations. Actions, not words, then mark him as a qualified disciple, e.g., T. Ber. 1:6: These are the benedictions which one recites briefly: he who recites a benediction (I) upon eating produce cf. M. Ber. 6:1, and (2) upon the performance of the commandments cf. T. Ber. 6:9 (3) and the invitation to say a common grace after meals; cf. M. Ber. 7:3, (4) and the final benediction of the grace after meals. And there are the benedictions which one recites at length: (I) benedictions in the Prayer for fast—days, (2) and benedictions in the Prayer for the New Year, (3) and benedictions in the Prayer for the Day of Atonement. From a man's benediction viz., the way in which he recites benedictions one discerns whether he is a boor or a disciple of the sages.

The disciple of the sage has to conduct himself with great dignity, so b. Ber. 6:5-6/VI.13/43b: There are six things that are not befitting the dignity of a sage. He should not go out perfumed to the market place. He should not go out by himself at night. He should not go out in patched sandals. He should not talk with a woman in public. He should not recline in an eating club made up of ordinary people. He should not come last to the school house. And there are those who say, he should also not walk with giant steps. He should not go about stiffly erect.

After the destruction of the Temple in 70, words of prophecy have no legal standing, but sages inherit their authority, so b. B.B. 1:6 II.4-5/12a: Said R. Abdimi of Haifa, "From the day on which the house of the sanctuary was destroyed, prophecy was taken away from prophets and given over to sages." So are sages not also prophets? This is the sense of the statement: Even though it was taken from the prophets, it was not taken from sages. Said Amemar, "And a sage is superior to a prophet: 'And a prophet has a heart of wisdom' (Ps. 90:12). Who is compared to whom? Lo, the lesser is compared to the greater." Said Abbayye, "You may know that sages retain the power of prophecy, for if an eminent authority makes a statement, it may then be stated in the name of some other eminent authority who can have gotten it only by prophecy." Said R. Yohanan, "When the house of the sanctuary was destroyed, prophecy was taken away from the prophets and handed over to idiots and children."

One becomes a disciple of a sage by hearing and repeating and memorizing the words of the sage set forth as Torah. Reciting words of Torah is obligatory for the disciple, and doing so in constant interchange with colleagues is the sole valid way, b. Sot. 9:12 V.3: Said R. Ilai, son of Yebarekhia, "If two disciples of sages go along without words of Torah between them, they are worthy of being burned in fire, as it is said, 'And it came to pass, as they still went on, that, behold, a chariot of fire' (2 Kgs. 2:11). The reason that the chariot of fire appeared is that they were talking. Lo, if there had not been talk of Torah, they would have been worthy of being burned." Said R. Ilai, son of Yebarekhia, "If there are two disciples of sages who live in the same town and are not easy with one another in the law, one will die and the other will go into exile, as it is said, 'That the manslaughter may flee there, who slays his neighbor without knowledge' (Deut. 4:42). 'Knowledge' refers only to Torah, as it is said, 'My people are destroyed for lack of knowledge' (Hos. 4:6)." Said R. Judah, son of R. Hiyya, "Any disciple of a sage who occupies himself in Torah in conditions of poverty will have his prayer heard, as it is said, 'For the people shall dwell in Zion at Jerusalem; you shall weep no more; he will surely be gracious to you at the sound of your cry; when he shall be here, he will answer you' (Is. 30:19). And the passage continues, 'The Lord will give you bread in adversity and water in affliction' (Is. 30:20)." R. Abbahu says, "They give him satisfaction even from the splendor of God's presence, as it is said, 'Your eyes will see your teacher' (Is. 30:20)." R. Aha bar Hanina said, "It is even the case that the veil will not be closed before him, as it is said, 'Your teacher will no more be hidden' (Is. 30:20)."

It is a great privilege to marry a disciple of a sage, so b. Pes. 3:7-8 I.7 49a-b: A person should always sell everything he has so as to marry the daughter of a disciple of a sage, for if he should die or go into exile, he will be secure that his children will be disciples of sages. But he should not marry the daughter of an unlettered man, for if he should die or go into exile, his children will be unlettered." A person should always sell everything he has so as to marry the daughter of a disciple of a sage and marry off his daughter to a disciple of a sage. It is comparable to grafting grapes of a vine with grapes of a vine that is right and proper. But let him never marry the daughter of an unlettered man. It is comparable to grafting grapes of a vine with berries of a bush, which is disgusting disreputable." A person should always sell everything he has so as to marry the daughter of a disciple of a sage. If he cannot get the daughter of a disciple of a sage, he should marry the daughter of one of the principal authorities of the generation. If he cannot get the daughter of one of the principal authorities of the generation, he should marry the daughter of one of the heads of a synagogue. If he cannot get the daughter of one of the heads of a synagogue, he should marry the daughter of one of the charity collectors. If he cannot get the daughter of one of the charity collectors, he should marry the daughter of one of the primary school teachers. But he should not marry the daughter of an unlettered person, because they are an abomination, and their wives are dead creeping things, and concerning their daughters Scripture says, "Cursed be he who lies with any manner of beast" (Dt. 27:21).

A disciple of a sage should make special efforts to produce children who study the Torah, so b. B.M. 7:1 I.27/85a: Said R. Parnak said R. Yohanan, "Whoever is a disciple of a sage, with a son who is a disciple of a sage, and a grandson who is a disciple of a sage — Torah will never again depart from his seed for ever, as it is said, 'As for me, this is my covenant with them, says the Lord. My spirit is upon you, and my words which I have put in your mouth shall not depart out of your mouth, nor out of the mouth of your seed, nor out of the mouth of the seed of your seed, says the Lord, from now and for ever' (Is. 59:21)."

A sage exhibits traits of intelligence and civility, so M. Abot 5:7: There are seven traits to an unformed clod, and seven to a sage. (1) A sage does not speak before someone greater than he in wisdom. (2) And he does not interrupt his fellow. (3) And he is not at a loss for an answer. (4) He asks a relevant question and answers properly. (5) And he addresses each matter in its proper sequence, first, then second. (6) And concerning something he has not heard, he says, "I have not heard the answer." (7) And he concedes the truth when the other party demonstrates it. And the opposite of these traits apply to a clod.

Even the beasts that belong to saints or holy men act in accord with the Torah, so Y. Dem. 1:3. The story proves that the ass of Pinhas b. Yair was more scrupulous in the matter of doubtfully tithed produce than great sages of the day. The she-ass of R. Pinhas b. Yair was stolen at night by thieves. It remained hidden with them for three days, during which time it would not eat anything. Three days later, they decided to return it to its master. They reckoned, "Let us return it to its master lest it die while with us and our cave start to stink so that our hiding-place might thereby be discovered." They sent it out. It went and stood outside its master's gate and began to bray. He said to them his servants, "Open the gate for that poor creature that hasn't eaten anything in three days." They opened the gate for it, and it came in. He said to them, "Give her something to eat." They put some barley before it, but it refused to eat. They said to him, "Master, she refuses to eat." He said to them, "Has it the barley been set right?" I.e., has the priestly gift been removed from it? They said to him, "Yes." He said to them, "Have you removed from it its requisite tithes on account of doubt as to whether it had already been tithed?" They said to him, "But has not Master taught us thus, One who purchases (1) grain for seed or for fodder, (2) flour for dressing hides, (3) oil for the lamp, (4) oil for greasing utensils — the produce is exempt from tithing as *dema'i-produce*." (M. 1:3A-B) He said to them, "What can we do about this poor creature, since she is so stringent with herself?!" So they removed the requisite tithes due from the barley on account of doubt, and the she-ass ate.

The sage when angered could curse with fatal effect, so Y. Ber. 2:8 I:3: The young Kahana was a prodigy in rabbinic learning. When he arrived here in the Land of Israel, a scoffer saw him and said to him, "What did you hear up in heaven?" He said to him, "Your fate is sealed." And so it was. He died. Another scoffer met him and said, "What did you hear up in heaven?" He said to him, "Your fate is sealed." And so it was. He Kahana said, "What is this? I came here to gain merit and study Torah. And now I have sinned. Did I come here to kill the inhabitants of the Land of Israel? I must go back to whence I came." He went before R. Yohanan. He said to him, "Where should a person go whose mother mocks him and whose step-mother honors him?" He said to him, "He should go to whomever honors him." So Kahana went back to Babylonia whence he came.

The laws governing conduct with sages underscore their eminence, so T. San. 7:8-9: When the patriarch enters, everyone rises and does not sit down until he says to them, "Sit down." And when the head of the court enters, they set up for him two rows, one on one side, one on the other side, through which he goes, and he sits down in his place. When a sage who comes in, one rises as another sits down, until he comes in and sits down in his place. Younger sages and disciples of sages, when the public requires their services, even step over the heads of the people. If one needed to leave to the privy, he reenters and takes his place without disrupting the proceedings. And even though they have said, "It is no praise for a disciple of a sage to come in last," if he went out for need, he comes back and sits down in his place. Younger sages and disciples of sages Bavli: sons of disciples of sages whose father was appointed administrator of the community, when they have a capacity to understand, turn toward their fathers on the court, with their backs toward the people. When they do not have the wit to understand, they enter and take their seats before their fathers, facing the people. R. Eleazar b. R. Sadoq says, "At a feast they treat them as his appendages" (T Sanhedrin 7:8-9).

Rabbis cannot be forced to share in the costs of the common defense, because through their supernatural merit they defend the city, so b. B.B. 1:5 III.3-4/7b-8a: R. Judah the Patriarch applied the wall tax to the rabbis. Said R. Simeon b. Laqish, "Rabbis don't need protection, since it is written, 'If I should count them they are more in number than the sand' (Ps. 139:18). Who are the ones that are counted? Shall I say that reference is made to the righteous? But are they more in number than the sand? Since of the whole of Israel it is written, 'they shall be like the sand on the sea shore' (Gen. 22:17), how can the righteous alone be more than the sand? The sense of the verse is, I shall count the deeds of the righteous, and they shall be more in number than the sand. Now, if the sand, which is the lesser, protects the land against the sea, then how much more must the deeds of the righteous, which are the more important, protect everybody?" When he came before R. Yohanan, he said to him, "But why not derive the same fact from the following: 'I am a wall and my breasts are like towers' (Song 8:10). 'I am a wall' refers to the Torah, 'and my breasts are like towers' refers to disciples of the sages." But R. Simeon b. Laqish interprets the verse in line with the manner in which Raba explained it: "'I am a wall' the community of Israel, 'and my breasts are like towers' refers to houses of assembly and houses of study." R. Nahman bar R. Hisda collected the head tax karga from rabbis. Said to him R. Nahman bar Isaac, "You have violated the rules of the Torah, the Prophets, and the Writings. The Torah: 'Although he loves the peoples, all his saints are in your hand' (Deut. 33:3). Said Moses before the Holy One, blessed be He, 'Lord of the world, even when you love the peoples, may all his holy ones be in your hand.'"

When a sage dies, he must be mourned with special sorrow, so b. Shab. 13:4 I.4/105b: Said R. Simeon b. Pazzi said R. Joshua b. Levi in the name of Bar Qappara, "Whoever sheds tears for a good man — the Holy One, blessed be He, counts them up and puts them away in his treasure house: 'You count my grievings, put my tears into your bottle, are they not in your book' (Ps. 56:9)." Said R. Judah said Rab, "Whoever is dilatory in lamenting a sage is worthy of being buried alive: 'And they buried him in the border of his inheritance in Timnath-serah, which is in the hill country of Ephraim, on the north of the mountain of Gaash' (Josh. 24:30) — since the word Gaash shares consonants with the root for rage this teaches that the mountain raged against them to kill them." Said R. Hiyya bar Abba said R. Yohanan, "Whoever is dilatory in lamenting a sage won't live a long time: measure for measure: 'In measure when you send her away you contend with her' (Isa. 27:8)."

The death of great sages marks the end of particular gifts and capacities, and the end will come only when matters cannot grow still more corrupt, so M. Sot. 9:15: When R. Meir died, makers of parables came to an end. When Ben 'Azzai died, diligent students came to an end. When Ben Zoma' died, exegetes came to an end. When R. Joshua died, goodness went away from the world. When Rabban Simeon b. Gamaliel died, the locust came, and troubles multiplied. When R. Eleazar b. Azariah died, wealth went away from the sages. When R. Aqiba died, the glory of the Torah came to an end. When R. Hanina b. Dosa died, wonder-workers came to an end. When R. Yosé, Qatnuta died, pietists went away. (And why was he called Qatnuta? Because he was the least of the pietists.) When Rabban Yohanan b. Zakkai died, the splendor of wisdom came to an end. When Rabban Gamaliel the Elder died, the glory of the Torah came to an end, and cleanness and separateness perished. When R. Ishmael b. Phabi died, the splendor of the priesthood came to an end. When Rabbi died, modesty and fear of sin came to an end. R. Pinhas b. Yair says, "When the Temple was destroyed, associates became ashamed and so did free men, and they covered their heads. "And wonder-workers became feeble. And violent men and big talkers grew strong. "And none expounds and none seeks learning and none asks. "Upon whom shall we depend? Upon our Father in heaven." R. Eliezer the Great says, "From the day on which the

Temple was destroyed, sages began to be like scribes, and scribes like ministers, and ministers like ordinary folk. "And the ordinary folk have become feeble. "And none seeks. "Upon whom shall we depend? Upon our Father in heaven." With the footprints of the Messiah: presumption increases, and dearth increases. The vine gives its fruit and wine at great cost. And the government turns to heresy. And there is no reproof. The gathering place will be for prostitution. And Galilee will be laid waste. And the Gablan will be made desolate. And the men of the frontier will go about from town to town, and none will take pity on them. And the wisdom of scribes will putrefy. And those who fear sin will be rejected. And the truth will be locked away. Children will shame elders, and elders will stand up before children. "For the son dishonors the father and the daughter rises up against the mother, the daughter-in-law against her mother-in-law; a man's enemies are the men of his own house" (Mic. 7:6). The face of the generation in the face of a dog. A son is not ashamed before his father. Upon whom shall we depend? Upon our Father in heaven.

No doctrine or teaching concerning sages and their disciples fails to express the main point that the category as a whole sets forth.

XXI

RIGHTEOUSNESS, CHARITY

RIGHTEOUSNESS, CHARITY: To be righteous is to love God. That love is best express through acts of charity (philanthropy), which define righteousness better than any other.

The mark of righteousness is to desire God, and the righteous always point their hearts to God, so Lev. R. XLI:I.1: "But the Lord afflicted Pharaoh and his house with great plagues because of Sarai, Abram's wife" (Gen. 12:17): "The righteous shall flourish like the palm-tree, he shall grow like a cedar in Lebanon" (Ps. 92:13). Just as a palm tree and a cedar produce neither crooked curves nor growths, so the righteous do not produce either crooked curves or growths. Just as the shade of the palm tree and cedar is distant from the base of the tree so the giving of the reward that is coming to the righteous seems distant. Just as, in the case of the palm tree and the cedar, the very core of the tree points upward, so in the case of the righteous, their heart is pointed toward the Holy One, blessed be he. That is in line with the following verse of Scripture: "My eyes are ever toward the Lord, for he will bring forth my feet out of the net" (Ps. 25:15). Just as the palm tree and cedar are subject to desire, so the righteous are subject to desire. And what might it be? What they desire is the Holy One, blessed be he.

Charity and righteousness are called by one and the same word, *sedeqah*, because the act of philanthropy represents righteousness above all else. T. Peah 4:18 contains a statement characteristic of this view: Monobases the king of Adiabene went and gave to the poor all of his treasures during years of famine. His brothers sent the following message to him: "Your ancestors stored up treasures and increased the wealth left for them by their ancestors. But you went and gave away all of these treasures, both your own and those of your ancestors!" He replied to them, "My ancestors stored up treasures for this lower world , but , through giving charity have stored up treasures for the heavenly world above…My ancestors stored up treasures for the material world , where the human hand can reach, but I have stored up treasures for the non-material world , where the human hand cannot reach. My ancestors stored up treasures of a type that produce no real benefits, but I have stored up treasures of the sort that do produce benefits. My ancestors stored up treasures of money, but I have stored up treasures of souls ...My ancestors stored up treasures that eventually, after their deaths, would benefit only others, but I have stored up treasures that will benefit myself both in life and in death ...My ancestors stored up treasures in this world, but I have stored up treasures for myself in the world-to-come." T. Peah 4:19 further states, Charity and righteous deeds outweigh all other commandments in the Torah. So too said R. Joshua b. Qorha, "From which verse may we derive the fact~ that anyone who loses sight of the importance of giving charity is viewed as if he worshipped idolatry? It is stated in Scripture, Take heed lest there be a base thought in your heart, and you say. 'The seventh year, the year of release, is near,' and your eye be hostile to your poor brother, and you give him nothing" (Deut. 15:9). And elsewhere Scripture states, If you hear ... that certain base men have gone out among you, ... saying, 'Let us go and serve other gods,' ... you shall surely put the inhabitants of that city to the sword, destroying it utterly ... (Deut. 13:12Ä15). Just as in the latter case 'base' explicitly refers to idolatrous worship, so too in the former case 'base' refers to something deemed equivalent to idolatrous worship."

Acts of righteousness/charity deliver from death, so b. B.B. 1:5 IV.42/10a: Said R. Hiyya bar Abba said R. Yohanan, "It is written, 'Riches do not profit in the day of wrath, but righteousness delivers from death' (Prov. 11:4), and further, 'Treasures of wickedness profit nothing, but righteousness delivers from death' (Prov. 10:2). Why make reference to righteousness two times? One delivers from an unnatural death, the other from punishment of Gehenna. Which one delivers from Gehenna? It is the one in which 'wrath' is used, as it is written, 'A day of wrath is that day' (Zeph. 1:15). Which delivers someone from an unnatural death? When someone gives without knowing to whom he is giving, when someone gets without knowing from whom he gets.'"

Acts of charity are to be conducted with dignity and respect for the poor, so b. B.B. 1:5 IV.28-29/9b: said R. Isaac, "Any one who gives a penny to the poor is blessed with six blessings, and anyone who speaks to him in a comforting manner is blessed with eleven. Any one who gives a penny to the poor is blessed with six blessings: 'Is it not to deal your bread to the hungry and bring the poor to your house...when you see the naked' (Isa. 58:7) 'then shall your light break forth... .' And anyone who speaks to him in a comforting manner is blessed with eleven: 'If you draw out your soul to the hungry and satisfy the afflicted soul, then shall your light rise in the darkness and your darkness be as noonday, and the Lord shall guide you continually and satisfy your soul in drought...and they shall build from you the old waste places and you shall raise up the foundations of many generations' (Isa. 58:10-12)." And said R. Isaac, "What is the meaning of the verse: 'he who follows after righteousness charity and mercy finds life, righteousness, and honor' (Prov. 21:21)? Because a man has followed after righteousness shall he find righteousness that is, because one has given to charity, will he get charity when he needs it? Rather, the purpose is to indicate to you, whoever pursues righteousness — the Holy One, blessed be He, sees to the money that he needs with which to do acts of righteousness." Nahman bar Isaac said, "The Holy One, blessed be He, provides him with people who are appropriate recipients of charity, so he may get a reward for helping them."

God responds to acts of charity, so b. B.B. 1:5 IV;37-38/10a: Said R. Eleazar b. R. Yosé, "Every act of charity and mercy that Israelites do in this world brings about peace and great reconciliation between Israel and their father in heaven: 'Thus says the Lord, do not enter into the house of mourning, nor go to lament, nor bemoan them, for I have taken away my peace from this people...even loving kindness and tender mercies' (Jer. 16:4) — loving kindness refers to acts of mercy, and 'tender mercies' to charity." R. Judah says, "Great is charity, for it draws redemption nearer: 'Thus says the Lord, keep judgment and do righteousness charity , for my salvation is near to come and my righteousness to be revealed' (Isa. 56:1)." He would say, "Ten strong things have been created in the world. Rock is strong, iron shatters it. Iron is strong, fire melts it. Fire is strong, water quenches it. Water is strong, clouds carry it. Clouds are strong, wind scatters them. Wind is strong, the body can withstand it. The body is strong. Fear crushes it. Fear is strong, wine overcomes it. Wine is strong, sleep removes it. Death is strongest of all, but charity saves from death: 'Righteousness delivers from death' (Prov. 10:2)." Expounded R. Dosetai b. R. Yannai, "Come and note that the trait of the Holy One, blessed be He, is not like the trait of a mortal. If someone brings a splendid gift to the king, it may or may not be accepted from him, and should it be accepted from him, he may or may not see the king. But the Holy One, blessed be He, is not that way. Someone gives a penny to a poor person, and he has the merit of receiving the face of the Presence of God: 'And I shall behold your face in righteousness, I shall be satisfied when I awake with your likeness' (Ps. 17:15)."

Not performing an act of righteousness/charity constitutes an act of idolatry, so b. Ket. 6:5 I.15/ 68a: R. Hiyya bar Rab of Difti set forth as a Tannaite statement: "R. Joshua b. Qorhah says, 'Whoever hides his eyes from the needs of philanthropy is as though he worships idols. Here it is written, "Beware that there not be a base thought in your heart and your eye will be evil against your poor brother" (Deut. 14:9), and with regard to idolatry, "Certain base fellows are gone out" (Deut. 13:14). Just as there, the ultimate sin is idolatry, so here, idolatry is involved.'"

The primary media for overcoming an unwanted fate are prayer, charity, and repentance. To these God may respond with an act of forgiveness, so Y. Ta. 2:1 III.5: Said R. Eleazar, "Three acts nullify the harsh decree, and these are they: prayer, charity, and repentance." And all three of them are to be derived from a single verse of Scripture: 'If my people who are called by my name humble themselves, pray and seek my face, and turn from their wicked ways, then I will hear from heaven and will forgive their sin and heal their land ' (2 Chron. 7:14). Pray — this refers to prayer. 'And seek my face'— this refers to charity, as you say, 'As for me, I shall behold thy face in righteousness; when I awake, I shall be satisfied with beholding thy form' (Ps. 17:15). 'And turn from their wicked ways'— this refers to repentance." The repetitiousness of the categories emerges with great force, since distinguishing one category from another proves increasingly difficult.

XXII

Sanctification

Sanctification: that which is set aside in a hierarchical structure for God's purposes and use. There are levels of sanctification, so that one classification of things may be at a higher or a lower level of sanctification when compared to some other. So too, there are corresponding levels of cultic uncleanness; the higher a level of sanctification that something may reach, the more sensitive that that same classification of matter is to cultic contamination.

This is expressed in the following ladder of ascending and descending levels of sanctification, M. Megillah 3:1: Townsfolk who sold (1) a street of a town buy with its proceeds a synagogue. If they sold (2) a synagogue, they buy an ark. If they sold (3) an ark, they buy wrappings. If they sold (4) wrappings, they buy scrolls of the prophets or writings. If they sold (5) scrolls, they buy a Torah scroll. But if they sold (5) a Torah scroll, they should not buy scrolls. If they sold (4) scrolls, they should not buy wrappings. If they sold (3) wrappings, they should not buy an ark. If they sold (2) an ark, they should not buy a synagogue. If they sold (1) a synagogue, they should not buy a street. And so with the surplus of the proceeds of any of these "They do not sell that which belongs to the public to a private person, because they thereby diminish its level of sanctity," the words of R. Judah They said to him, "If so, they should not sell from a large town to small one." M. Kel. 1:6-9 spells out the hierarchy of sanctification in locative terms, as follows: There are ten degrees of holiness: (1) The land of Israel is holier than all lands. And what is its holiness? For they bring from it the omer, and the firstfruits, and the Two Loaves, which they do not bring (thus) from all lands. (2) The cities surrounded by a wall are more holy than it the land. For they send from them the lepers, and they carry around in their midst a corpse so long as they like. But once it has gone forth, they do not bring it back. (3) Within the wall of Jerusalem is more holy than they For they eat there lesser sanctities and second tithe. (4) The Temple mount is more holy than it. For Zabim, and Zabot, menstruating women, and those that have given birth do not enter there. (5) The rampart is more holy than it. For gentiles and he who is made unclean by a corpse do not enter there. (6) The court of women is more holy than it. For a tebul-yom does not enter there, but they are not liable on its account for a sin offering. (7) The court of Israel is more holy than it. For one who yet lacks atonement offerings made in the completion of his purification rite does not enter there, and they are liable on its account for a sin offering. (8) The court of the priests is more holy than it. For Israelite(s) do not enter there except in the time of their cultic requirements: for laying on of hands, for slaughtering, and for waving.(9) The area between the porch and the altar is more holy than it. For those priests who are blemished or whose hair is unloosed do not enter there. (10) The sanctuary is more holy than it. For a priest whose hands and feet are not washed does not enter there. (11) The Holy of Holies is more holy than they. For only the high priest on the Day of Atonement at the time of the service enters there.

Gradations of sanctification matched by a hierarchy of susceptibility to uncleanness is expressed at M. Hag. 2:5ff:. They wash the hands for eating unconsecrated food, tithe, and heave offering; and for eating food in the status of Holy Things they immerse; and as to the preparation of purification water through the burning of the red cowl, if one's hands are made unclean, his entire body is deemed to be unclean as well. He who immerses for the eating of unconsecrated food and is thereby confirmed as suitable for eating unconsecrated food is prohibited from eating tithe. If he immersed for eating tithe and is thereby confirmed as suitable for eating tithe, he is prohibited from eating heave offering. If he immersed for eating heave offering and is thereby confirmed as suitable for eating heave offering, he is prohibited from eating food in the status of Holy Things. If he immersed for eating food in the status of Holy Things and is thereby confirmed as suitable for eating food in the status of Holy Things, he is prohibited from engaging in the preparation of purification water. If, however, one immersed for the matter requiring the more stringent rule, he is permitted to engage in the matter requiring the less stringent rule. If he immersed but was not confirmed, it is as though he did not immerse.

The counterpart to the hierarchy of sanctification involves a hierarchy of the relative virulence — capacity to impart uncleanness — of the various sources of uncleanness, twenty in all, as at M. Kel. 1:1-4: The

Fathers of Uncleannesses are (1) the creeping thing, and (2) semen of an adult Israelite, and (3) one who has contracted corpse uncleanness, and (4) the leper in the days of his counting, and (5) sin offering water of insufficient quantity to be sprinkled. Lo, these render man and vessels unclean by contact, and earthenware vessels by presence within the vessels' contained airspace. But they do not render unclean by carrying. Above them: (6) carrion, and (7) sin offering water of sufficient quantity to be sprinkled. For they render man unclean through carrying, to make his clothing unclean. But clothing is not made unclean through contact. Above them: (8) he who has intercourse with a menstruating woman, for he conveys uncleanness to what lies far beneath him in like degree as he conveys uncleanness to what lies above. Above them: (9) the flux of the Zab, and (10) his spittle and (11) his semen and (12) his urine, and (13) the blood of the menstruating woman, for they render unclean through contact and carrying. Above them: (14) the saddle, F for it the saddle is unclean under a heavy stone. Above the saddle: (15) the couch, for touching it is equivalent to carrying it. Above the couch: (16) the Zab, for the Zab conveys uncleanness to the couch, but the couch does not convey equivalent uncleanness to the couch. Above the Zab: (17) the Zabah, for she renders him that has intercourse with her unclean for seven days. Above the Zabah: (18) the leper, for he renders unclean by his coming into a house. Above the leper: (19) a bone about the size of a barley corn, for it renders unclean for a seven days' uncleanness. Weightiest of them all: (20) the corpse, for it renders unclean by overshadowing a mode of rendering uncleanness by which none of the rest conveys uncleanness.

    We note further that the category of sanctification encompasses relations between a man and a woman, from the act of betrothal, which is called an act of sanctification, onward. Heaven acknowledges that relationship, so that if on earth an act of adultery is committed, Heaven takes reprisal. When on earth a writ of divorce severs the relationship, Heaven recognizes that the sanctification of that woman to that man has concluded.

XXIII

Sin

SIN: an act of rebellion against God, for example, the failure to carry out one's obligation to God set forth in the Torah; to be avoided by imposing votive restrictions to avoid approaching the possibility of neglecting one's obligation, e.g., "As regards all commandments which sages said may be performed 'Until midnight' the obligation to perform them persists until the rise of dawn. If so why did sages say that these actions may be performed only until midnight? In order to protect man from sin" (M. Ber. 1:1). Sin is avoided through learning in the Torah, so M. Qid. 1:10: Whoever has learning in Scripture, Mishnah, and right conduct will not quickly sin, since it is said, "And a threefold cord is not quickly broken" (Qoh. 4:12). And whoever does not have learning in Scripture, Mishnah, and right conduct has no share in society. The three worst sins occur time and again, e.g., at Y. A.Z. 2:2 I.3: R. Jacob in the name of R. Yohanan: "With all sorts of things do they effect healing, except for an idol, fornication, or committing murder." These three — idolatry, fornication, and murder — are to be avoided at all costs, including one's life.

Sin comes about because of the innate inclination to do evil, so M. Suk. 5:1-4 II.3/b. 52a: With regard to "And the land shall mourn, every family apart; the family of the house of David apart, and their wives apart" (Zech. 12:12), What was the reason for the mourning to which reference is made in Zechariah's statement? R. Dosa and rabbis differed on this matter. One said, "It is on account of the Messiah, the son of Joseph, who was killed." And the other said, "It is on account of the evil inclination, which was killed." Now in the view of him who said, "It is on account of the Messiah, the son of Joseph, who was killed," we can make sense of the following verse of Scripture: "And they shall look on me because they have thrust him through, and they shall mourn for him as one mourns for his only son" (Zech. 12:10). But in the view of him who has said, "It is on account of the evil inclination, which was killed," should this be an occasion for mourning? It should be an occasion for rejoicing. Why then should the people have wept? The answer is in accord with the exposition of R. Judah: "In the time to come, the Holy One, blessed be he, will bring the evil inclination and slay it before the righteous and before the wicked. "To the righteous the evil inclination will look like a high hill, and to the wicked it will appear like a hair-thin thread. "These will weep, and those will weep. The righteous will weep, saying, 'How could we ever have overcome a hill so high as this one!' The wicked will weep, saying, 'How could we not have overcome a hair-thin thread like this one!' "And so too the Holy One, blessed be he, will share their amazement, as it is said, "'Thus says the Lord of Hosts. If it be marvelous in the eyes of the remnant of this people in those days, it shall also be marvelous in my eyes' (Zech. 8:6)."

The inclination to do evil bears a number of different names: M. Suk. 5:1-4 II.5/b. 52a: "The evil inclination has seven names. The Holy One, blessed be he, called it 'evil,' as it is said, 'For the inclination of man's heart is evil from his youth' (Gen. 8:21). Moses called it 'uncircumcised,' as it is said, "Circumcise therefore the foreskin of your heart' (Deut. 10:16). David called it 'unclean,' as it is said, 'Create in me a clean heart, O Lord' (Ps. 51:12), bearing the implication that there is an unclean one. Solomon called it, 'the enemy,' as it is said, 'If your enemy is hungry, give him bread Torah to eat, and if he is thirsty, give him water [Torah] to drink. For you will heap coals of fire upon his head, and the Lord will reward you' (Prov. 25:21-22). Do not read, 'will reward you' but 'will make him stay at peace with you. Isaiah called it 'stumbling block,' as it is said, 'Cast you up, cast you up, clear the way, take up the stumbling block out of the way of my people' (Is. 57:14). Ezekiel called it, 'stone,' as it is said, 'And I will take away the heart of stone out of your flesh, and I will give you a heart of flesh' (Ez. 36:26). Joel called it, 'the hidden,' as it is said, 'But I will remove far away from you the hidden one' (Joel 2:20)."

The inclination to do evil is constantly at work, M. Suk. 5:1-4 II.9/ b. 52a-b: "A man's inclination to do evil overcomes him every day. Said R. Simeon b. Laqish, "A man's inclination to do evil prevails over him every day and seeks to kill him. For it is said, 'The wicked watches the righteous and seeks to slay him' (Ps. 37:32). And if the Holy One, blessed be he, were not there to help him, he could not withstand it. For it is said, 'The Lord will not leave him in his hand nor suffer him to be condemned when he is judged' (Ps. 37:32)." But study of Torah drives the inclination to do evil away, so M. Suk. 5:1-4 II.10/52b: "If that vile one meets you, drag it to the house of study. If it is a stone, it will dissolve. If it is iron, it will be pulverized." If it is a stone, it will dissolve," as it is written, "Ho, everyone who is thirsty, come to water" (Is. 55:1). And it is written, "The water wears down stones" (Job. 14:19). If it is iron, it will be pulverized," as it is written, "Is not my word like fire, says the Lord, and like a hammer that breaks the rock into pieces" (Jer. 23:29). The evil inclination entices a man in this world and then gives testimony against him in the world to come.

The impulse to do evil competes with the impulse to do good, and the wise man will nurture the latter and try to contain the former, so b. Ber. 9:1 XVII.9-12/61a-b: Said Rab, "The impulse to do evil is like a fly. It sits between the two doors of the heart, as it is said, 'Dead flies make the ointment of the perfumes fetid and putrid' (Qoh. 10:1)." And Samuel said, "It is like a grain of wheat, as it is said, 'Sin couches at the door' (Gen. 4:7)." The kidneys counsel, the heart discerns, the tongue shapes words, the mouth expresses them, the gullet admits and gives out all sorts of food, the windpipe produces sound, the lungs take in all sorts of liquids, the liver produces anger, the gall drops a drop into it and calms it, the milt makes one laugh, the large intestine grinds food, the maw induces sleep, the nose wakes one up. If what produces wakening sleeps, or what produces sleep wakes one up, a person will pine away. R. Yosé, the Galilean says, "As to the righteous, the impulse to do good produces their judgments of what to do or not to do, for it is said, 'My heart is slain within me' (Ps. 109:22). As to the wicked, the impulse to do evil produces their judgments of what to do or not to do, for it is said, 'Transgression speaks to the wicked, I think, there is no fear of God before his eyes' (Ps. 36:2). As to people who fall in the middle, both impulses produce their judgments of what to do or not to do, for it is said, 'Because he stands at the right hand of the needy, to save him from them that judge his soul' (Ps. 109:31)."

The impulse to do evil can be overcome, specifically through Torah-study, so Gen. R. LIV:I.1: "When a man's ways please the Lord, even his enemies are at peace with him" (Prov. 16:7). R. Joshua b. Levi said, "The cited verse refers to the impulse to do evil. Under ordinary circumstances if someone grows up with a fellow for two or three years, he develops a close tie to him. But the impulse to do evil grows with someone from youth to old age, and, if one can, someone strikes down the impulse to do evil even when he is seventy or eighty. So did David say, 'All my bones shall say, "Lord, who is like unto you, who delivers the poor from him who is too strong for him, yes, the poor and the needy from him who spoils him'" (Ps. 35:10)." Said R. Aha, "And is there a greater thief than this one? And Solomon said, 'If your enemy be hungry, give him bread to eat' (Prov. 25:21). The meaning is, the bread of the Torah which will help a person resist the enemy that is the impulse to do evil, as it is said, 'Come, eat of my bread' (Prov. 9:5). 'If he is thirsty give him water to drink' (Prov. 25:21), that is, the water of the Torah, as it is said, 'Ho, everyone who is thirsty come for water' (Is. 55:1)."

It follows that what keeps man from sin is knowledge of who he is, and before Whom he is judged, so M. Abot 3:1: Aqabiah b. Mehallalel says, "Reflect upon three things and you will not fall into the clutches of transgression: Know (1) from whence you come, (2) whither you are going, and before whom you are going to have to give a full account of yourself. From whence do you come? From a putrid drop. Whither are you going? To a place of dust, worms, and maggots. And before whom are you going to give a full account of Yourself? Before the King of kings of kings, the Holy One, blessed be he."

What causes man to sin — the source of the impulse to do evil — is arrogance above all other motives, so T. Sot. 3:6-9 points to arrogance as the basis for sin, and arrogance comes about when people do not acknowledge that God is the source of the blessings that they enjoy: The generation of the Flood acted arrogantly before the Omnipresent only on account of the good which he lavished on them, since it is said, Their houses are safe from fear, neither is the rod of God upon them (Job 21:9). Their bull genders and fails not, their cow calves and casts not her calf (Job 21:10). They send forth their little ones like a pock, and their children dance (Job 21:11). They spend their days in prosperity and their years in pleasures (Job 36:11). That is what caused them to say to God, "Depart from us, for we do not desire knowledge of thy ways. What is the Almighty, that we should serve Him, and what property should we have, if we pray to him" (Job 21:14). They said, "Do we need Him for anything except a few drops of rain? But look, we have rivers and wells which are more than enough for us in the sunny season and in the rainy season, since it is said, And a mist rose from the earth (Gen. 2:6)." The Omnipresent then said to them, "By the goodness which I lavished on them they take pride before me? By that same good I shall exact punishment from them!" What does it say? And 1, behold, I bring a flood of water upon the earth (Gen. 6: 17). R. Yosé, b. Durmasqit says, "The men of the Flood took pride only on account of the covetousness of the eyeball, which is like water, as it is said, The sons of God saw that the daughter of men were fair, and they took them wives from all which they chose (Gen. 6:2). Also the Omnipresent exacted punishment from them only through water, which is like the eyeball, as it is written, All the fountains of the great deep were broken up, and the windows of heaven were opened (Gen. 7:11)."

Israelite sin is what estranges God from Israel, so b. Sot. 1: IV.9-10/3b: And R. Hisda said, "In the beginning, before the Israelites sinned, the Divine Presence rested upon every one of them, as it is said, 'For the Lord your God walks with you in the midst of the camp' (Deut. 23:15). Once they had sinned, the Divine Presence went away from them, as it is said, 'That he see no unclean thing in you and turn away from you' (Deut. 23:15)." Said R. Samuel bar Nahmani said R. Jonathan, "Whoever does a religious duty in this world — that deed goes before him to the world to come, as it is said, 'And your righteousness shall go before you' (Is. 58:8). And whoever commits a transgression in this world -- that act turns aside from him and goes before him on the Day of Judgment, as it is said, 'The paths of their way are turned aside, they go up into the waste and perish' (Job 6:18)." R. Eliezer says, "It attaches to him like a dog, as it is said, 'He did not listen to her to lie by her or to be with her' (Gen. 39:10). 'To lie by her' in this world 'Or to be with her' in the world to come."

Just as a principal sin is arrogance, as a principal virtue is humility, so b. Sot. 1:1 V.13-25//5b-6a: Whence in Scripture do we derive an admonition against the arrogant? Said Raba said Zeiri, "'Listen and give ear, do not be proud' (Jer. 13:15)." Nahman bar Isaac said, "From the following: 'Your heart will be lifted up, and you will forget the Lord your God' (Deut. 8:14). "And it is written, 'Beware, lest you forget the Lord your God' (Deut. 8:11)." And that accords with what R. Abin said R. Ilaa said. For R. Abin said R. Ilaa said, "In every place in which it is said, 'Beware lest... that you not...,' the meaning is only to lay down a negative commandment so that one who does such a thing violates a negative admonition." R. Avira expounded, sometimes in the name of R. Assi and sometimes in the name of R. Ammi, "Whoever is arrogant in the end will be diminished, as it is said, 'They are exalted, there will be a diminution' (Job. 24:24). And lest you maintain that they continue in the world alive, Scripture states, 'And they are gone' (Job. 24:24). But if the arrogant person repents, he will be gathered up in death at the time allotted to him and not before, as was the case with our father, Abraham, as it is said, 'But when they are lowly, they are gathered in like all' (Job 24:24) — like Abraham, Isaac, and Jacob, concerning whom 'all' is written at Gen. 24:1, 27:33, 33:11. And if not: 'They are cut off as the tops of the ears of corn' (Job 24:24)." "With him also who is of a contrite and humble spirit" (Is. 57:15). Huna and R. Hisda: One said, "I God am with the contrite." The other said, "I God am the contrite." R. Joseph said, "A person should always learn from the attitude of his Creator, for lo, the Holy One, blessed be he, neglected all mountains and heights and brought his Presence to rest on Mount Sinai, and he neglected all valuable trees and brought his Presence to rest in the bush." Said R. Eleazar, "Whoever is arrogant is worthy of being cut down like an asherah a tree that is worshipped. Here it is written, 'The high ones of stature shall be cut down' (Is. 10:33), and elsewhere it is written, 'And you shall hew down their Asherim' (Deut. 7:5)." And R. Eleazar said, "Whoever is arrogant — his dust will not be stirred up in the resurrection of the dead. For it is said, 'Awake and sing, you that dwell in the dust' (Is. 26:19). It is stated not 'you who lie in the dust' but 'you who dwell in the dust,' meaning, one who has become a neighbor to the dust by constant humility even in his lifetime." And R. Eleazar said, "For whoever is arrogant the Presence of God laments, as it is said, 'But the haughty he knows from afar' (Ps. 138:6). R. Avira expounded, and some say it was R. Eleazar, "Come and take note of the fact that not like the trait of the Holy One, blessed be he, is the trait of flesh and blood. The trait of flesh and blood is that those who are high take note of those who are high, but the one who is high does not take note of the one who is low. But the trait of the Holy One, blessed be he, is not that way. He is high, but he takes note of the low, as it is said, 'For though the Lord is high, yet he takes note of the low' (Ps. 138:6). Said R. Hisda, and some say it was Mar Uqba, "Concerning whoever is arrogant said the Holy One, blessed be he, he and I cannot live in the same world, as it is said, 'Whoever slanders his neighbor in secret — him will I destroy; him who has a haughty look and a proud heart I will not endure' (Ps. 101:5). o not read, 'him I cannot endure' but 'with him I cannot endure.'" Said R. Alexandri, "Whoever is arrogant — even the slightest breeze shakes him, as it is said, 'But the wicked are like the troubled sea' (Is. 57:20). Now if the sea, which is so vast — the slightest breeze shakes it, a man, who is not so vast — all the more so that the slightest breeze would shake him. Said R. Hiyya bar Ashi said Rab, "A disciple of a sage should have one eighth of an eighth of pride. Said R. Nahman bar Isaac, "He should have no part of it, nor even of part of part of it." Is it a small thing that it is written in connection with arrogance, 'Everyone who is proud of heart is an abomination to the Lord' (Prov. 16:5)?" Said Hezekiah, "The prayer of a person is heard only if he makes his heart as soft as flesh, as it is said, 'And it shall come to pass, that from one new moon to the next, all flesh shall come to worship' (Is. 66:23). Said R. Zira, "In regard to flesh, it is written, 'And it is healed' (Lev. 13:18). In regard to man, it is not written, 'And he is healed.' Said R. Yohanan, "The letters for the word Adam stand for dust, blood, and gall. The letters for the word for flesh stand for shame, stench, and worm. Some say, "Sheol," for its initial letter corresponds" "The initial of the word for 'stench' is *samek*, whereas the second letter in *basar* is similar in form to that of 'Sheol.'" Said R. Ashi, Whoever is arrogant in the end will be diminished, as it is said, 'For a rising and for a scab' (Lev. 14:56), and rising refers only to elevation, as it is said, 'Upon all the high mountains and upon all the hills that are lifted up' (Is. 2:14). Scab means only 'attachment,' as it is said, 'Attach me, I ask you, to one of the priests' offices, so that I may eat a piece of bread' (1 Sam. 2:36). Said R. Joshua b. Levi, "Come and take note of how great are the humble in the sight of the Holy One, blessed be he. For when the sanctuary stood, a person would bring a burnt-offering, gaining thereby the reward for bringing a burnt-offering, or a meal-offering, and gaining the reward for a meal offering. But a person who is genuinely humble does Scripture treat as if he had made offerings of all the sacrifices, as it is said, 'The sacrifices of God are a broken spirit' (Ps. 51:19). And not only so, but his prayer is not rejected, as it is said, 'A broken and contrite heart, O God, you will not despise' (Ps. 51:19). And R. Joshua b. Levi said, "Whoever properly sets his ways in this world will have the merit of witnessing the salvation of the Holy One, blessed be he, as it is said, 'To him who orders his way I will show the salvation of God' (Ps. 50:23). Do not read 'orders' but 'properly sets' his way." He calculates the loss incurred in fulfilling a precept against the reward it will bring him."

Among all types of sin, the two that predominate are idolatry and fornication. Of these, the impulse to do evil that exercises greatest power is sexual, so Song XCVI:i.1: "You are stately as a palm tree:" R. Hunia in the name of R. Dosa b. R. Tebet: "Two impulses to do evil did the Holy One, blessed be He, create in his world, the impulse to worship idols, and the impulse to fornicate. The impulse to worship idols has already been eliminated, but the impulse to fornicate still endures. Said the Holy One, blessed be He, 'Whoever can withstand the impulse to fornicate do I credit as though he had withstood them both.'" Said R. Judah, "The matter may be compared to the case of a snake-charmer who had two snakes. He charmed the larger and left the smaller, saying, 'Whoever can withstand this one is certainly credited as though he had withstood them both.' So the Holy One, blessed be He, eliminated the impulse to worship idols but left the impulse to fornicate. He said, 'Whoever can withstand the impulse to fornicate do I credit as though he had withstood them both.'" The impulse to do evil also bears a good side, so Gen. R. IX:VII.1: Nahman in the name of R. Samuel: "'Behold, it was very good' refers to the impulse to do good. 'And behold, it was very good' encompasses also the impulse to do evil. And is the impulse to do evil '*very* good'? Indeed so, for if it were not for the impulse to do evil, a man would not build a house, marry a wife, and produce children. So does Solomon say, 'Again I considered all labor and all excelling in work, that is rivalry with his neighbor' (Qoh. 4:4)."

A major sin is gossip, and all forms of wicked speech fall within that same category, so Lev. R. XVI:VI.1, XVI:VII.1: Said R. Joshua b. Levi, "The word 'torah' law occurs with regard to the leper on five different occasions: 'This is the Torah governing a spot of leprosy' (Lev. 13:59) 'This is the Torah governing him on whom is a spot of leprosy' (Lev. 14:32). 'This is the Torah governing every spot of leprosy and itch' (Lev. 14:54. 'This is the Torah And the encompassing reference: 'This will be the Torah governing the leper' (Lev. 14:2) — the Torah governing the common gossip. This teaches you that whoever repeats gossip violates all five scrolls of the Torah." Therefore Moses admonished the Israelites, saying to them, "This will be the Torah governing the leper (mesora)" (Lev. 14:2) — the Torah governing the gossip. "The priest shall command them to take for him who is to be cleansed two living clean birds and cedarwood and scarlet stuff and hyssop" (Lev. 14:4). Said R. Judah b. R. Simon, "Birds chirp a lot. This one who speaks gossip. Said the Holy One, blessed be he, 'Let the one with a voice the bird come and effect atonement for what the voice of the gossip has done.'"

God's presence is offended by displays of temper, and temper is a mark of arrogance, a source of sin, so M. Ned. 4:4 I.16-18/22b: Said Rabbah bar R. Huna, "Whoever loses his temper — even the Presence of God is not important to him: 'The wicked, through the pride of his countenance, will not seek God; God is not in all his thoughts' (Ps. 10:4)." R. Jeremiah of Difti said, "Whoever loses his temper — he forgets what he has learned and increases foolishness: 'For anger rests in the heart of fools' (Qoh. 7:9), and 'But the fool lays open his folly' (Prov. 13:16)." R. Nahman bar Isaac said, "One may be sure that his sins outnumber his merits: 'And a furious man abounds in transgressions' (Prov. 29:22)." Said R. Ada b. R. Hanina, "If the Israelites had not sinned, to them would have been given only the Five Books of the Torah and the book of Joshua alone, which involves the division of the Land of Israel. How come? 'For much wisdom proceeds from much anger' (Qoh. 1:18)." The anger of God caused him to send prophets with their wise teachings.

Sin exercises such power that on account of sin, various ailments commenced in Israel, so , so Sif. Num. I:X.2: R. Yosé, the Galilean says, "Come and take note of how great is the power of sin. For before the people had laid hands on transgression, people afflicted with flux and lepers were not located among them, but after they had laid hands on transgression, people afflicted with flux and lepers did find a place among them. Accordingly, we learn that these three events took place on one and the same day: transgression, the presence of those afflicted with flux, the development of leprosy among the people." R. Simeon b. Yohai says, "Come and take note of how great is the power of sin. For before the people had laid hands on transgression, what is stated in their regard? 'Now the appearance of the glory of the Lord was like a devouring fire on the top of the mountain in the sight of the people of Israel' (Ex. 24:17). Nonetheless, the people did not fear nor were they afraid. But once they had laid hands on transgression, what is said in their regard? 'And when Aaron and all the people of Israel saw Moses, behold, the skin of his face shone, and they were afraid to come near him' (Ex. 34:30)."

The impulse to do evil governed until Abraham entered the world, but he discovered how easy it is to overcome it, so Gen. R. XXII:VI.5: Explaining the sense of the phrase, "Sin is couching at the door," said R. Tanhum bar Merion, "There are dogs in Rome that know how to dissemble. A dog goes and sets down before a baker shop and pretends to doze. The owner of the shop dozes too, and then the dog knocks a loaf to the ground. While the people are collecting the bread, the dog snatches a loaf and makes its getaway. Thus sin pretends to sleep until it catches its victim off guard." Explaining the same phrase, said R. Abba bar Yudan, "The matter may be compared to the case of a threatening but feeble thug, who sat at the crossroads. Whoever came by he ordered, 'Give me everything you've got.' But a smart fellow came by and realized that the thug was in fact decrepit. So he beat him up. So for many generations the impulse to do evil caused destruction. The generation of Enosh, the generation of the Flood, and the generation of the Dispersion all were conquered by it. When Abraham arose and saw that the impulse to do evil in fact amounted to nothing, he began to knock it about. That is in line with the following verse of Scripture: 'And I will beat to pieces his impulse before him' (Ps. 89:24). Thus 'sin couches at the door' — his strength being only simulated." Said R. Ammi, "The impulse to do evil does not walk along the sides of the path but right down the center. When it sees a man blinking his eyes, smoothing his hair, skipping along arrogantly and generally preening himself about his good looks, he says, 'This one is mine.' Why so? 'Do you see someone wise in his own view? The fool meaning, sin has hope of seizing him' (Prov. 26:12)." Said R. Abin, "Whoever indulges his impulse to do evil in his youth in the end will be ruled by the evil impulse in his old age. What verse of Scripture so indicates? 'He who indulges his servant in youth shall have him as a master in the end' (Prov. 29:21)." R. Hanina said, "If your evil impulse comes to make you laugh, put it off with words of Torah: 'The evil impulse, when near you, you shall combat' (Is. 26:3). And if you do so, I shall credit it to you as if you had created peace: 'You shall create peace' (Is. 26:3). What is written is not 'you shall keep,' but 'you shall create.' And if you should say that the evil impulse does not lie within your domain, Scripture says, 'Surely it is safe in you' (Is. 26:3), and I have already written for your attention in the Torah: 'And its desire is for you, but you must master it' (Gen. 4:7)." R. Simon said, "If your impulse to do evil comes to make you laugh, give it reason to rejoice in the Torah: 'Your impulse is gladdened' (Is. 26:3). And if you do so, I shall credit it to you as if you had created two worlds. 'Peace' is not what is written here, but rather, 'Peace, peace' (Is. 26:3) referring therefore to two whole worlds."

Fear of sin is more important than acquisition of wisdom, so M. Abot 3:9 R. Haninah b. Dosa says, "For anyone whose fear of sin takes precedence over his wisdom, his wisdom will endure, And for anyone whose wisdom takes precedence over his fear of sin, his wisdom will not endure. Anyone whose deeds are more than his wisdom — his wisdom will endure. And anyone whose wisdom is more than his deeds — his wisdom will not endure." The stakes are very high, for it is sin that brings about not only pain, suffering, and misfortune, but the very givens of the human condition, the need to work, rather than exist off the abundance of nature, so M. Qid. 4:14: R. Simeon b. Eleazar says, "Have you ever seen a wild beast or a bird who has a trade? Yet they get along without difficulty. And were they not created only to serve me? And I was created to serve my Master. So is it not logical that I should get along without difficulty? But I have done evil and ruined my living." So to avoid sin it is a virtue to build a fence around the Torah, e.g., at M. Abot 3:13, R. Aqiba says, "Tradition is a fence for the Torah. Tithes are a fence for wealth. Vows are a fence for abstinence. A fence for wisdom is silence."

Sin is what diminishes man and estranges him from God, so Song R. XLI:ii.1-3: Before someone sins, he is paid awe and fear, and creatures fear him. But once he has sinned, he is subject to awe and fear, and he fears others. You may know that this is so, for so said Rabbi, "Before the First Man sinned, he heard the sound of the Divine Speech while standing on his feet, and he was not afraid. But once he had sinned, when he heard the sound of the Divine Speech, he was afraid and he hid: 'I heard your voice and I was afraid' (Gen. 3:10); 'And the man and his wife hid themselves' (Gen. 3:8)." R. Levi said, "Before the First Man sinned, he heard the sound of the Divine Speech in a mild way. But once he had sinned, when he heard the sound of the Divine Speech, it was fierce. Before the Israelites sinned, they saw seven fiery partitions pressing on one another, but they were not afraid nor did they tremble or concern themselves. But once they had sinned, even upon the face of the mediator Moses they could not gaze: 'The skin of Moses' face sent forth beams' (Ex. 34:35); 'And they were afraid to come near him' (Ex. 34:30).''

The same view comes to the surface in the proposition that before a man has sinned, people pay him reverence and awe. Once he has sinned, they impose on him reverence and awe, so PRK V:III.3: R. Ishmael taught on Tannaite authority, "Before a man has sinned, people pay him reverence and awe. Once he has sinned, they impose on him reverence and awe. Thus, before the first man had sinned, he would hear God's voice in an workaday way. After he had sinned, he heard the same voice as something strange. Before he had sinned, the first man heard God's voice and would stand on his feet: 'And they heard the sound of God walking in the garden in the heat of the day' (Gen. 3:8). After he had sinned, he heard the voice of God and hid: 'And man and his wife hid' (Gen. 3:8). Before the Israelites sinned, what is written in their regard? 'And the appearance of the glory of the Lord was like a consuming fire on the top of the mountain before the eyes of the children of Israel' (Ex. 24:17). But when they had sinned, even on the face of the intercessor Moses they could not look: 'And Aaron and all the children of Israel feared...to come near' (Ex. 34:40)." Before the deed of David with Bath Sheba took place, what is written? 'For David: The Lord is my light and my salvation, of whom shall I be afraid?' (Ps. 27:1). But after that deed took place, what is written? 'I will come upon him while he is weary and weak-handed' (2 Sam. 17:2). Before Solomon sinned, he could rule over demons and demonesses: 'I got for myself...Adam's progeny, demons and demonesses' (Qoh. 2:8). But after he had sinned, he brought sixty mighty men to guard his bed: 'Lo, the bed of Solomon, with sixty mighty men around it, all of them holding a sword and veterans of war' (Song 3:7-8). Before Saul had sinned, what is written concerning him? 'And when Saul had taken dominion over Israel, he fought against all his enemies on every side, against Moab, against the Ammonites, against Edom, against the kings of Zobah, and against the Philistines; wherever he turned he put them to the worse' (1 Sam. 14:47). After he had sinned what is written concerning him? 'And Saul saw the camp of the Philistines and was afraid' (1 Sam. 28:5)."

A person has to see himself as in danger by reason of sin, and should not be confident of his situation, so T. Qid. 1:13-15: One should always see himself as if he is half meritorious and half guilty. If he did a single commandment, happy is he, for he has inclined the balance for himself to the side of merit. If he committed a single transgression, woe is he, for he has inclined the balance to the side of guilt. Concerning this one it is said, "One sinner destroys much good" (Qoh. 9:18), for on account of a single sin that he commits, much good is lost to him. R. Eleazar b. R. Simeon says, "For the world is judged by the conduct of the majority in it, and an individual is judged by the majority of the deeds that he has done; if he did a single commandment, happy is he, for he has inclined the balance for himself and for the world as well to the side of merit. If he committed a single transgression, woe is he, for he has inclined the balance to the side of guilt for himself and for the world, for it is said, 'One sinner destroys much good' (Qoh. 9:18) — for on account of a single sin that he commits, much good is lost to him and to the whole world." R. Simeon b. Yohai says, "If a man was righteous his entire life but at the end he rebelled, he loses the whole, for it is said, 'The righteousness of the righteous shall not deliver him in the day of his transgression' (Ezek. 33:12). And even if one is completely wicked all his life but repents at the end, he is not reproached with his wickedness, for it is said, 'And as for the wickedness of the wicked, he shall not fall thereby in the day that he turns from his wickedness' (Ezek. 33:12)."

The punishment for sin varies, depending on the character of the sin. In general one may pay for sin in suffering in this world and hold on to his portion in the world to come, but under some circumstances, that is not possible, so Y. San. 10:1 I.2: As to idolatry and fornication, R. Jonah and R. Yosah — One of them said, "These are among the lesser violations of the law which are punished in this world only." The other of them said, "They are among the greater violations of the law which are punished in the world to come." Concerning one who did not repent and died through extirpation — if the greater part of his record consisted of honorable deeds, and the smaller part, transgressions, they exact punishment from him in this world. If the smaller part of the transgressions which he has done are of the lesser character, he is punished in this world so as to pay him his full and complete reward in the world to come. If the greater part of his record consisted of transgressions and the lesser part of honorable deeds, they pay him off with the reward of the religious deeds which he has done entirely in this world, so as to exact punishment from him in a whole and complete way in the world to come. If the greater part of his record consisted of honorable deeds, he will inherit the Garden of Eden. If the greater part consisted of transgressions, he will inherit Gehenna. If the record was evenly balanced — Said R. Yosé, b. Haninah, "'... forgives sins... ,' is not written here, but rather, '... forgives a sin' (Num 14:18). That is to say, the Holy One, blessed be he, tears up one bond recorded among the transgressions, so that the honorable deeds then will outweigh the others." Said R. Eleazar, "'And that to thee, O Lord, belongs steadfast love. For thou do requite a man according to his work' (Ps. 62:13). 'His deed' is not written here, but 'like his deed' — if he has none, you give him one of yours."

The marks of the skin disease ("plagues of leprosy") come about for specific sins, so Lev. R. XVII:III.1ff: For ten reasons do plagues of leprosy come: idolatry, promiscuity, murder, profanation of God's name, blasphemy of God's name, robbing from the community, stealing what does not belong to a person, arrogance, gossiping, and grudging ("the evil eye"). On account of idolatry: The case derives from Israel, which gave false testimony against the Holy One, blessed be he, by going and saying to a calf, "This is your God, O Israel" (Ex. 32:4). How do we know that they were afflicted with leprosy? As it is said, "And Moses saw the people, that it had broken out, for Aaron had made it break out" (Ex. 32:25). For an epidemic of leprosy and discharge had broken out among them. Promiscuity: The case derives from the daughters of Zion: "Because the daughters of Zion are haughty" (Is. 3:16). How do we know that they were afflicted with leprosy? As it is said, "The Lord will smite with a scab the heads of the daughters of Zion" (Is. 3:17). Murder: The case derives from Joab: "And the Lord will return his blood upon his own head" (1 Kgs. 2:32). How do we know that he was smitten with leprosy? "May it fall upon the head of Joab and upon all his father's house and may the house of Joab never be without one who has a discharge or who is leprous" (2 Sam. 3:29). Profanation of God's name: The case derives from Gehazi: "Gehazi, the servant of Elisha, the man of God, said, 'See, my master has spared this Naaman, the Syrian, in not accepting from his hand what he brought. As the Lord lives, I will run after him and get something (*meumah*) from him'" (2 Kgs. 5:20). What is the meaning of "something (*meumah*)?" From the blemish (*mumah*) which afflicts him. And how do we know that he was smitten with leprosy? "Therefore the leprosy of Naaman will cleave to you and to your descendants forever. So he went out from his presence a leper, as white as snow" (2 Kgs. 5:27). On account of blasphemy of God's name: The case derives from Goliath: "And the Philistine cursed David by his God" (1 Sam. 17:43). And how do we know that he was smitten with leprosy? As it is said, "This day the Lord will shut you up as a leper through my hands" (1 Sam. 17:46). And "shutting up" can mean only leprosy, in line with the following verse of Scripture: "And the priest will shut him up for seven days" (Lev. 13:21). On account of robbing from the community: The case derives from Shebna, who made personal use of things that had been consecrated to the Temple. And how do we know that he was smitten with leprosy? "Behold, the Lord will hurl you away violently. O you strong young man, he will wrap you around and around" (Is. 22:17). This "wrapping around" can refer only to leprosy, as it is said, "And he will wrap around his upper lip" (Lev. 13:45). Stealing what one does not own: The case derives from Uzziah, who planned to plunder the high priesthood. And how do we know that he was smitten with leprosy? As it is said, "And Uzziah the king was a leper" (2 Chron. 26:21). And how do we know that leprosy comes on account of arrogance? "But when he was strong, he grew proud, to his destruction. For he was false to the Lord his God and entered the temple of the Lord to burn incense on the altar of incense" (2 Chron. 26:16). On account of gossiping: The case derives from Miriam: "And Miriam and Aaron spoke against Moses" (Num. 12:1). And how do we know that she was smitten with leprosy? As it is said, "And when the cloud was removed from the tent, behold Miriam was leprous" (Num. 12:10). And on account of grudging? That is in accord with that which R. Isaac b. Eleazar said, "Deep green (*sheqaarurot*)" (Lev. 14:37) — the house sinks because of the curse." Therefore Moses admonished Israel, saying to them, "When you come into the land of Canaan" (Lev. 13:3-4).

Since God punishes sin with suffering, if a person sees that sufferings afflict him, let him examine his deeds, but God also shows favor by inflicting suffering, so b. Ber. 1:1 III.10-11/5a: In line with the statement, Upon whoever has the possibility of taking up the study of Torah and does not do so, the Holy One, blessed be he, brings ugly and troubling suffering, said Raba, and some say, R. Hisda, "If a person sees that sufferings afflict him, let him examine his deeds. For it is said, 'Let us search and try our ways and return to the Lord' (Lam. 3:40). If he examined his ways and found no cause for his suffering, let him blame the matter on his wasting time better spent in studying the Torah. For it is said, 'Happy is the man whom you chastise, O Lord, and teach out of your Torah' (Ps. 94:12). If he blamed it on something and found after correcting the fault that that had not, in fact, been the cause at all, he may be sure that he suffers the afflictions that come from God's love. For it is said, 'For the one whom the Lord loves he corrects' (Prov. 3:12)." Said Raba said R. Sehorah said R. Huna said, "Whomever the Holy One, blessed be he, prefers he crushes with suffering. For it is said, 'The Lord was pleased with him, hence he crushed him with disease' (Is. 53:10). Is it possible that even if the victim did not accept the suffering with love, the same is so? Scripture states, 'To see if his soul would offer itself in restitution' (Is. 53:10). Just as the offering must be offered with the knowledge and consent of the sacrifier, so sufferings must be accepted with knowledge and consent. If one accepted them in that way, what is his reward? 'He will see his seed, prolong his days' (Is. 53:10). Not only so, but his learning will remain with him, as it is said, 'The purpose of the Lord will prosper in his hand' (Is. 53:10)." R. Jacob bar Idi and R. Aha bar Hanina differed. One of them said, "What are sufferings brought on by God's love? They are any form of suffering which does not involve one's having to give up studying Torah. For it is said, 'Happy is the man whom you chasten, O Lord, and yet teach out of your Torah' (Ps. 94:12)." The other said, "What are sufferings brought on by God's love? They are any form of suffering which does not involve having to give up praying. For it is said, 'Blessed be God, who has not turned away my prayer nor his mercy from me' (Ps. 66:20)."

Sin brings about death, transgression brings about suffering, so b. Shab. 5:4 XII.12/55a-b: Said R. Ammi, "Death comes about only through sin, and suffering only through transgression. Death comes about only through sin: The soul that sins, it shall die; the son shall not bear the iniquity of the father, neither shall the father bear the iniquity of the son; the righteousness of the righteous shall be upon him and the wickedness of the wicked shall be upon him' (Ezek. 18:20). And suffering only through transgression: 'Then will I visit their transgression with the rod and their iniquity with stripes' (Ps. 89:33)." An objection was raised: Said the ministering angels before the Holy One blessed be He, "Lord of the universe, how come you have imposed the penalty of death on the first Adam?" He said to them, "I commanded him one easy commandment, but he violated it." They said to him, "But isn't it the fact that Moses and Aaron, who kept the entire Torah, also died?" He said to them, "There is one fate to the righteous and to the wicked, to the good..." (Qoh. 9:2). Ammi concurs with the following Tannaite authority, as has been taught on Tannaite authority: R. Simeon b. Eleazar says, "So, too, Moses and Aaron died on account of their sin: 'Because you didn't believe in me...therefore you shall not bring this assembly into the land that I have given them' (Num. 20:12) — lo, if you had believed in me, your time would not yet have come to take leave of the world." An objection was raised: Four died on account of the snake's machinations and not on account of their own sin: Benjamin the son of Jacob, Amram the father of Moses, Jesse the father of David, and Caleb the son of David. But all of them are known by tradition except for Jesse, the father of David, in which case Scripture makes it clear, as it is written, "And Absalom set Amasa over the host instead of Joab. Now Amasa was the son of a man whose name was Itra the Israelite, who went in to Abigail the daughter of Nahash, sister of Zeruiah Joab's mother" (2 Sam. 17:25). Now was she the daughter of Nahash? Surely she was the daughter of Jesse: "And their sisters were Zeruiah and Abigail" (1 Chr. 2:16). But she was the daughter of him who died on account of the machinations of the snake. Now who is the authority here? Shouldn't we say, the Tannaite authority who stands behind the story of the ministering angels? But there were Moses and Aaron, too. So it must be R. Simeon b. Eleazar, and that proves that there can be death without sin, and suffering without transgression. Isn't that a refutation of the position of R. Ammi? It is a solid refutation.

Sin may be punished in the world to come as well as in this world, and eternal punishment is the result, so T. Peah 1:2: For these things they punish a person in this world, while the principal i.e., eternal punishment remains for the world-to-come: (1) for acts of idolatrous worship, (2) for incest, (3) for murder, (4) and for gossip, which is worse than all of them together.

Sin in public is worse than sin in private, since in public one's sin profanes God's name, so b. Qid. 1:10 I.10/40a: Said R. Abbahu in the name of R. Hanina, "It is better for someone to transgress in private but not profane the Name of Heaven in public: 'As for you, house of Israel, thus says the Lord God: Go, serve every one his idols, and hereafter also, if you will not obey me; but my holy name you shall not profane' (Ezek. 20:39)." Said R. Ilai the Elder, "If someone sees that his impulse to sin is overpowering him, he should go somewhere where nobody knows him and put on ordinary clothing and cloak himself in ordinary clothing and do what he wants, but let him not profane the Name of Heaven by a public scandal." Is that so now! And hasn't it been taught on Tannaite authority: Whoever has no concern for the honor owing to his Creator is worthy of not having come into the world. And what would be such a case? Rabbah says, "This refers to someone who stares at a rainbow." R. Joseph says, "This refers to someone who commits a transgression in secret." There is no contradiction, the one speaks of a case in which he can control his urge, the other, a case in which he cannot control his urge.

Various specific sins are linked to the general ruin of Jerusalem, e.g. by Shab. 16:2 II.42/119b: Said Abbayye, "Jerusalem was ruined only because they violated the Sabbath therein: 'And they have hidden their eyes from my Sabbaths, therefore I am profaned among them' (Ezek. 22:26)." Said R. Abbahu, "Jerusalem was ruined only because they stopped reciting the Shema morning and evening: 'Woe to them that rise up early in the morning, that they may follow strong drink...and the harp and the lute, the timbrel and the pipe and wine are in their feasts, but they do not regard the works of the Lord,' 'Therefore my people have gone into captivity for lack of knowledge' (Isa. 5:11-13)." Said R. Hamnuna, "Jerusalem was ruined only because they neglected the children in the schoolmaster's household: 'pour out...because of the children in the street' (Jer. 6:211). Why pour out? Because the children are in the streets." Said Ulla, "Jerusalem was ruined only because they were not ashamed on account of one another: 'Were they ashamed when they committed abomination? No, they were not at all ashamed, therefore they shall fall' (Jer. 6:15)." Said R. Isaac, "Jerusalem was ruined only because they treated equally the small and the great: 'And it shall be, like people like priest' and then, 'the earth shall be utterly emptied' (Isa. 24:2-3)." Said R. Amram b. R. Simeon bar Abba said R. Simeon bar Abba said R. Hanina, "Jerusalem was ruined only because they did not correct one another: 'Her princes are become like harts that find no pasture' (Lam. 1:6) — just as the hart's head is at the side of the other's tail, so Israel of that generation hid their faces in the earth and didn't correct one another." Said R. Judah, "Jerusalem was ruined only because they humiliated disciples of sages therein: 'But they mocked the messengers of God and despised his words and scoffed at his prophets, until the wrath of the Lord arose against his people till there was no remedy' (2 Chr. 36:16)."

A remarkably coherent theory of sin emerges, matching rebellion and arrogance, humility and submission, sin and atonement, attitude and action. The whole holds together with the other principal components of the system.

XXIV.

The Soul

Soul: The animating component of the person, sentient and enduring. The soul is responsible for the person's intentionality and for the decisions that one makes. It bears the burden for one's sins. The soul relates to the body as God relates to the world, so b. Ber. 1:2 I.11/10a: "Just as the Holy One, blessed be he, fills the whole world, so the soul fills the whole body. Just as the Holy One, blessed be he, sees but is not seen, so the soul sees but is not seen. Just as the Holy One, blessed be he, sustains the whole world, so the soul sustains the whole body. Just as the Holy One, blessed be he, is pure, so the soul is pure. Just as the Holy One, blessed be he, sits in the innermost chambers, so the soul dwells in the innermost chambers."

This same matter is spelled out more elaborately as follows: Why did the soul of David praise the Holy One, blessed be he (B. Ber. 10a)? David said, "Just as the soul fills the body, so the Holy One, blessed be he, fills the whole world, as it is written, 'Do I not fill the entire heaven and earth? says the Lord' (Jer. 23:24). So let the soul, which fills the body, come and praise the Holy One, blessed be he, who fills the world. The soul supports the body, the Holy One blessed be he supports the world, for it is written, 'Even to your old age I am he, and to gray hairs I will carry you' (Is. 46:4). So let the soul, which supports the body, come and praise the Holy One, blessed be he, who supports the world. The soul outlasts the body, and the Holy One, blessed be he, outlasts the world: 'They will perish, but you do endure, they will all wear out like a garment. You change them like a garment and they pass away, but you are the same, and your years have no end' (Ps. 102:26-27). So let the soul, which outlasts the body, come and praise the Holy One, blessed be he, who outlasts the world. The soul in the body does not eat, and as to the Holy One, blessed be he, there is no eating so far as he is concerned, as it is written, 'If I were hungry, I would not tell you, for the world and all that is in it is mine' (Ps. 50:12). Let the soul in the body, which does not eat, come and praise the Holy One, blessed be he, before whom there is no eating. The soul is singular in the body, and the Holy One, blessed be he, is singular in his world, as it is said, 'Hear, O Israel, the Lord our God is a singular Lord' (Deut. 6:4). Let the soul, which is singular in the body, come and praise the Holy One, blessed be he, who is singular in his world. The soul is pure in the body, and the Holy One, blessed be he, is pure in his world: 'You who are of eyes too pure to behold evil' (Hab 1:13). Let the soul, which is pure in the body, come and praise the Holy One, blessed be he, which is pure in his world. The soul sees but is not seen, and the Holy One, blessed be he, sees but is not seen, as it is written, 'Am I a God at hand says the Lord, and not a God afar off? Can a man hide himself in secret places so that I cannot see him? says the Lord. Do I not fill heaven and earth? says the Lord' (Jer. 23:23-24). Let the soul, which sees but is not seen, come and praise the Holy One, blessed be he, who sees but is not seen. The soul does not sleep in the body, and the Holy One, blessed be he, is not subject to sleep, as it is said, 'Lo, the Guardian of Israel neither slumbers nor sleeps' (Ps. 121:4). Let the soul, which does not sleep in the body, come and praise the Holy One, blessed be he, who is not subject to sleep: 'Lo, he slumbers not nor sleeps.'"

The soul and the body cannot be separated, but the soul is responsible for the sin that a person does, so Lev. R. IV:V.2: R. Ishmael taught, "The matter of the soul's and body's guilt for sin may be compared to the case of a king, who had an orchard, in which were excellent early figs. So he set up two guards to keep watch over the orchard, one lame, one blind. He told them, 'Keep watch over the early figs.' He left them there and went his way. The lame guard said to the blind one, 'I spy some wonderful figs.' The other said, 'Come on, let's eat.' The lame one said, 'Now can I walk around?' The blind one said, 'And can I see a thing?' What did they do? The lame one rode on the blind one and they picked the figs and ate them. Then they went back and each one took his original place. After a while the king came back and said to them, 'Where are my figs?' The blind one said to him, 'Can I see a thing?' The lame one said, 'And can I walk around?' Since the king was smart, what did he do? He had the lame one climb onto the blind one, and he judged the two of them as a single defendant. He said to them, 'This is how you did it when you went and ate the figs.' So in time to come, the Holy One will say to the soul, 'Why did you sin before me?' And the soul will say before him, 'Lord of the ages, am I the one that sinned before you? It is the body that sinned. From the day that I left it, have I committed a single sin?' So the Holy One will say to the body, 'Why did you sin?' And it will say before him, 'Lord of the ages, it is the soul that committed the sin. From the day on which it left me, have I not been cast down before you like a shard on a garbage dump?' What will the Holy One, blessed be he, do? He will put the soul back into the body and judge them as a single defendant. That is in line with the following verse of Scripture: 'He calls to the earth above, heavens above, and to the earth, that he may judge his people' (Ps. 50:4). 'He calls to the heaven' — to produce the soul. 'And to the earth' — to bring forth the body. And then: 'To judge with him' all together, reading as if it read not *amo* but *imo*." R. Hiyya taught, "The matter of the soul's guilt for sin may be compared to the case of a priest who had two wives, one the daughter of a priest, the other the daughter of an Israelite. He gave them a piece of dough in the status of heave offering which was to be kept in conditions of cultic cleanness, but they rendered it cultically unclean. He went and remonstrated with the daughter of the priest, but he left the daughter of the Israelite alone. She said to him, 'Our lord, priest, you gave it to both of us simultaneously. Why do you remonstrate with me and leave that one alone?' He said to her, 'You are a priest's daughter and experienced on account of growing up in your father's house in dealing with the rules of cultic cleanness, but that one is an Israelite's daughter and not experienced from her upbringing in her father's house. 'Therefore I remonstrate with you.' So in time to come, the Holy One, blessed be he, will say to the soul, 'Why have you sinned before me?' And the soul will say before him, 'Lord of the ages, the body and I sinned simultaneously. Why then are you remonstrating with me but leaving that one alone?' He will then say to the soul, 'You come from the upper world, a place in which people do not sin, while the body comes from the lower world, a place in which people sin. Therefore I remonstrate with you.'"

    One should preserve one's own soul in purity, so that after death, he may render it back to God in the same condition, so b. Shab. 23:5 I.36-7/152b: "And the dust return to the earth as it was and the spirit returns to God" (Qoh. 12:7) — Give it back to him: Just as it was given to you, in purity, so give it back to him in purity. The matter may be compared to the case of a mortal king who divided up royal garments among his staff. The intelligent ones among them folded them up and laid them away in a chest. The stupid ones went and did their daily work in them. Some time later the king wanted his garments back. The intelligent ones among them returned them to him immaculate. The stupid ones returned them dirty. The king was pleased to great the intelligent ones but angry with the stupid ones. To the intelligent ones he said, "Let the garments be sent back to storage, and they will go home in peace." On the stupid ones he said, "Let the garments be sent to the laundry, and let them be sent to prison." So the Holy One, blessed be He, concerning the bodies of the righteous, says, "He enters into peace, they rest in their beds" (Isa. 57:2). Concerning their souls, he says, "Yet the soul of my lord shall be bound up in the bundle of life with the Lord your God" (1 Sam. 25:29). But of the bodies of the wicked he says, "There is no peace, says the Lord, for the wicked" (Isa. 58:22), and of their souls: "And the souls of your enemies, them shall he sling out, as from the hollow of a sling" (1 Sam. 25:29). R. Eliezer says, "The souls of the righteous are hidden away under the throne of glory: 'Yet the soul of my lord shall be bound up in the bundle of life with the Lord your God' (1 Sam. 25:29). And those of the wicked are kept in prison. One angel stands at one end of the world, and another angel stands at the other end of the world, and they sling their souls from one to the other: 'And the souls of your enemies, them shall he sling out, as from the hollow of a sling' (1 Sam. 25:29)."

One should always prepare for death, b. Shab. 23:5 I.45-6/152b: We have learned in the Mishnah there: R. Eliezer says, "Repent one day before you die" (M. Abot 2:10D). His disciples asked R. Eliezer, "So does someone know just what day he'll die?" He said to them, "All the more so let him repent today, lest he die tomorrow, and he will turn out to spend all his days in repentance." And so, too, did Solomon say, "Let your garments be always white and don't let your head lack ointment" (Qoh. 9:8). "Let your garments be always white and don't let your head lack ointment" (Qoh. 9:8)) — said R. Yohanan b. Zakkai, "The matter may be compared to the case of a king who invited his courtiers to a banquet, but he didn't set a time. The smart ones among them got themselves fixed up and waited at the gate of the palace, saying, 'Does the palace lack anything?' They can do it any time. The stupid ones among them went about their work, saying, 'So is there a banquet without a whole lot of preparation?' Suddenly the king demanded the presence of his courtiers. The smart ones went right before him, all fixed up, but the fools went before him filthy from their work. The king received the smart ones pleasantly, but showed anger to the fools. He said, 'These, who fixed themselves up for the banquet, will sit and eat and drink. Those, who didn't fix themselves up for the banquet, will stand and look on.'" R. Meir's son in law in the name of R. Meir said, "They, too, would appear as though in attendance. But, rather, both parties sit, the one eating, the other starving, the one drinking, the other in thirst: 'Therefore thus says the Lord God, behold, my servants shall eat, but you shall be hungry, behold, my servants shall drink, but you shall be thirty, behold, my servants shall rejoice, but you shall be ashamed; behold, my servants shall sing for joy of heart, but you shall cry for sorrow of heart' (Isa. 65:13-14)."

The soul survives death and is sentient, so that after death, the soul knows how the body has been treated, until the grave is closed, so b. Shab. 23:5 I.34-6/152a-b:Said R. Judah, "In the case of a deceased for whom there is no survivor to be comforted, ten people go and sit in the place in which he died and do the obsequies." There was the case of someone who died in the neighborhood of R. Judah. There was no survivor to be comforted. Every day Rab Judah assembled ten men and they sat in his place. After seven days the deceased appeared to him in a dream and said to him, "May your mind be at rest, for you set my mind at rest." Said R. Abbahu, "Whatever they say in the presence of the deceased he knows until the sealing stone closes his grave." None of these doctrines contradicts any other that we have examined.

XXV.

Suffering

SUFFERING: A gift from God sought for by the patriarchs, suffering is a principal mode of atonement for sin. Suffering is to be accepted gratefully, as a step in reconciliation with God.

The patriarchs asked for old age, suffering, and sickness, and these represent gifts from God, so Gen. R. LXV:IX.1: "When Isaac was old, and his eyes were dim, so that he could not see, he called Esau his older son, and said to him, 'My son,' and he answered, 'Here I am'" (Gen. 27:1): Said R. Judah bar Simon, "Abraham sought the physical traits of old age so that from one's appearance, people would know that he was old. He said before him, 'Lord of all ages, when a man and his son come in somewhere, no one knows whom to honor. If you crown a man with the traits of old age, people will know whom to honor.' Said to him the Holy One, blessed be he, 'By your life, this is a good thing that you have asked for, and it will begin with you.' From the beginning of the book of Genesis to this passage, there is no reference to old age. But when Abraham our father came along, the traits of old age were given to him, as it is said, 'And Abraham was old' (Gen. 24:1).' Isaac asked God for suffering. He said before him, 'Lord of the age, if someone dies without suffering, the measure of strict justice is stretched out against him. But if you bring suffering on him, the measure of strict justice will not be stretched out against him. Suffering will help counter the man's sins, and the measure of strict justice will be mitigated through suffering by the measure of mercy.' Said to him the Holy One, blessed be he, 'By your life, this is a good thing that you have asked for, and it will begin with you.' From the beginning of the book of Genesis to this passage, there is no reference to suffering. But when Isaac came along, suffering was given to him: his eyes were dim.' Jacob asked for sickness. He said before him, 'Lord of all ages, if a person dies without illness, he will not settle his affairs for his children. If he is sick for two or three days, he will settle his affairs with his children.' Said to him the Holy One, blessed be he, 'By your life, this is a good thing that you have asked for, and it will begin with you.' That is in line with this verse: 'And someone said to Joseph, "Behold, your father is sick"' (Gen. 48:1)." Said R. Levi, "Abraham introduced the innovation of old age, Isaac introduced the innovation of suffering, Jacob introduced the innovation of sickness. Hezekiah introduced the innovation of chronic illness. He said to him, 'You have kept a man in good condition until the day he dies. But if someone is sick and gets better, is sick and gets better, he will carry out a complete and sincere act of repentance for his sins.' Said to him the Holy One, blessed be he, 'By your life, this is a good thing that you have asked for, and it will begin with you.' 'The writing of Hezekiah, king of Judah, when he had been sick and recovered of his sickness' (Is. 38:9)."

Suffering is a mark of divine love, so Gen. R. XCII:I.2-3: Said R. Alexandri, "You have no one without troubles. Happy is the person whose Torah brings about his sufferings that is, because of his hard work in studying the Torah." Said R. Joshua b. Levi, "All sufferings that come upon a person and prevent him from his Torah-study constitute sufferings that serve to rebuke. But all forms of suffering that do not prevent a person from studying the Torah are sufferings that come out of love that a person may suffer in this world and joy all the more the age to come." Rabbi saw a blind man who was laboring in Torah-study. He said to him, "Peace to you, free man." He said to him, "Did you hear that I used to be a slave?" He said to him, "No, but you will be a free man in the age to come." Said R. Yudan, "It is written, 'And if he smite out his slave's tooth or his slave-woman's tooth, he shall let him go free for his tooth's sake' (Ex. 21:27). He upon whom troubles come, how much the more so!"

R. Yosé, b. R. Judah says, "Beloved is suffering, for the name of the Omnipresent rests upon the one upon whom suffering comes, as it is said, 'So the Lord your God chastens you' (Dt. 8:5)." R. Nathan b. R. Joseph says, "Just as a covenant is made through the land, so a covenant is made through suffering, as it is said, 'The Lord, your God" chastens you' (Dt. 8:7). And it says, 'For the Lord your God brings you into a good land' (Dt. 8:7)." R. Simeon b. Yohai says, "Suffering is precious. For through suffering three good gifts were given to Israel, which the nations of the world desire, and these are they: the Torah, the land of Israel, and the world to come. How do we know that that is the case for the Torah? As it is said, 'To know wisdom and chastisement' (Prov. 1:2). And it is said, 'Happy is the man whom you chastise O Lord and teach out of your Torah'

(Ps. 94:12). How do we know that that is the case for the land of Israel? 'The Lord your God chastens you...for the Lord your God brings you into a good land' (Dt. 8:5, 7). How do we know that that is the case for the world to come? 'For the commandment is a lamp and the Torah is a light, and reproofs of chastisement are the way of life' (Prov. 6:23). What is the way that brings a person to the world to come? One must say it is suffering." R. Nehemiah says, "Beloved is suffering, for just as offerings appease, so does suffering appease. In the case of offerings, Scripture says, 'And it shall be accepted for him to make atonement for him' (Lev. 1:4). And in the case of suffering: 'And they shall be paid the punishment for their iniquity' (Lev. 26:43). And not only so, but suffering appeases more than do offerings. For offerings are a matter of property, but suffering, of one's own body. And so Scripture says, 'Skin for skin, yes, all that a man has will he give for his life' (Job 2:4)."

The fact that suffering is precious is demonstrated, also, in the following colloquy, Mekh. LVI:I.11: Now when R. Eliezer was sick, four sages, R. Tarfon, R. Joshua, R. Eleazar b. Azariah, and R. Aqiba, came to visit him. Responded and said to him R. Tarfon, "My lord, you are more precious to Israel than the sun's orb. For the sun's orb gives light to this world, but you give light to us in this world and the world to come." Responded and said to him R. Joshua, "My lord, you are more precious to Israel than the gift of rain, for rain gives life in this world, but you give life to us in this world and the world to come." Responded and said to him R. Eleazar b. Azariah, "My lord, you are more precious to Israel than a father or a mother. For a father or mother bring one into this world, but you bring us into this world and the world to come." Responded and said to him R. Aqiba, "My lord, suffering is precious." R. Eliezer said to his disciples, "Lift me up." R. Eliezer went into session, saying to him, "Speak, Aqiba." He said to him, "Lo, Scripture says, 'Manasseh was twelve years old when he began to reign, and he reigned for fifty-five years in Jerusalem. And he did what was evil in the eyes of the Lord' (2 Chr. 33:1). And it further says, 'These are the proverbs of Solomon, which the men of Hezekiah, king of Judah, copied out' (Prov. 25:1). Now can anyone imagine that Hezekiah taught Torah to all Israel, while his son, Manasseh, he did not teach Torah? But one must conclude that, despite all of the learning that his father taught him, and all the work that he put into him, nothing worked for him except suffering. For it is said, 'And the Lord spoke to Manasseh and to his people, but they gave no heed. Therefore the Lord brought upon them the captains of the host of the king of Assyria, who took Manasseh with hooks and bound him with fetters and carried him to Babylonia. And when he was in distress, he besought the Lord, his God, and humbled himself greatly before the God of his fathers and prayed to him, and he was entreated of him and heard his supplication and brought him back to Jerusalem into his kingdom' (2 Chr. 33:10-13). That proves that suffering is precious."

That suffering is a valued gift explains why one should accept whatever God metes out to him, even suffering, so Sif. Dt. XXXII:V.1-12: R. Aqiba says, "Since it is said, 'with all your soul,' it is an argument *a fortiori*; that we should encompass, 'with all your might.' Why then does Scripture say, 'with all your might'? It is to encompass every single measure that God metes out to you, whether the measure of good or the measure of punishment." So does David say, "How can I repay the Lord for all his bountiful dealings toward me? I will lift up the cup of salvation and call upon the name of the Lord" (Ps. 116:12-13). "I found trouble and sorrow but I called upon the name of the Lord" (Ps. 116:3-4). So does Job say, "The Lord gave and the Lord has taken away. Blessed be the name of the Lord" (Job 1:21). If that is the case for the measure of goodness, all the more so for the measure of punishment. What does his wife say to him? "Do you still hold fast your integrity? Blaspheme God and die" (Job 2:9). And what does he say to her? "You speak as one of the impious women speaks. Shall we receive good at the hand of God and shall we not receive evil?" (Job 2:10). The men of the generation of the flood were churlish as to the good, and when punishment came upon them, they took it willy nilly. And is it not an argument *a fortiori*: if one who was churlish as to the good behaved with dignity in a time of punishment, we who behave with dignity in response to good should surely behave with dignity in a time of trouble. And so did he said to her, "You speak as one of the impious women speaks. Shall we receive good at the hand of God and shall we not receive evil?" (Job 2:10). And, furthermore, a person should rejoice in suffering more than in good times. For if someone lives in good times his entire life, he will not be forgiven for such sin as may be in his hand. And how shall he attain forgiveness? Through suffering. R. Eliezer b. Jacob says, "Lo, Scripture says, 'For whom the Lord loves he corrects, even as a father corrects the son in whom he delights' (Prov. 3:12). "What made the son be pleasing to the father? You must say it was suffering on account of correction.' R. Meir says, "Lo, Scripture says, 'And you shall consider in your heart, that as a man chasten his son, so the Lord your God chastens you' (Dt. 8:5). "'You know in your heart the deeds that you did, and also the suffering that I brought upon you, which was not in accord with the deeds that you did at all.'" Acceptance of suffering therefore marks one's attitude as correct and appropriate, consistent with the tendencies of the system overall, and rejection of suffering signifies rebellion against God.

XXVI.

Temple, Holy Place

TEMPLE, HOLY PLACE: the place, in Jerusalem, at which God and holy Israel meet. That is the highest point n earth, where God receives His share of the natural gifts of the Holy Land, meat, grain, wine, and olive oil; and where through the presentation of these gifts, the Israelite fulfills his obligations to God, inclusive of atoning for sin. Concomitantly, prayers are to be recited in the direction of the Temple, for instance, M. Ber. 4:6 A: If he was travelling in a ship or on a raft, he should direct his heart towards the Chamber of the Holy of Holies. The priority of the Land of Israel over all other lands, and Jerusalem over all other places, and the Temple over the rest of Jerusalem, is expressed in this language at T. Ber. 3:15 Those who are outside the Land turn toward the Land of Israel. Those who are in the Land of Israel turn toward Jerusalem. Those who are in Jerusalem turn toward the Temple. Those who are in the Temple turn toward the Chamber of the Holy of Holies and pray. It turns out that those standing in the north face south, those in the south face north, those in the east face west, and those in the west face east. Thus all Israel turn out to be praying toward one place.

The world rests upon the Temple service, so ARN IV:IV.1: ...on the Temple service: how so? So long as the Temple service of the house of the sanctuary went on, the world was blessed for its inhabitants and rain came down in the proper time. For it is said, To love the Lord your God and to serve him with all your heart and with all your soul that I will provide the rain of your land in its season, the former rain and the latter rain...and I will provide grass in your fields for your cattle (Deut. 11:13-14). But when the Temple service of the house of the sanctuary ceased to go on, the world was not blessed for its inhabitants, and rain did not come down in the proper time, as it is said, Take heed to yourselves lest your heart be deceived...and he shut up the heaven so that there shall be no rain (Deut. 11:16-17).

The mere entry within the walls of Jerusalem serves to impose the status of sanctification within Jerusalem upon produce that is brought there.

Produce in the status of second tithe that is to be eaten in Jerusalem is automatically consecrated for that purpose once it comes within the walls. But Coins in the status of second tithe enter Jerusalem and go out after they have been brought into Jerusalem they may be taken out again, but produce which is in the status of second tithe enters Jerusalem and does not go out it must remain in the city until it is consumed (M. Maaser Sheni 3:5).

The garments that the priest wore signified atonement and forgiveness for sins of various classifications, so Song R. XLVIII:v.3: The high priest serves in eight garments, and an ordinary priest in four: tunic, underpants, head-covering, and girdle. The high priest in addition wears the breastplate, apron, upper garment, and frontlet (M. Yoma 7:5A-C). The tunic would atone for bloodshed: "And they dipped the coat in the blood" (Gen. 37:31). Some say, "It atoned for those who wear mixed varieties: 'And he made him a coat of many colors' (Gen. 37:3)." The underpants atone for fornication: "And you shall make them linen underpants to cover the flesh of their nakedness" (Ex. 27:42). The head-covering atones for arrogance: "And he set the head-covering on his head" (Lev. 8:9). For what did the girdle atone? For the double-dealers. Others say, "For thieves." The one who says that it was for thieves maintains that view because the garment was hollow, standing for thieves, who work in hiding. The one who says that it was for the double-dealers is in accord with that which R. Levi said, "It was thirty-two cubits long, and he would twist it on either side." The breastplate would atone for those who pervert justice: "And you shall put in the breastplate of judgment the Urim and the Thummim" (Ex. 28:30). The apron ephod would atone for idolatry: "And without ephod or teraphim" (Hos. 3:4). The upper garment robe would atone for slander. The frontlet would atone for impudence. Some say, "It was for blasphemy." The one who says it was for impudence cites the following verse of Scripture: "And it shall be upon Aaron's forehead" (Ex. 28:38), and also, "Yet you had a harlot's forehead" (Jer. 3:3). The one who says it was for blasphemy cites the following verse of Scripture: "And it shall always be upon his forehead" (Ex. 28:38) along side, "And the stone sank into his forehead" (1 Sam. 17:49).

Israel's history and the history of the world are divided into periods, and these are marked by what happens to the Temple in particular: before the Temple was destroyed, after the Temple was destroyed marking time. The fate of the Temple introduced consideration, also, of differentiation among gentiles — Babylonia, Persia, Greece, Rome, but particularly Rome, so b. A.Z. 1:1 II.1-2/8b-9a: For twenty-six years the Romans kept their faith with Israel. From that point on, they subdued them. Now do we know that for twenty-six years the Romans kept their faith with Israel. From that point on, they subdued them? For said R. Kahana, "When R. Ishmael b. R. Yosé, fell ill, Rabbi sent word to him, 'Tell us two or three of the things that you said to us in your father's name.' He said to them, 'One hundred and eighty years before the house of the Temple was destroyed, the wicked kingdom took over the dominion over Israel; eighty years prior to the destruction of the Temple the decree was made that the lands of the peoples around the Land of Israel and utensils made out of glass were subject to uncleanness; forty years prior to the destruction of the Temple the sanhedrin went out into exile from the Temple and held its sessions in a stall on the Temple mount.'" One hundred and eighty years before the house of the Temple was destroyed, the wicked kingdom took over the dominion over Israel: but was it not a longer span of time than that? Did not R. Yosé, b. Rabbi repeat as a Tannaite version, The Persian government lasted for thirty-four years after the building of the Temple; Greek rule lasted one hundred eighty years during the time that the Temple stood; Hasmonean rule was for one hundred three years during the time the Temple stood; the house of Herod ruled for one hundred three years. From that point one should go on counting the years as from the destruction of the Temple. Thus we see that it was two hundred six years, and yet you say it was one hundred eighty years! Rather, it was for twenty-six years that the Romans kept faith with Israel and did not subjugate them, and those years are not counted in the period during which Rome was in fact ruling over Israel."

A synagogue also is deemed a holy place, enjoying some of the protections accorded to the Temple. A place at which a synagogue has been located is treated with reverence, so M. Megillah 3:3 A. And further did R. Judah state, "A synagogue which was destroyed — they do not (1) carry out a lamentation for the dead in it. And they do not (2) twist ropes in it, and they do not (3) spread out nets to dry in it, and they do not (4) spread out produce on its roof, and they do not (5) make it into a public shortcut. For it is written, I will bring your sanctuaries to desolation (Lev. 26:31) —

they remain sanctified even when they are desolated. If grass grew up in it, one should not cut it, because of grief." But the location of any particular synagogue bears no consequence, e.g., imposes no taxonomic traits, in the way in which the location of the Temple in Jerusalem does. One synagogue location is no different from any other, and once the synagogue has been removed from the spot, under ordinary circumstances the spot no longer is revered. But "the synagogue" in no way corresponds in systemic function to the Temple. In light of what we have examined in connection with Land of Israel, sanctification, and the like, nothing in this entry presents surprises.

XXVII.

Torah

TORAH: the medium of God's self-manifestation and revelation to humanity through Moses to Israel at Sinai. The Torah is comprised by a written and an oral part. Both parts represent God's statement of his will and plan for the world, but while the former is read as a verbatim record of God's word of his will, the latter, as written down in the sayings of the great sages, is not represented as a verbatim record, since much that is deemed part of the Torah is assigned to named sages, upward to Moses himself.

The world was created on account of the Torah, so Song R. XIX.i.5: R. Azariah in the name of R. Judah in the name of R. Simon interpreted the cited verse to speak of Israel before Mount Sinai. "'a lily among brambles': The matter may be compared to a king who had an orchard. He planted in it rows upon rows of figs, grapevines, and pomegranates. After a while the king went down to his vineyard and found it filled with thorns and brambles. He brought woodcutters and cut it down. But he found in the orchard a single red rose. He took it and smelled it and regained his serenity and said, 'This rose is worthy that the entire orchard be saved on its account.' So too the entire world was created only on account of the Torah. For twenty-six generations the Holy One, blessed be He, looked down upon his world and saw it full of thorns and brambles, for example, the Generation of Enosh, the generation of the Flood, and the Sodomites. He planned to render the world useless and to destroy it: 'The Lord sat enthroned at the flood' (Ps. 29:10). But he found in the world a single red rose, Israel, that was destined to stand before Mount Sinai and to say before the Holy One, blessed be He, 'Whatever the Lord has said we shall do and we shall obey' (Ex. 24:7). Said the Holy One, blessed be He, 'It is worthy that the whole world should be saved for the sake of the Torah and those who study it....'"

The Torah provided God's plan when he created the world, so Gen. R. ë:I.2: "In the beginning God created" (Gen. 1:1) "'Then I was beside him like a little child, and I was daily his delight rejoicing before him always, rejoicing in his inhabited world, and delighting in the sons of men'

(Prov. 8:30-31). The word means "workman." In the cited verse the Torah speaks, "I was the work-plan of the Holy One, blessed be he." In the accepted practice of the world, when a mortal king builds a palace, he does not build it out of his own head, but he follows a work-plan. And the one who supplies the work-plan does not build out of his own head, but he has designs and diagrams, so as to know how to situate the rooms and the doorways. Thus the Holy One, blessed be he, consulted the Torah when he created the world. So the Torah stated, "By means of 'the beginning' that is to say, the Torah did God create..." (Gen. 1:1). And the word for "beginning" refers only to the Torah, as Scripture says, "The Lord made me as the beginning of his way" (Prov. 8:22).

That the Torah comes from Heaven and that the resurrection of the dead is a teaching of the Torah is defined as an article of Israel's faith, so M. San. 10:1A-D: All Israelites have a share in the world to come, as it is said, Your people also shall be all righteous, they shall inherit the land forever; the branch of my planting, the work of my hands, that I may be glorified (Is. 60:21). And these are the ones who have no portion in the world to come: (1) He who says, the resurrection of the dead is a teaching which does not derive from the Torah, (2) and the Torah does not come from Heaven; and (3) an Epicurean. The revelation to Moses at Sinai encompasses everything that would be discovered later on, e.g., by processes of reasoning, so Y. Hag. 1:8 II.3: With reference to Deut. 9:10:"And on them was written according to all the words that the Lord spoke with you in the mount," said R. Joshua b. Levi, "He could have written 'On them,' but wrote 'And on them.' He could have written 'All,' but wrote 'According to all.' He could have written 'Words,' but wrote 'The words.' These then serve as three including clauses, serving to include Scripture, Mishnah, Talmud, laws, and lore. Every decision that an experienced student in the future will render before his master already has been stated to Moses at Sinai." What is the scriptural basis for this view? There is no remembrance of former things, nor will there be any remembrance of later things yet to happen among those who come after" (Qoh. 1:11). If someone says, "See, this is a new thing," his fellow will answer him, saying to him, "This has been around before us for a long time."

The Torah is revealed not out of the past, but in the acutely-present tense, so PRK XII:V.1: R. Abun commenced his discourse by citing the verse: "Here have I not written out for you three-fold sayings, full of knowledge and wise advice, to impart to you a knowledge of the truth, that you may take back a true report to him who sent you" (Prov. 22:20-21)." Bar Hoté, said, "The word that we read as three-fold in three-fold sayings of full of knowledge and of wise advice yields 'the day before yesterday'.'" Said R. Eleazar, "It is so that the words of the Torah should not appear to you like a dated decree, but they should appear to you like a new one which everyone is running to read. That is in line with this verse of Scripture: 'On this very day the Lord your God is commanding you to do... ' (Deut. 26:16)."

The Torah was set forth in ways in which Man cannot otherwise communicate or be communicated with, the very possibility of receiving the Torah serving as evidence of its supernatural character, so Y. Ned. 3:2 II.3: "You shall not take the name of the Lord your God in vain" (sw') (Deut. 5:11)."You shall not take the name of the Lord your God in vain" (Ex. 20:7). Both of them were stated in a single act of speech, which it is not possible for a mortal mouth to speak or a mortal ear to hear. "Remember the Sabbath day, to keep it holy" (Ex. 20:8)."Observe the Sabbath day, to keep it holy" (Deut. 5:12). Both of them were stated in a single act of speech, which it is not possible for a mortal mouth to speak or a mortal ear to hear. "You shall keep the Sabbath, because it is holy for you; everyone who profanes it shall be put to death" (Ex. 31:14)."And you shall say to them, 'This is the offering by fire which you shall offer to the Lord: two male lambs a year old without blemish'" (Num. 28:3). Both of them were stated in a single act of speech, which it is not possible for a mortal mouth to speak or a mortal ear to hear. "You shall not uncover the nakedness of your brother's wife; she is your brother's nakedness" (Lev. 18:16)."If brothers dwell together, and one of them dies and has no son, the wife of the dead shall not be married outside the family to a stranger; her husband's brother shall go in to her" (Deut. 25:5). Both of them were stated in a single act of speech, which it is not possible for a mortal mouth to speak or a mortal ear to hear. "So no inheritance shall be transferred from one tribe to another" (Num. 36:9)."And every daughter who possesses an inheritance in any tribe of the people of Israel shall be wife to one of the family of the tribe of her father" (Num. 36:8). Both of them were stated in a single act of speech, which it is not possible for a mortal mouth to speak or a mortal ear to hear. "You shall not wear a mixture of materials, wool and linen together" (Deut. 22:11)."You shall make yourself tassels on the four corners of your cloak with which you cover yourself" (Deut. 22:12). Both of them were stated in a single act of speech, which it is not possible for a mortal mouth to speak or a mortal ear to hear. And so too it says: "Once God has spoken; twice I have heard this; that power belongs to God" (Ps. 62:12). And it is written, "Is not my word like fire, says the Lord, and like a hammer which breaks the rock in pieces?" (Jer. 23:29).

The one thing God cannot forgive is rejection of the Torah, so PRK XV:V.3ff: R. Hunah, R. Jeremiah in the name of R. Simeon bar R. Isaac: "We find that the Holy One, blessed be He, showed forgiveness for idolatry, fornication, and murder, but did not forgive rejection of the Torah. For it is said, 'Why is the land ruined and laid waste like a wilderness, so that no one passes through?' What is written is not, because of idolatry, fornication, and murder, but, 'It is because they forsook my Torah, which I set before them; they neither obeyed me nor conformed to it.'" R. Huna, R. Jeremiah in the name of R. Hiyya bar Abba: "It is written, 'Me have they abandoned' (Jer. 16:11). Is it possible that they have kept my Torah? Would that they would abandon Me but keep my Torah. For if they had abandoned Me but kept my Torah, then in the course of their study of the Torah, the yeast that is in it would have brought them back to Me." R. Huna said, "Study Torah even though it is not for its own sake, for while you are studying Torah not for its own sake, since you are occupied with it, you will go and do it for its own sake." Said R. Joshua b. Levi, "Every day an echo comes forth from Mount Horeb and says, 'Woe for you, created beings of the world, because of the disgrace that has come to the Torah."

Israel meets God in the Torah, and it is through study of the Torah with the sage that the encounter takes place. Listening to the teachings of the sage is tantamount to listen to God's instruction, so Sifra CCLXIV:I.1: "But if you will not hearken to me" means, if you will not listen to the exposition of sages. Might one suppose that reference is made to Scripture rather than sages' teachings? When Scripture says, "and will not do all these commandments, "lo, reference clearly is made to what is written in the Torah. Then how shall I interpret, "But if you will not hearken to me"? It means, if you will not listen to the exposition of sages. "But if you will not hearken": What is the point of Scripture here? This refers to one who knows God's lordship and intentionally rebels against it. And so Scripture says, "Like Nimrod, a mighty hunter before the Lord" (Gen. 10:9). Now what is the point of saying "before It really means, rebellion, for the letters of the name for Nimrod can spell out "rebel," so that this refers to one who knows God's lordship and intentionally rebels against it.

One who denies that the Torah comes from Heaven loses his portion in the world to come, which is to say, is excluded from Israel, so b. San. 11:1 II.1/99a: And he who says, "The Torah does not come from heaven" (M. 11:1D): "Because he has despised the word of the Lord and broken his commandment, that soul shall utterly be cut off" (Num. 15:31): This refers to one who says, "The Torah does not come from heaven." And even if he had said, "The entire Torah comes from heaven, except for this one verse, which the Holy One, blessed be he, did not say, but which Moses said on his own," such a one falls under the verse, "Because he has despised the word of the Lord" (Num. 15:31). And even if he had said, "The entire Torah comes from heaven, except for one minor point, an argument a fortiori, an argument based on analogy," such a one falls under the verse, "Because he has despised the way of the Lord" (Num. 15:31).

The gentiles had the chance to accept the Torah, but they refused, each nation for its own characteristic reason, so Mekh. LI:I.8ff.: Therefore the nations of the world were approached to accept the Torah, so as not to give them an excuse to say, "If we had been approached, we should have accepted responsibility for carrying out the Torah." Lo, they were approached but did not accept responsibility for them, as it is said, "The Lord came from Sinai" (Dt. 33:2). "The Lord came from Sinai" (Dt. 33:2): When the Omnipresent appeared to give the Torah to Israel, it was not to Israel alone that he revealed himself but to every nation. First of all he came to the children of the wicked Esau. He said to them, "Will you accept the Torah?" They said to him, "What is written in it?" He said to them, "'You shall not murder' (Ex. 20:13)." They said to him, "The very being of 'those men' namely, us and of their father is to murder, for it is said, 'But the hands are the hands of Esau'"(Gen. 27:22). 'By your sword you shall live' (Gen. 27:40)." So he went to the children of Ammon and Moab and said to them, "Will you accept the Torah?" They said to him, "What is written in it?" He said to them, "'You shall not commit adultery' (Ex. 20:13)." They said to him, "The very essence of fornication belongs to them (us), all of us are the children of fornication, for it is said, 'Thus were both the daughters of Lot with child by their fathers' (Gen. 19:36)." So he went to the children of Ishmael and said to them, "Will you accept the Torah?" They said to him, "What is written in it?" He said to them, "'You shall not steal' (Ex. 20:13)." They said to him, "This is the blessing that was stated to our father: 'And he shall be a wild ass of a man' (Gen. 16:12) 'For indeed I was stolen away out of the land of the Hebrews' (Gen. 409:15)." But when he came to the Israelites: "At his right hand was a fiery law for them" (Dt. 33:2). They all opened their mouths and said, "All that the Lord has spoke we shall do and we shall hear" (Ex. 24:7). "He stood and measured the earth, he beheld and drove asunder the nations" (Hab. 3:6). R. Simeon b. Eleazar says, "If the seven religious duties that were assigned to the children of Noah they could not uphold, how much the more so all the religious duties that are in the Torah! "The matter may be compared to the case of a king who set up two administrators, one in charge of the supply of straw, the other in charge of the supply of silver and gold. The one in charge of the supply of straw was suspected of thievery, and he complained that he had not been appointed over the supply of silver and gold. They said to him, 'Fool! If you have been suspected of stealing from the straw-supply, how are people going to entrust to you charge of the supply of silver and gold!' Now this yields an argument a fortiori: If the seven religious duties that were assigned to the children of Noah they could not uphold, how much the more so all the religious duties that are in the Torah!" How come the Torah was not given in the land of Israel? It was so as not to give an excuse to the nations of the world to say, "It is because the Torah was given in their land, therefore we did not accept responsibility for it upon ourselves."

In the Mishnah's system Torah had served as a taxic indicator, that is, the status of Torah as distinct from other (lower) status, hence, Torah-teaching in contra-distinction to scribal-teaching. The category-formation attested in the successor-documents, by contrast, conceived that what the sage said was in the status of the Torah It was Torah because the sage was Torah incarnate. Knowledge of the Torah yields power over this world and the next, capacity to coerce to the sage's will the natural and supernatural worlds alike, on that account. The Torah is thus transformed from a philosophical enterprise of the sifting and classification of the facts of this world into a gnostic process of changing persons through knowledge. It is on that basis that in the Yerushalmi and related writings we find in the Torah the counterpart-category to philosophy in the Mishnah. In what follows, the Torah turns out to form not the post facto description of the facts of the world, but the design of the world that God followed in creation. The Torah comes prior to reality, that of nature as much as that of history, and its rules prove descriptive of how later on things were made. Genesis Rabbah I:I.1 expresses this view: "In the beginning God created" (Gen. 1:1): Oshaia commenced discourse by citing the following verse: "'Then I was beside him like a little child, and I was daily his delight rejoicing before him always, rejoicing in his inhabited world, and delighting in the sons of men' (Prov. 8:30-31). The word for 'child' uses consonants that may also stand for 'teacher,' 'covered over,' and 'hidden away.' Some hold that the word also means 'great.' "The word means 'teacher,' in line with the following: 'As a teacher carries the suckling child' (Num. 11:12). "The word means 'covered over,' as in the following: 'Those who were covered over in scarlet' (Lam. 4:5). "The word means 'hidden,' as in the verse, 'And he hid Hadassah ' (Est. 2:7). "The word means 'great,' in line with the verse, 'Are you better than No-Ammon?' (Nah. 3:8). This we translate, 'Are you better than Alexandria the Great, which is located between rivers.'" Another matter: The word means "workman." In the cited verse the Torah speaks, "I was the work-plan of the Holy One, blessed be he." In the accepted practice of the world, when a mortal king builds a palace, he does not build it out of his own head, but he follows a work-plan. And the one who supplies the work-plan does not build out of his own head, but he has designs and diagrams, so as to know how to situate the rooms and the doorways. Thus the Holy One, blessed be he, consulted the Torah when he created the world. So the Torah stated, "By means of 'the beginning' that is to say, the Torah did God create..." (Gen. 1:1). And the word for "beginning" refers only to the Torah, as Scripture says, "The Lord made me as the beginning of his way" (Prov. 8:22). The list before us — the initial proposition, then "another matter" — makes the simple point that the Torah comes prior to creation and reveals the plan of creation. If people appeal to the facts of nature, therefore, they err, because it is in the Torah, not in natural philosophy, that we find out how things are meant to be and actually are. Now we see the link between the Torah and Israel, which explains why the special rules governing Israel derive from the Torah in particular.

The main points of insistence of the whole of Israel's life and history come to full symbolic expression in that single word. If people wanted to explain how they would be saved, they would use the word Torah. If they wished to sort out their parlous relationships with gentiles, they would use the world Torah. Torah stood for salvation and accounted for Israel's this-worldly condition and the hope, for both individual and national alike, of life in the world to come. For the successor-system, therefore, the word Torah stood for everything. The Torah symbolized the whole, at once and entire. There is no counterpart in the Mishnah, a symbol that captures in itself the entire sense of "world-view," the whole weight of what we must now categorize as "knowledge," "learning," and "science" in the broadest sense. The generative symbol, the total, exhaustive expression of the system as a whole, the Torah stood for these things then: knowledge, learning, and science — all God's own gift to Israel.

XXVIII.

Oral Torah

Torah, Oral: That part of the revelation by God to Moses our Rabbi at Mount Sinai that was formulated orally and transmitted in memory and not in writing, forming the tradition that sages, through discipleship, master and hand on.

Sages stood in a line of direct tradition, from master to disciple, extended from God to Moses, Moses to Aaron, and onward down, from Sinai. That is alleged at M. Abot 1:1-4: Moses received Torah at Sinai and handed it on to Joshua, Joshua to elders, and elders to prophets. And prophets handed it on to the men of the great assembly. Simeon the Righteous was one of the last survivors of the great assembly. Antigonos of Sokho received [the Torah] from Simeon the Righteous. Yosé, b. Yoezer of Seredah and Yosé, b. Yohanan of Jerusalem received [it] from them.

Some laws of the Oral Torah rest on deep foundations in the written Torah, others do not, so M. Hag. 1:8: The release of vows hovers in the air, for it has nothing in the Torah upon which to depend. The laws of the Sabbath, festal-offerings, and sacrilege — lo, they are like mountains hanging by a hair, for they have little Scripture for many laws. Laws concerning civil litigations, the sacrificial cult, things to be kept cultically clean, sources of cultic uncleanness, and prohibited consanguineous marriages have much on which to depend. And both these and those equally are the essentials of the Torah.

This claim concerning an oral part of the Torah is concrete, pertaining to specified laws, e.g., M. Peah 2:6 A. M'SH b: R. Simeon of Mispah sowed his field with two types of wheat . The matter came before Rabban Gamaliel. So they went up to the Chamber of Hewn Stone, and asked about the law regarding sowing two types of wheat in one field . Said Nahum the Scribe, "I have received the following ruling from R. Miasha, who received it from his father, who received it from the Pairs, who received it from the Prophets, who received the law given to Moses on Sinai, regarding one who sows his field with two types of wheat: If he harvests the wheat in one lot, he designates one portion of produce as peah..

Y. Hagigah 1:7 refers to the assertion at M. Hag. 1:8D that the laws on cultic cleanness presented in the Mishnah rest on deep and solid foundations in the Scripture. R. Zeira in the name of R. Yohanan: "If a law comes to hand and you do not know its nature, do not discard it for another one, for lo, many laws were stated to Moses at Sinai, and all of them have been embedded in the Mishnah." The Mishnah now is claimed to contain statements made by God to Moses. Part of the Torah was written down, and part was preserved in memory and transmitted orally. That the Torah is in two media, written and oral, is indicated in Scripture itself, so Sifra CCLXIX:II.14: "These are the statutes and ordinances and Torahs": "...the statutes": this refers to the exegeses of Scripture. "...and ordinances": this refers to the laws. "...and Torahs": this teaches that two Torahs were given to Israel, one in writing, the other oral. The oral and the written parts of the Torah are one and cogent, so Sif. Dt. CCCVI:XXV.1: "May my discourse come down as the rain, my speech distill as the dew, like showers on young growths, like droplets on the grass ": Just as rain falls on various trees and gives to each its appropriate flavor in accord with its species, to the vine in accord with its species, to the olive in accord with its species, to the fig in accord with its species, so the words of the Torah are whole and one, encompassing Scripture, the Mishnah, Talmud, laws, lore.

The oral part of the Torah is greater than the written, so Y. Hag. 1:8 II.2: R. Zeira in the name of R. Eleazar: "'Were I to write for him most of my laws, would they not be regarded as a strange thing? ' (Hos. 8:12). Now is the greater part of the Torah written down? Surely not. The oral part is much greater. But more abundant are the matters that are derived by exegesis from the written Torah than those derived by exegesis from the oral Torah." The oral part is not to be written down, and the written part is not to be learned orally, so Y. Hag. 1:8 II.3: R. Haggai in the name of R. Samuel bar Nahman, "Some teachings were handed on orally, and some things were handed on in writing, and we do not know which of them is the more precious. But on the basis of that which is written, 'And the Lord said to Moses, Write these words; in accordance with lit., the mouth of these words I have made a covenant with you and with Israel' (Exod. 34:27), that is to say that the ones that are handed on orally are the more precious." R. Yohanan and R. Yudan b. R. Simeon — One said, "If you have kept what is preserved orally and also kept what is in writing, I shall make a covenant with you, and if not, I shall not make a covenant with you." The other said, "If you have kept what is preserved orally and you have kept what is preserved in writing, you shall receive a reward, and if not, you shall not receive a reward."

The division of the Torah, oral and written, is unequal; the two parts must be kept separate, each having its own tasks, but the oral part is principal, so B. Git. 5:8 I.9-10/60b: Said R. Eleazar, "As to the Torah, the larger part is in writing, and the smaller part is oral: 'Though I wrote for him the major portion of my law, they were counted a strange thing' (Hos. 8:12)." And R. Yohanan said, "The larger part was oral, the smaller part in writing: 'For orally, these words...' (Ex. 34:27)." R. Judah bar Nahmani, the interpreter of R. Simeon b. Laqish, expounded, "One version of Scripture says, 'Write these words' Ex. 34:27), and another verse of Scripture says, 'For in accord with these words' (Ex. 34:27). Since the word 'in accord' can be translated, 'by the oral version...,' it means to tell you, matters that are to be memorized you have not got the right to state in writing, and those that are to be in writing you have not got the right to state from memory." And a Tannaite authority of the household of R. Ishmael states, "Scripture says, 'Write these words for yourself,' meaning, these are the words that you may write, but you may not write down laws." Said R. Yohanan, "The Holy One, blessed be He, made a covenant with Israel only on account of words that are memorized: 'For by memorizing these words, I have made a covenant with you and with Israel' (Ex. 34:27)."

The reason that the Torah was given in part orally was to preserve Israel's claim to unique access to God's revelation, so Pes. R. V.2: Said R. Judah b. R. Shalom, "Moses wanted the Mishnah to be handed on in writing. The Holy One, blessed be he, foresaw that the nations were going to translate the Torah, proclaiming it in Greek, saying that they are Israel. Said the Holy One, blessed be he, to Moses, "Now Moses, the nations of the world are destined to claim, 'We are Israel, we are the true children of the Omnipresent,' while Israel will say, 'We are the children of the Omnipresent.' And then the scales will be evenly balanced.' Said the Holy One, blessed be he, to the nations, 'Now if you say that you are my children, I shall know the truth only by reference to who has my mysteries in his position. They are the ones who are my children.' Then the nations will say to him, 'And what are these mysteries of yours?' He will say to them, 'These mysteries are the Mishnah.'"

XXIX

Torah-Study

TORAH-STUDY: The systematic study of the Torah, written and oral, pursued by a disciple with a master, involving learning of the Torah from both what the master says and what he does.

The initial pattern of Torah-study was set when God taught Torah to Moses, and Moses handed on what he learned to Aaron. The matter is defined in the following way (B. Erub. 5:1 I.43/54b): What is the order of Mishnah teaching? Moses learned it from the mouth of the All-Powerful. Aaron came in, and Moses repeated his chapter to him and Aaron went forth and sat at the left hand of Moses. His sons came in and Moses repeated their chapter to them, and his sons went forth. Eleazar sat at the right of Moses, and Itamar at the left of Aaron. R. Judah says, "At all times Aaron was at the right hand of Moses." Then the elders entered, and Moses repeated for them their Mishnah chapter. The elders went out. Then the whole people came in, and Moses repeated for them their Mishnah chapter. So it came about that Aaron repeated the lesson four times, his sons three times, the elders two times, and all the people once. Then Moses went out, and Aaron repeated his chapter for them. Aaron went out. His sons repeated their chapter. His sons went out. The elders repeated their chapter. So it turned out that everybody repeated the same chapter four times. On this basis said R. Eliezer, "A person is liable to repeat the lesson for his disciple four times. And it is an argument a fortiori: If Aaron, who studied from Moses himself, and Moses from the Almighty —so in the case of a common person who is studying with a common person, all the more so!" R. Aqiba says, "How on the basis of Scripture do we know that a person is obligated to repeat a lesson for his disciple until he learns it however many times that takes? As it is said, 'And you teach it to the children of Israel' (Deut. 31:19). And how do we know that that is until it will be well ordered in their mouth? 'Put it in their mouths' (Deut. 31:19). And how on the basis of Scripture do we know that he is liable to explain the various aspects of the matter? 'Now these are the ordinances which you shall put before them' (Ex. 31:1)."

Man was created in order to study the Torah, so ARN XIV:II.1: If you have learned much Torah, do not puff yourself up on that account, for it was for that purpose that you were created. For people were created only on the stipulation that they should occupy themselves with the Torah. Everyone should study the Torah, both poor and rich alike, so ASRN III:I.1: Raise up many disciples. For the House of Shammai say, "A person should teach only one who is wise, modest, well-born, and rich." And the House of Hillel say, "A person should teach everybody, for there were many sinners in Israel who drew near to the study of the Torah, and from such as they came forth righteous, pious, and wholly acceptable persons. Study of the Torah is an exercise in humility and an act of virtue, so ARN XI:II.2-3: Said R. Aqiba, "Whoever raises himself over teachings of the Torah — to what is such a one to be compared? To a carcass left lying on the road. Whoever passes be holds his nose and steps away from it. For it is said, 'If you have done foolishly in lifting yourself up or if you have planned devices put your hand on your mouth' (Prov. 30:32)." Said to him Ben Azzai, "Interpret the passage in its own context. If a person humbles himself for the sake of the teachings of the Torah, eating dried dates and wearing dirty clothing and sitting and watching at the door of sages, whoever passes by will say, 'This one is a fool,' but in the end you will find that the whole of the Torah is with him." R. Yosé, says, "Going down is going up, and going up is coming down. Whoever raises himself over teachings of the Torah in the end will be thrown down, and whoever lowers himself over teachings of the Torah in the end will be raised up."

Study of the Torah involves discipleship, and much that is learned is learned by imitation of the master. Study of the Torah involves a variety of human relationships, far transcending intellectual activity, M. Suk. 4:9-10 V.7-10/49A: Said R. Eleazar, "Greater is the one who carries out an act of charity more than one who offers all the sacrifices. For it is said, 'To do charity and justice is more desired by the Lord than sacrifice' (Prov. 21:3)." And R. Eleazar said, "An act of loving kindness is greater than an act of charity. For it is said, 'Sow to yourselves according to your charity, but reap according to your loving kindness' (Hos. 10:12). If a man sows seed, it is a matter of doubt whether he will eat a crop or not. But if a man harvests the crop, he most certainly will eat it." And R. Eleazar said, "An act of charity is rewarded only in accord with the loving kindness that is connected with it. For it is said, 'Sow to yourselves according to your charity, but reap according to your loving kindness' (Hos. 10:12)." Our rabbis have taught on Tannaite authority: In three aspects are acts of loving kindness greater than an act of charity. An act of charity is done only with money, but an act of loving kindness someone carries out either with his own person or with his money. An act of charity is done only for the poor, while an act of loving kindness may be done either for the poor or for the rich. An act of charity is done only for the living. An act of loving kindness may be done either for the living or for the dead. And R. Eleazar has said, "Whoever does an act of charity and justice is as if he has filled the entire world with mercy. "And R. Eleazar said, "What is the sense of the following verse of Scripture: 'She opens her mouth with wisdom, and the Torah of loving kindness is on her tongue' (Prov. 31:26)? Now is there such a thing as a Torah that is one of loving kindness and a Torah that is not one of loving kindness? But rather the study of Torah done for its own sake falls into the category of Torah of loving kindness, and Torah not studied for its own sake falls into the category of Torah that is not of loving kindness." There are those who say, "Study of Torah in order to teach it is Torah of loving kindness, while Torah learned not so as to teach it is Torah that is not of loving kindness."

The disciple is required to defer to the master and may not give decisions in the presence of the master, so b. Erub. 6:1-2 I.14, 16/63a: R. Eliezer had a disciple who gave a legal decision in his presence. Said R. Eliezer to Imma Shalom his wife, "I'll be surprised if this one finishes out the year," and he didn't live out the year. She said to him, "So are you a prophet?" He said to her, "I'm not a prophet or the disciple of a prophet, but this I have as a tradition: Whoever teaches a law before his master is liable to death." Said R. Hiyya bar Abba said R. Yohanan, "Whoever gives a legal decision in the presence of his master is worthy of being bitten by a snake: 'And Elihu the son of Barachel the Buzite answered and said, I am young...wherefore I held back' (Job 32:6), and further, 'With the venom of crawling things of the gust' (Deut. 32:24)." Zeiri said R. Hanina said, "He is called a sinner: 'Your word have I laid up in my heart that I might not sin against you' (Ps. 119:11)."

Study of the Torah corresponds to the offering of sacrifices in the Temple in Jerusalem, and the acts of disciples are equivalent to those of priests; when disciples of sages study the Torah concerning the Temple service, it is as though the Temple were rebuilt and the offerings presented, so b. Men. 13:10 II.7-12: "And in every place offerings are burned and presented to my name" (Mal. 1:11): Do you really think that this is in every place! Said R. Samuel bar Nahmani said R. Jonathan, "This refers to the disciples of sages who engaged in Torah-study in every place. I regard them as though they burned up incense and made offerings to my Name. "'Even pure obligations:' this refers to one who in a state of purity studies the Torah, meaning, someone who first gets married and then studies the Torah." "A song of ascents: behold, bless you the Lord, all you servants of the Lord, who stand in the house of the Lord in the night seasons" (Ps. 134:1): What is the meaning of "in the night seasons"? Said R. Yohanan, "This refers to the disciples of sages who engaged in Torah-study by night. Scripture regards them as though they engaged in the Temple service." "This is an ordinance for ever to Israel" (2 Chr. 2:3): Said R. Giddal said Rab, "This refers to the altar that has been built, where Michael, the lead angelic prince, is standing and presented thereon an offering." And R. Yohanan said, "This refers to disciples of sages who are engaged in the study of the laws of the Temple service. Scripture regards them as though the Temple were rebuilt in their days." Said R. Simeon b. Laqish, "That is the meaning of the verse, 'This is the Torah for the burnt offering, meal offering, sin offering, and guilt offering' (Lev. 7:37)? Whoever is engaged in Torah-study is as though he offered a burnt offering, meal offering, sin offering, and guilt offering." Said Raba, "Why does the verse say, 'for the burnt offering, for the meal offering,' when it could as well have said, a burnt offering, a meal offering'?" Rather, said Raba, "Whoever engages in Torah-study has no need for either burnt offering, meal offering, sin offering, or guilt offering." Said R. Isaac, "What is the meaning of the verse, 'This is the Torah of the sin offering' (Lev. 7:16), 'This is the Torah of the guilt offering' (Lev. 7:1)? "Whoever engages in the study of the Torah of the sin offering is as though he had offered a sin offering, and whoever engages in the study of the Torah of the guilt offering is as though he had offered a guilt offering."

Along these same lines, a disciple of a sage as a sanctified utensil, so b. Men. 11:6 IV.9-13/99a-b: "Which you broke and you shall put them into the ark" (Dt. 10:2): This teaches that both the tablets and the broken pieces of the tablets were placed into the ark. On this basis we learn that a disciple of a sage who for no fault of his own forgot his learning is not to be humiliated." Said R. Simeon b. Laqish, "On occasions the nullification of the Torah may serve as a foundation for the Torah by ceasing to study in order to perform a religious deed: 'which you did break,' for the Holy One, blessed be he, said to Moses, 'You did well to break them.'" And said R. Simeon b. Laqish, "A disciple of a sage who turned sour is not to be humiliated in public: 'Therefore you shall stumble in the day, and the prophet also shall stumble with you in the night' (Hos. 4:5). Cover it up in darkness." And said R. Simeon b. Laqish, "Whoever forgets a single thing that he has learned transgresses a negative commandment: 'Only take heed for yourself and keep your soul diligently, lest you forget the things' (Dt. 4:9)." Both R. Yohanan and R. Eleazar said, "The Torah was given in forty days, and the soul was formed in forty days. Whoever guards his Torah-learning has his soul guarded, and whoever does not guard his Torah learning does not have his soul guarded." A Tannaite authority of the household of R. Ishmael: "The matter may be compared to the case of a man who handed a swallow over to his servant and said to him, 'Do you think that if you let it perish, I will take from you for its value only an issar? I will take your soul from you! I'll kill you."

God has a heavy stake in Torah-study and rewards those who do it, so B. Hag. 2:1 III.18: /12b Said R. Simeon b. Laqish, "For whoever engages in study of the Torah by night — the Holy One, blessed be he, draws out the thread of grace by day: 'By day the Lord will command his loving kindness, and in the night his song shall be with me' (Ps. 42:9). Why is it that 'By day the Lord will command his loving kindness'? Because 'in the night his song shall be with me.'" Some say, said R. Simeon b. Laqish, "For whoever engages in study of the Torah in this world, which is like the night, — the Holy One, blessed be he, draws out the thread of grace in the world to come, which is like the day: 'By day the Lord will command his loving kindness, and in the night his song shall be with me' (Ps. 42:9). Why is it that 'By day the Lord will command his loving kindness'? Because 'in the night his song shall be with me.'" Along these same lines, B. Nid. 10:8 II.4/73A states, "Whoever repeats laws every day is guaranteed to belong to the world to come, for it is said, 'his ways — the world is his' (Hab. 3:6). Read not, 'his ways,' but 'his laws,' meaning, the one who makes the laws his own will belong to the world to come."

Since God has a stake in Torah-study, he contributes to its success, so b. Shab. 6:4 II.5-6, 9/63a: Said R. Jeremiah said R. Eleazar, "Two disciples of sages sharpen one another in law. The Holy One, blessed be He, gives them success: 'And in your majesty be successful' (Ps. 45:5) — read the letters for 'in your majesty' as though they yielded, 'your sharpening.' Not only so, but they rise to greatness: 'Ride on prosperously.' Might one suppose that that is the case even if it is not disinterested? Therefore Scripture states, 'in behalf of truth.' Might one suppose that that is the case even if he becomes conceited? Therefore it is taught, 'and meekness of righteousness.' And if they do this properly, they gain the merit of the Torah that was given by the right hand: 'And your right hand shall teach you awe-inspiring things' (Ps. 45:5)." R. Nahman bar Isaac said, "They have the merit of getting the things that were given at the right hand of the Torah." Said R. Jeremiah said R. Simeon b. Laqish, "To disciples of sages who are gentle with one another in the law Ä the Holy One, blessed be He, pays close attention to them: 'Then they that feared the Lord spoke with one another, and the Lord listened and heard' (Mal. 3:16) — the sense of 'spoke' is only, gently, as in the usage, 'He shall subdue the peoples under us' (Ps. 47:3) where the same word occurs." Said R. Abba said R. Simeon b. Laqish, "Two disciples of sages who pay close attention to one another in law Ä the Holy One, blessed be He, listens to what they say: 'You that dwell in the gardens, the companions hear your voice, cause me to hear it' (Song 8:13). But if they don't do so, they make the Presence of God remove from Israel: 'Flee my beloved...' (Song 8:14)." Said R. Abba said R. Simeon b. Laqish, "Two disciples of sage who compete with one another for a banner position eminence in the law — the Holy One, blessed be He, loves them: 'And his banner over me was love' (Song 2:4)."

The disciple of the sage, through his study of Torah, gives Heaven a good name and sanctifies God's name, so b. Yoma 8:9 III.5/86b: "And you will love the Lord your God" (Dt. 6:4) — that the Name of Heaven may be made beloved through you, that one should recite Scripture and repeat Mishnah-teachings and serve as a disciple to disciples of sages, and so that one's give and take be done in serenity with other people. Then what will people say about him? "Happy is this one's father, who taught him Torah, happy is his master, who taught him Torah. Who for those people who have not studied Torah. Look at Mr. So-and-so, to whom they taught Torah — see how lovely are his ways, how orderly his deeds! Concerning him, Scripture says, "And he said to me, you are my servant, Israel, in whom I will be glorified" (Is. 49:3). But as to him who studies Scripture and repeats Mishnah and who serves as a disciple to disciples of sages but whose give and take is not in good faith and his speech is not serene with other people — what do people say about him? Who is Mr. So-and-So, who has studied Torah, woe is his father, who taught him Torah, woe is his master, who taught him Torah. As to Mr. So-and-so, who has studied Torah — see how disreputable are his deeds and how ugly his ways, and concerning him Scripture says, "In that men said of them, These are the people of the Lord and are gone forth out of his land" (Ez. 36:20).'"

Not only adults, but children who study Torah in the most elementary way, also represent God's chosen, so b. Shab. 16:2 II.43/119b: Said R. Judah said Rab, "What is the meaning of the verse of Scripture, 'Do not touch my anointed and do my prophets no harm' (1 Chr. 16:22)? 'Do not touch my anointed': This refers to the schoolchildren in the household of their teacher. '...And do my prophets no harm': This refers to disciples of sages." Said R. Simeon b. Laqish in the name of R. Judah the Patriarch, "The world endures only for the breath of the children in the schoolhouse of their teacher." And said R. Simeon b. Laqish in the name of R. Judah the Patriarch, "They don't dismiss the schoolchildren from the house of their schoolteacher even for the sake of building the house of the sanctuary." And said R. Simeon b. Laqish in the name of R. Judah the Patriarch, "This is what I have received as a tradition from my mothers, and some say, from your fathers: 'Any town that has no children in the household of their teacher do they wipe out.'"

Israel also has a heavy stake in Torah-study. The reason that Israel suffers and that the gentiles conquer is that Israel neglects the Torah, so PRK XV:IV.7-8: Said R. Abba bar Kahana, "No philosophers in the world ever arose of the quality of Balaam ben Beor and Abnymos of Gadara. The nations of the world came to Abnymos of Gadara. They said to him, 'Do you maintain that we can make war against this nation?' He said to them, 'Go and make the rounds of their synagogues and their study houses. So long as there are there children chirping out loud in their voices and studying the Torah, then you cannot overcome them. If not, then you can conquer them, for so did their father promise them: 'The voice is Jacob's voice' (Gen. 27:22), meaning that when Jacob's voice chirps in synagogues and study houses, The hands are not the hands of Esau so Esau has no power. 'So long as there are no children chirping out loud in their voices and studying the Torah in synagogues and study houses, The hands are the hands of Esau so Esau has power.'" Samuel said, "The host was given over to it together with the continual burnt-offering through transgression (Dan. 8:12). It is through the transgression against the Torah. So long as the Israelites toss words of the Torah to the earth, this wicked kingdom makes decrees and succeeds in carrying them out. What verse of Scripture indicates it? And the truth is thrown to the ground (Dan. 8:12). And the word truth refers only to teachings of Torah, as it is said, Acquire truth and do not sell it' (Prov. 23:23)."

Study of the Torah is critical for the salvation of Israel collectively, as well as of each individual Israelite, so b. A.Z. 1:1 I.5-6/3b: Said R. Levi, "To whoever stops studying the words of the Torah and instead takes up words of mere chatter they feed glowing coals of juniper: 'They pluck salt-wort with wormwood and the roots of juniper are their food' (Job 30:4)." Said R. Simeon b. Laqish, "For whoever engages in study of the Torah by night Ä the Holy One, blessed be He, draws out the thread of grace by day: 'By day the Lord will command his loving kindness, and in the night his song shall be with me' (Ps. 42:9). Why is it that 'By day the Lord will command his loving kindness'? Because 'in the night his song shall be with me.'" Said R. Judah said Samuel, "What is the meaning of the verse of Scripture, 'And you make man as the fish of the sea and as the creeping things, that have no ruler over them' (Hab. 1:14)? Why are human beings compared to fish of the sea? To tell you, just as fish in the sea, when they come up on dry land, forthwith begin to die, so with human beings, when they take their leave of teachings of the Torah and religious deeds, forthwith they begin to die."

Study of Torah involves much effort and anguish, so Sif. Dt. CCCVI:XXI.1: "May my discourse come down as the rain, my speech distill as the dew, like showers on young growths, like droplets on the grass. For the name of the Lord I proclaim." Sages say, "Moses said to Israel, 'Don't you know how much anguish I endured for the sake of the Torah, and how much labor I invested in it, and how much effort I poured into it?'" That is in line with this verse: "And he was there with the Lord forty days and forty nights; he did not eat bread or drink water" (Ex. 34:28). "Then I stayed in the mountains forty days and forty nights, I did not eat bread or drink water" (Ex. 9:9). "Moses said, 'I went among the angels, I went among wild beasts, I went among the serafim. One of these could burn up the whole world with all its inhabitants.'" So it is said, "Above him stood the seraphim" (Is. 6:2). "'I gave my life for it, I gave my blood for it. 'Now just as I have learned it through much anguish, so you must learn it through anguish.'" Or perhaps one might say, just as you have learned it in anguish, so you must teach it in anguish? Scripture states, "...my speech distill as the dew." "You should regard it as if it is as cheap as one sela for three or four seahs.

But study of the Torah also contains great rewards. Study of Torah makes the disciple unafraid of death, and its reward comes about in the world to come, so Gen. R. LIX:II.1: "Strength and dignity are her clothing, and she laughs at the time to come" (Prov. 31:25): "Strength and dignity are her clothing," namely, the clothing of the Torah. When is that the case? When "she makes a person laugh at the time to come." That is, the Torah makes a person unafraid of death. When does God give the reward for Torah-study? In the age to come. From whom do you derive that lesson? From Abraham. Since it is written concerning him, "That they may keep the way of the Lord, to do righteousness and justice" (Gen. 18:19), he had the merit of attaining old age: "Now Abraham was old, well advanced in years." "Length of days are in her right hand" (Prov. 33:16) in the world to come. "In her left hand are riches and honor" (Prov. 3:16) in this world. From whom do you derive that lesson? From Abraham. Since it is written concerning him, "That they may keep the way of the Lord, to do righteousness and justice" (Gen. 18:19), he had the merit of attaining old age: "Now Abraham was old, well advanced in years."

Repeating words of the Torah affords protection and healing: b. Erub. 5:1 I.30/54a: Said R. Joshua b. Levi, "He who goes along the way without an escort should occupy himself with Torah. For it is said, 'For they shall be escort of grace for your head and chains about your neck' (Prov. 1:9). If he has a headache, let him occupy himself with Torah: 'For they shall be escort of grace for your head and chains about your neck' (Prov. 1:9). If he has a sore throat, let him occupy himself with Torah:

'For they shall be escort of grace for your head and chains about your neck' (Prov. 1:9). If he has a bellyache, let him occupy himself with Torah: 'It shall be a healing to your navel' (Prov. 3:8). If he has a pain in the bones, let him occupy himself with Torah: 'And marrow to your bones' (Prov. 3:8). If he has pain all through his body, let him occupy himself with Torah: 'And healing to all his flesh' (Prov. 4:22)."

Upon proper study of the Torah all virtue rests, and without Torah-study there is no possibility of proper conduct, so ARN XXII:III.1: R. Eleazar b. Azariah says, If there is no learning of Torah, there is no proper conduct, if there is no proper conduct, there is no learning in Torah. If there is no wisdom, there is no reverence. If there is no reverence, there is no wisdom. He would say, A person who has good works and has studied much Torah Ä to what is he likened? To a tree that stands by water, with few branches but deep roots. Even though the four winds of the world come, they cannot move it from its place. A person in whom are no good deeds but who has studied much Torah — to what is he compared? To a tree that stands in the wilderness, with abundant branches but shallow roots. When the winds blow, they will uproot it and blow it down.

Involved in Torah-study is constant repetition of teachings of the Torah, so that they are reaffirmed verbally and orally. This is clear in the view that God wants Israel to work at Torah-study above all else, so Sifra CCLX:I.1-3: "If you walk in my statutes": This teaches that the Omnipresent desires the Israelites to work in the Torah. And so Scripture says, "O that my people would listen to me, that Israel would walk in my ways! I would soon subdue their enemies and turn my hand against their foes" (Ps. 81:13-14). O that you had hearkened to my commandments! Then your peace would have been like a river, and your righteousness like the waves of the sea; your offspring would have been like the sand, and your descendants like its grains; their name would never be cut off or destroyed from before me" (Isa. 48:18). And so Scripture says, "Oh that they had such a mind as this always, to fear me and to keep all my commandments, that it might go well with them and with their children forever" (Dt. 5:29). This teaches that the Omnipresent desires the Israelites to work in the Torah. "If you walk in my statutes": Might this refer to the religious duties? When Scripture says, "and observe my commandments and do them," lo, the religious duties are covered. Then how shall I interpret, "If you walk in my statutes"? It is that they should work in the Torah. And so it is said, "But if you will not hearken to me." Might that refer to the religious duties? When Scripture says, "and will not do all these commandments," lo, the religious duties are covered. If so, why is it said, "But if you will not hearken to me"? It is that they should be working in the Torah. And so Scrip Might one suppose that what is involved is only to do so in your heart? When Scripture says, "Observe the Sabbath day" (Dt. 5:12), lo, keeping it in the heart is covered. How then am I to interpret "remember"? It means that you should repeat with your mouth the teachings concerning the Sabbath day. And so Scripture says, "Remember and do not forget how you provoked the Lord your God to wrath in the wilderness, from the day you came out of the land of Egypt until you came to this place" (Dt. 9:7). Might one suppose that what is involved is only to do so in your heart? Scripture says, "and do not forget." Lo, forgetting in the heart is covered. How then am I to interpret "remember"? It means that you should repeat with your mouth the record of your behavior in the wilderness. And so Scripture says, "Take heed, in an attack of leprosy, to be very careful to do according to all that the Levitical priests shall direct you; as I commanded them, so you shall be careful to do. Remember what the Lord your God did to Miriam on the way as you came forth out of Egypt" (Dt. 24:9). Might one suppose that what is involved is only to do so in your heart? When Scripture says, "Take heed, in an attack of leprosy, to be very careful to do," lo, forgetting in the heart is covered. How then am I to interpret "remember"? It means that you should repeat with your mouth the lessons to be learned in respect to Miriam. And so Scripture says, "Remember what Amalek did to you on the way as you came out of Egypt...you shall blot out the remembrance of Amalek from under heaven; you shall not forget" (Dt. 25:17, 19). Might one suppose that what is involved is only to do so in your heart? When Scripture says, "you shall not forget," lo, forgetting in the heart is covered. How then am I to interpret "remember"? It means that you should repeat with your mouth the record of Amalek.

Study of the Torah is the best way to live a life, so M. Qid. 4:14: Abba Gurion of Sidon says in the name of Abba Gurya, "A man should not teach his son to be an ass driver, a camel driver, a barber, a sailor, a herdsman, or a shopkeeper For their trade is the trade of thieves." Some held that one should both study Torah and work at a craft, others that it sufficed to study the Torah and God would provide. Rabban Gamaliel, son of R. Judah the Patriarch, took the former view, so M. Abot 2:2: "Fitting is learning in Torah along with a craft, for the labor put into the two of them makes one And all learning of Torah which is not joined with labor is destined to be null and cause sin." But contrast, at M. Qid. 4:4, R. Nehorai says, "I should lay aside every trade in the world and teach my son only Torah. For a man eats its fruits in this world, and the principal remains for the world to come. But other trades are not that way. When a man gets sick or old or has pains and cannot do his job, lo, he dies of starvation. But with Torah it is not that way. But it keeps him from all evil when he is young, and it gives him a future and a hope when he is old." Man was made to study the Torah, so Rabban Yohanan b. Zakkai, M. Abot 2:8: "(1) If you have learned much Torah, (2) do not puff yourself up on that account, (3) for it was for that purpose that you were created."

Study of Torah also relieves a person of vices, so ARN XX:I.1: R. Hananiah, prefect of the priests, says, "Whoever places the teachings of the Torah upon his heart is relieved of many preoccupations: Those of hunger, silliness, libido, impulse to do evil, a bad woman, idle nonsense, the yoke of mortals. For so it is written in the book of Psalms by King David of Israel: "The precepts of the Lord are right, rejoicing the heart, the commandment of the Lord is pure, enlightening the eyes" (Ps. 19:9). And whoever does not place the teachings of the Torah upon his heart is burdened by many preoccupations: those of perpetual hunger, silliness, libido, the evil impulse, a bad woman, idle nonsense, the yoke of mortals. For so it is written in the Repetition of the Torah the book of Deuteronomy by Moses, our lord, "And they shall be upon you for a sign and for a wonder, and upon your descendants forever, because you did not serve the Lord your God with joyfulness, and with gladness of heart, by reason of the abundance of all things, therefore you shall serve your enemy whom the Lord shall send against you, in hunger and in thirst and in nakedness and in want of all things" (Deut. 28:46-48).

Disciples of sages accept penury in order to study the Torah, so b. Er. 2:1-3 V.16/21b: Expounded Raba, "What is the meaning of the verse of Scripture, 'Come my beloved, let us go forth into the field, let us lodge in the villages, let us get up early to the vineyards, let us see whether the vine has budded, whether the vine blossom be opened, and the pomegranates be in flower; there will I give you my love' (Song 7:12)? 'Come my beloved, let us go forth into the field': Said the congregation of Israel before the Holy One, blessed be He, 'Lord of the world, don't judge me like those who live in the cities, who are full of thievery and fornication and vain oaths and false swearing.' 'Let us go forth into the field': 'Come and I shall show you disciples of sages, who are engaged in the Torah in the midst of want.' 'Let us lodge in the villages': Read the letters for villages as though they bore vowels to yield, 'among the infidels,' 'come and I shall show you those upon whom you have bestowed much good, and who have denied you.' 'Let us get up early to the vineyards': This refers to the synagogues and study houses. 'Let us see whether the vine has budded': This refers to masters of Scripture. 'Whether the vine blossom be opened': This refers to masters of the Mishnah. 'And the pomegranates be in flower': This refers to the masters of analysis. 'There will I give you my love': 'I shall show you my glory, my greatness, the praise of my sons and my daughters.'"

Study of the Torah takes priority over wealth and other worldly goods, so B. Mak. 2:6 i.16/10a: Said R. Joshua b. Levi, "What is the meaning of the verse, 'Our feet stood within your gates, Jerusalem' (Ps. 122:2)? Who made our feet stand in war? The gates of Jerusalem, where students were engaged in the wars of the Torah." And said R. Joshua b. Levi, "What is the meaning of the verse, 'A song of ascents to David, I rejoiced when they said to me, let us go to the house of the Lord' (Ps. 122:1)? Said David before the Holy One, blessed be he, 'Lord of the world, I heard people say, "When is this old man going to die, so that his son Solomon will come and build the chosen house, so that we may go up there on a pilgrimage to the Temple that Solomon is going to build," but I rejoiced to hear it!' Said to him the Holy One, blessed be he, '"A day in your court is better than a thousand" (Ps. 84:11). Better for me is a single day on which you are engaged in the Torah before me than a thousand burnt offerings that Solomon, your son, is going to offer before me on the altar.'"

The disciple of the sage must be humble, and it is through humility that Torah is learned, so b. Erub. 5:1 I.36/54a: Raba b. R. Joseph bar Hama: R. Joseph had a grievance against him. On the eve of the Day of Atonement, he said, "I shall go and appease him." He went and found his attendant mixing a cup of wine before him. He said to him, "Give it to me to mix for him." He gave it to him and he mixed the cup of wine for him. When he was tasting it, he said, "This mixture is like the kind that Raba b. R. Joseph bar Hama makes." He said to him, "That's me." He said to him, "Don't sit down until you've told me the explanation of this matter, namely, the verse of Scripture, 'And from the wilderness, Mattanah and from Mattanah Nahaliel and from Nahaliel Bamot' (Num. 31:19-20)." He said to him, "If someone treats himself as an utter wasteland, available to everyone, the Torah is given to him as a gift, as it is said, 'And from the wilderness, Mattanah a gift,' and once it is given to him as a gift, God gives it to him as an inheritance, in line with the language, 'And from Mattanah Nahaliel.' And when God gives it to him as an inheritance, he ascends to the heights: 'and from Nahaliel Bamot.' But if he exalts himself, the Holy One, blessed be He, throws him down: 'And from Bamot, the valley.' And he is made to sink into the earth: 'Which is pressed down into the desolate soil.' But if he repents, the Holy One, blessed be He, raises him up: 'Every valley shall be exalted' (Isa. 40:4)."

A disciple of a sage must share what he learns, so ARN XXIX:V.1: Abba Saul b. Nannos says, "There are four traits in a disciple of a sage: There is one who studies for himself but does not teach others, there is one who teaches others but does not teach himself, there is one who teaches himself and others, and one who does not teach himself or others. There is one who studies for himself but does not teach others: how so? If someone repeats one or two or even three divisions of the Mishnah but does not repeat them to others, occupying himself with them and not forgetting them, this is someone who one who studies for himself but does not teach others. There is one who teaches others but does not teach himself: how so? If someone studied a division or two or three and repeated them for others, but did not occupy himself with them and ultimately forgot them, this is someone who teaches others but does not teach himself. There is one who teaches himself and others: how so? If someone repeated a division, two or three, and repeated them for others and occupied himself with them and did not forget them, held on to them and the others do too, that is one who teaches himself and others. And one who does not teach himself or others: how so? If someone repeated a division two or three times but did not repeat them for others and did not occupy himself with them and ultimately forgot them, this is one who does not teach himself or others."

Theological Grammar of the Oral Torah. Vol. I 355

Which takes precedence, study or deed? No value accrues for studying the Torah without carrying out the commandments and teachings thereof, so Lev. R. XXXV:VIII.2: "If you walk in my statutes and keep my commandments and do them" (Lev. 26:3). R. Hiyya taught, "The reference to doing them refers to one who studies Torah in order to practice it and not to one who studies it not in order to practice it. For he who studies not in order to practice the teachings of the Torah would have been better off had he not been born." Said R. Yohanan, "He who studies not in order to practice would have been better off had his afterbirth been turned over his face and he not come out into the world." Said R. Aha, "He who studies in order to practice the commandments attains sufficient merit to receive the Holy Spirit. What is the proof text? 'This book of the law shall not depart out of your mouth, but you shall meditate on it day and night, that you may be careful to do according to all that is written in it, for then you shall make your way prosperous and then you shall have good success' (SKL) (Josh. 1:8). The reference to having 'good success' alludes only to the Holy Spirit, in line with the following verse of Scripture: 'Successful inspiration (SKL) for Ethan the Ezrahite'" (Ps. 89:1).

Deed, not study, is of greater importance, and study matters only because it brings about right action, so b. Qid. 1:10 I.2/40b: Once R. Tarfon and the elders were reclining at a banquet in the upper room of the house of Nitezeh in Lud. This question was raised for them: "Is study greater or is action greater?" R. Tarfon responded: "Action is greater." R. Aqiba responded: "Study is greater." All responded, saying, "Study is greater, for study brings about action." But that is all the more reason to value study of Torah, so b. Qid. 1:10 I.3/40b: R. Yosé, says, "Great is study, for it preceded the commandment to separate dough-offering by forty years, the commandments governing priestly rations and tithes by fifty-four years, the commandments covering remission of debts by sixty-one years, the commandment concerning the Jubilee Year by one hundred and three years." The Torah was given to Israel two months after the Exodus from Egypt, but liability to dough-offering came into force forty years later, and so throughout. And just as study of the Torah came prior to the actual practice of it, so judgment on that account takes precedence over judgment concerning practice of the Torah. And just as judgment concerning study takes priority over judgment concerning practice, so, too, the reward for studying the Torah takes priority over the reward for practice: "And he gave them the lands and nations, and they took the labor of the people in possession, that they might keep his statutes and observe his laws" (Ps. 105:44-45).

Study of Torah without good deeds yields no firm results, but study of Torah joined with good deeds produces solid results, so ARN XXIV:I.1-IV.1: Elisha b. Abuyyah says, "One who has good deeds to his credit and has studied the Torah a great deal — to what is he to be likened? To someone who builds first with stones and then with bricks. Even though a great flood of water comes and washes against the foundations, the water does not blot them out of their place. One who has no good deeds to his credit but has studied the Torah — to what is he to be likened? To someone who builds first with bricks and then with stones. Even if only a little water comes and washes against the foundations, it forthwith overturns them." He used to say, "One who has good deeds to his credit and has studied the Torah a great deal — to what is he to be likened? To lime spread over stones. Even if vast rain storms come down on them, they do not stir the lime from its place. One who has no good deeds to his credit but has studied the Torah a great deal — to what is he to be likened? To lime spread over bricks. Even if a sporadic rain falls on the lime, it is forthwith melted and disappears." He used to say, "One who has good deeds to his credit and has studied the Torah a great deal — to what is he to be likened? To a cup with a base. One who has no good deeds to his credit but has studied the Torah a great deal — to what is he to be likened? To a cup with no case. When the cup is filled, it turns on its side and whatever is in it pours out." He used to say, "One who has good deeds to his credit and has studied the Torah a great deal — to what is he to be likened? To a horse that has a bridle. One who has no good deeds to his credit but has studied the Torah a great deal — to what is he to be likened? To a horse without a bridle. When someone rides on the horse, it throws him off."

Study of the Torah is the sole way of learning how to attain merit and do things right. Mere good intention does not suffice. If one does not intend to do things right, all the more so will one suffer blame. So intention to do the right thing must be joined to Torah-study, that is, discipleship, so Y. Naz. 7:1 I.13: He who finds a neglected corpse, lo, this one must attend to him and bury him where he is lying. Under what circumstances? When he has found him outside of the boundary of a town. But if he found him in the boundary of the town, lo, this one brings him to the place of burial and buries him in the normal cemetery. Said R. Aqiba, "Thus was the beginning of my labor of learning before sages. One time I was walking along the way, and I found a neglected corpse, and I attended to him for about four mils, until I brought him to the graveyard, and I buried him there. Now when I came to R. Eliezer and to R. Joshua, I told him them what I had done. They said to me, 'For every step you took, you were credited as if you had shed blood for taking the neglected corpse away from the spot in which he should have been buried.' Now I said, 'If when I intended to acquire merit, I suffered blame for not doing things right, when I do not intend to acquire merit, how much the more so do I suffer blame. From that time I have not ceased to serve and study with sages.'" He would say, "He who does not serve sages is worthy of death."

Study of the Torah through oral repetition should go on without interruption, so Y. Shab. 1:2 VI.1: R. Simeon b. Yohai said, "If I were standing at Mount Sinai at the time that the Torah was given to Israel, I would have beseeched the Merciful God to create for that man me two mouths so that I might perpetually engage in the repetition of Torah traditions, one with which to labor in Torah, the other to serve all my needs in general." But the purpose of Torah-study is to carry out the teachings of the Torah, not simply to repeat them, thus Y. Shab. 1:2 VI.1: Said R. Yohanan, "He who studies not with the intention of carrying out what he learns — it would have been better for him if his backbone had been turned on his face, and if he had not come forth into the world."

A disciple of sages or master who learns something new in the Torah will be overjoyed by that fact and his face will glow, thus Y. Shab. 8:1 I.3: R. Abbahu went down to Tiberias. Disciples of R. Yohanan saw that his face was glowing. They reported before R. Yohanan that R. Abbahu had found some sort of treasure. He said to him, "How do you know?" They said to him, "His face is glistening." He said to them, "Perhaps he has learned some new teaching of the Light Torah." He went up to him and said to him, "What new teaching in the Light have you heard recently?" He said to him, "An ancient passage of a Supplement to the Mishnah," and he recited in this regard, "A man's wisdom makes his face shine" (Qoh. 8:1).

Disciples of sages are a source of peace in the world, so b Yeb. 16:7 I.4/122b: Said R. Eleazar said R. Hanina, "Disciples of sages make peace abundant in the world, as it is said, 'And all your children shall be taught by the Lord, and great will be the peace of your children.' Do not read the letters that spell 'your children' as though that is their meaning, but rather, read them to say, 'those who build you.'"

XXX.

WILL OF GOD

WILL OF GOD, THE: In place of fate or impersonal destiny, the Oral Torah identifies God's will as the active and causative force in the lives of individuals and nations. What happens happens by God's will, so, for instance, when it is time for a person to die, nothing will postpone the event, and anything may turn out to carry out God's will, so b. Ned. 4:4 I.21-3/40b: R. Alexandri also said in the name of R. Hiyya bar Abba, and some say, said R. Joshua b. Levi, "When the end time of a person has come, everything conquers him: 'And it will be that whosoever finds me will slay me' (Gen. 4:14)." They said to Rabbah bar Shila that a tall man died. He was riding a small mule, and when he came to a bridge, the mule shied and threw the man, and he was killed. To him Rabbah applied this verse: "They stand forth this day to receive your judgments, for all are your servants" (Ps. 119:91). Samuel saw a scorpion carried across a river by a frog. Then it stung someone who died. He cited this verse: "They stand forth this day to receive your judgments, for all are your servants" (Ps. 119:91).

Destiny dictated by God, not chance, governs Israel, specifically, God's plan. For God has a purpose in what he does with Israel. He sent them down into Egypt so that he would have occasion to perform miracles, so that the whole world would know that He is God and there is no other, so Sif. Dt. CCCVI:XXX.1-4: "And how on the basis of Scripture do you say that our ancestors went down to Egypt only so that the Holy One, blessed be He, might do wonders and acts of might, and so that his great name might be sanctified in the world? As it is said, 'And it came to pass in the course of that long time that the king of Egypt died...and God heard their groaning, and God remembered his covenant' (Ex. 2:23-24). And it is said, 'For the name of the Lord I proclaim; give glory to our God.' And how on the basis of Scripture do we know that the Omnipresent brought punishments and the ten plagues on Pharaoh and on the Egyptians only so that his great name might be sanctified in the world? For to begin with it is said, 'Who is the Lord, that I should listen to his voice?' (Ex. 5:2). But in the end: 'The Lord is righteous, and I and my people are wicked' (Ex. 9:27). And how on the basis of Scripture do we know that the Omnipresent did wonders and acts of might at the sea and at the Jordan and at the Arnon streams only so that his great name might be sanctified in the world? As it is said, 'And it came to pass, when all the kings of the Amorites that were beyond the Jordan westward, and all the kings of the Canaanites that were by the sea, heard how the Lord has dried up the waters of the Jordan from before the children of Israel until they had passed over, their heart melted ' (Josh. 5:1). And so Rahab says to the messengers of Joshua, 'For we have heard how the Lord dried up the water of the Red Sea before you' (Josh. 2:10). Scripture says, 'For the name of the Lord I proclaim; give glory to our God.' And how on the basis of Scripture do we know that Daniel went down into the lions' den only so that the Holy One, blessed be He, might have occasion to do wonders and acts of might, and so that his great name might be sanctified in the world? As it is said, 'For the name of the Lord I proclaim; give glory to our God.' And Scripture says, 'I make a decree, that in all the dominions of my kingdom men tremble and fear before the God of Daniel...' (Dan. 6:27-28). And how on the basis of Scripture do you maintain that Hananiah, Mishael, and Azariah went into the fiery oven only so that the Holy One, blessed be He, might have occasion to do for them wonders and acts of might, and so that his great name might be sanctified in the world? As it is said, 'It seems good to me to declare the signs and wonders that God Most High has done for me...how great are his signs, and how mighty are his wonders, his kingdom is an everlasting kingdom' (Dan. 3:32-33)."

Proof of Israel's election lies in Israel's destiny; when Israel suffers, it is because of their own sin, and when Israel prospers, it is because of service to God, acceptance of God's will, so b. Ket. 6:4 II.4/66b: There was the case of Rabban Yohanan b. Zakkai, who was riding on his ass leaving Jerusalem, and his disciples were following him. He saw a girl who was picking barley seeds from the shit of Arab cattle. When she saw him, she covered herself with her hair, stood before him, and said to him, "My lord, give me some food." He said to her, "My daughter, who are you?" She said to him, "I'm the daughter of Naqdimon b. Gurion." He said to her, "My daughter, what ever happened to the money of your father's house?" She said to him, "My lord, doesn't the Jerusalem proverb go,

'The salt that keeps money secure is distributing it to the poor?'" Others say, "...acts of loving kindness done with the money ...." "And what ever happened to the money of your father-in-law's house pledged to your marriage contract?" She said to him, "The funds were mingled, and one came and destroyed the other." She said to him, "My lord, do you remember when you signed my marriage contract?" He said to his disciples, "I remember full well, when I signed her marriage contract, I read in it, 'A thousand gold denars from the house of her father, not counting what comes from her father-in-law....'" Rabban Yohanan ben Zakkai wept and said, "Happy are you, Israel! When you do what the Omnipresent wants, no nation or alien tongue can rule you, and when you don't do what the Omnipresent wants, he hands you over to the most degraded nation, and not only into the power of the most degraded nation, but into the power of their cattle."

God decrees from year to year, on the New Year, just what would happen to individuals and to the entire holy people, thus Y. Yoma 5:2 II.1: This was the prayer of the high priest on the Day of Atonement, when he left the holy place whole and in one piece: "May it be pleasing before you, Lord, our God of our fathers, that a decree of exile not be issued against us, not this day or this year, but if a decree of exile should be issued against us, then let it be exile to a place of Torah. May it be pleasing before you, Lord, our God and God of our fathers, that a decree of want not be issued against us, not this day or this year, but if a decree of want should be issued against us, then let it be a want of the performance of religious duties. May it be pleasing before you, Lord, our God and God of our fathers, that this year be a year of cheap food, full bellies, good business; a year in which the earth forms clods, then is parched so as to form scabs, and then moistened with dew, so that your people, Israel, will not be in need of the help of one another. And do not heed the prayer of travelers that it not rain." Rabbis of Caesarea say, "And concerning your people, Israel, that they not exercise dominion over one another." Along these same lines, M. Bes. 2:1 I.5/16a: A person's entire allotment for the year is determined by God between New Year's Day and the Day of Atonement, except for the expenses of celebrating Sabbaths and the expenses of celebrating festivals and the expense of educating his sons in Torah. For if he spends less on these things than he should, he is given less. While if he spends more than is expected, he is given more."

Because Israel is governed by God's will, Israel is not subject to astrological influences, so b. Shab. 24: 3 III.9-/156b-157a: R. Yohanan said, "Israel is not subject to the stars." And R. Yohanan is consistent with views expressed elsewhere, for said R. Yohanan, "How on the basis of Scripture do we know that Israel is not subject to the stars? As it is said, 'Thus says the Lord, Do not learn the way of the gentiles, nor be dismayed at the signs of the heavens, for the nations are dismayed at them' (Jer. 10:2). They are dismayed, but the Israelites are not dismayed." And so Rab takes the view that Israel is not subject to the stars, for said R. Judah said Rab, "How on the basis of Scripture do we know that Israel is not subject to the stars? As it is said, 'And he brought him forth outside' (Gen. 15:5). Said Abraham before the Holy One, blessed be He, 'Lord of the world, "Someone born in my household is my heir" (Gen. 15:3).' He said to him, 'Not at all. "But he who will come forth out of your own loins" (Gen. 1:4).' He said before him, 'Lord of the world, I have closely examined my star, and I have seen that I am destined to have no children.' He said to him, 'Abandon this astrology of yours — Israel is not subject to astrology. It is also the position of Samuel that Israel is not subject to the stars. For Samuel and Ablat were in session, and some people going along to a lake. Said Ablat to Samuel, "That man is going but won't come back, a snake will bite him and he'll die." Said to him Samuel, "Yeah, well, if he's an Israelite, he will go and come back." While they were in session, he went and came back. Ablat got up and took of the man's knapsack and found in it a snake cut up and lying in two pieces. Said Samuel to the man, "What did you do today in particular ?" He said to him, "Every day we tossed our bread into one pot and ate, but today one of us had no bread, and he was shamed. I said to him, 'I will go and collect the bread.' When I came to him, I made as if to go and collect the bread, so he shouldn't be ashamed." He said to him, "You have carried out a religious duty." Samuel went forth and expounded, "'But charity delivers from death' (Prov. 10:2) — not from a grotesque death, but from death itself." It is also the position of Aqiba that Israel is not subject to the stars. For R. Aqiba had a daughter. Chaldaeans astrologers told him, "On the day that she goes into the bridal canopy, a snake will bite her and she'll die." This worried him a lot. On that day she took a brooch and stuck it into the wall, and by chance it sank into the eye of a snake. The next day when she took it out, the snake came trailing along after it. Her father said to her, "What did you do today in particular ?" She said to him, "In the evening a poor man came to the door, and everyone was busy with the banquet so no one could take care of him, so I took some of what was given to me and gave it to him." He said to her, "You have carried out a religious duty." R. Aqiba went forth and expounded, "'But charity delivers from death' (Prov. 10:2) — not from a grotesque death, but from death itself." It is also the position of R. Nahman bar Isaac that Israel is not subject to the stars. For to the mother of R. Nahman bar Isaac the Chaldaean said, "Your son will be a thief." She didn't let him go bareheaded, saying, "Keep your head covered, so fear of Heaven may be upon you, and pray for mercy." He didn't know why she said that to him. One day he was in session, studying under a palm tree. His head covering fell off. He lifted his eyes and saw the palm tree, and was overcome by temptation; he climbed up and bit off a cluster of dates with his teeth.

In the Oral Torah, casting of lots and other forms of chance yield God's decision.. How the lot falls then reflects how God wants things, since to begin with God commands and fate conforms. Nothing in fact takes place by chance, so by allowing the dice to fall where they will, man discovers God's wishes. That is the preferred mode of identifying that which God desires, e.g., within a given batch of produce. When the farmer wishes to designate God's share (the heave-offering or priestly ration) of the crop, so that he may then retain the rest as his own, secular food, he must do so in a random manner. The volume must not be measured; the designation should not be subject to the will of the farmer. Thus M. Ter. 1:7: They do not separate heave offering by (1) a measure of volume , or by (2) weight, or by (3) a count of the number of pieces of fruit being separated as heave offering . But he separates the heave offering of (1) produce which has been measured, of (2) that which has been weighed, and of (3) that which has been counted. They do not separate heave offering in a basket or in a vessel which hold a known measure. But he separates heave offering in them if they are one-half or one-third part filled . He may not separate heave offering in a basket which holds one seah, if it is one-half part filled , since the half thereof is a known measure. The matter of chance likewise governs the designation of produce for the poor in the former of the forgotten sheaf, an estimate being made of whether or not it is likely that the farmer intended to go back and collect a sheaf that is left in the field. If he intended to leave the sheaf, it is not regarded as a forgotten sheaf that God has assigned to the poor. So M. Peah 6:4: And these are the rules which apply to sheaves left at the ends of rows in a field : (1) Two men who began to harvest a crop from the middle of a row, one facing north and the other facing south, and they forgot sheaves in front of them toward the edge of the field, and at their backs in between them — a sheaf which they forgot in front of them is subject to the restrictions of the forgotten sheaf, for it is in clear view while they harvest — But a sheaf which they forgot at their backs is not subject to the restrictions of the forgotten sheaf, for neither of the workers had the sheaf in plain view while they harvested the field. (2) An individual who began to harvest a field from the end of a row, and forgot sheaves in front of himself and behind himself — a sheaf which he forgot in front of himself is not subject to the restrictions of the forgotten sheaf, for he can gather it when he harvests that part of the row — But a sheaf which he forgot behind himself is subject to the restrictions of the forgotten sheaf, because it is under the law, When you reap your harvest in your field, and have forgotten a sheaf in the field, you shall not go back to get id (Dt. 24:19). This is the general principle : Whatever sheaf is under the law 'You shall not go back' is subject to the law of the forgotten sheaf. But what is not under the law 'You shall not go back' is not subject to the law of the forgotten sheaf.

God decides who follows an easy trade and who does heavy lifting, who prospers and who does not, so M. Qid. 4:14: R. Meir says, "A man should always teach his son a clean and easy trade. And let him pray to him to whom belong riches and possessions. For there is no trade which does not involve poverty or wealth. For poverty does not come from one's trade, nor does wealth come from one's trade. But all is in accord with a man's merit."

Whatever happens comes about by reason of the character of a given generation and the presence of the righteous or the wicked. The righteous bring goodness to the world, and when they die, retribution follows; the wicked bring retribution to the world, and when they die, goodness returns, so T. Sot. 10:1: When righteous people come into the world, good comes into the world and retribution departs from the world. And when they take their leave from the world, retribution comes into the world, and goodness departs from the world. When bad people come into the world, retribution comes into the world, and goodness departs from the world. And when they depart from the world, goodness comes back into the world, and retribution departs from the world. How do we know that, when righteous people come into the world, goodness comes into the world, and retribution departs from the world? Since it is said, "And he called him Noah, saying, This one will comfort us in our work and in the toil of our hands" (Gen. 5:29). And how do we know that, when they take their leave of the world, retribution comes into the world and goodness departs from the world? Since it is said, "The righteous man perishes and no one lays it to heart" (Is. 57:1), and it says, "he enters into peace, they rest in their beds who walk in their uprightness" (Is. 57:2) — He goes in peace to the grave. And it says, "But you, draw near hither, sons of the sorceress, offspring of the adulterer and the harlot" (Is. 57:3). And how do we know that when bad people come into the world, retribution comes into the world and goodness departs from the world? Since it is said, "When the wicked comes, then comes also contempt, and with ignominy, reproach" (Prov. 18:3). And how do we know that, when he departs from the world, goodness comes into the world and retribution leaves the world? Since it says, "And when the wicked perish, there is exultation" (Prov. 11:10). And it says, "So that the Lord may turn from the fierceness of his anger and show you mercy and have compassion on you" (Deut. 13:17).

Satan brings about the prosecution and punishment of Man, but much that he is able to do comes about by reason of Man's own fault, e.g., Y. 2:6 I:1: Said R. Levi, "In three situations Satan is waiting to prosecute: he who makes a trip all by himself, he who sleeps by himself in a closed-up house, and he who sets sail on the Great Sea."

God's will then forms the governing power of reality, and God's will is made known in the Torah. A rational plan encompasses all things, and rules, which are self-fulfilling, explain all being.

XXXI.

Women

WOMEN: Along with slaves and minors, women form a classification of Israelites deemed not fully capable of independent will, intentionality, entire responsibility, and action and therefore subject not only to God's will but also to the will of another, the husband or father in the case of the woman, the master in the case of the slave, and the parent in the case of the child, thus M. Ber. 3:3: Women, slaves, and minors are exempt from the recitation of the *Shema* and from the obligation to wear phylacteries, but are obligated to the recitation of the prayer, and to post a *mezuzah* and to recite the blessing over the meal. But they do not form part of the community of holy Israel that is obligated to recite blessings publicly, thus M. Ber. 7:2: Women, slaves or minors who ate together with adult Israelite males — they may not invite others to bless on their account.

When Scripture refers to "man," it may cover both man and woman, but special conditions yield the word-choice, so Sifra CXCV:II.1-2: "Every one Hebrew: man of you shall revere his mother and his father, and you shall keep my Sabbaths": I know only that a man is subject to the instruction. How do I know that a woman is also involved? Scripture says, "...shall revere" using the plural. Lo, both genders are covered. If so, why does Scripture refer to "man"? It is because a man controls what he needs, while a woman does not control what she needs, since others have dominion over her.

In a number of specific contexts, moreover, a man and woman are differentiated in the functions that they perform or to which they are obligated, e.g., M. Sot. 3:8: What is the difference between a man and a woman? A man goes around with unbound hair and torn garments, but a woman does not go around with unbound hair and torn garments (Lev. 13:44-5). A man imposes a Nazirite vow on his son, and a woman does not impose a Nazirite vow upon her son (M. Naz. 4:6). A man brings the hair offering for the Nazirite vow of his father, and a woman does not bring a hair offering for the Nazirite vow of her father. The man sells his daughter, and the woman does not sell her daughter Ex. 21:6. The man arranges for a betrothal of his daughter, and the woman does not arrange for the betrothal of her daughter (M. Qid. 2:1). A man who incurs the death penalty is stoned naked, but a woman is not stoned naked. A man is hanged after being put to death, and a woman is not hanged (M. San. 6:3-4). A man is sold to make restitution for having stolen something, but a woman is not sold to make restitution for having stolen something (Ex. 22:2).

The matter is further amplified at M. Qid. 1:7-8: For every commandment concerning the son to which the father is subject-men are liable, and women are exempt. And for every commandment concerning the father to which the son is subject, men and women are equally liable. For every positive commandment dependent upon the time of year, men are liable, and women are exempt. And for every positive commandment not dependent upon the time, men and women are equally liable. For every negative commandment, whether dependent upon the time or not dependent upon the time, men and women are equally liable, except for not marring the comers of the beard, not rounding the corners of the head (Lev. 19:27), and not becoming unclean because of the dead (Lev. 21:1). The cultic rites of laying on of hands, waving, drawing near, taking the handful, burning the incense, breaking the neck of a bird, sprinkling, and receiving the blood apply to men and not to women, except in the case of a meal offering of an accused wife and of a Nazirite girl, which they wave. This matter is clarified at T. Qid. 1:10-11: What is a positive commandment dependent upon the time of year, for which men are liable and women are exempt (M. Qid. 1:7C)? For example, building the Sukkah, taking the lulab, putting tefillin. What is a positive commandment not dependent upon the time of year (M. Qid. 1:7D)? For example, restoring lost property to its rightful owner, sending forth the bird, building a parapet, and putting on show-fringes. What is a commandment pertaining to the son concerning the father to which men and women are equally liable (M. Qid. 1:7B)? Giving him food to eat and something to drink and clothing him and covering him and taking him out and bringing him in and washing his face, his hands, and his feet. All the same are men and women. But the husband has sufficient means to do these things for the child, and the wife does not have sufficient means to do them, for others have power over her. So too, a woman is not obligated to study the Torah or to wear tefillin, so Y. Er. 10:1 I.2: He who is liable to study Torah also is liable to wear *tefillin*.

women, who are not liable to study Torah, also are not liable to wear *tefillin*.

It is taken for granted that women are subject to men, daughters to fathers, then wives to husbands; widows are assumed to return to their fathers' households. Marriage is the natural condition of man and woman, so b. Yeb. 6:6 II.19-21 Said R. Hanilai, "Any man who has no wife lives without joy, blessing, goodness: Joy: 'and you shall rejoice, you and your house' (Dt. 14:26). Blessing: 'to cause a blessing to rest on your house' (Ez. 44:30). Goodness: 'it is not good that man should be alone' (Gen. 2:18)." In the West they say: without Torah and without a wall of refuge. without Torah: "Is it that I have no help in me and that sound wisdom is driven entirely out of me" (Job 6:13). without a wall of refuge: "A woman shall form a wall about a man" (Jer. 31:22). Raba bar Ulla said, "Without peace: 'and you shall know that your tent is in peace, and you shall visit your habitation and shall miss nothing' (Job 5:24)." He who loves his wife as he loves himself, he who honors her more than he honors himself, he who raises up his sons and daughters in the right path, and he who marries them off close to the time of their puberty Ä of such a one, Scripture says, "And you shall know that your tabernacle shall be in peace and you shall visit your habitation and you shall not sin" (Job 5:24).

In marriage a woman is expected to observe the law of Moses, and if she does not, she may be divorced without financial penalty to her husband, losing the alimony to which she would otherwise be entitled. How is that law defined? M. Ket. 7:6 states matters in these terms: What is the law of Moses which she has transgressed? If (1) she feeds him food which has not been tithed, or (2) has sexual relations with him while she is menstruating, or if (3) she does not cut off her dough offering, or (4) if she vows and does not carry out her vow. And what is the Jewish law? If (1) she goes out with her hair flowing loose or (2) she spins in the marketplace, or (3) she talks with just anybody. Abba Saul says, "Also: if she curses his parents in his presence." R. Tarfon says, "Also: if she is a loudmouth."

As to sexual relations, women's rights are to be carefully respected; marital rape is forbidden, and a woman who invites sexual relations is highly praised and will produce remarkable children, so b. Er. 10:10:8 II.9/100b: And said R. Ammi bar Abba said R. Assi, "It is forbidden for someone to rape his wife force his wife to carry out the religious duty (of sexual relations): 'And he that hastes with his feet sins' (Prov. 19:2)." And said

R. Joshua b. Levi, "Whoever rapes his wife will have unworthy children." Said R. Samuel bar Nahmani said R. Jonathan, "Any man whose wife calls him to sexual relations will have children of the like of which the generation of our lord, Moses, didn't have, as it is said, 'Take you men wise, understanding, and known among your tribes and I will make them rulers over you' (Deut. 1:13); and 'So I took the chiefs of your tribes, wise men and known' (Deut. 1:15) Ð without reference to 'understanding.' And with reference to Leah, it is written, 'And Leah went out to meet him and said, you must come to me, for I have surely hired you' (Gen. 30:16), and it is written, 'Issachar is a large-boned ass' (Gen. 49:14), and elsewhere, 'And of the children of Issachar, who were men that had understanding of the times' (1 Chr. 12:33)." This was Leah's reward, proving that it is meritorious for a woman to demand sexual relations. Is that so? And didn't R. Isaac bar Abdimi say, "Eve was assigned ten curses, as it is said, 'To the woman he said, I will greatly multiply your pain and your travail; in pain you shall bring forth children; and your desire will be to your husband; and he shall rule over you' (Gen. 3:16). "'I will greatly multiply your pain' refers to the two kinds of blood that a woman discharges, one the pain of menstrual blood, the other that of hymeneal blood. "'And your travail' refers to the pain of pregnancy. "'In pain you shall bring forth children' bears the obvious meaning and refers to the pain of giving birth. "'And your desire will be to your husband' refers to the fact that a woman lusts after her husband when he goes off on a journey. "'And he shall rule over you' refers to the fact that a man asks explicitly for what he wants, while a woman just aches in her heart for it, cloaked as in mourning, imprisoned, cut off from all men other than her husband" (Fathers According to R. Nathan I:VIII.4)? So is that a good quality for women? When we made the statement that we did, it means, she seduces him but doesn't solicit him in so many words.

Sages and their disciples do not talk too much to women but keep their distance, so M. Abot 1:5: Yosé, b. Yohanan of Jerusalem says, "Don't talk too much with women." (He spoke of a man's wife, all the more so is the rule to be applied to the wife of one's fellow. In this regard did sages say, "So long as a man talks too much with a woman, (1) he brings trouble on himself, (2) wastes time better spent on studying Torah, and (3) ends up an heir of Gehenna.") Correct behavior with women requires modesty and deference, so b. Er. 2:3 I.8/18b:He who counts out coins into a woman's hand from his own in order to have a chance to stare at her, even if such a one has in hand Torah and good deeds like Moses, our master, will not be quit of the judgment of Gehenna. For it is said, "Hand to hand, he shall not escape from evil" (Prov. 11:21). He shall not escape from the judgment of Gehenna. Correct conduct with women involves modesty and chastity, so b. Ber. 9:1 XVII.6, 8/61b: He who counts out coins into a woman's hand from his own in order to have a chance to stare at her, even if such a one has in hand To For it is said, "Hand to hand, he shall not escape from evil" (Prov. 11:21). He shall not escape from the judgment of Gehenna." Said R. Yohanan, "Walk after a lion but not after a woman, after a woman but not after a gentile, after a gentile but not behind a synagogue when the community is saying prayers.

Women come to listen to the study of the Torah, and bring their children as an act of merit as well, so ARN XVIII:II.1: When R. Joshua got old, his disciples came to visit him. He said to them, "My sons, what was the new point that you had today in school?" They said to him, "We are your disciples, and your water alone do we drink." He said to them, "God forbid! it is impossible that there is a generation of sages that is orphaned and without suitable guidance. Whose week was it to teach?" They said to him, "It was the week of R. Eleazar b. Azariah." He said to them, "And what was the topic of the narrative today?" They said to him, "It was the passage that begins, Assemble the people, the men and the women and the children (Deut. 31:12)." He said to them, "And what did he expound in that connection?" They said to him, "This is how he interpreted it. 'The men come to learn, the women to listen, but why do the children come? It is to provide the occasion for the gaining of a reward for those who bring them.'"

XXXII.

ZEKHUT

ZEKHUT: the empowerment of a supernatural character that derives from the virtue of one's ancestry or from one's own virtuous deeds of a very particular order. Such remarkable deeds involve actions favored by God but not subject to God's power to compel or command, e.g., love of God, which must be given freely or makes no difference; remarkable abstinence or generosity beyond the expectations of the commandments of the Torah. Whence then the lien on Heaven? It is through deeds of a supererogatory character — to which Heaven responds by deeds of a supererogatory character: supernatural favor to this one, who through deeds of ingratiation of the other or self-abnegation or restraint exhibits the attitude that in Heaven precipitates a counterpart attitude, hence generating *zekhut*, rather than to that one, who does not. The simple fact that rabbis cannot pray and bring rain, but a simple ass-driver can, tells the whole story. The relationship measured by *zekhut* — Heaven's response by an act of uncoerced favor to a person's uncoerced gift, e.g., act of gentility, restraint, or self-abnegation — contains an element of unpredictability for which appeal to the *zekhut* inherited from ancestors accounts. So while man cannot coerce heaven, he can through *zekhut* gain acts of favor from Heaven, and that is by doing what Heaven cannot require of me. Heaven then responds to his attitude in carrying out his duties — and more than his duties. That act of pure disinterest — giving the woman one's means of livelihood — is the one that gains Heaven's deepest interest.

The character of *zekhut* such as is attained by an individual's actions is best defined by exemplary accounts of the matter, e.g., cases in which ordinary persons are endowed with supernatural power (prayers for rain being answered, for instance), which cannot be attributed to Torah-study. Ordinary folk, not disciples of sages, have access to *zekhut* entirely outside of study of the Torah. In stories not told about rabbis, a single remarkable deed, exemplary for its deep humanity, sufficed to win for an ordinary person the *zekhut* — "the heritage of virtue and its consequent entitlements" — that elicits the same marks of supernatural favor enjoyed by some rabbis on account of their Torah-study. Even though a man was degraded, one action sufficed to win for him that heavenly glory to which rabbis in lives of Torah-study aspired. The mark of the system's integration around *zekhut* lies in its insistence that all Israelites, not only sages, could gain *zekhut* for themselves (and their descendants). A single remarkable deed, exemplary for its deep humanity, sufficed to win for an ordinary person the *zekhut* that elicits supernatural favor enjoyed by some rabbis on account of their Torah-study. The advantages or privileges conferred by *zekhut* may be inherited and also passed on; it stresses "entitlements" because advantages or privileges always, invariably result from receiving *zekhut* from ancestors or acquiring it on one's own; and "virtue" refers to those supererogatory acts that demand a reward because they form matters of choice, the gift of the individual and his or her act of free will, an act that is at the same time (1) uncompelled, e.g., by the obligations imposed by the Torah, but (2) also valued by the Torah. But *zekhut* may be attained, also, through performance of religious duties and good deeds, so Gen. R. IX:X.1: Said R. Samuel bar R. Isaac, "'Lo, it was very good' refers to the angel of life. 'And lo, it was very good' refers to the angel of death. And can anyone say that the angel of death is 'very good'? Rather, the matter may be compared to the case of a king who made a banquet and invited guests and set before them a spread of every good thing. He said, 'Whoever eats and says a blessing for the king may eat and enjoy himself, but whoever eats and does not say a blessing for the king will have his head cut off with a sword.' So here, for whoever stores up a treasury of merit attained through performance of religious duties and good deeds, lo there is the angel of life. And for whoever does not store up a treasury of merit attained through performance of religious duties and good deeds, lo, there is the angel of death."

Specifically, deeds beyond the strict requirements of the Torah, and even the limits of the law altogether, transform the hero into a holy man, whose holiness served just like that of a sage marked as such by knowledge of the Torah. Merit is achieved through an act of philanthropy, and that fact enters the language, so Lev. R. XXIV:VII.1: Said R. Zeira, "Even the ordinary speech of the inhabitants of the Land of Israel is Torah. How so? Someone says to his fellow, 'Attain merit by giving me charity.' 'Acquire merit for yourself through me by giving me charity.' 'Add merit to yourself through me.' In these usages the ordinary folk reflect the teaching of the Torah that through giving charity a person acquires merit." The following stories, all of them at Y. Taanit 1:4.I, deny in favor of a single action of surpassing power sages' lifelong devotion to what the sages held to be the highest value, knowledge of the Torah:

A certain man came before one of the relatives of R. Yannai. He said to him, "Rabbi, attain *zekhut* through me by giving me charity." He said to him, "And didn't your father leave you money?" He said to him, "No." He said to him, "Go and collect what your father left in deposit with others." He said to him, "I have heard concerning property my father deposited with others that it was gained by violence so I don't want it." He said to him, "You are worthy of praying and having your prayers answered."

The point is self-evidently a reference to the possession of entitlement to supernatural favor, and it is gained, we see, through deeds that the law of the Torah cannot require but must favor: what one does on one's own volition, beyond the measure of the law. Here I see the opposite of sin. A sin is what one has done by one's own volition beyond all limits of the law. So an act that generates *zekhut* for the individual is the counterpart and opposite: what one does by one's own volition that also is beyond all requirements of the law.

A certain ass driver appeared before the rabbis the context requires: in a dream and prayed, and rain came. The rabbis sent and brought him and said to him, "What is your trade?" He said to them, "I am an ass driver." They said to him, "And how do you conduct your business?" He said to them, "One time I rented my ass to a certain woman, and she was weeping on the way, and I said to her, 'What's with you?' and she said to me, 'The husband of that woman (=me) is in prison for debt, and I wanted to see what I can do to free him.' So I sold my ass and I gave her the proceeds, and I said to her, 'Here is your money, free your husband, but do not sin by becoming a prostitute to raise the necessary funds.'" They said to him, "You are worthy of praying and having your prayers answered."

The ass-driver clearly has a powerful lien on Heaven, so that his prayers are answered, even while those of others are not. What he did to get that entitlement? He did what no law could demand: impoverished himself to save the woman from a "fate worse than death."

In a dream of R. Abbahu, Mr. Pentakaka (="Five sins") appeared, who prayed that rain would come, and it rained. R. Abbahu sent and summoned him. He said to him, "What is your trade?" He said to him, "Five sins does that man do every day, for I am a pimp: hiring whores, cleaning up the theater, bringing home their garments for washing, dancing, and performing before them." He said to him, "And what sort of decent thing have you ever done?" He said to him, "One day that man was cleaning the theater, and a woman came and stood behind a pillar and cried. I said to her, 'What's with you?' And she said to me, 'That woman's my husband is in prison, and I wanted to see what I can do to free him,' so I sold my bed and cover, and I gave the proceeds to her. I said to her, 'Here is your money, free your husband, but do not sin.'" He said to him, "You are worthy of praying and having your prayers answered."

The named man has done everything sinful that one can do, and, more to the point, he does it every day. So the singularity of the act of *zekhut*, which suffices if done only one time, encompasses its power to outweigh a life of sin — again, an act of *zekhut* as the mirror-image and opposite of sin. Here again, the single act of saving a woman from a "fate worse than death" has sufficed.

A pious man from Kefar Imi appeared in a dream to the rabbis. He prayed for rain and it rained. The rabbis went up to him. His householders told them that he was sitting on a hill. They went out to him, saying to him, "Greetings," but he did not answer them. He was sitting and eating, and he did not say to them, "You break bread too." When he went back home, he made a bundle of faggots and put his cloak on top of the bundle instead of on his shoulder. When he came home, he said to his household wife, "These rabbis are here because they want me to pray for rain. If I pray and it rains, it is a disgrace for them, and if not, it is a profanation of the Name of Heaven. But come, you and I will go up to the roof and pray. If it rains, we shall tell them, 'We are not worthy to pray and have our prayers answered.'" They went up and prayed and it rained. They came down to them and asked, "Why have the rabbis troubled themselves to come here today?" They said to him, "We wanted you to pray so that it would rain." He said to them, "Now do you really need my prayers? Heaven already has done its miracle." They said to him, "Why, when you were on the hill, did we say hello to you, and you did not reply?" He said to them, "I was then doing my job. Should I then interrupt my concentration on my work?"

They said to him, "And why, when you sat down to eat, did you not say to us 'You break bread too'?" He said to them, "Because I had only my small ration of bread. Why would I have invited you to eat by way of mere flattery when I knew I could not give you anything at all?" They said to him, "And why when you came to go down, did you put your cloak on top of the bundle?" He said to them, "Because the cloak was not mine. It was borrowed for use at prayer. I did not want to tear it." They said to him, "And why, when you were on the hill, did your wife wear dirty clothes, but when you came down from the mountain, did she put on clean clothes?" He said to them, "When I was on the hill, she put on dirty clothes, so that no one would gaze at her. But when I came home from the hill, she put on clean clothes, so that I would not gaze on any other woman." They said to him, "It is well that you pray and have your prayers answered."

The pious man finally enjoys the recognition of the sages by reason of his lien upon Heaven, able as he is to pray and bring rain. What has so endowed him with *zekhut*? Acts of punctiliousness of a moral order: concentrating on his work, avoiding an act of dissimulation, integrity in the disposition of a borrowed object, his wife's concern not to attract other men and her equal concern to make herself attractive to her husband. None of these stories refers explicitly to *zekhut*; all of them tell us about what it means to enjoy not an entitlement by inheritance but a lien accomplished by one's own supererogatory acts of restraint. *Zekhut* represents the power of the weak. People who through their own merit and capacity can accomplish nothing, can accomplish miracles through what others do for them in leaving a heritage of *zekhut*. And *zekhut* also is what the weak and excluded and despised can do that outweighs in power what the great masters of the Torah have accomplished. *Zekhut* also forms the inheritance of the disinherited: what you receive as a heritage when you have nothing in the present and have gotten nothing in the past, that scarce resource that is free and unearned but much valued.

The systemic statement made by the usages of *zekhut* speaks of relationship, function, the interplay of humanity and God. One's store of *zekhut* derives from a relationship, that is, from one's forebears. That is one dimension of the relationships in which one stands. *Zekhut* also forms a measure of one's own relationship with Heaven, as the power of one person, but not another, to pray and so bring rain attests. What sort of relationship does *zekhut*, as the opposite of sin, then posit? It is not one of coercion, for Heaven cannot force us to do those types of deeds that yield *zekhut*, and that, story after story suggests, is the definition of a deed that generates *zekhut*: doing what we ought to do but do not have to do. But then, we cannot coerce Heaven to do what we want done either, for example, by carrying out the commandments. These are obligatory, but do not obligate Heaven.

Zekhut also derives from the founding saints of Israel, Abraham, Isaac, Jacob, their wives and children, and, by extension, one may acquire *zekhut* via the otherwise-unrequited actions of one's own forebears. God remembers the merit of the ancestors and counts it to the advantage of their heirs, e.g., in the liturgy for praying for rain, M. Taanit 2:4 A. (1) For the first ending he says, "He who answered Abraham on Mount Moriah will answer you and hear the sound of your cry this day. Blessed are you, O Lord, redeemer of Israel." (2) For the second he says, "He who answered our fathers at the Red Sea will answer you and hear the sound of your cry this day. Blessed are you, O Lord, who remembers forgotten things." (3) For the third he says, "He who answered Joshua at Gilgal will answer you and hear the sound of your cry this day. Blessed are you, O Lord, who hears the sound of the shofar " (4) For the fourth he says, "He who answered Samuel at Mispeh will answer you and hear the sound of your cry this day. Blessed are you, O Lord, who hears a cry." (5) For the fifth he says, "He who answered Elijah at Mount Carmel will answer you and hear the sound of your cry this day. Blessed are you, O Lord, who hears prayer." (6) For the sixth he says, "He who answered Jonah in the belly of the fish will answer you and hear the sound of your cry this day. Blessed are you, O Lord, who answers prayer in a time of trouble." For the seventh he says, "He who answered David and Solomon, his son, in Jerusalem, will answer you and hear the sound of your cry this day. Blessed are you, O Lord, who has mercy on the Land."

The sound of the shofar is heard by God; God is reminded of the readiness of Abraham and Isaac at Moriah to make the supreme sacrifice, and so God's mercies are aroused. Hence the shofar is sounded at every turning, so M. Taanit 3:5: On account of the appearance of these do they sound the shofar in every locale: (1) blasting or (2) mildew, (3) locust or (4) caterpillar (I Kings 8:27), (5) wild beasts, and (6) the sword (Lev. 26:6).

Everywhere do they sound the shofar on their account, because it is an affliction which spreads.

Zekhut thus extends to the heirs of the saints, and that is in proportion to the actions of the patriarchs, thus b. B.M. 7:1 IV.6/87b: Said R. Judah said Rab, "Whatever Abraham himself did for the ministering angels, the Holy One, blessed be he, himself did for his children. Whatever Abraham did for the ministering angels through an errand-boy, the Holy One, blessed be he, did for his children through an angel. 'And Abraham ran to the herd' is matched by 'And there went forth a wind from the Lord' (Ex. 16:4). 'And he took butter and milk' is matched by 'Behold I will rain bread from heaven for you' (Ex. 17:6). 'And he stood by them under the tree' is matched by 'Behold, I will stand before you there upon the rock' (Ex. 17:6). 'And Abraham went with them to bring them on the way' is matched by 'And the Lord went before them by day' (Ex. 13:21). 'Let a little water, I pray you, be gotten' is matched by 'And you shall hit the rock, and water will come out of it that the people may drink' (Ex. 17:6)." "As a reward for three things that Abraham did, his heirs got three things. As a reward for 'and he took butter and milk,' they got the manna. As a reward for 'and he stood by them,' they received the pillar of cloud. As a reward for ''let a little water, I pray you, be brought,' they got Miriam's well."

The notion of inheriting the entitlements bequeathed by the patriarchs and matriarchs is spelled out in a specific context. God remembers the deeds of the patriarchs and credits their descendants with the merit thereby earned, so with Abraham and Isaac on Mount Moriah (M. Ta. 2:4). This is spelled out in the following way, Y. Ta. 2:4 I.1: R. Bibi, Abba in the name of R. Yohanan: "Said Abraham before the Holy One, blessed be he, 'Lord of the ages! It is self-evident to you that when you told me to offer up Isaac, my son I had a good answer to give you: Yesterday you said to me, "Be not displeased because of the lad and because of your slave woman; whatever Sarah says to you, do as she tells you, for through Isaac shall your descendants be named" (Gen. 21:12) 'And now you tell me: "Take your son, your only son Isaac, whom you love, and go to the land of Moriah and offer him there as a burnt offering upon one of the mountains of which I shall tell you" (Gen. 2:22). 'But I, God forbid, I did not give you that answer, but I overcame my impulse and did what you wanted. Now may it be pleasing to you, O Lord my God, that when the children of Isaac, my son, come to a time of trouble and will have no one to speak in their behalf, you will speak in their behalf.' And Abraham said, 'God will see to the sheep for his burnt offering, my son. So they went both of them together (Gen. 22:8).' You remember in their behalf the binding of Isaac, their father, and have mercy upon them." What is written thereafter? "And Abraham lifted up his eyes and looked behind, and behold, there was a ram caught in a thicket by his horns; and Abraham went and took the ram and offered it up as a burnt offering instead of his son" (Gen. 22:13). What is the meaning of "behind 'after'?" Said R. Judah b. R. Simon, "After all generations your children are going to be caught up in sins and entrapped in troubles. But in the end they will be redeemed by the horn of this ram." R. Hunah in the name of R. Hinenah bar Isaac: "For that entire day Abraham saw now the ram would get caught in one tree and free itself and go forth, then it got caught in a bush and freed itself and went forth, and then it got caught in a thicket and freed itself and went forth. Said to him the Holy One, blessed be he, 'Abraham, this is how your children in the future will be caught by their sins and trapped by the kingdoms, from Babylonia to Media, from Media to Greece, from Greece to Edom Rome.' He said to him, 'Lord of the ages! Is that how it will be forever?' He said to him, 'In the end they will be redeemed by the horn of this ram. 'Then the Lord will appear over them, and his arrow will go forth like lightning; the Lord God will sound the trumpet, and march forth in the whirlwinds of the south'" (Zech. 9: 14).

  The merit of the patriarchs forms an inheritance of entitled grace for Israel, but how long does this last? Y. San. 10:12 I.6 responds in these terms: How long did the merit of the patriarchs endure to protect Israel? R. Tanhuma said in the name of R. Hiyya the Elder, Bar Nahman stated in the name of R. Berekiah, R. Helbo in the name of R. Ba bar Zabeda: "Down to Joahaz." But the Lord was gracious to them and had compassion on them, because of his covenant with Abraham, Isaac, and Jacob, and would not destroy them; nor has he cast them from his presence until now" (2 Kings 13:23). Up to that time the merit of the patriarchs endured." Samuel said, "Down to Hosea." Now I will uncover her lewdness in the sight of her lovers, and no man shall rescue her out of my hand" (Hos. 2:12). Now 'man' can refer only to Abraham, as you say, 'Now then restore the man's wife; for he is a prophet, and he will pray for you, and you shall live. But if you do not restore her, know that you will surely die, you, and all that are yours' (Gen. 20:7). And 'man' can refer only to Isaac, as you say, 'Rebekkah said to the servant, "Who is the man yonder, walking in the field to meet us?" The servant said, "It is my master." So she took her veil and covered herself' (Gen. 24:65). And 'man' can refer only to Jacob, as you say, 'When the boys grew up, Esau was a skilful hunter, a man of the field, while Jacob was a quiet man, dwelling in tents'" (Gen. 25:27). R. Joshua b. Levi said, "It was down to Elijah." And at the time of the offering of the oblation, Elijah the prophet came near and said, 'O Lord, God of Abraham, Isaac, and Israel, let it be known this day that thou art God in Israel, and that I am thy servant, and that I have done all these things at thy word'" (1 Kings 18:36). R. Yudan said, "It was down to Hezekiah." Of the increase of his government and of peace there will be no end, upon the throne of David, and over his kingdom, to establish it, and to uphold it with justice and with righteousness from this time forth and for evermore. The zeal of the Lord of hosts will do this" (Is. 9:6). Said R. Aha, "The merit of the patriarchs endures forever to protect Israel." For the Lord your God is a merciful God; he will not fail you or destroy you or forget the covenant with your fathers which he swore to them" (Deut. 4:31). This teaches that the covenant is made with the tribes.

Zekhut governs in every corner of life, so that those that enjoy *zekhut*, either on their own account or by reason of that inherited from their ancestors, God's presence will come among them, and the effects of zekhut are detailed and permeate the whole of existence, so b. Sot. 2:3 I.2/17a: R. Aqiba expounded, "When a man and woman have merit, the Presence of God is among them. When they do not have merit, the word for man loses a letter and so turns into the word for fire, which consumes them." Said Raba, "That fire which comes from the woman is more severe than that which comes from the man. How so? In the case of the woman, the letters for fire are consecutive, but not for the man. Since the first two letters for the word of woman, by themselves, spell fire, the rest follows." Said Raba, "Why is it that the Torah has said to bring dirt for the accused wife? Because if she merits a decree of innocence, surviving the ordeal, a son will come forth from her like Abraham, our father, concerning whom it is written, 'Dirt and ashes' (Gen. 18:27). If she does not emerge meritorious, she will return to the dirt." Raba interpreted, "On account of the merit of

Abraham, our father, who said, 'And I am dirt and ashes' (Gen. 18:27), his children gained the merit of two religious duties: the ashes of the red cow, and the dirt used for the accused wife." But is there not also the matter of the dirt used for covering up the blood of a beast one has slaughtered? That sort of dirt is used only for the preparation of the doing of a religious duty but itself does not constitute dirt through which a religious duty is carried out and there is no advantage to the one who does it. The dust in the ceremony of the ordeal helps to restore the confidence of a husband in his wife or punishes immorality and the ashes of the red heifer serve to cleanse the unclean." Raba expounded, "On account of the merit of Abraham, our father, who said, 'I will not take a thread nor a shoe-latchet' (Gen. 14:23), his children had the merit of two religious duties involving a thread, the thread of blue used in the show-fringes and the strap of the phylacteries." Now to be sure, the strap of the phylacteries poses no problem, for it is written, "And all the peoples of the earth shall see that you are called by the name of the Lord" (Deut. 28:10). In this connection it has been taught on Tannaite authority: R. Eliezer the Great says, "This refers to the phylactery used on the head."

Zekhut defines the point at which the supererogatory action takes over, and the commandments no longer govern; that is why even the learned sage and disciple of sages do not enjoy the favor of Heaven that a person who attains *zekhut* does. It is the point of systemic reversal, the heart of the system as a whole.

Cross References

Native categories encompass a variety of subjects, and this list of cross-references points to the abundance of topics that a given category may include. Some of the categories intersect with others, e.g., repentance occurs in the category of atonement.

Topic	See the entry under
Aaron	Torah-study
Abraham	Land of Israel, Jerusalem
Abraham	sin
Abraham	suffering
Abraham, Isaac, and Jacob	*zekhut*
acceptance	suffering
accidents	will of God, the
action	intentionality
actions, not words	sage, disciple of sages
Adam and Eve	creation
Adam	Israel
Adam	justice and mercy
Adam	Land of Israel
Adam	repentance
alienation	sin
angels	creation
angels	God
angels	man
angels	Revelation, giving of the Torah at Sinai
anguish, suffering	Torah-study
animals and Torah-law	sage, disciple of sages
anointed	Messiah, the
antidote to sin	sin
apostates	gentiles
arrogance	repentance
arrogance	sin

ascent to Heaven	God
astrology	will of God, the
Atonement for sin	Land of Israel, Jerusalem
atonement	gentiles
atonement	Israel
atonement	Land of Israel
atonement	repentance
atonement	suffering
atonement	Temple, Holy Place
attitude	commandment
attitude	God
attitude	intentionality
attitude	repentance
mercy, attribute of	creation
justice, attribute of	creation
attribute of justice	creation
attribute of mercy	creation
attributes	God
authority, sages'	prophecy
beasts	sage
beneficence	creation
bestiality	gentiles
blessings	kingdom of Heaven
body	soul
burial	Land of Israel, Jerusalem
Cain	repentance
Canaan	gentiles
Canaan	Land of Israel
casting lots	will of God, the
cause and effect	justice and mercy
causes of sin	sin
cemetery, blessing in	resurrection, eternal life, world to come
chain of tradition	Torah, oral
chance	will of God, the
chaos	Messiah, the

character	will of God, the
charity	loving kindness
charity	prayer
charity	Torah-study
charity	will of God, the
charity	*zekhut*
charity/righteousness	repentance
chastisement, penitential	resurrection of the Dead, judgment, world to come
Christians	gentiles
circumcision	Israel
classification	intentionality
commandment	kingdom of Heaven
commandments	gentiles
commandments	repentance
commandments to Noah's heirs	gentiles
commandments	*zekhut*
Commandments, Ten	commandment
contrition	sin
corporeality of God	God
court, earthly	prophecy
court, heavenly	prophecy
covenant	suffering
creation	God
creation	justice and mercy
creation	Land of Israel
creation	man
creation	Messiah, the
creation	Revelation, giving of the Torah at Sinai
creation	Torah
crime and penalty	justice and mercy
cultic contamination	Sanctification
curses	sage, disciple of sages
cursing God	gentiles
David	commandment

Day of Atonement	Atonement
Day of Atonement	repentance
death of death, the	resurrection, eternal life, world to come
death	resurrection, eternal life, world to come
death	righteousness, charity
death	sage
death	sage, disciple of sages
death	sin
death	sin
death	soul
death	suffering
death	Torah-study
death	will of God, the
death, death of	resurrection of the Dead, judgment, world to come
death, delivery from	righteousness, charity
declarations of faith	Land of Israel
decrees, divine	will of God, the
deed	intentionality
deed vs. study	Torah-study
deeds, authoritative	sage
descent from Heaven	God
destiny of man	resurrection of the Dead, judgment, world to come
destiny	will of God, the
destruction of the Temple	justice and mercy
differentiation of sexes	women
direction of the heart	intentionality
disciple of sages	sage
disciple of sages	Torah-study
disciple of sages	women
disciple	sage
discipleship	Torah-study
disobedience	Israel

Theological Grammar of the Oral Torah. Vol. I

echoes, heavenly	prophecy
Eden	Land of Israel
Eden	Land of Israel, Jerusalem
Eden	man
Egypt	gentiles
election of Israel	will of God, the
emotions	God
end of days	Land of Israel
end-time	redemption
entitlement	*zekhut*
estrangement from God	sin
estrangement from God	Torah
estrangement	God
estrangement	repentance
Eve	man
evil	intentionality
exile	commandment
exile	God
exile	Israel
exile	justice and mercy
exile	Land of Israel
exile	Messiah, the
exile of Israel	God
fairness	justice and mercy
faith	intentionality
Fall of Man	man
fall of Adam and Eve	creation
false messiah	Messiah
fate	will of God, the
fear of God	intentionality
fear of sin	sin
fear of sin	sin
firmament	God
First Man	Israel
forbearance	loving kindness
forgiveness	Atonement

forgiveness	God
forgiveness	Israel
forgiveness	justice and mercy
forgiveness	prayer
forgiveness	righteousness, charity
fornication	gentiles
fornication	sin
free will	justice and mercy
Garden of Eden	creation
garments of priest	Temple, Holy Place
Gehenna	resurrection, eternal life, world to come
Gehenna, the	creation
gender differentiation	women
generation of Enosh	sin
generation of the Dispersion	sin
generation of the Flood	sin
generosity	Israel
generosity	loving kindness
gentiles	Israel
gentiles	Land of Israel, Jerusalem
gentiles	Torah
gentiles	Torah, oral
gentiles' merit	gentiles
gentiles, nations	Messiah
giving of the Torah	God
God	creation
God	Land of Israel, Jerusalem
God	prayer
God	repentance
God	Revelation, giving of the Torah at Sinai
God	righteousness, charity
God	sage, disciple of sages
God	sin
God	Torah

God	Torah-study
God's image	God
God's love	Israel
God, mind of	sage
Gog and Magog	redemption
Gog and Magog	resurrection, eternal life, world to come
good deeds (*ma'asim tobim*)	commandment
good deeds	prayer
good life, the	Torah-study
goodness of God	creation
gossip	atonement
gossip	sin
grace	Israel
grace	*zekhut*
grace, divine	Land of Israel
grudge-bearing	loving kindness
hatred of Israel	gentiles
hatred, God's for	gentiles
healing	Torah-study
heart	intentionality
Heaven	kingdom of Heaven
Heaven	Torah
heavenly voice	Prophecy, Echoes, and Other Media
hell	resurrection, eternal life, world to come
heretics	God
heritage of grace	*zekhut*
hierarchization	sanctification
hierarchy of sanctification	Land of Israel, Jerusalem
hierarchy of virtues	resurrection, eternal life, world to come
high priest	Temple, Holy Place
history	Temple, Holy Place
holiness	Israel

holiness	Land of Israel
Holy of Holies	Temple, holy place
Holy Spirit	Prophecy, Echoes, and Other Media
Horeb	Revelation, giving of the Torah at Sinai
house of the sanctuary, the	creation
humiliation of others	resurrection, eternal life, world to come
humility	intentionality
humility	Israel
humility	Messiah
humility	resurrection, eternal life, world to come
humility	sin
humility	Torah-study
idolatry	gentiles
idolatry	God
idolatry	Israel
idolatry	Land of Israel, Jerusalem
idolatry	righteousness, charity
idolatry	sin
ignorant men	*zekhut*
imitation of master	Torah-study
inclination to do evil	commandment
inclination to do evil	sin
inclination to do good	sin
incorporeality	God
infants	resurrection of the Dead, judgment, world to come
intent to do evil	intentionality
intentionality	atonement
intentionality	commandment
intentionality	God
intentionality	repentance
intentionality	righteousness, charity

intentionality	sanctification
intentionality	soul
intentionality	women
Isaac	suffering
Israel	God
Israel	justice and mercy
Israel	kingdom of Heaven
Israel	Land of Israel, Jerusalem
Israel	Prophecy, Echoes, and Other Media
Israel	redemption
Israel	repentance
Israel	resurrection, eternal life, world to come
Israel	Revelation, giving of the Torah at Sinai
Israel	righteousness, charity
Israel	sage, disciple of sages
Israel	sin
Israel	Torah
Israel	Torah, oral
Israel	Torah-study
Israel	Torah-study
Israel, salvation of	*zekhut*
Jacob	suffering
Jerusalem	Temple, Holy Place
Jerusalem, fall of	sin
judgment	gentiles
judgment in world to come	sin
judgment	repentance
judgment	resurrection, eternal life, world to come
judgment	soul
judgment, last	repentance
justice and mercy	God
justice, attribute of	God

Kapparah	Atonement
kavvanah	intentionality
king	sage, disciple of sages
Kingdom of God	Revelation, giving of the Torah at Sinai
land of Israel	resurrection, eternal life, world to come
land of Israel	Temple, Holy Place
languages other than Hebrew	Revelation, giving of the Torah at Sinai
law	sage, disciple of sages
Lord of the dance	resurrection, eternal life, world to come
lots (dice)	will of God, the
love	God
love of God	intentionality
love of neighbor	loving kindness
love of the other	loving kindness
love, divine	suffering
love, God's for Israel	commandment
love, God's	Israel
love, God's	suffering
love, uncoerced	*zekhut*
loving kindness	Torah-study
Man	creation
man	God
man	man
man	Torah-study
man	women
man, counterpart in nature	man
man, creation of	creation
man, creation of	Torah-study
marriage	sage, disciple of sages
marriage	women
martyrdom	commandment
martyrdom	gentiles

master	sage
master-disciple	Torah, oral
master-disciple	Torah-study
measure for measure	justice and mercy
memory, God's	*zekhut*
Menachem	Messiah, the
mercy, attribute of	God
merit	gentiles
merit	Torah-study
merit	*zekhut*
Messiah	redemption
Messiah	resurrection, eternal life, world to come
Messiah son of Joseph	sin
Messiah's time, length of	Messiah, the
Messiah, false	Messiah, the
Messiah, name of	creation
Messiah, pangs of	Messiah, the
Messiah, royal	Messiah, the
Messiah, son of David	Messiah, the
Messiah, son of Joseph	Messiah, the
Messianic banquet	resurrection, eternal life, world to come
Minim (heretics)	gentiles
minor	intentionality
minors	women
miracles	Israel
Mishnah, the	Torah
modesty	Israel
Moses	Torah-study
Moses	Torah, oral
Moses, law of	women
murder	gentiles
murder	sin
name of the Messiah	Messiah
nations of the world	atonement

nations of the world	Gentiles
nations of the world	Land of Israel
Noah	creation
Noah	gentiles
Noah	man
Noah, children of	commandment
Noah, children of	gentiles
number of Messiahs	Messiah
offerings	intentionality
offerings	repentance
offerings	Temple, Holy Place
old age	suffering
past	Torah
patience	God
patriarchs	creation
patriarchs	prayer
patriarchs	suffering
peace	Torah-study
penitence	resurrection, eternal life, world to come
penury	Torah-study
personality-traits	sage
plan of world	Torah
power of God	*zekhut*
prayer	intentionality
prayer	repentance
prayer	righteousness, charity
prayer	Temple, Holy Place
prayer	*zekhut*
Presence (Shekhinah)	God
pride	sin
priest	Temple, Holy Place
priesthood	Torah-study
private action	sin
prophecy	sage, disciple of sages
prophets	Israel

providence	justice and mercy
public sin	sin
punishment & reward	justice and mercy
punishment	Atonement
punishment	commandment
punishment	gentiles
punishment	sin
punishment, divine	justice and mercy
purify the heart	commandment
purpose	intentionality
purpose	will of God, the
pursued	Israel
rabbi	sage
random outcomes	will of God, the
rebellion	God
rebellion	Israel
rebellion	sin
rebellion	sin
rebellion	sin
reconciliation	God
redemption	repentance
redemption	*zekhut*
regret	repentance
remorse	repentance
repentance	atonement
repentance	Israel
repentance	Messiah
repentance	prayer
repentance	redemption
repentance	righteousness, charity
repetition	Torah-study
responsibility	women
resurrection of the dead	Israel
resurrection of the dead	repentance
resurrection of the dead	Revelation, giving of the Torah at Sinai

resurrection of the dead	Torah
resurrection	repentance
resurrection	Torah
revelation	God
revelation	sage, disciple of sages
reward	commandment
reward of Torah-study	women
reward	Torah-study
righteous	gentiles
righteous, presence of	will of God, the
righteous, the	resurrection, eternal life, world to come
righteous, the	will of God, the
righteousness	loving kindness
righteousness of God	will of God, the
righteousness	prayer
righteousness	redemption
righteousness/philanthropy	prayer
Rome	Temple, Holy Place
rule, God's	kingdom of Heaven
Sabbath	creation
Sabbath	sin
sacrifice	atonement
sacrifice	prayer
sacrifices	Temple, Holy Place
sacrifices	Torah-study
sage	Torah-study
sage, disciple of	Torah-study
sages	Torah, oral
sages	women
sages, conduct of	women
saints	prayer
salvation	redemption
salvation	sage, disciple of sages
salvation	Torah-study
sanctification	Israel

sanctification	Land of Israel
sanctification of God's name	Torah-study
sanctification of Israel	commandment
sanctification	Temple, Holy Place
sanctuary	sanctification
Satan	will of God, the
scriptural interpretation	prophecy, echoes, and other media
self-indulgence	resurrection, eternal life, world to come
service	Temple, Holy Place
sexual relations	women
sexual rights	women
Shekhinah	God
Shema	kingdom of Heaven
sickness	sin
sickness	suffering
sin and penalty	justice and mercy
sin and punishment	justice and mercy
sin	gentiles
sin	Israel
sin	repentance
sin	righteousness, charity
sin, types of	sin
Sinai	Israel
Sinai	kingdom of Heaven
Sinai	Revelation, giving of the Torah at Sinai
Sinai	Torah
sincerity	commandment
sincerity	intentionality
sins, cardinal	gentiles
slavery	kingdom of Heaven
slaves	women
Sodom	gentiles
song	Atonement

soul	suffering
speech	prayer
stars	will of God, the
status	Torah
study of Torah	God
study vs. deed	Torah-study
submission to God's will	intentionality
suffering in this world	resurrection, eternal life, world to come
suffering	sin
suffering	Torah-study
sustenance, annual	will of God, the
symbol	Torah
synagogue	Temple, Holy Place
synagogues	God
taxes, obligation to pay	sage, disciple of sages
temper	sin
Temple	creation
Temple	Land of Israel
Temple sacrifices	Torah-study
Temple service	Temple, Holy Place
Temple	Torah-study
Temple, destruction of	Land of Israel, Jerusalem
Temple, destruction of	Messiah, the
teshubah	repentance
this world, world to come	justice and mercy
throne of glory	creation
time of the Messiah	Messiah
Torah	gentiles
Torah	God
Torah	Israel
Torah	Messiah, the
Torah	sage, disciple of sages
Torah	sin
Torah	Torah, oral
Torah, rejection of	gentiles

Torah, rejection of	Torah
Torah, revelation of	gentiles
Torah, study of	sage, disciple of sages
Torah, the	creation
Torah, written	resurrection, eternal life, world to come
Torah-learning	Land of Israel, Jerusalem
Torah-learning	sin
Torah-study	Land of Israel
Torah-study	sin
Torah-study	suffering
Torah-study	women
Torah-study	*zekhut*
Torah, oral	Land of Israel, Jerusalem
tradition	Torah, oral
ubiquity	God
uncleanness	Sanctification
unity of God	kingdom of Heaven
unlettered person	*zekhut*
vengeance	Israel
vice, avoiding	Torah-study
vice, virtue	Torah-study
violation of the law, intentional	intentionality
virtue	Israel
virtue	Torah-study
virtue	*zekhut*
wealth	Torah-study
wicked, presence of	will of God, the
wicked, the	resurrection of the Dead, judgment, world to come
wicked, the	will of God, the
will	women
wisdom	sin
woman	man
woman	sanctification
women	*zekhut*

women's source of zekhut   women
world to come   gentiles
world to come   sin
world to come   Torah
world, this   resurrection, eternal life, world to come

yoke of the commandments   Kingdom of Heaven
yoke of the kingdom of Heaven   Kingdom of Heaven